Implementing Codes of Conduct
How Businesses Manage Social Performance in Global Supply Chains

IMPLEMENTING CODES OF CONDUCT

How Businesses Manage
Social Performance in Global Supply Chains

Ivanka Mamic
Management and Corporate Citizenship Programme,
International Labour Office

Funding for this research was provided by
the United States Department of State

International
Labour Office

2 0 0 4

International Labour Office, CH-1211 Geneva 22, Switzerland
in association with
Greenleaf Publishing, Aizlewood's Mill, Nursery St, Sheffield S3 8GG, UK

First published 2004

Printed on paper made from at least 75% post-consumer waste using TCF and ECF bleaching.
Printed in Great Britain by William Clowes Ltd, Beccles, Suffolk.
Cover by LaliAbril.com.

HD
60
.M347
2004

British Library Cataloguing in Publication Data:
A catalogue record for this book is available from the British Library.

ISBN 92-2-116270-2 (International Labour Office)
ISBN 1-874719-89-6 (Greenleaf Publishing)

Contents

Figures

Tables

Preface

This book details the findings of International Labour Office (ILO) field research conducted under funding from the United States Department of State on the global sports footwear, apparel and retail sectors between 2000 and 2002. The goal of this research was to identify and examine the ways in which companies adopt, implement and evaluate policies regarding codes of conduct in their global business operations. The main objective was to illustrate the different methods and strategies by which multinational enterprises achieve their labour practice objectives and thereby provide a learning platform.

The research was conducted in two parts. The pilot phase of the research focused on the sports footwear sector and was conducted during the second half of calendar year 2000. Subsequently our understanding of the issues under consideration increased as is reflected in our fine-tuning of areas of focus in the apparel and retail sectors. The purpose of the pilot research was to help identify issues and provide a focal point for our analysis, rather than a definitive platform of findings, while simultaneously strengthening the capacity of the ILO team to carry out the research. Consequently, there were a number of changes made to the original research approach including a revision of the methodology as well as a broadening of inputs to incorporate expert advice from leading academics and practitioners active in this field.

The footwear sector was chosen for the pilot phase of research due to the fact that the relevant policies and management systems in that sector are relatively well developed. It is acknowledged that the selection of multinational enterprises reviewed in this sector was limited to a subsection of firms that have been actively involved in code implementation for a number of years. An attempt was made to widen the scope of our coverage in the apparel and footwear sectors by increasing sample size. However, given the specific objective of this research, namely to document the management systems in use, our focus was limited to those firms that actually have codes of conduct together with an established implementation process.

In conducting the research, the ILO research team, together with assistance from various academic experts, interviewed managers regarding the techniques and systems used by three sports footwear multinationals, nine apparel multinationals and eight retail multinationals in carrying out their social performance objectives, tracking progress, and determining the means by which enterprises respond to shortcomings when they are identified. Particular emphasis was placed on understanding the institutionalised structures of corporate oversight, ranging from those dedicated systems explicitly focused on achieving social objectives, to adaptations of pre-existing corporate institutions, including human resource management, quality assurance, communications and personnel evaluation systems. The research also included interviews with government representatives, employers' organisations, workers' organisations, non-governmental organisations (NGOs) and others actively involved in this field.

There are many difficulties involved with the assessment of the effect of corporate codes of conduct. Like other private-sector initiatives, codes of conduct are not created in a vacuum, but are developed and negotiated against a backdrop of international and national laws and regulations within the context of the management and operations of the enterprise. For this reason, the scope of this research was limited to the identification of the key characteristics of the management practices and systems established rather than an assessment of the effects of the codes of conduct themselves.

Foreword

The last 15 years have witnessed the birth of a new, privatised mode of workplace regulation integrated into global production and supply chains. The emergence and rapid spread of corporate codes of conduct—setting forth a list of workplace rights and standards for the factories in those chains—is only the most visible element of the new mode of regulation. Along with the codes themselves, multinational manufacturers and retailers have developed elaborate managerial systems for formulating, enforcing and revising the norms contained in the codes.

These managerial systems for 'labour monitoring', 'labour auditing' or 'social compliance' are embedded in the multinational corporations' complex array of structures and functions for production, sourcing, information, quality control, legal compliance and so on. And those overall corporate structures and functions are situated, in turn, in an organisational environment that now includes not only familiar forms of worker representation—unions and works councils—but also new kinds of intermediaries that apply pressure, offer services and provide arenas for managerial learning and co-ordinated action, all with a view to improving conditions for factory workers. Among the new intermediaries are for-profit auditing firms, not-for-profit consultants, multi-stakeholder consortia, foundations, and a variety of non-governmental organisations dedicated to the campaign against global sweatshops. The new workplace initiatives of both managers and intermediaries are ultimately impelled and inflected by the concerns and interests of national and global unions, consumers and investors.

Calling the new managerial systems a privatised mode of 'regulation' does not presuppose any particular view about their desirability, or about the relation between these new activities and traditional public regulation of workplaces. Some view the managerial systems simply as a more high-powered vehicle for corporations' internal compliance with external legal norms—a new, unobjectionable mechanism serving a familiar compliance function. At the other extreme, some see the managerial systems as a substitute for sovereign legal institutions and a threatening rival to trade unions. Either of these views is consistent with the fact that most of the corporate codes explicitly or implicitly require factories to comply with the rights and standards set forth in international labour law (as promulgated by the International Labour Organization) and in relevant domestic labour law.

I refer to the managerial systems as a new mode of regulation solely for heuristic purposes: to highlight some important features of the systems and to suggest parallels with emerging forms of transnational standard-setting in areas other than workplace conditions, such as environmental controls, financial risk management and technical standards. In all of these areas, decision-makers formulate, specify and implement norms, in the form of standards, rights or rules. Decision-makers (social compliance managers, in the case of labour standards) therefore face the common dilemma of ensuring that norms (codes of conduct) are applied consistently even while ensuring that norms are flexibly adapted to local circumstances (specific factory workplaces). This familiar dilemma of domestic, sovereign labour regulation is only heightened when norms have to be specified and enforced across borders by private managers facing a wide variety of national labour-relations systems, legal regimes and workplace cultures. The multinational corporation is, in effect, an administrative apparatus for formulating and applying workplace norms, and that apparatus spans the national and international regulatory mechanisms serving an analogous function.

This heightened dilemma, and the surprising speed with which the privatised mode of workplace regulation has emerged and diffused in the last 15 years, are symptoms of the current era of economic globalisation. The time is ripe for empirical research and analysis that begins to map comprehensively the managerial systems and intermediaries comprising the new mode of workplace regulation. In this book, Ms Ivanka Mamic has done an extraordinary job of launching that endeavour. The unique access to managerial personnel she enjoyed under the auspices of the International Labour Office produced a very rich harvest of in-depth interviews and analysis. Her book will be indispensable to managers, unionists, policy-makers and academics who seek a better understanding of managerial systems for social compliance, as well as those who wish to comprehend the broader phenomenon of transnational, private standard-setting across many fields.

Mark Barenberg
Professor of Labor and International Law, Columbia University, New York
Director, Governing Board, Worker Rights Consortium, Washington, DC

I
Overview of the research

This book provides a review of the findings from field research into the sports footwear, apparel and retail sectors. Conducted over a two-year period between 2000 and 2002, this research looked at the management approaches to implementing corporate social responsibility (CSR) and corporate codes of conduct and was carried out in two parts. The first part encompassed an examination of the sports footwear sector and was undertaken on a pilot basis with a view to providing an opportunity to refine the approach for the remainder of the research. It also provided an opportunity to develop a framework for the presentation of the findings. The second part of the research involved an in-depth analysis of the implementation of the myriad voluntary corporate codes of conduct in the apparel and retail sectors. The goal of the research was to identify and examine ways in which companies adopt, implement and evaluate the effect of policies regarding CSR and the voluntary commitment to labour, social and ethical practices in the context of globalised business operations. The approach of our analysis was to consider the dynamics of multinational enterprises (MNEs) at all of their relevant levels, along with related developing country firms linked into MNE supply chains.

1. Background

Considerable resources are being devoted to tracking the recent exponential increase in the voluntary initiatives of MNEs to promote objectives reflecting principles in the ILO Declaration on Fundamental Principles and Rights at Work, CSR and related labour, social and ethical practices. Emphasis has rightly fixed on their content: for example, which behaviour or performance principles are endorsed, and on arrangements for verification of the implementation of codes. By contrast, comparatively little is known about the methods that enterprises use to advance their labour policy objectives, or to ascertain whether they are being observed in practice. Even less is known about the extent to which the scope of implementation is being enlarged to include the enterprises' commercial partners up and down the supply chain: affiliates with common shareholding, suppliers of goods and services, contractors and subcontractors, customers, joint venture partners and partners in strategic alliances. Knowledge is especially scant about the way in which developing country enterprises, be they principals or partners of larger firms, are setting and pursuing their performance objectives regarding labour practices under the influence of MNE codes of conduct.

2. Purpose and impact

The research aimed to shed light on the techniques and systems in use by sports footwear, apparel and retail MNEs to implement their voluntarily established code of conduct objectives, to track the progress being made and to determine the means by which enterprises adjust to shortcomings when they are identified. As will be highlighted later in this book, these objectives are not set in a vacuum but rather are impacted by national legislation, international legislation and regulations, and other guidelines such as the ILO Tripartite Declaration for MNEs and OECD Guidelines on MNEs.

The goal was to better understand the dedicated systems explicitly focused on labour, social and ethical objectives, or adaptations of existing systems such as those relating to strategic goals, human resource management, quality assurance, communications and dialogue strategies, and evaluation systems. It is hoped that this documentation of the management systems used will help illuminate how the objectives pertaining to labour practice are translated into practice and the consequences of such actions.

Our intent is that the knowledge gained can be used by enterprises to ensure that their commitments to labour, social and ethical goals and their legal obligations are met. Furthermore, public policy-makers may find value in understanding the interaction of business operations and corporate social commitments in order to better integrate private initiatives with public systems of regulation. Specific research questions addressed were:

1. What are the management systems that enterprises use at MNE and supplier levels to set, communicate, implement and evaluate progress in attaining social (code of conduct) objectives?

2. How are management systems that are related to social (code of conduct) performance linked between MNE and supplier levels, and how do they interact?

As is clear from the above questions, the focus of the research was on management systems for CSR and codes of conduct. Looking to one of the leading theorists in terms of organisations, such systems are those 'responsible for directing and coordinating the other subsystems of the organisation. In addition, these systems are responsible for developing organisation structure and directing tasks within each [of the other various organisational] subsystems' (Daft 1995). It is important to recognise that management systems, addressing things such as vision setting—for example the development of a code of conduct—or the allocation of resources to support compliance or establishing reporting and monitoring approaches, stretch beyond the involvement of managers, and in most cases directly and indirectly concern the actions of and the impacts on workers. While managers in suppliers and brand/buyer companies may have a greater direct role in, and impact on, many of these systems, the ILO in general promotes the importance of establishing and maintaining a role for workers. Such a role, we heard repeatedly, is central to meeting code elements in general as well as boosting the productivity of the firms concerned. At the same time, as becomes clear in this book, management systems are those that determine how firms comply with labour law, both at the international and the national level, and establish labour norms in the workplace as well as implementing the social commitments reflected in CSR and voluntary codes of conduct.

3. Scope of research

This research focused on MNE/buyer and developing country/supplier inputs to address the issues identified above, and the research scope in general. The footwear sector was chosen for the pilot phase of research because the policies and management systems in this sector are well developed and labour issues have generated considerable interest and debate. Given the involvement of a number of leading MNE footwear brands in the apparel sector, there appeared to be useful synergies to be gained by focusing on this sector in the next stage of our research. Prior to a conclusive decision being achieved on this point, a research trip was undertaken to a number of apparel supplier factories based in Turkey, supplying to both well-known apparel brands and sports footwear brands.

This visit revealed that many of the issues that emerged through the research on the footwear sector are replicated in the apparel industry. However, our discussions there confirmed our background research, indicating that there were marked differences in the evolution of the management systems used to implement codes of conduct, both at the supplier and MNE level, that merited further study in this sector. Finally, after considerable background research and preliminary findings from the apparel sector, a decision was made to include the retail sector as the third sector of focus. However, due to time constraints and the vastness of this sector, it was decided the focus would be limited to a specific set of retailers, namely large diversified retailers who carry both 'soft' (apparel) and 'hard' (non-apparel) line products. The rationale for this decision was the desire to examine the different approaches MNEs take when implementing their codes of conduct with respect to different product areas.

As with the research into the footwear sector, the focus of attention in the apparel and retail sectors was on several MNEs and their commercial partners in the supply chain. Particular attention was paid to the extent to which, and the manner in which, the management systems were applied or transferred to all relevant firms in the supply chain. Research on the three sectors was conducted in a sequential, yet overlapping, manner, so that the lessons learned from the first sector could be applied to the other sectors, while also compressing the time required for the study.

The findings from the pilot phase of the research have been aggregated with the results of research into other sectors, allowing a cross-sectoral analysis and providing an overview of different practices adopted. For all three sectors extensive co-operation was received from MNEs and suppliers, workers, worker representatives at the factory level, government representatives and local trade unions.

4. Methodology

The research carried out has been one of inductive theory building based on multiple case studies.[1] In this approach, the research process involved the use of multiple data sources—particularly interviews and the collection of documents made available by firms—to develop findings within cases, and between cases within the sectors reviewed. A qualitative research approach was adopted based on our aim to develop rich explanations of the processes under study and on the explanatory nature of the research (Glaser and Strauss 1967; McGrath 1982). Our desire was to provide well-developed theories that could then be tested in the future.

Interviews with managers and workers within MNEs and suppliers, as well as a limited number of other interested parties, were the primary data source. Attention was focused on supplier firms as well as MNEs. Initial contact with MNE representatives occurred through existing contact lists at ILO headquarters and through numerous networking opportunities: for instance, attending various code-related conferences. To the extent possible, a deliberate attempt was made to include a cross sample of MNEs from both the United States and Europe with a view to examining whether there were differences in approach based on geographical location. Introductions to supplier factories were facilitated by the MNEs under study in order to help us with the objective of understanding code of conduct implementation across MNE supply chains. In some instances, assistance was sought via ILO constituents, who contacted local employer and trade union organisations and suggested particular local firms that might be willing to participate in the study.

In many of the factories a regional or local compliance manager from an MNE, who was usually one of the factory's major customers, introduced us. Several criteria for selection of the factories existed:

- **Geographical location**: due to time restrictions, an attempt was made to organise interviews in clusters of factories located within a two-hour driving proximity of each other

- **Product**: production of items falling within the product categories of the three sectors under study

- **Size**: in order to gain an understanding of the challenges involved with code implementation, the size of supplier factories visited ranged from 200 employees to 10,000 employees

- **Requirement to adhere to a code of conduct**

Further details of the supplier firms studied are included in the individual sectoral reports. As Table 1 reveals, MNEs that participated in our study range from small, for example in the apparel sector, to relatively large, for example in the retail sector.

At the MNE level, interviews were conducted with a range of senior and middle managers involved in the compliance process including: compliance, purchasing, legal, information technology, communications, logistics and human resource managers. A

---

1   For a more in-depth discussion of this methodological approach, see Eisenhardt 1989: 532-50. See also Yin 1994.

	Footwear	Apparel	Retail
No. of MNEs interviewed	3	11	8
Range in no. of employees	2,400–25,000	200–150,000	24,000–400,000
Median no. of employees	15,000	12,300	127,500
Revenue range (US$ million)	1,100–12,000	50–16,000	2,800–72,000
Median revenue (US$ million)	8,000	3,500	18,500
Average revenue (US$ million)	7,000	4,000	28,800
Product categories	Primarily footwear; also apparel and accessories	Footwear, apparel and sporting goods	Hard and soft lines including apparel, footwear, accessories, home-furnishings, etc.

TABLE 1   DATA ON COMPANIES REVIEWED

total of 107 interviews were conducted with MNE representatives. Interviews at the supplier level were focused on production, compliance, health and safety, and human resource managerial level. In many instances, directors and/or owners of the supplier factory were also interviewed. A total of 135 interviews were conducted with supplier factory representatives. In most instances, interviews were conducted one-on-one with the respective interviewee and our research team, so that, for example, within one factory, three or four interviews may have been held. As there is no set heuristic as to the number of interviews needed to reach saturation, we did not determine the total number of interviews to be conducted a priori. Instead, we continued with our interviews until we reached a point of saturation or 'redundancy' in each of the research questions under consideration (Patton 1990; Marshall and Rossman 1995).

We employed a semi-structured interview approach, based on questions displayed in Appendix 2. The ILO developed these questions but it should be noted that, as the research progressed and discrepancies between the sectors emerged, the focus of our questions was refined. It should also be noted that the original interview questions were targeted broadly at the notion of social performance objectives. As we conducted the pilot phase of the research it became apparent that there was a need to focus our questions specifically to the issues relevant to code of conduct implementation. Also, additional areas for exploration were provided by each of the participating experts. Interviewees were not provided with a copy of the interview questions prior to the interview and interviews were conducted face to face.

MNE interviews generally commenced with the compliance manager and then progressed to other functional areas depending on the structure of the organisation. Interview length was dependent on the knowledge of the interviewee and their role in the compliance process, with variations of length from 45 minutes to four hours. The typical interview lasted one hour. Supplier factory interviews were carried out sequentially, commencing with general questions regarding the history of the factory and current management strategy and later addressing specific code-related issues in more detail. The supplier factory interviews usually lasted between one and one-and-a-half hours. In most instances, hand-written notes were taken with the exception of some research conducted in China and Thailand where notes were directly transcribed onto a computer. Additionally, a limited amount of documentary data was collected such as organisational charts, copies of codes of conduct, and other related code data and reports. Where there was less formality, greater use was made of interviews and observation. The role of upstream suppliers was emphasised.

Interviewee	Footwear	Apparel	Retail
Agent	...	5	1
Employers' organisation	...	4	...
Government representatives	2	1	...
Multinational enterprise	47	40	20
Multi-stakeholder initiative	...	4	2
NGO	...	4	1
Supplier	30	70	47
Third-party auditor	...	10	1
Trade association	...	10	...
Trade union	1	27	0
Other	...	2	...

TABLE 2 INTERVIEWS CONDUCTED

As shown in Table 2, interviews were also conducted with others involved or active in the compliance process, including government representatives as well as those from trade unions, employers' organisations, trade organisations and NGOs. This was done in a deliberate attempt to obtain as broad an understanding and range of perceptions as possible regarding the systems used to implement codes of conduct. Where possible, independent documentation or reports regarding the companies under study were obtained. It was our hope that this documentation and these external interviews would aid in triangulation with the interviewees' verbal responses (Silverman 1993).

We did not create coding for data in advance of the interviews, adopting instead a more grounded approach of developing coding that represented the data as we conducted our research. Similarly, we did not utilise any specific qualitative data analysis software, opting instead to develop our own 'matrix of findings'. The initial version of this matrix was created on completion of our pilot phase of research into the footwear sector. Based on our findings in this sector, we created specific coding for findings pertaining to the systems used by MNEs and their supplier factories. This coding is represented in this book in the following style, for example: FMNE I, CSR Director.

The following table provides a synopsis of the coding used throughout this book:

Interviewee	Coding		Numbering system
Example	F	MNE	1
Agent	Agent		
Expert report	E		
Industry association	IA		
Multinational enterprise	F Footwear A Apparel R Retail	MNE	
NGO	NGO		
Supplier factory	CA Cambodia CH China G Guatemala H Honduras SL Sri Lanka TH Thailand TU Turkey UK United Kingdom USA United States of America VI Viet Nam	S	Number based on number of MNEs, suppliers, agents, NGOs, third-party auditors, trade unions and industry associations interviewed
Third-party auditor	TPA		
Trade union	U		
Other	0		

TABLE 3 INTERVIEW CODING

As the research progressed, there were several iterations of our matrix, until, at the conclusion, it became an invaluable tool with more than 900 pages that linked all of the interviews together to create meaningful thematic links and enable higher-level analyses.[2]

The results from our interviews are reported in Chapters IV–VI utilising a framework explained in Chapter III consisting of the following broad elements:

---

2   This is a common phenomenon that results with all approaches to the coding of qualitative data. Often as new understandings and insights into the data emerge or as codes become decayed or too general, new codes will be developed. For further details see Lincoln and Guba 1985 and Miles and Huberman 1994.

- Creating a shared vision

- Developing understanding and ability

- Implementing the code in operations

- Feedback, improvement and remediation

This framework is introduced with the goal of both mapping out the findings for the two research questions under consideration and providing an outline to help guide future research endeavours in this area. Further, adoption of this framework facilitates comparison across and between the sectors studied.

Staff from the Job Creation and Enterprise Department and the Management and Corporate Citizenship Programme of the ILO carried out the research. The pilot phase of the research was conducted solely by ILO officials with helpful comments and suggestions being obtained on completion of the research from:

- Jill Murray, Lecturer, Melbourne University, Australia

- Bennett Freeman, Principal, Sustainable Investment Strategies, former US Deputy Assistant Secretary of State for Democracy, Human Rights and Labor

Interviews in the apparel and retail sectors were predominantly carried out in conjunction with leading academic experts experienced in code-of-conduct issues and the sectors under review. Participating academics in the research were:

- Mark Barenberg, Professor of Law, Columbia University, USA

- Stephen Frenkel, Professor of Organisation and Employment Relations, Australian Graduate School of Management, UNSW, Australia

- Jan Hammond, Unit Head, Technology and Operations Management Unit, UPS Professor of Business Logistics, Harvard Business School, USA

- Alyson Warhurst, Professor and Chair of Strategy and International Development, Director, Corporate Citizenship Unit, Warwick University, UK

Input was also obtained from the following:

- Liu Kaiming, Director, Institute for Contemporary Observation, China

These experts provided valuable and insightful inputs into this research: guiding the research questions and focus, providing detailed reports after each of the field visits and verifying the findings contained herein. Support was also provided by a number of external consultants including several for language assistance/translation services at the supplier level. The research team was further assisted by participation of labour ministry and productivity centre personnel in some of the developing countries visited.

5. A note on the presentation of data/transcriptions

The research team believes that it would be particularly useful for practitioners to see and 'hear' the voice of the managers, workers and government representatives interviewed during this project, rather than just having a summary of their comments. For that reason, many of the more interesting and useful quotations are provided here. At the same time, a number of comments on these quotes need to be made.

Due to interviewee concerns and with the goal of maintaining an open dialogue, the research team did not record the interviews. Transcriptions were made as accurately as possible. An attempt was made to capture both the content and tone of comments made. Between the companies some of the common terminology varied and has been standardised here for easier understanding. As one example, the organisations' social performance objectives, referred to by different names in the different companies, have all been standardised to the terms 'codes' or 'codes of conduct' in this book. Similarly, while the core groups responsible for implementing these codes are referred to in different ways, here this has been standardised to the CSR (corporate social responsibility) group.

As mentioned elsewhere in this book and made clear to all participants at the start of their involvement in the research project, the inclusion of firms in the project should not be seen as recognition of their overall good practice. Along these same lines, a comment or example of problems described should not be seen as an indication of poor overall performance. The MNE sports footwear brands, their suppliers and their managers and workers have extensive experience—relative to other sectors—in developing and implementing codes across their supply chains and therefore were considered a good starting point for the pilot phase of this project. As mentioned above, to focus on the apparel and retail sectors after conducting this initial review seemed like a logical extension of our study.

In writing this book, an attempt was made to ensure the non-disclosure of the identities of the participating firms as well as of the interviewees. Mutual non-disclosure was agreed on by the ILO and the participating companies prior to the start of the field research. As such, some of the comments that referred to management systems or approaches used to implement social objectives, approaches that could by those in the industry be linked to specific participating companies, have been modified, giving generic names to the practices in question. Similarly, dates, locations or other items that would identify the company or the individual interviewed have been modified where it appeared necessary to avoid identification. In each of these cases, the basic content of the comments made has been retained.

6. Limitations

As with any piece of research, there are some limitations worth noting.

   1.   **Scope**. We were limited in the scope of our research by the research questions themselves. We aimed to obtain an understanding of the code implementa-

tion process and the management systems used therein by reasonably well-known MNEs. We were not seeking a representative sample, choosing instead to focus on those MNEs and supplier factories familiar with codes. Our objective in this exercise was primarily to understand *how* codes were being implemented and what systems were being introduced or used by management rather than focusing on how codes were received by workers. The effect of codes was also of concern to us, so this was included in our inquiry, as is explained in this chapter; however, it was not a central objective, as looking into such effects would have required a different set of research questions and methodology.

2. **MNE and factory selection.** As indicated above, we were limited to a fairly small sample size of MNEs and their supplier factories based on our desire to study firms with a reputation for being experienced in the code implementation process. Furthermore, the selection of supplier factories was a matter beyond our control, often left in the hands of the MNE albeit according to criteria requested by us. This biases our sample in the direction of better practice. While it is important to take into account any possible bias in analysing research of this nature, we contend that the effect of this bias is limited due to our desire to obtain an understanding of the good practices that are adopted in the implementation process.

3. **Research process.** Due to the lack of detailed documentary information and the proprietary nature of some documentation requested, we did not always obtain enough information to enable the comparison of one supplier factory against another on every single point in our matrix of findings. In an effort to compensate for this, we increased our sample size and broadened our geographical coverage. Additionally, in some countries we experienced multiple tiers of translation, which may have resulted in the loss of some detail and nuances of information being conveyed.

Acknowledgements

First of all, given the ILO's efforts at ensuring decent work for all employees, we would like to acknowledge the support of the workers in the factories, who often provided important insights during our factory visits and who labour to provide goods worn and used around the globe. Second, the work carried out in this research was made possible by the support of the participating companies, both MNEs and suppliers, and in particular their managers, CSR personnel and employees who provided us with their insights. It appeared to the research team that, time and again, these people went out of their way to be open and honest with the researchers, presenting both the successes and difficulties that they had faced—and continue to face—in implementing the codes of conduct. This is demonstrated by the range of comments that have been included in this book and for that we are very grateful. In addition, we received the support of various governmental and local groups in China, Viet Nam, Turkey, Guatemala, Honduras, Sri Lanka, Cambodia and Thailand, who provided background, helped with understanding of local laws and context, and assisted with communicating with local managers and workers. To them we would also like to express our greatest appreciation.

This research could not have been conducted without the contribution of several people throughout various phases including assistance with research, drafting and editing: Mark Barenberg, Charles Bodwell, Mary-Jeanne Cabanel, Lanny Entrekin, Bennett Freeman, Stephen Frenkel, Yevgeniy Gorakin, Janice Hammond, Jennifer Higgins, Mark Hilborne, Peter Illig, Cornelia Jesse, Katrina Kropa, Anthony Miller, Jill Murray, Nikolai Rogovsky, Alyson Warhurst and Lynette Yeo.

Finally, we would like to thank the United States Department of State for its support and funding, without which this research would not have been possible.

II
Review of the environment and content of codes

1. Context

Today's realm of globalisation and trade liberalisation has led to a constantly changing and unstable scene of international business operations. Individual corporations now command budgets and organisational systems that far surpass those of many individual nation states. How to manage the behaviour of these entities has become a serious concern of global stakeholders. The purpose of this chapter is to set the context of codes of conduct against the current conditions of the world business environment.

According to data published by the United Nations Conference on Trade and Development (UNCTAD), world foreign direct investment (FDI) inflows in 2001 declined to US$735 billion, which is half of what it was in 2000. In 2002, FDI declined by approximately 27% to about US$651 billion, continuing a downward trend from a peak in the late 1990s of nearly US$1.5 trillion.

Interestingly, FDI has slowed more significantly in developed countries, while continuing to remain strong in the developing countries of the world. Worth noting is the fact that UNCTAD predicts China may soon overtake the United States to become the largest FDI host country in the world.[3]

Regarding control and distribution of FDI, the role of MNEs is significant. One hundred of the world's largest multinationals make up approximately one-third of FDI (Kyloh and Murray 1998: 16). Such investment takes many forms: that of joint ventures, often in minority positions; subcontracting and production sharing; and non-equity arrangements, for example turnkey operations and long-term contracting. These statistics highlight the dramatically increasing global reach of firms, the lengthening of supply chains and the outsourcing and disaggregation of multinationals' operations.

There have been several driving factors in the move of many firms' operations to developing countries, including lower production costs and significantly lower labour rates for both high- and low-skilled workers. Considering the information technology sector, at the low end of the educational/skill spectrum, in 1994 computer typing contract rates in the Philippines were US$0.50 per 10,000 characters, while in China

---

3 Personal communication from Masataka Fujita, Officer-in-Charge, Investment Trends Section, Division on Investment, Technology and Enterprise Development, United Nations Conference on Trade and Development (UNCTAD).

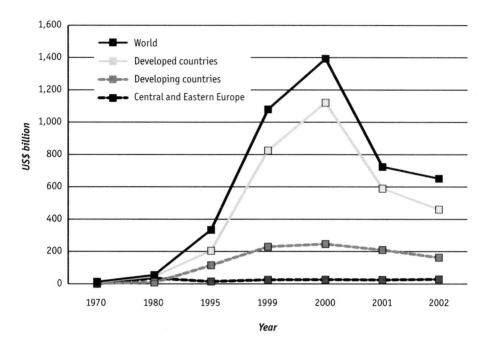

FIGURE 1 GLOBAL INFLOWS OF FDI 1970–2002, BY GROUP OF COUNTRIES
Source: UNCTAD, FDI database

they were only US$0.20 for the same amount (White and Munger 1998: 103). At the other end of the educational spectrum, an Indian PhD in computer science can be hired for US$9,000 a year or less to write software code, with the results shipped back to the United States or Europe by e-mail, over the Internet or through satellite links (*The Washington Post* 1996).

In 2002 exports of Indian IT and software grew to US$6.9 billion, with McKinsey & Co. estimating that the trade could reach US$50 billion by 2008. The Indian software industry is multi-faceted, providing everything from mundane data entry and maintenance work to the management of increasingly complex projects for European and US-based multinationals. Infosys Technologies is an example of a software service provider that allows these developed country firms to outsource operations at cut-rate prices. Recruiting new hires at salaries in the US$400 to 500 range per month, while having access to a huge and talented labour pool—in 1999 Infosys received over 183,000 applications for fewer than 3,000 open positions—this firm and companies like it in India are mounting a growing challenge to firms such as EDS or IBM as regards both price and quality.

Similar stories of the move of production and services to developing countries, whether due to labour costs, differences in regulatory frameworks or access to markets, are mirrored in a wide variety of industries. Most prominent are the consumer products industries dominated by brand names, for example Reebok, Adidas, Levi, C&A, Nike, The Gap and other footwear and apparel manufacturers. Less prominent but just as directly connected to global supply chains are other sectors, such as toy manufacturing (Mattel and others) and retailing (examples include store chains such as Ikea, Wal-Mart, Sainsbury's and Carrefour). Similar reports of the impact of globalised value chains and disaggregated supply chains could be made regarding a range of manufacturing operations and service industries, for example the software operations discussed above or the increasingly international food service chains. The burgeoning call centre industry in the Philippines is one example linking the trend of globalisation with both a move into developing economies and developments in information and communications technologies. Due to a large pool of English-speaking, well-educated and computer-literate potential employees, as well as a liberal business environment and decreasing telecommunication charges, call centre employment is increasing rapidly. Specialist firms such as Sykes, one of the largest global call centre operators with business in Africa, Canada, China, Europe, Latin America and the United States, as well as other multinationals such as America Online, have already established large operations in the country, with annual business growth in the sector estimated at over 50% (Villamor 2001: 1).

The shifts in value chains and trade patterns reflected by the growth in FDI also reflect a fundamental shift in the relationships in and governance of corporate production chains. As the nature of business relations changes, from the formerly dominant model (rigidly hierarchical firms manufacturing goods within wholly owned facilities in national operations for local markets) to transnational operations of alliances and supplier-based manufacturing that serve a range of global markets, CSR is seeing a related transformation. No longer is CSR the domain of the individual firm operating in a local regulatory framework, with perhaps a localised single-enterprise-based code of conduct governing operations. Increasingly, private voluntary social initiatives govern the range of transactions that are encompassed by joint ventures, licensees and disaggregated supply chains, with their varying degrees of attachment between business partners and involvement of stakeholders.

2. Emergence of corporate initiatives

a. Background

In the context of the frenetic economic and trade activity of the last decade, the emergence of corporate initiatives to address the voluntary labour, social and ethical commitments embodied in codes of conduct grew increasingly important. Several reasons are behind this trend. First of all, news media exposés and general public awareness of labour and social issues heightened in the 1990s. In the first half of the decade a number of United States firms received extensive negative coverage. This type of news coverage, often documenting alleged supply chain-based infractions of international labour standards, has continued. At the same time, communication technologies have provided a further impetus to the rapid distribution of brand image-damaging information. A variety of NGOs, workers' representative organisations and organisations supporting CSR initiatives have established websites, each of which can quickly and easily distribute information or reports on the labour and social practices of companies.[4] These developments have taken place during a time of increasing debate concerning the benefits and costs of globalisation, resulting in an unprecedented focus on the issues covered by CSR. Student protests in the United States concerning labour practices in the manufacture of university-licensed sportswear, as well as actions in Europe such as the Clean Clothes Campaign, have also added momentum to the development of CSR initiatives.

Many firms have initiated voluntary, code-based programmes in part due to a desire to limit such exposure as stated in a United States Department of Labor study of codes of conduct, 'companies adoption of codes of conduct serve to ease consumer concerns—and their own—that they may be contributing to the exploitation of child labour'. It is highly likely that they also ease concerns about other questionable practices covered by codes (United States Department of Labor 1996: 8). The danger to a company's reputation, and the image held by consumers resulting from stories covered nationally or internationally of child labour, abusive work practices or dangerous workplaces, is clear. Branding has become a crucial element of competitiveness in global economies (Ries and Trout 1997). Of course, the brand image of any firm operating transnationally stretches far beyond the borders of its home country; protecting it from damage is central to maintaining a competitive position. For some firms, enhancing brand image through positive actions and linkage to best labour practices is an emerging trend.

Other reasons also exist for firms implementing voluntary initiatives. Many organisations have found that employees increasingly want to work for firms that are considered ethical and that play a positive role in their communities. At the same time, a growing number of researchers have documented the business case for social responsibility (Hopkins 1999; Waddock 2001), highlighting the benefits to firms of working closely with their communities, improving stakeholder dialogue and valuing their employees. As this book shows, the development of codes of conduct forms part of a range of initiatives that firms adopt in implementing their CSR objectives. It is possible, however, to have a socially responsible firm which has not adopted a written or formal code. Shorter delivery times and pressures to reduce costs, as well as an increasing tendency towards transnational supply chains, are in part dependent on maintaining good relations with supply chain partners, avoiding production disruptions and speeding the ability to make improvements by empowering workers to address problems at the source (Levy 1997). This research shows that labour disputes, employee illness or government intervention can result in disruptions apart from other ill-effects that would make lean production approaches difficult if not impossible.

At the individual company level, codes of conduct are a relatively new development with, for example, the well-known apparel company code of conduct, that of Levi's, having only been adopted in 1991 (United States Department of Labor 1996: ii). Among certain leading firms' attempts have been made to operationalise codes of conduct across MNE production chains rather than merely regarding them as a statement of broad corporate principles. One writer in a United States Department of Labor study shared the view that the most important developments today do not lie so much in

---

4   See International Labour Rights Fund, www.laborrights.org, International Confederation of Free Trade Unions, www.icftu.org, and Business for Social Responsibility, www.bsr.org, as just three examples.

adopting codes that are already widespread, but in the ways companies are devising to implement codes (United States Department of Labor 1996: 9). However, other experts in this area have stated contradictorily that codes are in fact not widespread, but are limited to a few proactive MNEs within a few specific sectors (Jenkins 2001: 12). We do not seek to address this debate within this book but rather focus primarily on the experiences of MNEs and suppliers in the implementation of CSR and code standards.

Increasingly, the implementation of codes is becoming an activity that is central to the operations of the organisation, requiring an integrated approach that touches on many areas, including communication, training, reward systems, reporting, purchasing and logistics, and monitoring, to name a few. This last point has received particular attention, linked as it is to the belief of diverse stakeholders in the effectiveness of various corporate efforts; boosting transparency—and stakeholder support of monitoring—has become an objective of many firms. The general acceptance of this can be seen in the comments of CEOs at the 2001 World Economic Forum's annual meeting in Davos, where the panel discussion addressing this issue stated that:

> It would be difficult to overstate the consensus, almost the passion, among these CEOs of the leading global companies [on the Davos panel] that the time is at hand for transparency.[5]

However, in our view, there is progress to be made, as in our experience companies do not always embrace transparency if it conflicts with business goals. At a broader level, companies are often opposed to government intervention.[6]

Increasingly, another form of initiative is evolving, this involving a range of actors, sometimes including stakeholders other than the firms themselves, with a more generalised set of principles or social performance objectives. These hybrid associations may involve NGOs, workers' organisations, student groups and investors as well as enterprises. Examples would include the UK-based Ethical Trading Initiative (ETI), an alliance of companies, unions and NGOs that has established a programme of independent verification, and carried out numerous studies to determine best practices for implementing codes, and the US-based Fair Labor Association (FLA), an initiative initially created with the support of President Clinton with the participation of manufacturers, consumer groups, labour and human rights organisations, and universities. The Global Compact, a more recent and broader effort initiated by the United Nations, is centred on ten principles addressing human rights, labour conditions, the environment and anti-corruption. While not a code, the Compact does set expectations for firms that need to be included in their strategic objectives if they are to meet its requirements.

The complexity of these issues, the varying goals of initiatives and the range of actors and viewpoints, makes a short review difficult. From the ILO perspective, a primary objective would be that firms act in ways that support core labour standards and, with regard to codes of conduct, that

> **The Global Compact, a more recent and broader effort initiated by the UN, is centred on ten principles addressing human rights, labour conditions, the environment and anti-corruption.**

---

5   Summary of 2001 WEF panel 'The Corporation and the Public: Open For Inspection'. This can be found by searching the title at the WEF website: www.weforum.org.

6   In the view of Nobel prize-winning economist Milton Friedman 'there is only one social responsibility of business . . . to increase its profits so long as it stays within the rules of the game' (Friedman 1970).

these codes support such action. At the same time, core labour standards are part of some of the more prominent initiatives, with overlap existing between the Global Compact, the Organisation for Economic Co-operation and Development (OECD) Guidelines for Multinational Enterprises, and ETI, each calling for firms to respect and implement the ILO's Declaration on Fundamental Principles and Rights at Work. It should also be recognised that some initiatives, including those of the ILO that are based on tripartite consensus between governments, workers' organisations and employers' organisations, have more weight than others. For example, the OECD Guidelines, which were developed with input from the Business and Advisory Committee to the OECD (BIAC) and the Trade Union Advisory Committee to the OECD (TUAC), have an important status as recommendations made by OECD Governments to MNEs, while the ILO Tripartite Declaration of Principles concerning Multinational Enterprises and Social Policy, which references the ILO's Fundamental Principles and goes beyond these Principles in its recommendations, is a universal instrument offering guidelines to MNEs, governments, and employers' and workers' organisations.

Considering the nature of voluntary private initiatives, the content of corporate social performance objectives and codes of conduct, the means of implementing these codes and of verifying the efficacy of approach chosen all have led to a lively debate. In particular, the process of globalisation and the blurring of corporate boundaries, together with the shifting expectations of national publics concerning responsibility for supply chains that stretch into developing countries, have proved confusing for many companies. According to a leading columnist in *The Guardian* newspaper, 'many business leaders warn of "market confusion", with a blizzard of new ethical, social and environmental standards' (Elkington 2001). The challenge for those working on these issues is how to achieve the objectives of these various codes, alliances and schemes in the most effective and efficient manner—typically to ensure decent work for employees while meeting needs of various stakeholders—without getting overwhelmed by the plethora of possible approaches.

b. Role of international frameworks

Our research revealed that there is extensive documentation, research and analysis that exists which continues to provide a foundation for initiatives related to codes of conduct. Studies and research have occurred on the international, national and local levels, and have included analysis and evaluation by public, private and non-profit sector organisations representing the full spectrum of diverse stakeholders. Some of the most authoritative information exists within international organisations such as the ILO, the OECD and the United Nations.

A search of the 'Business and Social Incentives' database[7] of the ILO (BASI) turned up no less than 400 Web-based resources related to codes of conduct. The existence of general as well as authoritative resources may be used to counter criticism that parties developing codes are drawing on inconsistent or disparate resources for content. While the actual intent of a code, or the rationale for inclusion or exclusion of specific provisions of a code, may be the subject of debate or speculation, the fact remains that vast amounts of literature exist to assist in defining the aims and objectives of all

7   Business and Social Incentives (BASI); see www.ilo.org/basi.

aspects of codes of conduct. This supports the ILO contention that codes, including the broad content of codes, have not been developed in a vacuum.

The following sections summarise pertinent provisions of key international organisation documents related to codes of conduct. This material includes frameworks for the development of codes, systems and procedure related to the activities of MNEs that are or may be incorporated into individual codes of conduct. The provisions referenced in this section are embodied in public international law that may include a ratified treaty or convention, or the express provisions contained therein. Accordingly, the ILO, OECD and UN provide a historical basis and authoritative source for negotiated language that seeks to balance the divergent interests of governments, workers and employers.

A complete listing of applicable ILO and OECD documents related to labour standards is contained in Appendix 1.

Labour provisions of the ILO

Tripartite Declaration

The primary document embodying the ILO's labour principles for MNEs is the 'Tripartite Declaration of Principles Concerning Multinational Enterprises and Social Policy' (hereinafter 'Tripartite Declaration').[8] In this document, the ILO lays out a basic framework of labour principles, from which the intent for implementation may be inferred, interpreted and debated. In the Tripartite Declaration, the ILO invites governments, employers, workers' organisations and MNEs to observe its principles so as to maximise the positive contributions of MNEs, particularly those related to economic and social development. It calls for appropriate laws and policies, along with co-operation between government and trade unions, and recommends the principles as a guide to be observed on a voluntary basis by all parties.

All parties are admonished to respect the sovereign rights of states, obey national laws and regulations, give due consideration to local practices and respect relevant international standards. Specific mention is made of the United Nations Universal Declaration of Human Rights (also covered in this section), international covenants adopted by the UN, and the Constitution of the ILO, with special emphasis placed on the freedom of expression and association.[9]

The Tripartite Declaration seeks to promote a consistent standard for both domestic and international companies, calling for 'good practices' for conduct in general, and social practices in particular. It states that national governments should promote good social practice and have regard to 'social and labour law, regulations and practices in host countries as well as to relevant international standards', including consultations among all concerned parties, as appropriate.

Disputes under the ILO Tripartite Declaration

The ILO has established a system for resolving disputes or conflicts arising under the terms or provisions of the Tripartite Declaration. Specifically, the ILO provides for the

---

8   Adopted by the Governing Body of the International Labour Office at its 204th Session, Geneva, November 1977, as amended at its 279th Session, Geneva, November 2000.

9   *Ibid.*, Art. 8.

'examination of disputes' arising from the application of the Tripartite Declaration by means of a process of formal interpretation.[10]

This provision states that '[t]he purpose of the procedure is to interpret the provisions of the Declaration when needed to resolve a disagreement on their meaning, arising from an actual situation, between parties to whom the Declaration is commended.' The ILO is careful to avoid duplication or conflicts with either national law and practice, or existing ILO procedures, prohibiting the invocation of this interpretive process when other dispute mechanisms are already provided for.[11]

Table 4 provides a listing of the specific labour-related activities of the General Policies provisions of the Tripartite Declaration, along with the applicable ILO Convention and Recommendation referenced in the provision.

ILO Declaration on Fundamental Principles and Rights at Work

The Governing Body of the ILO at its 277th Session, Geneva, March 2000, adopted the 'Declaration on Fundamental Principles and Rights at Work' (which had been adopted by the International Labour Conference in June 1998). This Declaration called for a renewed 'commitment to respect, promote and realise the following fundamental principles and rights at work, namely:

a. Freedom of association and the effective recognition of the right to collective bargaining;

b. The elimination of all forms of forced or compulsory labour;

c. The effective abolition of child labour; and

d. The elimination of discrimination in respect of employment and occupation.'

The Declaration makes clear that these four categories of fundamental rights and principles are universal and apply to the entire tripartite membership, whether or not member states have ratified the relevant ILO Conventions. Explicit mention is also made to the contributions of MNEs as 'an important element' in attaining the Declaration's objective. Further, the Declaration states that these fundamental rights and principles should be taken fully into account when interpreting and applying the principles of the Tripartite Declaration. Consistent with avoiding prescriptive language, the ILO reaffirms here the voluntary character and meaning of the Tripartite Declaration.[12]

---

10   Adopted by the Governing Body of the International Labour Office at its 232nd Session, Geneva, March 1986.

11   For additional information, see the *Official Bulletin*, Vol. LXIX, Series A, No. 3, ILO, Geneva, 1986, pp. 196-97, and *Official Bulletin*, Vol. LXIV, Series A, No. 1, 1981, pp. 89-90.

12   Copies of ILO Conventions and Recommendations referred to in the Tripartite Declaration are available on request from ILO Publications or at www.ilo.org.

Labour area	Labour activity	Applicable Convention	Applicable Recommendation
Conditions of Work and Life	Age, Benefits and Conditions of Work		No. 116: Reduction of Hours of Work
		No. 110: Conditions of Plantation Workers	No. 110: Conditions of Plantation Workers
			No. 115: Workers' Housing
			No. 69: Medical Care
		No. 130: Medical Care and Sickness Benefits	No. 134: Medical Care and Sickness Benefits
	Minimum Wage	No. 131: Minimum Wage	No. 135: Minimum Wage
	Minimum Age	No. 138, Art. 1: Minimum Age	
		No. 182, Art. 1: Child Labour	
	Safety and Health	No. 119: Guarding of Machinery	No. 118: Guarding of Machinery
		No. 115: Ionising Radiation	No. 114: Ionising Radiation
		No. 136: Benzene	No. 144: Benzene
		No. 139: Occupational Cancer	No. 147: Occupational Cancer
Employment	Employment Promotion	No. 122: Employment Policy	No. 122: Employment Policy
	Equality of Opportunity and Treatment	No. 111: Discrimination	No. 111: Discrimination
		No. 100: Equal Remuneration	No. 90: Equal Remuneration
	Security of Employment		No. 119: Termination of Employment
Industrial Relations	Freedom of Association and Right to Organise	No. 87: Freedom of Association and Right to Organise	
		No. 98: Principles of the Right to Organise and Bargain	
	Collective Bargaining	No. 98: Principles of the Right to Organise and Bargain	
		No. 135: Workers' Representatives	
			No. 129: Communications, Management and Workers
	Consultation		No. 94: Consultation and Co-operation
			No. 129: Communications
	Examination of Grievances		No. 130: Examination of Grievances
		No. 29: Forced or Compulsory Labour	
		No. 105: Abolition of Forced Labour	
			No. 35: Indirect Compulsion of Labour
	Settlement of Industrial Disputes		No. 92: Voluntary Conciliation and Arbitration
Training	Training	No. 142: Vocational Guidance and Training	No. 150: Vocational Guidance and Training

TABLE 4 APPLICABLE ILO CONVENTIONS AND RECOMMENDATIONS

OECD Guidelines for Multinational Enterprises[13]

The Guidelines for MNEs were adopted by the governments of the 29 member countries of the OECD and Argentina, Brazil, Chile and the Slovak Republic at the OECD Ministerial Meeting on 27 June 2000.

The OECD Guidelines for MNEs are recommendations generated by governments that provide voluntary principles and standards for responsible business conduct. The Guidelines aim to ensure that the operations of MNEs make positive contributions to the societies in which they operate. The Guidelines state that their aim is 'to encourage the positive contributions that multinational enterprises can make to economic, environmental and social progress and to minimise the difficulties to which their various operations may give rise'.

Key government action in this regard includes effective domestic policy frameworks; stable macroeconomic policy; non-discriminatory treatment of firms; appropriate regulation and prudential supervision; an impartial system of courts and law enforcement; and efficient and honest public administration. In addition to referencing the promotion of sustainable development, the Guidelines state, 'Governments adhering to the Guidelines are committed to continual improvement of both domestic and international policies with a view to improving the welfare and living standards of all people.'

The general provisions enumerate various behavioural goals and objectives for MNEs, including:

1. Economic, social and environmental progress

2. Respect of human rights

3. Local capacity building, and domestic and foreign market development

4. Human capital formation, including employment opportunities and training

5. Exemptions to environmental, health, safety, labour, taxation, financial incentives, or other issues

6. Good corporate governance principles and practices

7. Self-regulatory practices and management systems

8. Awareness of, and compliance with, company policies

9. Action against employees who report practices that contravene the law

10. Business partners, suppliers and subcontractors compliance with the Guidelines

11. Improper involvement in local politics

Unique to the OECD Guidelines, a meritorious attempt is made to address the issue of bribery. Specifically, MNEs 'should not, directly or indirectly, offer, promise, give, or demand a bribe or other undue advantage to obtain or retain business or other improper advantage. Nor should enterprises be solicited or expected to render a bribe

---

13   Text adapted from www.oecd.org.

or other undue advantage'. The Guidelines include six sections that outline a variety of steps, actions, behaviours and policies that should be undertaken by MNEs to discourage and fight bribery, extortion and corrupt practices.

National Contact Points (Ncps)

The OECD espouses a formal programme of promotion, management, interpretation and dispute settlement arising from the Guidelines in the form of Ncps for each country adhering to the Guidelines. Responsible for clarification of the Guidelines, this body is empowered to seek advice from a variety of entities, including business and trade union advisory committees, and in general is tasked with ensuring the effective functioning of the Guidelines.

Explicit procedural guidance regarding Ncps is provided relating to the objectives of 'visibility, accessibility, transparency and accountability'. These include such matters as the appointment and organisation of Ncps, dissemination of information and promotion of the Guidelines. Further, the detailed process for the handling and resolving of issues arising under the Guidelines is outlined, along with the requirement that Ncps submit annual reports.

United Nations

United Nations Universal Declaration of Human Rights[14]

Adopted and proclaimed by the General Assembly of the United Nations, the Universal Declaration of Human Rights calls upon all member countries to publicise the text of the Declaration and 'to cause it to be disseminated, displayed, read and expounded principally in schools and other educational institutions, without distinction based on the political status of countries or territories'.

For the purposes of this book, the operative articles of the UN Universal Declaration of Human Rights applicable or related to issues of labour and employment include:

Article 7
All are equal before the law and are entitled without any discrimination to equal protection of the law. All are entitled to equal protection against any discrimination in violation of this Declaration and against any incitement to such discrimination.

Article 8
Everyone has the right to an effective remedy by the competent national tribunals for acts violating the fundamental rights granted him by the constitution or by law.

Article 20

1. Everyone has the right to freedom of peaceful assembly and association.

2. No one may be compelled to belong to an association.

---

14   United Nations Universal Declaration of Human Rights, adopted by UN General Assembly resolution 217 A (III) of 10 December 1948. For full text see www.un.org.

Article 22
Everyone, as a member of society, has the right to social security and is entitled to realisation, through national effort and international co-operation and in accordance with the organisation and resources of each State, of the economic, social and cultural rights indispensable for his dignity and the free development of his personality.

Article 23

1. Everyone has the right to work, to free choice of employment, to just and favourable conditions of work and to protection against unemployment.

2. Everyone, without any discrimination, has the right to equal pay for equal work.

3. Everyone who works has the right to just and favourable remuneration ensuring for himself and his family an existence worthy of human dignity, and supplemented, if necessary, by other means of social protection.

4. Everyone has the right to form and to join trade unions for the protection of his interests.

Article 24
Everyone has the right to rest and leisure, including reasonable limitation of working hours and periodic holidays with pay.

Article 25

1. Everyone has the right to a standard of living adequate for the health and well-being of himself and of his family, including food, clothing, housing and medical care and necessary social services, and the right to security in the event of unemployment, sickness, disability, widowhood, old age or other lack of livelihood in circumstances beyond his control.

United Nations Global Compact[15]
The Global Compact is an initiative of the Secretary General that promotes CSR by seeking to advance universal values. The Global Compact presents business with the challenge to adopt and apply ten universal principles in the areas of human rights, labour and the environment and to integrate these principles into daily practices and management systems.

The underlying objective of the Global Compact is to enhance economic progress, foster corporate responsibility, global citizenship and institutional learning in addressing a variety of present-day issues. By its efforts, the Global Compact creates a common forum for enterprises, labour and civil-society organisations with the aim of expanding the benefits of economic development as well as limiting their negative impacts.

The universal document upon which the ten principles of the Global Compact are based include the UN Universal Declaration of Human Rights, the ILO's Declaration on Fundamental Principles of Rights at Work, and the Rio Principles on Environment and

15　For further information see www.unglobalcompact.org.

Development. The organisational partners involved with dissemination and implementation of the provisions of the Global Compact include the UN Secretary General, UN Environment Programme (UNEP), the ILO and the UN High Commissioner for Human Rights.

Other international frameworks

Other related international initiatives include the United Nations Subcommission on the Promotion and Protection of Human Rights, which has drafted a document entitled 'Human rights principles and responsibilities for transnational corporations and other business enterprises', which explicitly incorporates the principles of ILO Conventions.[16] The International Finance Committee (IFC), a division of the World Bank, has established a corporate citizenship facility to assist in demonstrating the business case for good corporate behaviour. The IFC also has a framework for measuring the sustainability of private-sector investments, which includes an assessment of the health, safety and welfare of the labour force (ILO 2003: 12).

3. Distinguishing features of codes

In this section, we review a variety of factors that influenced the initial development as well as the continued evolution of codes. Foundational issues relating to code development include definition and scope of the subject matter to be managed, the specific legal parameters within which the entity seeks to operate, as well as the initial motivations for establishing a code. Further, the breadth of stakeholders involved in the creation of a respective code is a significant factor for its acceptance and credibility.

> *The bottom line is that corporate codes of conduct—whether drafted by individual companies or by groups of them, whether independently monitored mechanisms or useless pieces of paper—are not democratically controlled laws. Not even the toughest self-imposed code can put the multinationals in the position of submitting to collective outside authority.*
> (Klein 2002: 437)

Corporate codes of conduct are not mandated by legislation. By and large, they are voluntary initiatives undertaken by the private sector to address a variety of operational and social issues, including labour standards. They may be developed with or without input from diverse stakeholders such as employees, trade unions, NGOs and governments. In many respects, codes of conduct have evolved in response to a lack of (or enforcement of) national regulatory schemes to manage global corporate behaviour. Within this context, it is noteworthy that great emphasis has been placed on the implicit shortcomings of non-governmental regulatory programmes: 'the bottom line is that corporate codes of conduct—whether drafted by individual companies or by groups of them, whether independently monitored mechanisms or useless pieces of paper—are not democratically controlled laws. Not even the toughest self-imposed code can put the multinationals in the position of submitting to collective outside authority' (Klein 2002: 437).

16   For more information see www.unhcr.ch.

Historically, companies have relied on national laws and regulations to guide them in the development of operational procedures and management systems, the purpose of which was to meet the required standards prescribed by the legislation. The common-law and civil-code traditions under which the majority of MNEs were created and operate provided the measure for corporate behaviour. The challenge that codes typically seek to address is the voluntary application of prescriptive standards from the home countries of MNEs to the overseas operations of suppliers, subcontractors and other business partners where standards may be non-existent, incomplete, not enforced or ignored.

In the absence of highly developed regulatory structures, codes reflect an attempt to address the operational challenges of globalisation and extend accountable MNE behaviour overseas. Codes attempt to define and apply a performance standard to a complex web of foreign supply chains, inexperienced workforces, differing local custom and cultural values, conflicting legislation and inconsistent enforcement. Motivated initially by public pressure to real and perceived abuses in overseas operations, some MNEs developed codes in an attempt to address or resolve these concerns. However, the lack of express standards developed and overseen by an appropriate governmental authority has led to often-acrimonious relations among diverse stakeholders. Conflict arises in attempting to balance competing interests related to code content and the practical implementation thereof, with the need for meaningful, effective and verifiable results.

Generally, any voluntary limitation to corporate power occurs only when the value proposition shows a return or benefit. Uniquely, codes present the paradoxical position of limiting the power of the entity that creates it. Essentially a form of self-regulation, codes derive from the interaction of normally competing interests of various workplace, community and regulatory forces.

a. Definition and development

Codes of conduct do not have a fixed definition. They include a broad array of goals, formulations, benchmarks and approaches to implementation. They address a wide range of issues, including relations between MNEs in the world market, labour matters such as terms and conditions of work and equality, environmental standards, and health and safety issues related to individual products. In the most general sense, a code of conduct may be understood as a statement of business principles defining a set of relationships on a range of topics between an entity and its stakeholders (ILO 2002a: ch. 1). Codes are largely voluntary, though some trade and industry organisations make adoption of a code a precondition for membership.

The first formal corporate code of conduct, authored by the International Chamber of Commerce (ICC) in 1937, was created to restrict competition between companies and to help prevent competition from damaging the environment or society.

The first formal corporate code of conduct, authored by the International Chamber of Commerce (ICC) in 1937, was created to restrict competition between companies and to help prevent competition from damaging the environment or society in locations where members of the ICC operated (ILO 2002a: 3). During the late 1960s and 1970s, the public drive to eliminate unethical business practices led several international organisations and national governments to adopt ethical codes addressing corporate conduct. The most significant of these are the OECD Declaration on International Investment and Multinational Enterprises, issued in 1976, and the ILO Tripartite Declaration, issued in 1977.

These declarations have been pivotal in promoting responsible labour practices, primarily because they provide clear, precise and broadly applicable definitions and standards. Representing the only internationally agreed principles on the operations of MNEs and their implications for labour rights, they have played a prominent role in the development of CSR and codes of conduct. Since the late 1980s, the majority of code development has been on the part of individual companies. As systems of global production have replaced trade as the principal international economic interaction and questions about the internal and external regulation of MNEs continue to gain prominence, companies have responded by formulating their own codes to address issues such as labour practices and the environment.

b. Factors influencing codes

Many factors contribute to the development of a code. The motivation of an MNE to create or adopt a code varies greatly. Further, the specific methodology employed in developing, selecting and implementing a code greatly influences the effectiveness and credibility of the code before diverse stakeholders such as fellow industry members, trade unions, consumers and governments. Factors that influence a code include diversity of participants involved, scope of issues, standards used to evaluate corporate behaviour or performance, level of detail in substantive provisions, effective implementation and ongoing management, resources devoted to training, monitoring and enforcement; transparency and disclosure, real or anticipated costs of compliance and public relations factors.

Soliciting input from a broad range of stakeholders in drafting the code is often interpreted as demonstrating a strong commitment to a company's social obligations. Just criticism can be directed at codes developed with no or minimum input from stakeholders. While MNEs are arguably free to establish their own internal governance and are primarily responsible to employees and shareholders, our research indicates that it is highly beneficial to consult widely in making policy decisions directed towards the larger community.[17] Given that many factories affected by code commitments do not have functioning union representation, soliciting input from sources such as the Global Union Federations (GUFs) may provide useful information regarding practices and pressures affecting workers in similar factories. Similarly, governmental departments, labour rights NGOs, and organisations such as the OECD and the ILO can provide valuable insight into the internal and external factors affecting MNE operations, and can help in the creation of a code that is both appropriate and effective to their circumstances.

> **Factors influencing codes include:**
> * Diversity of participants involved
> * Scope of issues
> * Standards used to evaluate corporate behaviour or performance
> * Level of detail in substantive provisions
> * Effective implementation and ongoing management
> * Resources devoted to training, monitoring and enforcement
> * Transparency and disclosure
> * Costs of compliance
> * Public relations factors

---

17   This topic is dealt with later in this book, in Chapters IV, V and VI.

A variety of factors may give expression to a code. For example, our findings highlight that a public commitment to the code by the chief executive and the involvement of upper-level management in all required departments suggests a thorough integration of the code. Adoption of international labour standards also may enhance the credibility of a code as such provisions enjoy unparalleled international legitimacy. Perhaps the most important issues relate to the specific provisions and the resources dedicated to code implementation. The more clear, concise and specific the code is regarding key aspects such as training, compliance verification, supplier behaviour, working conditions and labour practices, the more legitimate the code appears. Finally, the transparency of the code is critical, and is a function of the extent to which code commitments, means of implementation, ongoing management systems, performance records and reports, and compliance verification are publicly available.

c. Codes specific to a sector or issue

Codes have been developed to address both narrow and broad purposes, specific industry sectors and specific types of work. For example, the adoption of the Sullivan Principles in 1977 was intended to promote equal opportunity in then-segregated South Africa. Other examples include initiatives begun by the Fédération Internationale de Football (FIFA), the ILO and others, to implement a programme to eliminate child labour in the production of soccer balls in Pakistan (ILO 2002a: 7). However, corporate codes most often address a range of labour and environmental issues and are meant to apply broadly to all company operations.

A variety of drivers may motivate an MNE to develop a code. Jill Murray notes:

> One set of reasons may be to do with internal management, particular across geographically far-flung sites: a code of conduct provides a framework for consistent managerial conduct and is thus a useful tool of internal governance. Another set of reasons may have to do with the benefits which would accrue to an organisation (or industry grouping) through the proper application of fair labour practices. Ethical reasons may form the basis of the code, reflecting management's desire to be, or portray itself as, a good corporate citizen. A firm may want to use a code of conduct to extend or protect its reputation, which in some industries will be an important asset (Murray 1998: 12).

Since the late 1980s, some MNEs in the footwear, apparel and retail sectors have come under increased scrutiny because of scandals in their supplier factories involving child labour, excessive working hours, low wages, harassment and abuse, denial of the right to organise, and other violations of international labour standards. As the importance of brand reputation is especially acute in these industry sectors, these companies were among the first to adopt codes addressing the practices of their suppliers. Since the inception of codes, 'available information suggests that the world's largest multinational enterprises, and in particular US-based multinational enterprises in the textile, apparel, footwear, and related commerce sectors, have led the trend towards the usage of codes as a means of responsible sourcing' (Urminsky 2001: 16). Businesses in these industries have also developed a larger number of codes in conjunction with industry organisations, labour unions, and NGOs, than in other sectors.

Supplier codes are of primary interest in the debate on codes, as they represent a fundamental shift in the function of codes. As Jill Murray observes in her discussion on these codes:

> Perhaps the greatest conceptual innovation of modern codes is their expansion to include employees of suppliers and subcontractors who are not direct hires of the company authoring the code.

> Most codes developed before this period were directed at internal company behaviour, and as such were largely 'inappropriate to the diverse cross-cultural demands of the international marketplace'. Those codes which were externally directed were 'aimed primarily at social critics, the government, and the media,' and lacked 'operations specificity or credibility' (Murray 1998: 3).

In contrast to internally directed codes, this current trend is fundamentally different in several important ways. Codes are largely formulated and applied unilaterally. In most cases MNEs cite their own internal standards rather than directly applying recognised international guidelines such as those outlined by the ILO or OECD. Similarly, monitoring and remediation efforts conducted by the company are not necessarily co-ordinated with their counterparts in the existing state regulatory systems (United States Department of Labor 2002). Further, the purpose of these codes is not to protect the sovereignty of governments, as was the case with international agreements in the 1970s. Instead, modern codes have been adopted in response to gaps and shortcomings of existing regulatory systems. Perhaps the greatest conceptual innovation of modern codes is their expansion to include employees of suppliers and subcontractors who are not direct hires of the company authoring the code.

These innovations may imply recognition by MNEs of the inherent responsibilities created by the realities of a global business operation. The complexity of these production systems has challenged the jurisdiction and efficacy of existing national and international regulatory schemes. In economic and political environments that do not provide a strong external and independent system of regulation, codes may provide a significant means for workers to secure treatment no less favourable than those stipulated in the legislation of MNE home countries and international labour agreements.

Importantly, it must be emphasised that corporate codes of conduct cannot be considered an adequate substitute for effective national labour regulation. Groups as disparate as the International Organisation of Employers (IOE) and the International Confederation of Free Trade Unions (ICFTU), as well as numerous labour rights theorists, maintain that private codes can complement, but never replace, adequate national provisions. Thus, the point is strongly emphasised that 'codes of conduct should be seen as an area of political contestation, rather than as a solution to the problems created by the globalisation of economic activity' (Jenkins 2002b: 70).

4. Language used in a code

In this section, we evaluate the importance of selecting appropriate language for a code of conduct, as a variety of challenges are posed in developing a code for application in diverse localities across the globe. Given the broad aims and objectives of the code, along with the various audiences to which it is to be communicated, language and message arise as critical concerns. Specific code language is not a reliable indication of actual practice. It is possible for companies without codes to work to ensure that their suppliers act in accordance with applicable legal, labour, social or ethical standards. Nevertheless, codes do represent a discernable demonstration of a company's commitment to certain business practices, and an examination of the specific language used in a code provides useful insight into the attitudes and motivations underlying it.

a. Ambiguity and clarity

The substantive content of a code has two primary linguistic parts. The first is the expression of the standard to be complied with. The second is the expression of how strictly the MNE holds itself or its supplier to that standard. The utility of a statement in implementing standards functions on a scale. At one end is an absolute and unqualified commitment to abide by the standard, thereby setting a mandatory obligation for itself and its suppliers. At the other end of the scale is the promotion of a standard, which leaves a firm definition and clear implementation measures to the discretion of suppliers.

Standards that provide little or no definition of their terms and reference no external body of practice are problematic. The following is an example from our research of an unclear standard regarding wage levels:

> We believe in the betterment of wage and benefit levels that address the basic needs of workers and their families, so far as possible and appropriate, in light of national practices and conditions. We will seek suppliers who share this commitment.

This statement has several components that inhibit effective implementation. Though the statement endorses wage levels, it provides no definition of the key term 'basic needs', and no guidance for establishing a definition. In this case, an explicit reference to national or regional minimum-wage laws would provide clarity, since minimum-wage levels are established in part through the thorough examination of the goods and services that constitute 'basic needs'. In addition, by framing wage levels 'in light of national practices and conditions' rather than with respect to national labour laws, the statement creates a potential conflict between the code and national legislation. Finally, the inclusion of the clause 'so far as possible and appropriate' effectively limits the standard, providing a caveat through which even wages that do not meet 'basic needs' of workers may be deemed acceptable by the language of the statement. A more effective code element addressing wage levels might be:

> In all cases, wages must equal or exceed the minimum wage or the prevailing industry wage, whichever is higher, and legally mandated benefits shall also be provided.

This statement makes a clear commitment to adequate wage and benefit levels by aligning each with national labour laws. The language of the standard itself is absolute, and does not allow for interpretations regarding the authority of the national legislation cited. However, the statement does not define 'prevailing industry wage', which leaves discretion to the company in making its own determination as to what is 'prevailing' in this industry. Further, the utility of national labour law in setting code standards extends to other labour issues. For example, the following health and safety standard would be considered unclear due to its lack of any independently verifiable benchmark:

> We believe that factories should be safe and that the risk of harm from dangerous activities should be minimised through the provision of safety equipment, training, and a safe factory infrastructure.

Though the statement does detail several factors impacting workplace health and safety, it provides no definitions or examples for evaluating these influences. Its ambiguity is further compounded by its lack of reference to any body of knowledge, such as national law or ILO Convention that could clarify its meaning. A better statement might read:

> Suppliers must ensure that they abide by all local laws relating to health and safety in the workplace and residentially where facilities are provided.

This statement is equally concise, but by framing workplace health and safety in the context of national laws, this provision references a larger body of explicit practices that can be invoked as measurements of a factory's progress.

b. Hard and soft language

In addition to its impact on standards, the language chosen in drafting a code can suggest the level of responsibility taken on by an MNE regarding the degree to which the provisions will be enforced. 'Hard' code language is specific, precise, fully-defined, and provides a high level of commitment to the standard. 'Soft' code language is general, broad, loosely defined, and displays a low level of commitment.[18]

As has been noted, MNEs have often drafted codes in response to the increased scrutiny of their global production systems by consumers, investors and advocacy groups. The concerns and perceptions of domestic audiences in turn influence the expression of various labour issues. With emotional issues such as child labour, the language of code statements seems more likely to be strong and unambiguous and include potential consequences for code violations. Examples include:

---

18   The terms 'hard' and 'soft' are used in two instances in this book. The first is with reference to the language used in codes of conduct, as outlined in this section. The second usage is to distinguish between product categories in the retail sector. It should be noted, however, that within those involved in the compliance industry there is a further, third application of the two terms. Sometimes auditors and academics use the term 'hard' to refer to technical issues encapsulated in a code, such as EHS, which have clear and easily measurable performance criteria. The term 'soft' is then left to describe those aspects of the code, such as discrimination and freedom of association, which cannot be measured empirically but instead require in-depth probing through various avenues, including face-to-face interviews with workers. The term 'soft' is used in this instance to describe the skills that the interviewer requires to obtain the requisite information and originates from terminology commonly used in the field of human resources. It does not refer to the standards themselves.

> We will not work with partners who use the labour of children. We define 'child' as younger than 15 years of age (or 14 where the local law allows) or younger than the compulsory age for school attendance.

> We will not work with business partners that use child labour. The term 'child' generally refers to a person who is younger than 15 (or 14 where the law of the country of manufacture allows) or younger than the age for completing compulsory education in the country of manufacture where such age is higher than 15.

> Business partners shall not employ children who are less than 15 years old, or who are younger than the age for completing compulsory education in the country of manufacture where such age is higher than 15.

The strength of these statements resides in the explicit definition of terms such as 'child', and the explicit reference to both an internal standard and national education laws. Similarly, by opening with the phrase 'we will not work with . . .' the first two statements make adherence to the provision a condition for a business relationship. The language of the third statement, though equally unambiguous, allows greater leeway in determining a response to a violation of the standard. Nevertheless, all of these statements exemplify the manner in which hard language can facilitate the clear interpretation and implementation of a given standard.

Child labour is a vivid and widely publicised labour problem, and so it is not surprising that a strong stance has been taken by enterprises towards its elimination. For less visible or more complex labour issues, however, codes seem more likely to use less specific wording and to distance the company from direct responsibility. For example, by prefacing code provisions with statements such as 'the company will never knowingly purchase from a supplier who' or 'the company will seek vendors who', an enterprise can effectively shift the responsibility for compliance, and associated guilt, to the supplier, which may be the aim or intent of the language selection. Similarly, by qualifying standards with statements such as 'so far as is possible and feasible' or 'in light of accepted custom or regional practice', a company's stated commitment may be limited, intentionally or otherwise.

c. Language nuances

For effective code implementation, it is important to determine the appropriate information and form of communication required to reach the necessary audiences. For example, our research indicated that the CEO message announcing the code might on its own be inadequate to communicate the specific duties to the overseas supplier. The detailed procedures that guide plant managers in implementing code provisions may also be inadequate for overseas workers to make a determination regarding their specific rights and responsibilities under a new code. Overly legalistic boilerplate language drafted in the office of the General Counsel in the home country may understandably address legal concerns, but is probably inappropriate or ineffective for communicating responsibilities to domestic or international technical staff. Our field research supports such claims. In our research, we learned from worker representatives that, in some overseas operations, workers simply do not understand the code.

Further, sensitivity to cultural norms, nuances and biases is required. Translation that takes into consideration regional and local dialects, the awareness of unwritten social norms regarding communication, and the actual levels of education and reading ability in the workforce are practical and necessary considerations for effective communication. The clear communication of the code's meaning and specific requirements to suppliers and their employees is arguably the single greatest challenge to code implementation.

5. Types of code of conduct

This section provides a brief introduction to the most prominent types of initiative related to codes of conduct. Additional detail is offered in following sections regarding those initiatives of most pertinence to the footwear, apparel and retail sectors, in particular the multi-stakeholder initiatives (MSIs).

a. Company codes

Company codes refer to those voluntary initiatives adopted unilaterally by individual corporations. Motivated in part by extreme public pressure directed at them for real and perceived abuses in overseas operations, some of the first MNEs to develop their own company codes were Levi's and Nike. Often developed with minimal, if any, participation from other stakeholders, company codes generally relate to their own operations. Increasingly, our research shows that these codes have evolved over time to apply specifically to the operations of MNE suppliers, subcontractors and other business partners. Representing the majority of codes that exist, much attention is placed on company codes due to the fact that MNEs generally have unparalleled technical, financial and human resources to deal with the labour, social and ethical issues sought to be addressed in codes. Further details regarding the functionality of company codes will be provided in ensuing chapters.

b. Multi-stakeholder initiatives (MSIs)

Some of the most innovative and highly studied developments related to codes are MSIs, which will be covered in much greater detail later in this chapter. Uniquely, MSIs are adopted through a process of negotiation among a variety of stakeholders, thereby providing a forum within which a significantly broad range of issues and concerns may be raised and addressed. While not increasing as rapidly as individual corporate codes of conduct, important inroads and developments continue to occur within the realm of MSIs. Developed through the co-ordination of diverse stakeholders including NGOs, trade unions, companies or industry associations and on occasion governmental bodies, these codes often represent a more progressive approach to addressing concerns such as independent monitoring and the overall effectiveness of codes. The inclusion of often-divergent interests in the development of these codes leads to a level of credibility not necessarily found in other codes.

A noteworthy example of an MSI is the London-based ETI, an alliance comprising companies, NGOs and trade unions working to identify and promote good corporate practices. ETI does not certify performance or conduct audits, but rather focuses on information exchange related to the experiences of companies in implementing labour standards throughout diverse supply chains. Companies that commit to ETI standards must adopt the ETI Base Code and submit annual reports on their experience (ILO 2003: 4).

Another example of an MSI is Social Accountability International (SAI), which has developed and continues to refine its SA8000 standard for evaluating workplaces across a broad spectrum of industry sectors. Highly developed with a significant level of detail, SAI accredits monitors to audit factories and certify their compliance with the SA8000 standard. It also publishes a list of certified companies on its website. Modelled after the International Organisation for Standardisation (ISO) system, SAI considers itself a certification system for all industries, not just apparel or textile.[19]

c. Intergovernmental codes

Intergovernmental codes generally fall within the purview of public international law as negotiated instruments developed and adopted by national governments. These codes originated during the 1970s with the OECD's Guidelines for Multinational Enterprises and the ILO's Tripartite Declaration of Principles Concerning Multinational Enterprises. With no binding effect on the domestic or global behaviour of MNEs, intergovernmental codes exist as a body of documentation founded on internationally recognised and accepted principles applicable to, among other things, labour and workforce activities. A critical debate currently exists regarding the evolution of these international agreements into a body of standards that can form the basis for defining and verifying accepted corporate conduct and practice. For greater detail on these legal instruments, refer to the previous section of this chapter entitled 'Role of international frameworks' (p. 28).

d. Framework agreements

The key players in the development of framework agreements are MNEs and GUFs. Some 20 framework agreements were signed between 1999 and 2001, and represent the natural progression of industrial relations within the context of global operations. Specific reference to international labour standards occurs in framework agreements more than any other type of code (ILO 2002b).

Similar to MSIs in their reference to monitoring and accreditation procedures, framework agreements are significant and differ from corporate codes in some instances by their incorporation of signatory GUFs in follow-up pro-

> Some 20 framework agreements were signed between 1999 and 2001, and represent the natural progression of industrial relations within the context of global operations.

19   Though SAI aspires to make SA8000 a pan-industry standard, the majority of factories that have implemented the standard and sought certification are producers in apparel, footwear and toy industries. Interest in SAI is reportedly growing in agriculture and electronics. See McIntosh *et al.* 2002: 26.

cedures such as complaints procedures and awareness-raising activities. Formalised review and follow-up mechanisms include requiring senior executives, management and worker representatives to work together in the implementation of the agreement, as well as outlining specific action that must be taken towards implementation. In some cases this action extends to the holding of regular meetings and the establishment of channels for urgent communication between the MNE and signatory GUF when needed (ILO 2002b: 4).

The involvement and reach of employer, employee and the union representative can be seen in those framework agreements that call for company-wide dissemination and translation of the agreement; the development of joint training programmes; and the monitoring of the agreement by local management, workers and their representatives. Further, it is also common for agreements to include mechanisms to deal with problems that cannot be solved at the local level (ILO 2003: 6).

Framework agreements have been reached in a wide range of sectors ranging from minerals and mining to retailing, telecommunications and manufacturing. In the retail sector, framework agreements have been signed between the Union Network International (UNI) and Carrefour as well as between the International Federation of Building and Wood Workers (IFBWW) and IKEA. Interestingly, this latter agreement has been renegotiated to include specific standards applicable to IKEA suppliers, along with joint monitoring to be conducted by international worker representatives and company management (IFBWW-IKEA 2001).

Along with the other types of code of conduct outlined in this chapter, framework agreements need to be considered in the context in which they are being created. As Anita Normark, Secretary General of the IFBWW, notes, while 'the verification of the efforts of the company to live up to international standards can be facilitated through the use of a global union network . . . it is also important for governments to provide a legal framework for the implementation of global ILO and OECD standards' (ILO 2002b: 5).

6. Selection of code content

a. Scope

The scope of labour issues covered by a code can vary widely between sectors and between enterprises. Further, 'labour issues included in codes of conduct often appear to reflect the nature of publicised labour problems in the various industry and service sectors' (Urminsky 2001: 21). The shaping of a code by prevalent industry trends and other external determinants is common, as companies respond to the particular labour issues manifest in their manufacturing sectors. Recognised labour problems in the textile, clothing and footwear sectors focus on child and forced labour because these are primary areas of public outcry.

Comparatively, codes for the extractive industries such as mining and forestry more often include provisions addressing environmental and community impact. Given its proposed impact on a company's business practice, our research indicates that a code should not be hastily cobbled together in response to publicised labour problems. Such an approach promotes an uneven implementation of fundamental labour rights, both within the company and across the global labour pool. Given the fundamental inter-dependence of labour rights, piecemeal treatment could make it difficult to sustain progress in one selected area while leaving others behind (Urminsky 2001: 22). For example, disregard for the issues of working hours and overtime can adversely affect the implementation of health and safety measures. Similarly, restrictions on workers' rights to association and collective bargaining, sometimes exhibited by their lack of inclusion in a code, could inhibit the reporting of worker harassment and abuse and other violations.

In attempting to grasp the full breadth of labour and workplace standards, our research suggests that any code, at a minimum, should include the four categories of universal rights and principles at work. These include prohibitions against forced labour (expressed in Conventions No. 29 and No. 105) and child labour (Conventions No. 139 and No. 182), protection of the freedom of association and collective bargaining (Conventions No. 87 and No. 98), and support of non-discrimination and equal remuneration (Conventions No. 100 and No. 111). In addition to these core standards, other provisions advocated by the ILO include those addressing health and safety, minimum wages, job security, hours and overtime, benefits, training, and adherence to national labour law. Sound economic and ethical reasons exist for extending codes to include these other labour standards: in particular, the positive benefits of the development of human resources are supported by standards in the areas of vocational training, family leave, health and safety, industrial democracy, and so on (Murray 1998: 14).

b. Adoption of standards

Establishing the standards by which a code will be evaluated is a delicate task. The substance of a standard must be both broad enough to be applicable to myriad labour situations and precise enough to be useful in judging an individual case. Given these requirements, it is crucial to the success of a code that the standards cited are clear, specific and precise. These criteria ensure that a standard can be enacted at the corporate level and tracked and measured throughout a corporation's operations.[20] The adoption of clear standards greatly facilitates training the company's supplier operations to effectively use the code and helps create a corporate atmosphere conducive to the implementation of the code's principles. In order for a standard to be considered clear, specific and precise, it must consist of, or at the very least include references to, explicit labour and environmental practices whose merits can be argued by the larger community of the company's stakeholders.

> In order for a standard to be considered clear, specific and precise, it must consist of, or at the very least include references to, explicit labour and environmental practices whose merits can be argued by the larger community of the company's stakeholders.

---

20   ILO 2002a: Chapter 1, section entitled 'The ILO Tripartite Declaration, ILO standards and their relevance for codes'.

Generally speaking, the explicit labour and environmental practices needed to establish the standards of a code may be drawn from a number of sources, including national legislation, international labour standards and industry benchmarks. They may also be determined internally by the company itself. It has been suggested that codes are increasingly basing their standards on international references. Groups such as the United States Council for International Business (USCIB) have argued that, in most cases, the 'internal policies, guidelines, and practices established by [individual enterprises' codes of conduct] are consistent with . . . international multilateral guidelines' (USCIB 1998). However, there are several reasons why explicit references to international conventions are more useful than internal standards merely 'consistent' with these instruments in establishing labour practice goals. The first benefit is widely recognised legitimacy. In particular, ILO Conventions and Recommendations that constitute the body of international labour standards are unparalleled in their international legitimacy among the ILO's tripartite membership, and provide a sound foundation for any code. Explicit reference to national and international standards also allows individual companies to draw on the experience of governments and organisations such as the ILO in interpreting and implementing complex labour rights. The body of jurisprudence that accompanies ILO Conventions helps ensure that the definition, meaning and expression of this labour terminology are clear, credible and defensible.

> The US Council for International Business (USCIB) has argued that, in most cases, the 'internal policies, guidelines, and practices established by [individual enterprises' codes of conduct] are consistent with . . . international multilateral guidelines'.

Adopting widely recognised labour standards also helps MNEs counter criticism voiced by union activists that there is a danger of codes becoming substitutes for national legislation, thereby impinging on the sovereignty of states (ICFTU 2001). Finally, evidence from our research suggests that the management of supplier factories often view code standards as an imposition of values and not as an expression of locally accepted standards.

Given the benefits of referencing national legislation and international standards in setting standards, it is somewhat distressing that our research indicated that these resources in code formulation appear limited. Organisations and standards that are cited in codes vary widely. These included such diverse sources as the United Nations Charter, Chapter IX, Article 55, governing international economic and social co-operation; the SA8000 standards created by SAI, which make extensive references to ILO and UN Conventions; and guidelines from the UN, OECD and Amnesty International. Explicit reference to Conventions adopted by the ILO, which is made up of a tripartite constituency of more than 170 member states, may facilitate code implementation by increasing the legitimacy of a company's code in the eyes of its suppliers.

Also, regular reference is made to the adherence to national law, which is often granted primacy over corporate standards or the code in the event of conflict or inconsistency. Some have argued that the provision to adhere to national laws is essentially meaningless, as it is already the minimum obligation of any legitimate enterprise (Justice 2000). However, the infrastructure for the enforcement of labour laws and the resources devoted to the monitoring of factories in many supplier countries are often extremely limited, creating the possibility for local manufacturers to operate largely without regulation. Thus while critics have quite reasonably argued against developing CSR as a 'privatisation of national labour regulation', such provisions are useful as a reinforcement of existing legislation, and would seem most useful as an addition to a set of clearly defined internal provisions based on widely recognised international instruments (ICFTU 2001).

c. Problems with unclear standards

The practice of inconsistent or random selection of code provisions from a diversity of sources is partially a reflection of the process of ad-hoc negotiation that drove the formulation of many of the first codes of conduct, particularly in the footwear, apparel and retail sectors. Such selective citation creates significant obstacles to code implementation. Multiple sources make interpretation of standards more laborious for suppliers and increase the possibility of gaps and conflicts between requirements of the code, as well as between the code and national law. Our research indicated that these problems in turn make effective and uniform implementation more difficult. As fundamental labour rights are interdependent both in scope and degree, holding suppliers to a lesser standard in one area likely inhibits the implementation of standards in other areas.

> The application of the concept of 'continuous improvement' to labour, social and ethical standards falls short of providing a meaningful substitute for the clear and fixed standards provided by international organisations and national legislation.

One of the primary impediments to effective code implementation is the attempt to apply performance criteria from one area of operation to another. Difficulties arise when a quantitative or objective measure is attempted to be applied to an area that requires qualitative or subjective analysis; to wit, the code standard 'continuous improvement'. This term designates one of the central organising principles of contemporary globalisation, and originated in company production guidelines for quality control and environmental practices. Some companies, pursuing a 'triple bottom line' approach to business that emphasises financial, environmental and labour responsibility, have extended the use of this phrase to the sphere of labour rights. Some companies maintained that it is a useful means of distinguishing between 'what was possible and what they felt was only aspirational in codes', and some NGOs have argued that the phrase could be used to forge ongoing relationships with MNEs (ICFTU 2001). Indeed, this phrase is arguably appropriate to the quality of a product and the industrial practices used in its manufacture, both of which partially depend on technologies that are constantly advancing. However, the application of the concept of 'continuous improvement' to labour, social and ethical standards falls short of providing a meaningful substitute for the clear and fixed standards provided by international organisations and national legislation.

7. Specific standards

This section elaborates on specific performance standards commonly incorporated into codes of conduct. Code standards can broadly address issues as diverse as meals, housing, transportation, health, environment and safety. This section also provides detail regarding the primary labour standards espoused by private and public initia-tives attempting to redress the more serious concerns facing workplace conditions throughout the MNE supply chain.

a. Forced labour

Along with child labour, statements against forced labour rank among the most common code provisions. However, many codes are characterised by self-definition, primarily by prohibiting 'forced labour' without any further definition of the term (Urminsky 2001: 25). The importance of clearly defining this term is observed when considering that 'forced labour' can broadly be defined to include such things as prison, indentured, involuntary, compulsory, bonded, or any labour that is the result of politi-cal coercion or punishment for peacefully holding and expressing political views.

Those codes that best addressed the full scope of forced labour included a clear definition of forced labour, and included examples of practices that may constitute forced labour, such as the withholding of personal identification documents for the duration of an employee's contract. Further, research has shown that issues of worker harassment and abuse are often included in the provisions of forced-labour statements (Urminsky 2001: 25).

b. Freedom of association and collective bargaining

There is a relatively high incidence of reference to the right to freedom of association and collective bargaining. Some codes make 'soft' commitments, such as stating that the company 'will seek business partners who share its commitment' to these rights, while other codes state that the MNE partners with suppliers dedicated to 'continuous improvement in management practices . . . [including] the freedom of association and collective bargaining'. Nuances in language may in effect function to absolve a company from responsibility for a violation of rights, or merely hold a company to a standard of 'improvement' with no specific benchmark. Most codes make provisions along the following lines:

> Our business partners must recognise and respect the right of workers to form and join associations of their own choosing, and to bargain collectively.

Codes may further stipulate that management must not discriminate against, penalise or interfere with workers or their representatives involved in union activity. Some codes also place a proactive obligation on the management of supplier factories to allow alternative means of worker representation in those countries that restrict the freedom of association and collective bargaining:

> Where law specifically restricts the right to freedom of association and collective bargaining, the employer must not obstruct alternative and legal means for independent and free association and bargaining.

> In those situations in which workers' right to freedom of association and collective bargaining is restricted under law, our business partners will facili-tate and not hinder the development of parallel means for independent and free association and bargaining.

In the realm of labour rights, the right to freedom of association and the right to collective bargaining are more abstract than an employer's obligations in some other areas: for example, wage rates and health and safety measures. Such rights, being more conceptual, are more likely to be expressed as a prohibition from interfering or restricting workers from pursuing means of collective representation. However, the absence of restriction or intimidation is difficult to quantify, making the protection of the freedom of association and of collective bargaining, along with other topics such as harassment and abuse, more problematic to implement and evaluate.

As noted in the example above, some codes make reference to 'parallel means' of worker representation. In some instances where national law does not permit the establishment of independent trade unions, a number of codes demand that companies establish alternative means or some other structure that may give some voice to the workers. According to Neil Kearney, General Secretary of the International Textile, Garment and Leather Workers' Federation, 'the parallel means provision is designed to encourage nascent forms of worker self-representation, such as the election of worker representatives to join health and safety committees, in countries such as China where independent unions are prohibited'. Examples of these other structures include the establishment of workers' councils, welfare committees, complaints resolution committees and basic-needs wage committees.

The concept of parallel means has existed for some time, encompassing situations such as the recognition of what were considered illegal trade unions of black workers in South Africa. However, it should be noted that the use of the concept is heavily criticised by some groups. It is sometimes used in countries that have legislation upholding the right to freedom of association but where in practice such rights are not upheld. There are also instances where parallel structures are used to undermine existing legal trade unions. Moreover, as the term is often broadly defined, it is not clear exactly what qualifies as an effective non-union means of representation, nor how independent of management these means might be. Often little guidance is provided by codes on this matter.

It must be remembered that the right to freedom of association is a core labour standard enshrined in the ILO's Constitution, which governments, employers' and workers' organisations of all its member states are bound to uphold and respect. As such, all parties need to exercise care and due diligence to ensure the application of freedom of association and not to promote the concept of parallel means in situations at the workplace or enterprise level. Otherwise, as workers' organisations point out, there is the potential for disempowerment of workers as a direct consequence of having been given so-called parallel-means representation but without the safeguards that they would be given if they were to have a legitimate voice through the fully fledged exercise of their right to associate freely.

c. Discrimination and equal remuneration

Provisions against discrimination are common in codes, though are most often formulated as self-definitions with no reference to international conventions (Urminsky 2001: 24). In the codes of the MNEs that participated in this study, many contained statements addressing discrimination. Some stated a weak adherence to the standard, promising only to 'seek business partners' who do not discriminate in their hiring and employment practices. Others contain strong commitments to non-discrimination, but include varying explanations about the term itself. Still others may best be characterised as general statements requiring that suppliers 'respect human rights and dignity'.

Many codes enumerate various grounds of discrimination, such as race, national origin, gender, religion, age, disability, marital status, membership of associations, sexual orientation or political opinion. Most did not include all of the grounds for discrimination embodied in ILO instruments. As found throughout most codes, this limited scope is problematic, as an incomplete catalogue of the grounds may cause confusion among suppliers about appropriate behaviour and code violations. Providing examples of unacceptable discriminatory grounds is important, but it must be recognised that these grounds evolve and develop over time.

Another distinction our research revealed pertained to code provisions calling for equal remuneration regardless of gender. Further, some codes that mention discrimination also include specific reference to equal remuneration, either by stating some form of the 'equal work for equal pay' principle, or by prohibiting discrimination in compensation based on a range of characteristics, including gender.

d. Health and safety

Health and safety provisions are the most common references found in corporate codes of conduct. However, there are significant differences in specificity and commitments to compliance, with some codes simply stating only that they 'will seek business partners' who will adhere to their standard. There is also great variation within substantive content of the standard itself. Codes may use general self-definitions that make no reference to national legislation or international standards, and include, by example:

> The supplier will provide a safe and hygienic working environment, and occupational health and safety practices shall be promoted.

> We will seek business partners who strive to assure employees a safe and healthy workplace and who make a significant effort toward continuous improvement of that environment.

While relatively few codes cite national law as a basis for their health and safety standards, some go into great detail regarding specific practices to be targeted for improvement. Further, inclusion of examples of related fire safety, adequate lighting and ventilation standards is significant in that it helps clarify to factory management the goals of a given MNE code. Code statements may also require that the health and safety standards applied in the factory be extended to any dormitory facilities maintained by the factory. While in theory the pertinence of such a stipulation may depend on the particular supply chain, the increased use of foreign contract labour in factories around the world makes specific recognition of this labour trend an important part of responsible sourcing.

e. Harassment and abuse

Specific reference to harassment and abuse is sometimes found in forced labour provisions or it may be addressed separately. MNE codes usually demonstrate a strong commitment to the standard. While relatively common, these provisions were not generally as well defined as other topics. When included, harassment in the workplace includes reference to 'words or actions by an individual or group towards another that bothers, troubles, or annoys, or action that prevents or interferes with a person performing their duties in the workplace'. Abuse is often defined as 'words or actions used by an individual or group towards another with the intent to attack, injure, or damage another person'. Both concepts may be considered as violations of the victim's dignity, and may occur physically, verbally, psychologically or sexually. Harassment and abuse are two of the most difficult labour violations to track in supply chains, particularly since definitions of these terms vary widely between countries and cultures. A code that seeks to adequately address these problems must clearly define unacceptable practices, as well as establish a verifiable system to address and resolve matters in an appropriate manner.

f. Minimum wage

Codes commonly refer to a minimum wage for workers and demonstrate a strong commitment to the standard. The majority of codes include statements similar to the following:

> The supplier must pay each employee at least the legal minimum wage, or the prevailing industry wage, whichever is higher.

Other codes contain nuances that specify or stipulate certain pay practices. These include such provisions as the compensation of workers for overtime in compliance with local laws; forbidding deductions from wages as a disciplinary practice; requiring suppliers to provide clear and accurate pay slips to employees for each pay period; prohibiting pay deductions not stipulated by law or agreed to by the worker; and requiring that workers be allowed to check themselves in and out of work. Another aspect of pay practices is the provision of legally mandated benefits.

Further, it is important to acknowledge the heated debate regarding the adequacy of a legislatively prescribed minimum wage. The underlying issue is whether the minimum wage is adequate. The reality of substandard living conditions and quality of life found in many developing economies where vast numbers of MNE suppliers operate is well documented. In response, many advocacy groups are advancing an agenda that includes a variety of concepts to establish a social safety net and ensure the fundamental needs of workers, particularly in developing economies, are met. These include the following:

- 'Living wage': a wage that meets basic requirements related to food, health, social, leisure and familial needs and obligations

- 'Prevailing wage': the average rate paid to workers in a particular sector, which is often higher than the minimum wage given that specialised skills may be required

- 'Fair wage': similar in intent to 'living wage', developed in response to what is perceived as unrealistically low minimum wage levels and taking into consideration the realities of daily life

- A wage that allows workers to meet their 'basic needs'—again, similar in its intent to provide for minimum requirements of an individual's life

g. Hours

Code language referencing hours of work is quite common. Many code statements reflect the aims and objectives of the following, though varying slightly in their adherence to the standard set:

> Employees shall not be required to work more than 48 hours of regular work and 12 hours of overtime per week. Employees shall have at least one day off in every seven-day period, and shall receive paid annual and sick leave.

This sample code statement includes some of the primary issues that should be covered in a provision on hours, such as clear limits on regular and overtime hours, the requirement of a day of rest a week, and the inclusion of paid annual and sick leave. Some codes also specify that overtime work must always be voluntary unless the worker's contract clearly stipulates some amount of mandatory overtime. The most comprehensive of the codes also require employers to provide maternity leave and nursing breaks for female employees. In drafting a code, all of these provisions would be important additions to a thorough and inclusive CSR programme.

> Both suppliers and trade unions have noted that the implementation of labour provisions addressing 'hours of work' and 'overtime' is made more difficult by the 'just-in-time' production methodology of many supplier factories.

Both suppliers and trade unions have noted that the implementation of labour provisions addressing 'hours of work' and 'overtime' is made more difficult by the 'just-in-time' production methodology of many supplier factories. Our research indicated that it is quite common for factory workers to, at times, work excessive hours to meet production deadlines (ILO 2002a: Chapter 11, Introduction). This practice is implicitly recognised in several codes by the inclusion of clauses that state that the limit on working hours must be respected 'except in extraordinary circumstances' or that limits on hours must not be exceeded 'on a regular basis'. It is important to note that such code provisions attempt to address the realities of the global production systems. In the absence of accepted industry-wide standards, it is important to have clear definitions and explicit examples, so as to remove ambiguity and limit inconsistent implementation. As is the case with many labour principles outlined in codes, it is incumbent on MNEs to work with suppliers to incorporate social goals into the company's business methodology.

h. Other standards

In addition to labour and workplace standards, such as those outlined in the preceding section, a variety of other issues and subjects may be addressed within a code. The most common of these areas include:

- Environmental stewardship
- Disclosure of information
- Competition
- Taxation
- Bribery and corruption
- Science and technology
- Consumer protection

Other than labour standards, the most frequent reference in codes is to environmental standards and performance, referred to as 'environmental stewardship'. Provisions contained under this category may be as diverse as employee education, awareness and training related to the subject matter, incorporating environmental performance into the production process or product itself, programmes to heighten community or public awareness, and performance obligations for suppliers, subcontractors and other business partners.

8. Implementing guidelines

Beyond the general parameters required for effective implementation of the standards outlined in codes of conduct, this section reviews the critical component of the supplemental material necessary to establish the systems for implementing, managing and ensuring compliance with the code. This is especially critical within the context of extension of the code to suppliers, subcontractors and other business partners. Usually necessitating great detail and the consideration of myriad scenarios of operation, these are referred to as 'implementing guidelines'. Basically, implementing guidelines represent what could be referred to as the 'standard operating procedures' (SOPs) for code implementation. It is common practice across most industry sectors to have SOPs for financial reporting and record-keeping, as well as for the treatment, storage and disposal of regulated wastes in manufacturing operations. By analogy, implementing guidelines attempt to standardise the procedures required to fulfil the objectives of the code.

The trend among the more progressive MNEs has been to develop and refine guidelines so as to efficiently work with suppliers, subcontractors and other business partners who are expected to fulfil the terms of the code.

The extent to which guidelines are offered by the parent company vary widely. Both MNEs and business associations have issued instruction manuals, audit checklists and other documentation that map out procedures for code implementation and follow up (OECD 2000: 26). However, the trend among the more progressive MNEs has been to develop and refine guidelines so as to efficiently work with suppliers, subcontractors and other business partners who are expected to fulfil the terms of the code. MNE motivation comes in part from the fact that they are increasingly being held accountable for the actions of overseas suppliers, regardless of the arm's-length contractual relationship.

The complexities of code implementation require a level of detail that takes into consideration different types of procedures and activities as diverse as product alterations, significant changes in the volume of production, equipment failures, and other issues that both directly and indirectly affect labour practices and the workforce. Finally, some would argue that the MNE, given its depth of financial, management and organisational resources, is in the best position to bear the burden and responsibility of effective implementation.

An example of an implementing guideline comes from a major retailer. In a provision that seeks to limit the labour hours of its suppliers, it provides a maximum limit on the number of hours to be worked. However, an exception is provided for instances of 'peak periods'. Importantly, the implementing guideline goes on to explicitly define and explain 'peak periods', thereby providing key guidance to the supplier regarding the specific parameters of this obligation. Further, this provides guidance to regional managers and auditors tasked with making a determination as to overall compliance with code provisions.

a. Confidentiality and transparency

A significant issue surrounding implementing guidelines has to do with the fact that they are largely internally developed documents and procedures, and the level of detail required for effective implementation may reflect proprietary systems and procedures. Often, they are conceived as instructional handbooks for supplier management and the company's own internal compliance officers, explaining in detail the requirements of the code to vendors and outlining the obligations of compliance officers in enforcing those requirements. As such, many MNEs argue these to be privileged communications, confidential business information or trade secrets, or as providing a competitive advantage, and therefore should not be disclosed.

Accordingly, many codes refer to accompanying guidance that may or may not be available to the larger community of stakeholders. This lack of transparency surrounding implementing guidelines, regardless of how legitimate, makes a quantitative comparison of current measures largely impossible.

b. Practicalities

As a supplement to a more general code, implementing guidelines should ideally be a handy reference tool for those internal and external individuals responsible for implementation. Some may restate relevant code provisions and provide additional explanations of the requirements of those provisions. For example, in a section on discrimination, this might include a comprehensive list of the prohibited grounds for discrimination, as well as specific examples and scenarios of prohibitions.

Several guidelines examined provided lists of common practices that violate the standard and management practices that facilitate compliance with the standard. For example, a section on wages and benefits listed 'falsified pay records', 'late payment of wages' and 'unauthorised wage deductions' as common violations. Good management practices might include 'provision for comprehensive pay stubs clearly detailing wage calculations and applicable deductions' and 'installation of automated time clocks for which workers swipe their own cards'. In addition to these examples, implementation guidelines may also include case studies that present sample labour situations accompanied by their interpretation under the requirements of the code of conduct. These methods are especially useful for training MNE and supplier staff on the application of the code because they help those involved view the code and guidelines as more than abstract concepts.

c. Paths toward implementation

A variety of paths forward exists for effective implementation. Some companies, particularly large, highly visible brands, have chosen to develop internal compliance departments devoted to pursuing the social goals of the enterprise. Other companies have chosen to incorporate labour practice goals into already existing corporate structures devoted to quality control or purchasing. Others have chosen to partner with accredited semi-independent third-party auditors, union officials or other international multi-stakeholder initiatives. Specific details regarding the management systems used to implement codes are provided in Chapters IV, V and VI.

9. Regulatory conflicts

This section focuses on the legal nuances that arise when companies and private entities attempt to prescribe and measure corporate behaviour. As the parameters and reach of codes of conduct increasingly extend to suppliers, subcontractors and other business partners not formally integrated into the legal structure of an MNE, legal implications and conflicts invariably arise. While voluntary, it is recognised in legal practice that public admissions regarding standards for corporate behaviour may have significant repercussions. As noted:

> By their very nature, voluntary codes contain commitments often made in response to market incentives with no legal or regulatory compulsion. However, as public statements, codes usually are considered to have legal implications (Urminsky 2001: 13).

Our research indicates that a significant number of labour issues encompassed in a code are covered to some degree by the labour law of a given country. However, the reality in many instances is that there is generally little regulation or training by government bodies regarding the enforcement of labour standards. In the absence of a strong national regulatory framework, the implementation of a code really does become a proactive measure borne by a private enterprise. Given the substantive overlap between obligatory labour laws and voluntary labour codes, a debate has developed about the responsibility of the MNE in ensuring labour rights. Given this somewhat precarious position, MNEs often seek to distinguish between promoting a set of standards to their suppliers and holding themselves responsible for the practices of those suppliers.

In a position paper on codes of conduct, the IOE emphasises the facultative character of corporate codes for suppliers, and argues that while companies can be criticised for the substandard practices of parties in their supply chain, they ultimately cannot be held responsible (ICFTU 2001: 25). Some NGO and advocacy groups counter that the overwhelming power of MNEs to influence labour trends makes them responsible for the social and environmental effects of their operations. Union groups warn that any sort of privatisation of labour regulation sets a dangerous precedent, removing the last vestiges of government control from the operations of global business. However, most stakeholders seem to agree that codes, if implemented in good faith with adequate accountability to the global community, could provide a useful complement to existing state regulatory systems.

> The International Organisation of Employers (IOE) emphasises the facultative character of corporate codes for suppliers, and argues that while companies can be criticised for the substandard practices of parties in their supply chain, they ultimately cannot be held responsible.

Despite the substantial overlap between codes and national legislation, there are cases in which these public and private measures will either be in conflict or place different requirements on suppliers. Supporting alternative representation in countries that either do not respect the right to organise or that tightly control the channels of such representation may put suppliers in difficult positions. Factory management may resist paying an 'industry' or 'prevailing' wage that is higher than the legal minimum wage, arguing that industry benchmarks are too capricious. For cases such as these, some codes specify that the supplier should defer to the highest standard. Other codes provide no guidance whatsoever surrounding such conflicts. Fundamentally, MNEs must work with suppliers to find solutions to conflicting requirements inherent in the adoption of diverse, foreign or incomplete workplace standards.

10. Assuring compliance

A variety of mechanisms, policies and procedures exist that can assist in verifying compliance with the performance standards of a corporate code of conduct. This section reviews what we were told are some of the more common items used both internally and externally, including a variety of procedures for monitoring, reporting and disclosure of information, along with inspection, auditing and corrective action.

a. Monitoring, reporting and disclosure

Internal monitoring systems are used primarily to ensure consistency in the ongoing management of implemented code provisions. Our research suggests that many of the existing internal structures for managing or measuring other operational activities, such as quality control, human resources and production throughputs, may lend themselves to adaptation for monitoring of the labour and social commitments embodied in a code. A key distinction is the monitoring of those elements of the code that are quantitatively measurable and those that are qualitatively measurable. The workplace activities addressed in labour standards are often a function of dynamic interpersonal processes, thereby posing the challenge to objectively measure subjective human interactions.

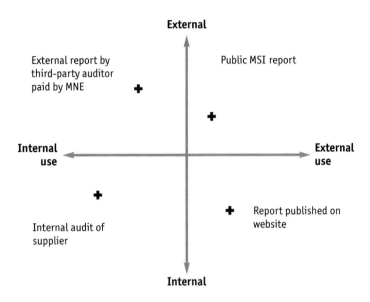

FIGURE 2   INTERNAL AND EXTERNAL REPORTING MECHANISMS

The degree to which information obtained from internal monitoring does or does not make its way into the public domain is the subject of much debate. As shown in Figure 2, there are varying uses of internal and external reporting mechanisms. Finding the balance between important conflicting principles such as confidential business information, transparency and meaningful disclosure, leads the debate on what is appropriate. Disclosure of information usually falls within three domains: product information, financial, and code commitments. Additionally, target audiences for disclosure may vary and include an internal audience, the general public, other vetted stakeholders or the government.

In the formal reporting arena, the trend has been for MNEs to report on the environmental and social impacts of their operations, to the point where many corporations, both domestic and international, now produce 'sustainability reports' as a standard industry practice. However, the inclusion of labour and employment information continues to be rather weak.

One particular initiative worth noting is the UN Global Reporting Initiative (GRI), which is 'an international multi-stakeholder effort to create a common framework for voluntary reporting of the economic, environmental and social impact of organisational-level activity'.[21] Demonstrative of the overall need for established, consistent and accepted criteria to measure performance, the GRI seeks to improve the comparability

21   See www.unglobalreporting.org.

and credibility of sustainability reporting, and has integrated the input of a broad sector of stakeholders in the private sector, and human rights, environmental, labour and governmental organisations. While meritorious in its approach, the GRI has yet to eliminate criticism regarding application of consistent criteria for reporting and their mandatory application, which would, in the view of employers' organisations, take it outside the domain of voluntary private initiatives.

b. Inspection, auditing and corrective action

A growing trend watched with great interest is the development of external verification services. Global auditing firms were some of the first to branch into this new market of non-financial verification, along with specialised technical monitoring and consulting firms, as well as a number of NGOs.[22]

A key issue regarding inspections and auditing relates to the independence of the individual or entity undertaking the task. Also significant is whether the inspection or audit is done internally or externally, or under the direct or indirect supervision of the MNE. For example, the MNE may conduct its own audits, and simply turn over the information to an independent third-party auditor for review. This is a common practice in financial auditing, though a critical difference is that established accounting standards have been around for decades. Further, even if an independent third-party auditing entity conducts the inspection, there may be an inherent conflict of interest if it is dependent on the MNE for payment. Supporting this concern, our research has revealed that auditors may hesitate to present truly damaging information, based on a desire to maintain good business relations and receive future work from the client. Further, the question of the competence and qualification of the auditor is a critical issue.

A primary purpose of an auditing standard is to remove discretion from the auditor so as to increase the credibility and effectiveness of the audit. According to the OECD, 'This means that, after undertaking standard steps to verify pre-agreed aspects of a firm's management procedures and of the information it proposes to publish, the auditor makes standardised statements about the adherence (or lack thereof) of these procedures and information to a given quality standard' (OECD 2001: 11). Accordingly, the development of generally accepted standards and a system for legitimate and independent verification is a critical phase of development for codes. This requires participation from stakeholders representing the employer, the employee and national governments. It is logical that existing OECD and ILO guidelines applicable to labour and social standards form the foundation from which to proceed.

The effectiveness of a code is also influenced by the steps taken to address inadequate performance with respect to code requirements. Our research indicated that, generally, there are three courses of action undertaken by MNEs:

- Work internally or with the business partner to correct the non-complying conduct

---

22 For additional information on the design and implementation of social responsibility programmes, see 'Business for Social Responsibility', www.bsr.org.

- Terminate the contract or business relationship

- Other measures including internal disciplinary actions such as employee dismissal, legal remedies, fines, expulsions or suspensions from membership in associations

Further, 'corrective action' often occurs as a mechanism that allows MNEs to work with suppliers or other business partners to make improvements necessary to meet code standards. However, in the absence of specific remedies for non-compliance, the effect of a code is relegated to voluntary self-obligation with no provision to deal with non-compliance (OECD 1999: 18). Many codes seek to address the performance issues of suppliers, subcontractors and other business partners. This may take the form of requiring them to sign a statement of understanding that contains language to the effect that sanctions are possible if the standard is not adhered to. However, many codes state that prior to enforcement of sanctions, remedial action may be allowed for in correcting the error and achieving compliance (OECD 2000: 13).

11. Multi-stakeholder initiatives (MSIs)

Primary MSIs that have appeared in the past decade:
- Clean Clothes Campaign
- Ethical Trading Initiative
- Fair Labor Association
- Forest Stewardship Council
- Global Compact
- Global Reporting Initiative
- Marine Stewardship Council
- Social Accountability International
- Workers' Rights Consortium

Within the context of corporate codes of conduct, this section of our report elaborates on the significant development of MSIs. While private voluntary codes continue to represent the vast majority of initiatives in place, MSIs have emerged as a response to the specific concerns of trade unions, employee activists and consumer groups, as well as MNEs genuinely concerned about workplace conditions or brand image. A significant number of the firms that participated in this research are participating in MSIs. This has partly to do with the fact that a number of the MNEs and their supplier factories in the footwear, apparel and retail sectors were the subject of vociferous criticism due to allegations of poor factory and workplace conditions. MSIs evolved as a response from a collection of stakeholders to address these issues.

Primary criticism of private voluntary codes has tended to focus on such issues as the lack of independent systems to verify or monitor compliance with the code.[23] Further, the existence of so many codes espoused by different companies makes it difficult for consumers to keep track of code provisions, code commitments and claims of compliance. As a result, various stakeholders, including human rights organisations and much of the public, suspected that many codes were mere public relations tools that would

23 'A US Department of Labor study of the codes of 42 companies found that "most of the codes . . . do not contain detailed provisions for monitoring and implementation, and many of the companies do not have a reliable monitoring system in place". The same study found that many corporate respondents "did not know whether workers were aware of the existence of their codes" ' (Connor 2004).

not produce tangible improvements in working conditions. As a result of this mistrust, a new approach to improve and police workplace conditions developed in the form of the MSI.

a. Development of MSIs

MSIs are not-for-profit organisations comprising coalitions of companies, unions and NGOs that have developed specific standards for workplace conduct. Each MSI advances its specific code among MNEs or industry sectors, with the express purpose of bringing the factories, subcontractors and related business partners along the MNE supply chain into compliance with the performance standards of the code.

> The OECD Inventory of Codes of Corporate Conduct shows that a far higher percentage of MSI codes than corporate codes incorporate the ILO's fundamental labour standards: freedom of association, right to collective bargaining, freedom from forced labour and discrimination, equal remuneration and minimum age.

MSIs have attempted to address some of the perceived weaknesses in unilaterally adopted corporate codes. Research indicates that the performance standards to which MSIs require compliance are consistently more stringent than those of corporate codes. The OECD Inventory of Codes of Corporate Conduct shows that a far higher percentage of MSI codes than corporate codes incorporate the ILO's core labour standards: freedom of association, right to collective bargaining, freedom from forced labour and discrimination, equal remuneration and minimum age. The Inventory also shows that the most frequently included standard in MSI codes is freedom of association and collective bargaining, while this has been found to be the least included standard in company codes (Jenkins 2002a: 18-20). A detailed chart summarising MSI codes of conduct is given in Appendix 4.

While many MSIs share a number of advances over traditional corporate codes, our research indicates that there are still differences and inconsistencies among MSIs:

- Some MSIs significantly involve unions and workers at many stages in their process,[24] while others are largely driven by companies.[25]

- Some MSIs monitor one industry or a few industries, while others monitor many industries.

- The codes adopted by some MSIs go beyond incorporating the ILO core labour standards, while others incorporate little else.

Further, other MSI requirements are more vague:

---

24 As Peter Utting points out, however, union participation needs to be interpreted with care. It may not mean that unions unreservedly and fully endorse the MSI, but rather that they wish to be 'critically engaged' and to have an opportunity to interact more directly with the senior management of the companies that employ their members (Utting 2002: 95).

25 See Jenkins 2002a for a detailed explication of the widely divergent goals of the various stakeholders (large corporations, unions, individual workers, exporters, NGOs, shareholders and investors, and institutional and individual consumers) who participate in these MSIs. Because the interests of the stakeholders are so far from each other, the balance struck among stakeholders in the governance of MSIs makes a significant difference.

- Some MSIs allow factories seeking certification to *choose* the monitor which will audit them, while others *assign* monitors to companies who have sought certification.

- Some MSIs certify individual factories, while others certify entire brands based on audits of a sampling of the factories that produce goods for those brands.

- Some MSIs disclose the results of audits or investigations (including the names of factories involved in this process), while others do not.

b. Accreditation and certification

Some MSIs have developed programmes through which they accredit independent monitors to audit factories and 'certify' that conditions at the factory comply with the requirements of the MSI code. 'Certified' factories can then advertise certification and thereby promote themselves as ethical or socially conscious to investors and consumers. A surprisingly large number of MSIs (and consequently CSR auditing firms) have sprouted up in the past five years and many companies have elected to be certified by not just one but by many of them (Rohitratana 2002: 8; Cestre 2002).

In practical terms, an MSI establishes a system that 'accredits' a monitoring or auditing entity to undertake audits to inspect facilities and make a determination as to whether the facility is in compliance with the performance standards of the MSI. A facility, such as a supplier factory, subcontractor or related business partner, upon successfully passing an audit, is awarded 'certification', thereby purporting to demonstrate that the facility is operating within the performance standards outlined by the MSI.

Our research indicates that, generally, certification is perceived to mean more when it comes from MSI-accredited independent monitors than when it comes from the company itself and is not independently verified. The degree to which MSI monitoring and certification is truly independent varies, but in most cases the monitors are entities that are not on the regular payroll of the companies whose factories they are auditing. This alone is a departure from the corporate code system.

Regarding the types of entity undertaking monitoring and auditing, almost all MSIs include provisions that 'invite' NGOs and unions to apply for accreditation to be monitors. While all MSIs claim to require certain core skills in monitors, our research indicates that a great deal of the monitoring is done by traditional financial auditing firms such as PricewaterhouseCoopers.[26]

Specific examples of accreditation and certification programmes include the FLA and SAI, which focus entirely on labour standards. Others, such as the Worldwide Responsible Apparel Production Program (WRAP) principles, integrate other concerns such as customs compliance and drug interdiction together with labour standards. The most common methods used for verification of compliance are on-site inspections, document review and interviews with a variety of stakeholders including employees, management and NGOs. Criticism of these programmes usually is directed at conflicting or

---

26 PricewaterhouseCoopers has become the world's largest private monitor of labour and environmental practices (O'Rourke 2002: 196).

MSI	Industries covered	Stakeholder representation	What is certified	Monitoring and certification	Public disclosure
CCC www.cleanclothes.org	Apparel industry	Coalitions of consumers, trade unions, human and women's rights organisations, researchers, solidarity groups and activists	Does not certify	Five pilot projects in monitoring and verification under way	CCC gathers information about workplace from a variety of sources (factory workers, independent research, media) and makes it public
ETI www.ethicaltrade.org	All industries including apparel, food, beverage, horticulture	Companies; unions; NGOs; observer from the Department for International Development (UK)	Does not certify	Pilot projects complete and several under way. Each pilot project operates according to a different model of internal or external monitors of academics, unions and NGOs	ETI 'support[s] the principle of public disclosure as a long-term goal', but does not require companies to make ETI annual reports public
FLA www.fairlabor.org	Apparel industry; college and university licensees	Industry; NGOs; colleges and universities; former US Secretary of Labor Glickman	Brands, colleges and universities	Monitors accredited and selected by FLA conduct announced and unannounced audits of 30% of a company's supplier factories (chosen by FLA staff) during initial three-year participation	FLA issues an annual public report on compliance record of each affiliated company. Names of individual factories and full monitor reports not disclosed
SAI www.cepaa.org	All industries	NGOs; trade unions; 'socially responsible investors' and government; industry	Individual factories	Monitors accredited and selected by SAI perform certification audits of factories; certification lasts for three years	SAI publishes certified facilities, locations on its website, list of complaints, corrective action, monthly newsletter
WRAP www.wrapapparel.org	Apparel industry	Non-apparel-industry-related individuals; top apparel industry executives	Individual factories	Factories choose a monitor and schedule an audit in advance. WRAP board decides on unannounced audits. Certification lasts one year	None. Audit reports given only to factories and WRAP board which do not disclose certified factories or factories that fail
WRC www.workersrights.org	College and university licensees	Colleges, universities; labour rights experts (academics, union officials, NGOs); students	Does not certify	WRC itself investigates factories about which it receives complaints. Investigations conducted by collaborative investigative team of local labour NGOs, academic experts and staff	WRC makes results of all investigations public; maintains web database of college and university affiliates; names and locations of factories producing goods bearing logos

TABLE 5 MSI PROGRAMMES

confidential methodologies used, the specificities of interviews and inspections, and the expertise, size and composition of the audit team.

12. Challenges facing MSIs

While much attention is currently being placed on MSIs as the next wave of non-governmental regulation of global MNEs, a number of challenges exist. Concerns include the fact that, as with some private corporate codes, by participating in MSIs, MNEs may themselves be creating conditions that make it nearly impossible for their suppliers to comply with the performance standards the companies are asking them to adopt. Our research showed that the apparel industry, for example, is characterised by flexibility, intensity, short-term employment and production cycles, competition and insecurity. This situation often results in the lengthening of supply chains and the further subcontracting of labour to the informal economy. Some critics argue that it is unrealistic to demand compliance with proper working hours standards and workplace conditions standards when simultaneously creating a situation in which workers have no choice but to put in intense periods of overtime and managers have no choice but to subcontract (see, for instance, Shaw and Hale 2002: 108; Utting 2002: 100).

Moreover, under both a corporate code system and an MSI system, contractors are usually asked to pay the costs necessary to implement measures that will bring a factory into compliance with a code. Contractors in the apparel industry are in intense competition with each other to produce at the lowest cost and win the largest contracts from MNEs and buyers. When market forces demand that contractors produce at the lowest cost, some would argue that it is unrealistic to expect contractors to bring wage levels and health and safety measures up to international standards (see, for instance, Shaw and Hale 2002: 108).

Additionally, some complain that MSIs have developed their codes in a top-down manner without any attempt to solicit the input of ordinary workers in producer countries. MSI codes and certification programmes are given credit for being legitimate in a way that corporate codes are not because non-industry groups such as NGOs and unions have participated in their development. These worker-friendly groups, it is argued, are still working at a distance from the factory floor, and are not necessarily in touch with the needs and desires of workers in producer countries,[27] or prepared to conceive of workers as agents of their own empowerment rather than as 'victims' (Utting 2002: 96, 103-107). Some have even warned that MSI efforts do not necessarily bolster workers' attempts to organise, pointing out that codes may be implemented by companies in conjunction with efforts to prevent workers from joining unions, and that

---

27   According to Shaw and Hale (2002: 104), 'Codes of conduct are typically introduced on behalf of workers, without their knowledge or consent. It is simply assumed that workers will see these initiatives as being in their interests.' Similarly, Utting (2002: 96-97) cites many case studies that conclude that the primary concerns of workers in, for example, Bangladesh and India, are not reflected in the standards developed by SAI and ETI.

auditing by outside monitors could even come to be seen by workers themselves as a substitute for self-organisation.[28]

Other critics have argued that MSI codes do not reach far enough down the supply chain, pointing out that most of them make no mention of homeworkers or workers in the informal economy despite the fact that these workers participate regularly in global supply chains as subcontractors (Barrientos 2002: 68). Further, the goal-oriented mind-set of certification programmes may work to the detriment of workers because rather than working with factory management to improve inadequate conditions, some companies might be tempted to abandon factories where working conditions are poor and move elsewhere, opting for a 'quick fix' that will leave thousands of workers jobless (ETI 2000: 5).

A final significant concern has to do with what some perceive to be the privatisation of a function that should rightfully be performed by government. One perspective of government is that the non-state, market-driven MSI system may be attractive as it can take up some of the demands placed on state agencies. Nevertheless, privatised regulators will by necessity always lack many of the powers that government regulators have. For example, because participation in MSIs is voluntary, management at factories are not under the same legal pressure to disclose facts to private monitors. Private monitors, unlike government, have no subpoena power, and there is no legal penalty for perjury or withholding information.

Naomi Klein, journalist and well-known critic of globalisation, writes,

> The bottom line is that corporate codes of conduct—whether drafted by individual companies or by groups of them, whether independently monitored mechanisms or useless pieces of paper—are not democratically controlled laws. Not even the toughest self-imposed code can put the multinationals in the position of submitting to collective outside authority (Klein 2002: 437).

Finally, some feel that there are legitimacy problems with a system that is powered primarily by consumer preferences. Many companies may be persuaded to participate in the MSI system because of the threat of consumer boycott. Research indicates that, currently, over 80% of consumers polled in the United States of America are willing to pay more for products that are made under 'good' conditions, and 51% of Americans reported 'punishing' a firm for bad social practices (O'Rourke 2003: 7).

---

28   Wick (2001: 84) states: 'One of the more dangerous aspects of the "independent monitoring" way of thinking is that, because monitoring needs to be an ongoing process, "independent monitoring" arrangements will introduce outside organisations into the workplace on a permanent basis with the effect of discouraging or preventing workers from joining or forming their own organisations.'

III
Background and framework of the report

1. Background

As stated, the objective of this research was to gain a better understanding of the management systems used by MNEs in the implementation of CSR and corporate codes of conduct across three sectors: footwear, apparel and retail. Before delving into our substantive findings regarding management systems, it would be useful to consider the nature of operations in the context of the sectors studied. In the following chapters we address each sector separately and offer a more detailed introduction regarding the historical development of the sector, along with the context for emerging commitments related to labour, social and ethical behaviour in that sector.

Increasingly, MNEs are engaged in a model of production where they must be flexible to address rapidly changing demands of the consumer and to compete on a global level. Typical of this model is a reliance on outsourcing of production to keep labour and material costs low. For the most part, MNEs based in the industrialised world no longer manufacture products such as footwear, apparel or retail goods such as jewellery, toys and gifts, but rather concentrate on core competences such as design, marketing and merchandising. Production is left to an increasingly complicated network of contractors, agents, vendors, suppliers and subcontractors in the developing world. The end result is that the brand-name manufacturers often find it challenging to identify where and by whom their products are produced. This can have serious repercussions for labour, social and ethical practices throughout the global production process. Our research indicated similarities in the industries of apparel, often called the 'stepping-stone' to industrial development; sports footwear, which has distinguished itself as having the leanest supply chains; and retail, which we define here as the manufacture of hard lines, specifically products other than garments and shoes, such as toys, jewellery and housewares, sold in leading discount or mass-merchandise chains. Also, due to its size and importance as a world exporter of consumer products, China will frequently be cited as an example. It should be noted that the focus of this chapter is the similarities across the three sectors. Matters of specific significance to individual sectors are discussed in greater depth in each of the sector reports in the ensuing chapters.

a. Evolution of global manufacturing operations

Originally, footwear, apparel and retail were primarily locally based manufacturing operations, created on what is referred to as the 'Fordist' business model of production. This term originated from fully vertically integrated enterprises such as the Ford Motor Company, which manufactured every aspect of the automobile from the tyres to the steering wheel. Fordism is presently being replaced by 'Post-Fordist' production, which is characterised by outsourcing production to ensure 'more flexible and "leaner" production (fewer workers) and the fabrication of small lots with greater product variety to meet the needs of different consumer groups' (Boje and Prieto 2000: section II, p. 1). In Post-Fordist production, also called 'Toyotaism',[29] the emphasis is on continuous improvement processes such as total quality management (TQM), shorter cycle times and just-in-time (JIT) inventory systems (Boje and Prieto 2000). Post-Fordist firms are characterised by flexibility to meet the changing demand of consumers and to capitalise on opportunities created by global labour-cost differentials. This has resulted in changes in supply chain management and the shifting of labour pools to overseas, often developing, markets.

b. Overseas production

Until the end of World War II the US and Europe dominated the world economy and controlled most industrial production, while lesser-developed countries tended to produce raw materials and agricultural products. Domestically, US companies were constantly in search of less expensive labour and the early 20th century witnessed many apparel companies moving from the relatively high wage, unionised northeast to the low wage, non-unionised south (Bonacich and Appelbaum 2000: 54). The offshore production of goods, notably apparel and textile products, began in earnest after World War II when financial and technical assistance from American aid programmes was provided to Japan and subsequently to the East Asian economies of the Republic of Korea, Hong Kong, China and Taiwan, China. As a result of these programmes, garment production flourished in these 'new' economies, while American and European companies and consumers benefited from an abundant supply of inexpensive labour that, even when coupled with international transportation expenses, kept costs low throughout the industry. These low labour costs were not lost to manufacturers of other products and soon a variety of industries such as sports footwear and retail goods were sourcing production abroad. By the 1970s the countries of the Republic of Korea, Japan, Hong Kong, China, and Taiwan, China, had massive trade surpluses with the US. By the 1980s these countries, called newly industrialised economies (NIEs),[30] were moving from being labour-intensive manufacturers to producers of capital-intensive, high-technology goods.

In the late 1980s, sourcing locations began to change. Taiwan, China, and the Republic of Korea suffered declining international competitiveness based on labour shortages that resulted in rising wages, international protectionism and competition from other developing countries. China's 'open-door policy', which began in 1978,

---

29 So named after the production practices of the Japanese auto manufacturer, Toyota.
30 At present, these countries are also referred to as first-tier NIEs to distinguish them as pace-setters in development.

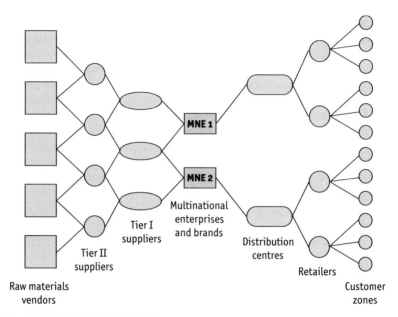

FIGURE 3   SUPPLY CHAIN NETWORK

Source: Adapted from Chandra and Kumar 2001

relaxed controls on foreign investment, which led companies based in Taiwan, China, and the Republic of Korea to move hundreds of production lines to mainland China and South-East Asia where labour and production costs were considerably lower. This foreign direct investment (FDI) in China took the form of wholly owned factories, joint ventures and outward processing plants (Lau and Chan 1994: 115). Thus the supply chain became even broader, as a European or American-based brand-name manufacturer would contract production with a supplier in Hong Kong, China, the Republic of Korea or Taiwan, China, only to have the order fulfilled in mainland China.

Today, MNEs in the footwear, apparel and retail sectors operate within a fluid global structure of supplier facilities. These can range from less than a dozen supplier factories, in the case of a footwear brand, to literally thousands of supplier factories in the case of a major retail chain.

c. The sweatshop issue

Perhaps no issue is as critical to the sectors of apparel, footwear and retail goods production as is the sweatshop issue. Indeed, hardly a month passes without allegations accusing suppliers of brand-name products as violators of human rights in the developing world. Historically, the word 'sweatshop' originated in the 19th century to describe a subcontracting system in which the middlemen earned profits from the margin between the amount they received for a contract and the amount they paid to workers. Workers, who received minimal wages for excessive hours worked under unsanitary conditions, were said to have 'sweated' this margin. Today, social activists, the media, NGOs and a myriad of watchdog organisations cite long working hours, inadequate factory working conditions and housing facilities, low wages, the lack of freedom of association and collective bargaining, and the use of forced and child labour as evidence of exploitation of workers in exchange for corporate profits. The US General Accounting Office has developed a working definition of a sweatshop as 'an employer that violates more than one federal or state labour, industrial homework, occupational safety and health, worker's compensation or industry registration law'.

There are several factors that influence the possibility of labour conditions that do not meet international labour standards in the developing economies of Asia and Latin America. First, as discussed, leading retail firms and brand-name manufacturers no longer own the means of production. Product manufacture occurs far from company headquarters, often under networks of contractors and subcontractors. 'These networks obstruct accountability as much by their flux as by their intricacy. Manufacturers of products such as garments regularly switch countries, or even continents as they switch suppliers' (Sabel *et al.* 2000: 3). Consequently, MNEs may be unaware of actual factory working conditions. Second, developing countries often lack trade unions or enforceable labour laws, therefore leaving the working population vulnerable to inadequate working conditions. Third, the pressure of JIT inventory practices has forced suppliers to take on more of the risk of inventory planning and control. As inventories on hand are costly, this may adversely affect the way in which suppliers handle production planning, which if left to the last minute may result in longer hours and less time off for workers. An example of how such a situation can arise was given to us by a vice-president of production at a large multinational retail enterprise.

> We drive time-lines that force our vendors to work overtime. Therefore it is my responsibility to control this. I will sign up to assist them (the vendors) to manage their time-lines, and where it is our responsibility we extend our time-lines. Convenient denial is more the state people live in and so production and international offices try to discipline what is occurring. The end result should be on time delivery to the stores. Production sets the entire calendar. You would be amazed by what we do. Imagine having 15 million pairs of pants all with the same label. So we try to build contingency planning, but most people know that we factor this in. You have to then expect the human factor and add that too. Finally, you have to have air and shipping deadline extensions (AMNE 4, Manager).

Contractors responding to the fluctuating need of buyers must manage their labour force based on a set of surmised conditions: for example, the actual demand for a particular product in season. If poorly forecast, this demand can have serious implications for the number of hours worked by employees and the retention of factory workers. Fourth, the tremendous competition among retailers in the developed world to offer a wider spectrum of products at increasingly lower prices means that in many instances suppliers are selected on the basis of price alone ignoring, perhaps, the actual conditions under which products are produced.

d. Future of the apparel, footwear and retail sectors

Given the rapid spread of global production and supply chains, and the current attention focusing on the alleged inequities produced by the workplace conditions of various footwear, apparel and retail operations, increased pressure may be placed on MNEs to adopt CSR and voluntary private initiatives such as codes of conduct as standard parts of their business operations. Many already have. This book explores in greater detail the experience of some MNEs and related supplier factories in adjusting their management structures to incorporate CSR and code-of-conduct commitments across the full spectrum of production. What remains to be seen, however, is the degree to which MNEs and their business partners are able to upgrade production to the next level, manufacturing more sophisticated products not only for export but also eventually for domestic demand. Indeed, global retailers such as Wal-Mart, Carrefour and Metro are already betting on the future of the market in China and are achieving good results. Similarly, companies such as J.C. Penney, Dillards and Sears are putting great emphasis on production in Mexico. As leading retailers relocate globally they may well find incentives to establish or strengthen local supplier networks for buyer-driven commodity chains (Gereffi and Hempel 1996: 8). Recognising that workers may one day be customers could prove influential in the manner in which retailers and brand manufacturers oversee production, and ensure, hopefully, a better work environment for all.

2. Report framework

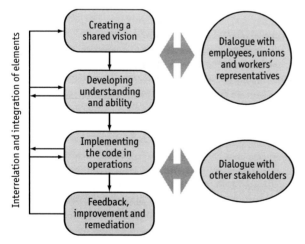

For the obligations of CSR and codes of conduct to be implemented effectively, our research indicates that such management systems require that appropriate knowledge, responsibility, authority, resources and motivation be distributed throughout the company in a manner that provides for the fulfilment of this objective.[31]

From our investigations, we learned that no single template exists that is applicable to all MNEs, and 'firms tend to tailor implementation measures to the

31   While the focus of this book is on understanding the management systems and processes used in implementing codes, it is important to consider the workers' perspective on this issue. This could also include that: the code content, and the process by which it was developed and implemented, includes and empowers the workers to whom it is directed; the code reflects local needs of workers and as a minimum guarantees the core standards of the ILO; the company adopting the code is genuinely committed to its implementation and provides adequate resources, training, monitoring and reporting mechanisms; and that the company's behaviour is transparent with regard to its treatment of employees and those in the employment of suppliers, contractors and subcontractors. For further details, see Murray 1998: 2.

type of commitment and to their own circumstances' (OECD 2001: 8). Within the context of code implementation, MNEs usually consider a variety of factors. The general methodology is to balance the available mechanisms for implementation against cost, effectiveness and implications for failure to comply with public commitments, in particular any legal, financial or public relations impacts.

We found that firms in the footwear, apparel and retail sectors utilised a great diversity of approaches to implement systems for the management of CSR and code requirements. As we organised the data generated from interviews conducted, factory visits, trips to headquarters and reviews of various reports and tools used by the participating companies, an attempt was made to find some common structure among the various approaches.

Our research suggested that a general framework existed for the presentation of findings as well as to guide those interested in the implementation of social policy across supply chains. The framework that we have adopted is presented in the diagram above. We have used this framework as the basis for analysis of all three sectors covered by the research. It should be noted that, in adopting this approach, we are not contending that all of the firms studied actually used this approach. Rather, the framework emerged with some consistency out of the data we gathered and provides a useful tool for the presentation of our findings.

a. Creating a shared vision

The commitment to labour, social and ethical standards begins with the creation of the individual code of conduct, namely the vision that is to be integrated throughout the MNE and its supply chain. We were repeatedly told that this is a task that is not accomplished in a vacuum but rather is the product of sustained effort by the MNE borrowing from the vast amount of information and research undertaken in part by international organisations such as the ILO and the United Nations. Further, MNEs draw on the experience and expertise of management and workers as well as, increasingly, the involvement of society at large.

One of the first steps undertaken by an MNE is to incorporate the commitments of CSR and the voluntary obligations of codes of conduct into their internal policies, strategies and operational processes. For this reason, the top management must be committed to the development of a coherent message and a thorough understanding of the business rationale behind the contents of the code. This helps to explain why one of the leading suggestions made by those interviewed was the need to change a corporation's view of itself and how it works with its supply chain partners; in short, the creation of a shared vision for the organisation that travels throughout the supply chain.

> We are 'an innovation-oriented company targeting developing leading edge products for sports'. Now, the CEO says we don't just want to be the best sports and fitness company, we are going to be the best company, period. Part of that is the [triple-bottom-line approach]. This means a lot of things. And that can't be just with regard to our core operations but must also apply to our supply chain, for all products we buy. It also stretches to consumers, colleges, athletes, suppliers, all our stakeholders (FMNE 2, Marketing Manager, Headquarters).

As our findings clearly demonstrate, the code of conduct must be integrated into the strategic direction of the organisation if it is to be successful.

b. Developing understanding and ability

In order to integrate the vision throughout the organisation and its supply chains, a process of communication and education needs to take place, and has to continue on an ongoing basis. In fact, taking the step of recognising the multiplicity of audiences to whom the code is addressed allows the challenge of adequate and appropriate communication to be addressed. Multiple layers of communication and training are required for domestic and foreign audiences. Both communication and training must occur at a level of sophistication and technicality that is appropriate for the recipient.

With a code in place and the organisation committed to its implementation, one of the challenges that must be addressed, we were told, is helping employees and others throughout the supply chain understand the purpose of the code and its implications for those areas under their responsibility. The following provide a good overview of the process, from developing new objectives to training managers and staff at all levels.

> Communication is huge. What is needed is, first, get a code and communicate what it is. You've got to work top down—with training programmes. In Indonesia we had a week-long training programme—with set time limits and deadlines. You've got to give some idea of where you are heading (FMNE 2, Manager).

> We [in the CSR group] have done training for country managers, presentations, and we have built a broader base of support. If it is only [a few dozen] people supporting this you will never have a success. You have to at least have understanding and support (FMNE 1, CSR Manager, Headquarters).

In the context of overseas operations, our research highlights the importance of undertaking communication and training with sensitivity towards regional or local dialects, non-verbal expressions, traditions of interpersonal communication, and the nuances associated with translation and interpretation as well as gender, age, religion or tribal customs. Language proficiencies must be taken into consideration, as it is common to have low levels of reading functionality and literacy in some overseas localities. A process to review, test or verify that those to whom the code is directed understand the information, along with their specific responsibilities and obligations, is essential.

Yet this process of developing commitment and understanding does not come easily, if at all, it would appear. A number of people interviewed highlighted the apparent lack of understanding and support, both by those within the MNEs and in particular those affected beyond the firm. As such, the process of developing understanding and commitment needs to be seen as continuous and long term if it is to succeed.

c. Implementing the code in operations

A broad range of management systems is used by MNEs in implementing the objectives of their codes of conduct and incorporating them throughout the firm as a whole. As outlined earlier in this book, one of the key responsibilities of a managerial system is the setting of organisational structure. In fact, one of the very first questions to consider when implementing a code into an organisation's operations and its supply chains is that of structure. In terms of assigning code-of-conduct responsibilities, various approaches have been adopted with either the establishment of new departments or the assignment of responsibilities to existing departments. Some illuminating examples are provided in the ensuing chapters.

Other processes utilised in the integration process include:

- Integration of code-of-conduct responsibilities into annual performance appraisals for the in-factory manufacturing managers of the MNEs

- Linkage to the decision-making processes of purchasing

- Incorporation into the job descriptions of quality inspectors and others involved in the implementation process

- Integration of code-related responsibilities into the policies and procedures of operating manuals

- Assimilation into human resource practices including training

- Streamlining with existing legal procedures

> At the start it is a bit of work to implement code requirements; you have to put more effort into monitoring, partner selection. But it gets easier over time; you have some best practices in place; you set up mentors for the suppliers (FMNE 2, CSR Manager, Headquarters).
>
> Multinationals need to consider that a code or compliance policy can reach way past their audit or compliance team. Training is needed for your QC and purchasing, who will have to provide crucial support to the code. You may have to consider your product design and the sampling process and what they can do to OSH or overtime at the supplier level. And, before you go anywhere, your top management has to understand the implications and support what needs to be done. If they send mixed messages about compliance versus low costs, then you might as well just walk away (O 17).

The integration of all of these processes, when it occurred in the firms studied, took many months, even years, and in almost all cases it remains an ongoing process. Furthermore, we were told that important decisions need to be made regarding the establishment of enabling mechanisms within an organisation to ensure successful integration and implementation. These can include the establishment of internal and/or external monitoring systems, which are discussed in the following section.

d. Feedback, improvement and remediation

Finally, we were told repeatedly that a process of monitoring, improvement or remediation should be in place, so that problems that are discovered are fed back to those managers or others who can adjust practice or take appropriate action to address problem areas. The internal/external distinction in monitoring approaches was discussed earlier in this chapter.[32] Understanding that the information and feedback obtained either internally or externally can be used either internally within a corporation or externally, for example, with its supply chain, is critical to the presentation of our findings. The management systems that support codes of conduct in the firms studied are dependent on several other processes; these include those that provide information, feedback and accountability for results. These systems appear to be focused internally, providing individual managers with results on their performance in carrying out their code-related activities and, externally, providing stakeholders with feedback on how the MNE and its suppliers are performing with respect to the objectives outlined in the code. However, it must be remembered that many of the code elements are difficult to measure due to their intangibility and subjectivity.

A number of the firms studied stated that internal monitoring systems are required primarily to ensure consistency in the ongoing management of implemented code provisions. It is suggested that many of the existing internal structures for managing or measuring other operational activities, such as quality control, human resources and production throughputs, may lend themselves to adaptation for monitoring of the labour and social commitments embodied in a code. A key distinction is the monitoring of those elements of the code that are quantitatively measurable and those that are qualitatively measurable. The workplace activities addressed in labour standards are often a function of dynamic interpersonal processes, thereby posing the challenge to objectively measure subjective human interactions. These were also found to be those elements of codes that are least amenable to monitoring by, for example, quality-control inspectors.

A growing trend exhibited by some of the firms studied is the development of external verification services. Global auditing firms have been some of the first enterprises to branch into this new market of non-financial verification, along with specialised technical monitoring and consulting firms, as well as a number of NGOs.[33] We were told of a number of approaches adopted in external monitoring and verification, details of which are provided in the subsequent chapters.

A key issue regarding inspections and auditing relates to the independence of the individual or entity undertaking the task. Also significant is whether the inspection or audit is done internally or externally, or under the direct or indirect supervision of the MNE. For example, the MNE may conduct its own audits, and simply turn over the information to an independent third-party auditor for review. This is a common practice in financial auditing, though a critical difference is that established accounting standards have been around for decades. Further, even if an independent third-party auditing entity conducts the inspection, there may be an inherent conflict of interest if they are dependent on the MNE for payment. Supporting this concern, our research has revealed that auditors may hesitate to present truly damaging information, based on a desire to maintain good business relations and receive future work from the client. Further, the question of the competence and qualification of the auditor is a significant issue.

---

32   Also, for further details on independent monitoring, see 'Almost everything you always wanted to know about independent monitoring', Clean Clothes Campaign, www.cleanclothes.org/codes/monitoring-long.htm.

33   For additional information on the design and implementation of social responsibility programmes, see Business for Social Responsibility (BSR) at www.bsr.org.

A primary purpose of an auditing standard is to remove discretion from the auditor in order to increase the credibility and effectiveness of the audit. This means that, after undertaking standard steps to verify pre-agreed aspects of a firm's management procedures and of the information it proposes to publish, the auditor makes standardised statements about the adherence (or lack thereof) of these procedures and information to a given quality standard (OECD 2001: 11). Accordingly, the development of generally accepted standards and a system for legitimate and independent verification would appear to be a critically important development for codes. This requires participation from stakeholders representing the employer, the employee and national governments. It is logical that existing OECD and ILO guidelines applicable to labour and social standards form the foundation from which to proceed.

The degree to which information obtained from internal monitoring does or does not make its way into the public domain is the subject of much debate. Finding the balance between important conflicting principles such as confidential business information, transparency and meaningful disclosure is a challenge for many companies. Disclosure of information usually falls within three domains: product information, financial and code commitments. Additionally, we were told that target audiences for disclosure might vary and include an internal audience, the general public, other vetted stakeholders or the government.

In the formal reporting arena, the trend has been for MNEs to increasingly report on the environmental and social impacts of their operations, to the point where many corporations, both domestic and international, now produce 'sustainability reports' as a standard industry practice. However, as we will see, the inclusion of labour and employment information continues to be rather weak. Further elaboration of these systems and processes will be made as appropriate in the following chapters.

Each of these sets of activities—namely the creation of a shared vision, the development of understanding and ability, integration of the code into operations, and feedback, improvement and monitoring—take place at both the supplier and MNE/buyer levels. Our findings show that, just as a buyer company may develop a code and establish it as the vision for the organisation, a supplier also needs to incorporate this code into its own vision of how it operates and what top management wants in the future. Without this reciprocity from suppliers, we were told that the code will not be fully implemented. Similarly, suppliers need to communicate the new vision, educate managers and implement the code into their various managerial systems. They also need the feedback and improvement systems in place in order to meet the rising standards to which they will be held accountable along with MNEs.

Finally, there are two other elements to the framework that are integral for presenting our findings.

e. Dialogue with employees, unions, workers' representatives and other stakeholders

It appears that an ongoing process of dialogue is central to the successful implementation of CSR and code commitments. At one level communication is essential between workers and their representatives. Workers are closest to operations and are best equipped to spot areas for improvement, whether this has to do with productivity or code compliance. The quality movement has long accepted the important, active role of the worker on the assembly line. The same is true of the worker when we consider meeting code requirements. Open channels of communication as well as support of the right to freedom of association and collective bargaining are essential for workers to be able to exercise their legal rights and point out any abuse, discrimination or pay problems. At the same time, a firm needs to maintain open channels of communication with other stakeholders in order to better understand their concerns, their challenges and their expectations—and then make decisions accordingly.

f. Interrelation and integration of elements

The final element is that of integration of CSR and code management requirements into the total operational structure of a firm. It was clear that integration was a theme running through all our interviews, from the factory floor of the supplier to the headquarters of the MNEs. Code objectives need to be integrated at the earliest stage of business planning, into strategic objectives of the firm, throughout human resource and training programmes and management systems and embedded as performance targets. The objectives of labour, social and ethical behaviour need to be fully integrated into all management systems and threaded throughout the entire organisation. As is evident from Figure 4, outlining some of the functional areas involved in the management of supply chains can be very complex. An issue explored by this research was where, within this web of functions and activities, the issues of compliance with code are addressed.

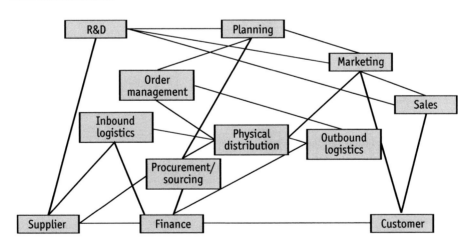

FIGURE 4 MAP OF FIRM INTERNAL SUPPLY CHAIN-RELATED SYSTEMS: WHERE DOES COMPLIANCE FIT?

Source: Alber and Walker 1997

Collectively, these elements provide the framework from which we will present our findings, summaries and conclusions from our research conducted in the footwear, apparel and retail sectors. The ensuing chapters will provide further details and practical examples of each of these elements as they pertain to the specific sector addressed.

IV
Review of the footwear sector

1. Background

Thirty years ago most production, distribution and sales of sports footwear were located in North America and Western Europe. In contrast, Asia now produces 99% of branded athletic footwear. Sports shoe production is a highly labour-intensive industry, involving 150 different stages or more in the manufacture of a single shoe. Enormous attention is devoted to product innovation and the crafting of a marketable image. In 2002, the top-selling five footwear manufacturers in the US (based on market share in dollars) were Nike (38.97%), Reebok (11.9%), New Balance (11.62%), Adidas (9.72%) and K-Swiss (3.18%). In the same year, these companies had annual turnover of almost US$8 billion, an increase of 4.47% from the previous year (Sporting Goods Intelligence 2003).

We found this high concentration of market share within a handful of brands to be particular to the footwear sector. This has led to interesting approaches by this sector to the management of its supply chain. The purpose of this section is to present our findings regarding how the footwear sector has evolved in its response to demands for CSR and voluntary commitments for labour, social and ethical behaviour. Fundamentally, evidence from our research visits suggests that the footwear sector outpaces the apparel and retail sectors in meeting such obligations, and offers significant lessons learned and best practices for application across other sectors. This can be attributed to historical reasons such as greater investment in this sector, a more stable supply base, greater leverage by MNEs due to an increased presence within the factories and intense public scrutiny due to alleged violations of workers' rights in overseas operations supplying MNEs.

a. Outsourcing

As shoe production involves high-volume and labour-intensive manufacturing, production is increasingly subcontracted to factories in the developing world, leaving firms to focus on what they consider their core competences. Footwear MNEs are consequently leaving, to a large degree, their subcontractors to decide the details of building and running factories, managing workplaces and workers, and dealing with local governments. On the other hand, in order to meet appropriate delivery standards, ensure high quality, and maintain international labour standards, MNEs often have their own manufacturing personnel on-site working closely with the subcontractor. These personnel may include staff from the departments of costing, planning, materials, development and quality who are present to monitor and assist the factories. In view of this delicate balance between complete autonomy and direct influence, some of the challenges associated with outsourcing are more than offset by low labour costs, less regulation and the possibility of focusing on core competences. Additionally, there is also some flexibility in placing orders in that some factories specialise in certain types of shoe, while others produce different kinds. Production bottlenecks at one facility or unanticipated growth in one type of shoe mean that the MNE can seek greater production at another factory.

At present, some research and development (R&D) is beginning to move to China and the Republic of Korea. For example, Hwaseung Ltd, a Republic of Korea company that first started as an original equipment manufacturer (OEM) for Nike, has captured 20% of the export market and has a dominant share domestically with its LECAF brand. Similarly, Li-Ning Sports Goods Co. in China (which is owned by three-times gymnastics Olympic gold medallist, Li Ning), has opened its own R&D centre in Beijing and is investing heavily in marketing and promotion in order to capture a share of the projected US$2.5 billion market by the time the Olympics come to Beijing in 2008 (Kahn 2003).

In the sports footwear sector, until the late 1980s, a great deal of the production occurred in Taiwan, China, and in the Republic of Korea. At this point, manufacturing practices in the sector began to change. As a result of the relaxation of controls on Taiwanese investments in the late 1980s and a sharp depreciation of the Taiwan dollar, as well as rising labour and production costs, companies began to move hundreds of production lines to mainland China and South-East Asia where such costs are considerably lower. By 1990, footwear exports from Taiwan, China, had fallen by 50% from 1988 to US$1.8 billion (Mooney 1991).

Similarly, in the Republic of Korea the footwear industry also succumbed to declining international competitiveness. By 1989, the Korean market share of the leather sports shoes market in the US fell to 45.7% from a high of 64.5% while at the same time China's share of the market rose to 18.9% from 5.5%. Today, the large footwear companies contract out only a negligible percentage of their total sports shoe production to the Republic of Korea and Taiwan, China. Sports shoes are now produced in China, Indonesia, Thailand, the Philippines, Viet Nam and India, admittedly by many Korean and Taiwanese suppliers. Along with the relocation of production facilities to low-wage countries has come associated labour, social and ethical behaviour issues that are complicated by such factors as a migrant workforce, high worker turnover, lack of training, lack of clear legal and regulatory programmes and levels of enforcement.

Of particular significance was the massive transfer of companies from Taiwan, China, to the mainland of China in the early 1990s. The Taiwanese footwear industry association estimates that by the end of 1991 about 400 of the network's 891 members had set up factories in China, employing approximately 100,000 workers (Abegglen 1994). The Taiwanese firms have tended to cluster in a few geographic areas (for example, Guangzhou and Shenzhen in Guangdong province and Xiamen and Fuzhou in Fujian province) (Chen 1999). Since then, this process has continued. The basis of this conglomeration results from a number of factors. Firstly, low labour costs, due to the availability of workers from other parts of the country, combined with proximity to shipping routes, acceptable infrastructure and the availability of land. Moreover, all the factors are made highly accessible by kin or 'guanxi' ties, similar language and customs which bind the two sides of the Taiwan Strait to make this area particularly attractive to the NIE-based, primarily Taiwanese, footwear suppliers who have set up operations in the area (Abegglen 1994).

b. Production process

The development of a sports shoe is a long process, taking between 12 and 16 months, followed by the relatively rapid manufacturing, distribution and sale of the product. The production process includes the development of the concept, design, testing of the concept, development of the construction and materials, engineering, agreement on design and production, and, finally, marketing, distribution and sale. Generally, the conceptual development and marketing decisions occur in the developed country base of the brand company, whereas those phases involving the actual manufacture of the shoe occur in suppliers' factories in the developing world. Increasingly, however, there is close communication between the global firms and the factories as regards the development of the shoe. In fact, a new shoe may be prototyped and costed through iteration between headquarters of the MNE and the factory's development department or section. We heard from some shoe designers who, after visiting assembly lines of overseas factories, were motivated to design new product lines that eliminated steps involving interaction with hazardous substances such as solvents or other chemicals. This closer interaction between the designer and supplier has led to some positive developments in health and safety. As such, interaction of this nature should be encouraged.

Offshore processing has become a profitable means of doing business for companies in the NIEs of South-East Asia, capitalising on the wage differentials between the NIEs and developing countries (Spinanger 1992). Companies use offshore processing to reduce costs and become more competitive in world markets. This approach cross-subsidises high-cost domestic activities and employment in the home countries of suppliers. Conversely, benefits from offshore processing for developing countries stem from gains in direct employment (something that must be considered from both a quality and quantity perspective), foreign direct investment and increased demand for intermediate inputs from the domestic market (Asia Research Centre, Murdoch University 1992). Another advantage is that local firms learn from MNEs, not only in terms of the technical aspects of production but also in terms of more tacit elements such as how to analyse markets and production, and the value placed on quality, on-time delivery and cost.

The production of athletic footwear is a labour-intensive process best considered as a vast sewing operation together with a number of supporting manufacturing systems. For example, a Chinese factory that we visited employed 6,000 people from 26 provinces, outputting between 500,000 and 600,000 shoes per month. The workers in these factories create shoes almost from scratch as the factories mainly purchase raw materials for further processing (tanned leather, rubber, adhesives, etc.), which exit a short while later as finished products.

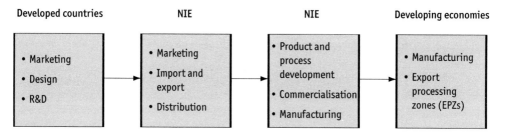

Developed countries	NIE	NIE	Developing economies
• Marketing • Design • R&D	• Marketing • Import and export • Distribution	• Product and process development • Commercialisation • Manufacturing	• Manufacturing • Export processing zones (EPZs)

FIGURE 5 GLOBAL SUPPLY CHAIN: SPORTS FOOTWEAR IN SOUTHERN CHINA

Source: Adapted from Frenkel 2001

While shoe production involves a variety of processes, such as rubber operations required in the construction of soles, in the factory mentioned above the majority of workers worked on eight double-sided stitching lines. In this process, skilled metal workers create moulds that bake the three-dimensional outsoles, workers in the chemical plant stretch and flatten quantities of raw rubber on heavy-duty rollers and cutters, then trim sheets of nylon, leather and other fabric for the uppers. Stitchers then sew cut pieces into a single upper, and the line workers attach the soles to these stitched uppers. Finally, workers lace and package the shoes. The development and production process is centred on three seasons, with a resulting swing in production, as demand rises and falls. The following comments provide a review of what and who is involved in production and development, as well as the challenges faced.

> In the development process, there are three seasons: fall, holiday and spring. We send several people from [the MNE] and factories back to our head-quarters. They grab the technical package and bring it back here; we spend eight months developing a test run. There are lots of modifications. Then, once designers, developers and manufacturing are happy with the product, it moves to RFC, ready for commercialisation. That is when we prepare it for the move to production. Here in [this factory] we do everything from concept through to putting it in the box and shipping. I wear two hats here. As [the person responsible for the sports category] I do concept to RFC; then as manufacturing manager I handle commercialisation and production. I try to bring as much of the manufacturing into the pre-RFC phase, so that we won't have any surprises. We've had a lot of problems in the past due to a lack of communication between design and manufacturing (FMNE 2, Manufacturing Manager).

> We have horrible swings in production, which makes it very hard. For local labour law they allow 84 hours of work. And I as the factory manager don't want to pay lots of overtime. But for the peak season we need to do something (THS 1, Factory Manager).

In general, purchasing begins with marketing: purchasers determine what items will be needed in each of the product ranges that each marketing group handles. The headquarters-based marketing team responsible for product ranges makes these decisions based on their work with the national marketing team, who provide input on future market needs. The marketing managers work with the sourcing team to determine how many of each item need to be made and where. These needs are then conveyed to country managers, generally with the sourcing manager making selections or suggestions as to the factory to be employed. The sourcing manager handling the factory chosen then negotiates the contract with this factory. Such a disparate structure highlights the need for better integration of CSR and voluntary commitments embraced in corporate codes of conduct across all functional areas within an MNE and its supply chain.

c. Costs of production

Production costs are dependent on the model of the shoe, the availability and price of raw materials and the skill of workers; for example, the efficiency of leather cutters. Generally, the largest part of the cost of production of the shoe (that is, the cost to the supplier of athletic shoes) is made up by the cost of materials (65 to 75%), while overheads, including labour, and factory profits contribute to the remainder of the price of the shoe. The cost breakdown presented here was provided as an illustrative example by an FMNE representative that we interviewed. Such a breakdown can vary depending on a variety of factors.

Breakdown of costs of production— factory price:

US$19.50	Materials (65%)
US$4.50	Labour (15%)
US$4.50	Overhead (15%)
US$1.50	Profit (5%)
US$30.00	Total production cost for the MNE
US$42.00	Delivery to retailer cost for the MNE

Average retail price: US$65.00

d. Worker base

While thousands of workers are managed directly under the umbrella of the major sports shoe brands, hundreds of thousands more work for their suppliers on the often-dedicated manufacture of their products. The ILO visited six factories in China and five factories in Viet Nam. The following data represents a summary of worker information provided by factory management, as shown in Table 6. This information could not, given the constraints of the research and the requirement for confidentiality, be independently verified.

In China, the average factory visited had nearly 10,000 workers. At each factory these workers were mainly female migrants generally from the provinces of Hunan, Sichuan and Guangdong, or from central China. On average, labour turnover was 3% per month or 36% per year. Employees worked an average of eight-and-a-half hours a day, six days a week and were entitled to anywhere from five to fifteen days off per year. Wage payments were typically on a monthly basis and averaged 600 RMB per month as a basic wage. Workers in five of the six factories visited were entitled to productivity bonuses, typically calculated by piece-rate production. In some factories, higher-skilled workers such as jumpers[34] were paid as much as 1,000 RMB per month.

In Viet Nam, in the five factories visited there were, on average, approximately 4,000 workers per factory. As in China, workers were typically female migrant workers from Central and North Viet Nam. Labour turnover was reportedly quite low, averaging 1–2%

---

34   The term 'jumper' refers to workers who are so named because they have the ability to perform several different tasks and may jump from task to task as needed or 'jump in' in case of worker absence.

	China 1	China 2	China 3	China 4	China 5	China 6
Staff composition	Female, migrant workers > 90% from Hunan, Sichuan and Guangdong	Female, migrant workers > 90% from central China	Female, migrant workers > 90% from Guangdong, Hunan and Sichuan	Female, migrant workers > 90% from Hunan, Sichuan and Guangdong	Female, migrant workers > 90% from central China	Female, migrant workers > 90% from Jiangxi, Hunan, Hubei and Sichuan
Average number of employees	9,000–10,000 employees	11,000 employees	6,000–6,500 employees of which 80% are women	8,000 workers	2,000 workers	22,032 employees
Labour turnover	2–3% per month	4–5% per month	2% per month	2–3% per month	4–5% per month	2.77% per month
Wage system and average monthly wage (AMW)	Basic + skill + bonus + overtime; AMW US$72.60–96.80; US$121.00 + for skilled workers; computerised payroll records	Basic + skill + productivity bonus + overtime; AMW US$60.50–84.70; US$121.00 + for skilled workers	Basic wage + production/efficiency incentive + allowance; AMW around US$66.55–78.65	Basic + skill + bonus + overtime; AMW US$72.60–84.70; computerised payroll records	Piece rate + overtime; AMW US$66.55–78.65; computerised payroll records	Basic wage + production/efficiency incentive + allowance; AMW around US$72.60–84.70
Maximum working hours per day/annual leave	11 hours, 2 rest days per week, 7–15 days paid holiday	11 hours, 2 rest days per week, 5 days paid holiday	8 hours per day, 1 rest day per week, 5–14 days paid? holiday	8 hours per day, 1 rest day per week, 5 days paid annual leave	8 hours per day, 1 rest day per week, 5 days paid annual leave	8 hours per day, 1 rest day per week, 5–14 days paid holiday
Workers' welfare deductions	Meals: N/A; Dormitory: US$3.00	Meals: US$0.61; Dormitory: US$3.63; Union subs: US$0.24	Meals: US$7.26; Housing: US$13.92 (food, water, electricity); Union subs: US$0.24–0.48; Transfer fee: US$0.24	Meals: US$16.34; Housing: US$5.44; Insurance: US$0.48; Cleaning: US$0.60; Medical: US$1.82	Meals: US$7.26; Dormitory: US$0.60; Hukou* fee: US$0.97	Meals: US$19.96; Housing: US$5.44; Insurance: US$0.48; Cleaning: US$0.60; Medical: US$1.82

Note: The information in this table was provided by factory management and could not be independently verified.

US$1 was approximately equal to 121 Chinese RMB at the time of this research.

* *Hukous*, symbolic of China's two-tiered (urban–rural) society are personal identification booklets issued for all Chinese and are inscribed to identify the carrier as a rural or urban resident. Each urban administrative entity issues its own *hukou*, which entitles only registered inhabitants of that entity full access to social services, such as education.

TABLE 6 FOOTWEAR FACTORIES VISITED IN CHINA AND VIET NAM *(continued over)*

	Viet Nam 1	Viet Nam 2	Viet Nam 3	Viet Nam 4	Viet Nam 5
Staff composition	Female, mainly from Cu-Chi district	Female, 80% from Dongnai and 20% from central/north Viet Nam	Female, mainly from Dongnai	Female, migrant workers > 60% from central/north Viet Nam	Female, migrant workers > 80% from central/ north Viet Nam
Average number of employees	5,000 employees	6,000 employees	N/A	6,000 employees	2,900 employees to date
Labour turnover	0.2% per month	0.2% per month	0.5–0.7% per month	0.8–1% per month	(new factory)
Wage system and average monthly wage (AMW)	Basic + skill + allowance + overtime; AMW US$50.48; computerised payroll records	Basic + position pay + bonus + allowance + overtime; AMW US$53.84; computerised payroll records	Basic + skill pay + production/efficiency incentive + allowances; AMW around US$53.84; computerised payroll records	Basic wage + bonus + overtime and allowances; AMW around US$53.84; computerised payroll records	Basic wage + production/efficiency incentive and allowances; AMW around US$43.75; computerised payroll records
Maximum working hours per day/annual leave	8 hours per day, 1 rest day per week, 12 days of annual leave according to Article 74 of the Vietnamese Labour Code	8 hours + 2 hours overtime, 1 rest day per week, 12 days of annual leave according to Article 74 of the Vietnamese Labour Code	8 hours per day, 1 day off per week, 12 days of annual leave according to Article 74 of the Vietnamese Labour Code	8 hours per day, 1 rest day per week, 12 days of annual leave according to Article 74 of the Vietnamese Labour Code	8 hours per day, 1 rest day per week, 12 days of annual leave according to Article 74 of the Vietnamese Labour Code
Workers' welfare deductions	Union subs: US$0.34 Social insurance: 5% Health insurance: 1% Share of medical expenses incurred: 20%	Union subs: US$0.13 Meals (less food allowance): approx VUS$1.34 Social insurance: 5% Health insurance: 1%	Union subs: US$0.13 Meals: US$4.37 Social insurance: 5% Health insurance: 1%	Union subs: US$0.34 Social insurance: 5% Health insurance: 1%	Meals: US$2.36 Social insurance: 5%

US$1 was approximately equal to 14,858 Vietnamese Dong at the time of this research.

TABLE 6 *(from previous page)*

per month. In general, management stated that employees worked eight hours per day six days a week and were entitled to 12 days off per year. Salaries were, on average, 760,000 VND per month plus productivity bonuses.

e. The industry in 2005

Closer ties between brand-name MNEs and suppliers are increasingly characterising the sports footwear industry. This is generally due to a global firm strategy that has the express goal of working more closely with the better factories and is enabled by improved and less expensive information and communications technology as well as the relatively low cost and efficiency of transportation. Similarly, the technical nature of production relative to the apparel sector and the enormous size of footwear factories make it difficult for firms to change location quickly. Hence MNEs, as previously noted, have often installed compliance or quality control managers on-site and tend to be reducing the number of suppliers and staying longer in existing supplier relationships. Such consolidation has had positive effects on the practice of CSR as it has led to better relationships with footwear factory managers and a much greater ability to influence supply chain management (as compared with other industries, such as the apparel industry for example, where small factory size and the practice of producing for several brands simultaneously makes closer ties with a particular brand more difficult). In the view of one FMNE manager, 'In footwear, we are moving away from being policemen towards being advisors.' It is exactly this kind of relationship that can be held up as an example for other industries to follow, in that it allows for the more effective implementation of the labour, social and ethical standards of CSR.

2. Creating a shared vision

In Chapter III we outlined the framework for the presentation of our findings based on the data generated in interviews we conducted. We found that one of the first steps in implementing a code of conduct was the creation of a shared vision. The following sections outline the various elements that may contribute to the creation of that vision. They explore the issues of top-management commitment to code development and its implementation, communication of the message and the potential for establishing a business case for code implementation.

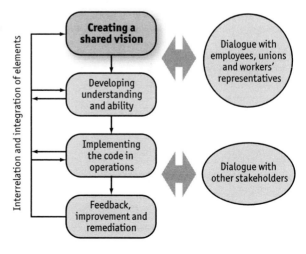

a. Top-management commitment

Without the commitment of the organisation's senior management, no major initiative can be successfully implemented. Top management sends a signal each time it speaks to stakeholders or communicates with its staff.

> With the code, you need to have buy-in from top management. Knowing that the president was behind it, it got into our performance objectives and made us roll it out with our leadership partners [supplier managers]. We started with the leadership partners. We had several people who travelled country to country explaining the code and its impact (FMNE 2, Headquarters).

Importantly, this commitment needs to be continually reaffirmed after it has been introduced. Implementing the objectives of a code can have extensive impact on the organisation; it may change the way an organisation does business, requiring shifts in priorities, management systems and stakeholder relations. As such, it depends on broad-based support emanating from the top of the firm and also stretching down through the organisation and out to business partners.

> Our biggest problem is getting full support internally. The concept of who are stakeholders, how do we deal with critics, and things like the NGO3, is really new—we need a stakeholder rather than a shareholder philosophy (FMNE I, CSR Manager Headquarters).

> [Following a discussion of the production pressures with a MNE CSR manager] That is why, if we don't get support from production and the [MNE country-level general manager], then the supplier won't care. We have to have their support (FMNE 2, Country-Level General Manager).

> The top level push has been very important to bring this about. With larger footwear suppliers, we have had more direct top support and, as such, we have been able to get work hours within the 60 we set in the code. But this has not been possible in apparel, in part due to the nature of the industry. We would have to change the industry (MNE, CSR Manager Headquarters).

> It really helps to have an impassioned CEO. It [successfully integrating CSR issues] depends on seeing competitive practices from a different viewpoint. Our CEO said we need to move toward greater innovation . . . if he would have said 'sustainable innovation' we would have seen a much greater impact (FMNE 2, CSR Manager Headquarters).

> Most of the senior management people, if you ask them what is the code, they would not be able to quote you back these points [of the content of the code]. Child labour, of course, but not the rest (FMNE I, Regional CSR Manager).

b. Development of the message on code

It is the responsibility of management to develop strategic plans and set corporate objectives. In the views of those interviewed, if social considerations are not an integral part of the company's long-term strategy and included in its overall objectives then impact of any CSR effort will be limited. Corporate codes of conduct can be an important step in this process—providing a clear commitment to CSR objectives.

> The code is your constitution, your principles and the way you operate (FMNE 2, CSR Manager Headquarters).

> You have to consciously make a decision about what your company values are. Not just talk about them. They have to be strong enough to make improvements in product, how you lead, and you have to demonstrate how they impact on you (FMNE 2, Headquarters).

Firms can support their social responsibility objectives through the culture and actions of management—setting clear ethical or social guidelines through a broad range of initiatives, changes in reward systems and structures, and the promotion of social issues. These, though, are dependent on a consistent strategy that typically needs to be supported by a consistent message. The following comment demonstrates the complexity of this process in the highly matrixed and dispersed sports footwear companies reviewed.

> To understand the company's approach, we first of all have a strategic plan. These are the five or six things that we will focus on as a company, and each group needs to know what these are to know what to focus on. Each region and product category has its own strategic plan. And with each, profit feeds into it. We have also a great deal more experience with fitting [environmental issues] into the plan, but not so much with [the people issues] (FMNE 2, Marketing Manager Headquarters).

One thing we heard from many managers was the need for broad applicability in the development of the code. Yet such applicability has several challenges. First, the firms themselves have many different market demands, varied product lines and various locations of production. In the view of the managers of the FMNEs interviewed, particularly those operating in the CSR teams that are typically responsible for both developing the code and supporting its communication throughout the organisation, it is difficult to balance the need for generality to make a code globally relevant and the specificity needed to make it useful.

> We want to make sure the code is globally relevant, the same from region to region. Suppliers need to know where you are coming from. Also, it needs to be a living document (FMNE 2, Headquarters).

> What we are trying to develop is some sort of global consistency. This is of course challenged by legal and cultural aspects. We have to have some leeway to interpret the code. While guidelines help ensure consistency to the degree possible, we are trying some different things to see what works. Asia has been at the forefront, due to the size of the teams. The development of the guidelines has been a good reality check—our health and safety guidelines were a very European viewpoint—fire extinguisher height was set, as one example, far too high for an Asian woman. So we have to consider this as a guideline, not a law (FMNE 1, Regional CSR Manager).

The law referred to above was not national but rather the companies' own internal 'law'. This complexity in interpretation of the code within the context of local or national conditions is particularly challenging. As in the case mentioned above, there are situations where the local law does not address issues covered by the code. In such instances, guidelines that address meeting the content of the code, for example that workers be provided with a safe workplace, mean that flexibility has to be present to allow adjustment to local realities, including in this case the height of workers.

Developing a code also requires its communication, outlining what the code means for the firm and its supply chain, with some means of consistently presenting this message to factories. Of course, the challenge thereafter is to ensure that there is consistency between what is communicated and what is actually occurring within the factories themselves. For example, some of the most challenging issues for businesses investing in China include the right to freedom of association and the right to collective bargaining. In particular, companies that back the ILO Declaration on Fundamental Principles and Rights at Work and choose to invest in China may find themselves in a dilemma. As discussed in Chapter II, some companies have opted to address the dilemma by undertaking special proactive policies with respect to the rights of freedom of association and collective bargaining. Under such policies, when the rights of freedom of association and collective bargaining are restricted, these companies seek to facilitate the development of parallel means for independent freedom of association and collective bargaining. Concrete exchanges of experience with such innovations can help build good management practice consistent with the universal values of freedom of association and collective bargaining, even in these difficult situations. Nonetheless, parallel means should not be seen as a substitute for the full respect for freedom of association and collective bargaining rights for workers.

In some cases, the development of a coherent code message has meant that the MNE manufacturing managers have had to be the final voice of authority on company CSR issues. We heard that this responsibility entails avoiding telling supply chain partners one thing and then later presenting different advice or requirements. It also means, as the quote below indicates, leading by example.

> Quality control people are sometimes too helpful; they may conflict with the CSR people, which can confuse the factory. So we have to make sure the factory hears one voice (FMNE 1, Regional CSR Manager).

> We [management] weren't leading by example—working every Saturday, going home at nine or ten at night. Now we have changed, and the quality of life here has improved. We know we have to finish by five-thirty; I kick them all out by that time. We also have all the systems here, not just in Guangzhou. It is good that [the senior manager at Headquarters] said that this would happen—he gave us a year, we didn't get it, so he said 'OK, get your act together, no working late.' And this allowed us to go to the factory and say now you have to do the same (FMNE 2, Manufacturing Manager).

Those interviewed, both in supplier firms and the MNEs themselves, emphasised the importance of involvement, of having those workers affected by codes take part in developing the code and translating it into reality. Yet, as several managers (including the last quoted here) indicated, in a diversified organisation, balancing varied interests—including the added focus on CSR—and working out agreement on this can be time-consuming.

> In any good code, in developing it everybody wins a little and everybody loses. In hammering it out, it needs to reflect a compromise document. It is important that both sides feel they got something out of it (FMNE 2, Headquarters).

> We developed a written code, and got some of our bigger partners back at [headquarters] to get involved in the process (FMNE 2, Senior Manager).

> Price and delivery are the concerns of one department in [the MNE]; quality is the concern of another and social responsibility is the concern of a third. That is why we have so many meetings (FMNE 2, Headquarters).

One issue that we heard repeatedly concerned the standardisation of codes. While several managers made suggestions that related to the role of international bodies and multi-company agreements, no consistent solution was presented. As the two excerpts below indicate, this challenge is not only at the MNE level but stretches down to the factory floor.

> We have two factories, one making for [one large MNE brand] and the other for [another MNE]. Since both of them have different codes, we are trying to establish our own company standard that meets the needs of both (VIS 1, CSR Manager).

> A bigger question is 'should there be a standardised code?' I have seen factories with codes wallpapering the entrance, so we have to wonder if this is right (FMNE 1, Regional Manufacturing Manager).

Finally, from the perspective of business, in its November 2002 statement on CSR, the USCIB advises that companies communicate their commitment to corporate responsibility in a variety of ways, depending on the unique situation or requirements of each firm. The statement highlights that while some firms within specific sectors have chosen to collectively embrace a particular social initiative in a very public manner, other firms have chosen to develop their policies and programmes internally without making them widely available outside the company. As has been pointed out by some critics, while such approaches respect the particular corporate personality, they do little to standardise the requirements for labour, social and ethical criteria of CSR and codes of conduct.

c. Make the business case

Managers at both MNEs and their suppliers are business people operating in a competitive environment, dealing with conflicting and complex goals. For example, increasing quality may require expenditures that may reduce profits, or implementing the practices required in a code may be seen to reduce flexibility. Yet quite a large number of managers (although not all) supported the view that being socially responsible—in large part by meeting the requirements of a code of conduct—can have long-term and even short-term competitive advantages for MNEs and their suppliers.

> The code is just a guideline; it is not the reason for doing these things. Doing these things helps make everything work smoothly. And if we opened a new factory tomorrow then we would do things the same way. I have to consider myself one of the employees. When you tour our factory you will see that our employees are shiny and bright, and that is good for business (VIS 5, Factory Manager).

> The companies realise at the end of the day that implementing the code is good for their business. People are happy to work here. At first, they thought

> it would cost them a lot, but later they didn't complain. There was a case of a fire in the assembly area; some of the heating units sparked the solvent, and because the guys had been trained they quickly put out the fire. The company realised then how important it was (FMNE 1, Manufacturing Manager).

> One of the other factories [a large supplier] loses 40% of their staff every season. And you can see real quality differences with experienced stitchers (FMNE 1, Product Designer).

Yet we also heard that the business case is not universally accepted, that implementing codes is not always seen as being in the best interest of the company, a view particularly held by suppliers.

> Business has not embraced the triple-bottom-line approach (FMNE 2, Marketing Manager, Headquarters).

> We [at the MNE] and our partners [the supplier firms] have seen the benefits of these CSR components. But I can imagine that many other companies might ask 'what will be the cost of really implementing all these things in a code? '(FMNE 2, Manufacturing Manager).

> If we stopped pushing the code tomorrow some of our factories would continue doing it, continue following labour practices that meet the code. And some would stop the same day (FMNE 1, Country Manager).

In seeking to generate support from suppliers in carrying through the requirements of their codes, and in seeking to develop support internally to the firm introducing a code, it was repeatedly suggested that the business case needs to figure more prominently.

> I always walk in and present 'this is the business case and this is the environment case'. At the same time, I have to adjust our story to the interests of the audience. So to a designer I push the opportunity [in supporting code] for creativity; for legal I push the legal (FMNE 2, Marketing Manager, Headquarters).

> Show people not just with PowerPoint presentations but with real-world experiences (FMNE 2, Marketing Manager, Headquarters).

> Train top management [of suppliers] and make sure they all understand what is the benefit, and in particular what is the benefit to [the supplier]. [The MNE] has been like a professor at showing why to do this (CHS 9, Factory Manager).

There are many drivers behind the business-case argument that are put forward. As mentioned above, this is sometimes due to the fact that quality improvements and greater worker commitment can result from code implementation—as can higher productivity. The business case can also sometimes be made clear by the potential of lost sales, both within the firm and with supplier relationships. However, notwithstanding the need to make a business case, there are some fundamental human rights in the workplace that must not be breached—no matter what the cost—namely those highlighted in the ILO Declaration on Fundamental Principles and Rights at Work.

For getting companies to realise the value of doing things the right way, top management has to be made aware that eventually it will benefit the company. Safe workplaces are more productive—and if you in the ILO can show this then companies will start to do this without so much prodding from the multinational. We improved the ventilation in the sole melt area and this resulted in defects falling to 2% from 7 or 8%, while productivity went up 20% (FMNE 2, Compliance Manager).

Doing the right thing reflects good business, not quarter to quarter but over the lifetime of the company. And it has to be measured that way (FMNE 2, Operations Manager, Headquarters).

We improved airflows, which resulted in a two-degree temperature drop. This along with other changes resulted in, according to our estimate, an increase in productivity of 10 to 15% while cutting defect rates by 75% (VIS 5, Factory Manager).

Bottom line for us is if you don't comply, we don't do business with you (FMNE 2, Manager).

Linking productivity and excessive overtime

In supporting the business case, one manager gave the example of a 7,000-employee footwear factory, which had workers putting in a 75-hour working week. With the code limiting working hours to 60 a week, the company pressured the supplier management to cut back on the time put in. They did cut back working hours by 12%, which resulted in a 5% drop in output. With better targeting of incentives, and lower turnover due in part to the code, within a month output was back to previous levels.

The question the manager then posed was, while this may work in large operations where some understanding can be developed with the managers, would it be more difficult in an industry such as apparel? The obvious answer to those familiar with the industry, the manager suggested, was 'yes, very much so'. The manager suggested then that perhaps this indicates the need to work with companies' head offices rather than with many small factories, but no clear answer seemed apparent. Again, similar sentiments with regard to the possible difference between footwear and apparel were heard in other discussions.

The important point is that from the MNE's perspective, integrating social responsibility into operations can in many circumstances lead to greater profits rather than just higher costs and less profit. We would suggest that at the individual firm level this type of real world example is useful in presenting the argument for following codes throughout supply chains.

Similar real-world examples of business arguments for social responsibility should continue to be developed by the ILO and others concerned with social responsibility. Of course, the business case is not the only thing that needs to be considered given the ILO's declarations and its support for fundamental principles and rights at work. Other considerations including the firms' desire to meet local and national laws must also be taken into account.

3. Developing understanding and ability

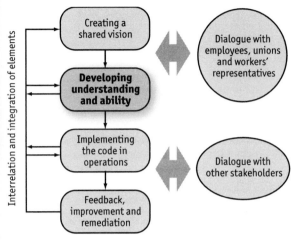

Apart from creating a shared vision of a code, one of the most critical elements of its implementation rests with the development of understanding and ability. We heard that in some cases this process extends beyond the boundaries of the MNE to encompass its supplier factories. Important decisions need to be made regarding the prioritisation of capacity building, education and training in support of the message being communicated. Furthermore, issues such as the internal capacity of staff, costs and external resources are often addressed as a result of attempting to develop understanding and ability. The following sections outline in greater detail our findings on this aspect of code-of-conduct implementation.

a. Make the code a priority throughout all components of the supply chain

Effective code implementation depends on generating and sustaining commitment not only from the MNE but also from suppliers, beginning at the senior-management level. This theme is highlighted in the following remarks.

> You have to have buy-off from senior management. If the GM here was not serious about this then it would be a real battle. It makes it very easy to get things done—and since many people don't understand yet you need top management to push it. Particularly the senior manager in the factory, since if the owner overseas buys in but the factory manager doesn't, it won't work (FMNE 2, Manufacturing Manager).

> There is an impact of the top manager [at a factory] on the managers down the chain of command (FMNE 2, CSR Manager).

> You need the support of top management; without this you don't have a chance. Whether you are a big dominant buyer or not (FMNE 1, Manufacturing Manager).

> The first thing we noticed was the change in [the factory manager] himself; he seems to care about the workers more (CHS 7, Workers' Representative).

> I'm sure at the top, with the general managers of the suppliers, there was some give and take, but by the time it got to us it was 'here is where we are going' (FMNE 2, Manager).

> When you enter a factory you can almost tell from the start whether their managers believe in this (FMNE 2, CSR Inspector).

> Key is to have the owner and senior management on your side; make sure that they personally believe in this, rather than take this 'when the cloud is [going] to pass' approach (FMNE I, Regional Manager).

While a number of managers in both MNEs and suppliers highlighted the business case for supplier firms as well as for the multinationals, in practice the business case often started with the potential loss of contracts. This would indicate a challenge for those sectors or firms that do not have buyer–supplier relationships where those implementing a code can link compliance with retaining business.

> The people at the top [for the supplier] at least see the code as a business advantage. If you don't master it, you don't do business with us. You have to hope that eventually they will see good in it (FMNE 2, Manufacturing Manager).

> The simple way for a company like one of these multinationals [to implement a code] is to say, 'you don't do it and we don't do business'. The code is written very clearly and it is a business decision (VIS 7, Factory Manager).

> Last year we worked with a military factory and they refused to post our code because they said they don't have to, they have the Viet Nam Labour code. We told them they post the code or we don't do business with them—so they did (FMNE 2, Labour Practices Inspector).

> If the buyer has the power to force the company to do this, they might do it, but I haven't seen many factories that would do it for benevolent reasons (FMNE 2, Manufacturing Manager).

At the same time, there were those managers who emphasised the power of making a business case not only based on possible loss of business—the stick approach—but also on the potential improvements in key factors such as productivity. Even so, it appeared that a combination was often necessary. The stick would figure prominently at the start, combined with the carrot of improved operations accompanied by clear explanations of the reasons for the changes and the reality faced by the MNE in its markets.

> The first thing you have to do is educate the shareholder or general manager at the factory of the benefits of the programme. [The MNE] brings top managers and country managers here to see us, how we operate (CHS 7, Manager).

> The bad publicity in the sector helped; it brought a sense of urgency to the task (FMNE 2, CSR Manager, Headquarters).

In working with these suppliers, as could be expected, those with effective management seem to be those most capable of adapting to code requirements. We feel that this is an important point, highlighting the need for an integrated management system together with managers who are truly committed to meeting CSR objectives.

> Our top-performing factories are those that have good management systems—an owner and top management that believe this is good for them, at

least from a business sense. If the top management believes it, it will work; if they don't then you will have a hard time getting it down through all levels (FMNE 2, Senior Manager).

We have to spend much more time with those factories that think this will eventually pass. This did cause some economic challenge for some of our suppliers—some couldn't adjust well, and the ones that 'got it' have adjusted better (FMNE 2, Senior Manager).

A number of suggestions were made with regard to developing commitment to a code of conduct throughout the supply chain. First, given the offshore nature of many suppliers, it is important to make sure their corporate headquarters, which may be located in the Republic of Korea or in Taiwan, China, are brought into the code and support its implementation, for whatever reason—negative or positive.

Whatever we ask for here, they go up the ladder and check things with Taiwan (FMNE 2, Manufacturing Manager).

Don't expect that you will get approval with the factory for spending half a million dollars for its improvement without the support of their headquarters (FMNE I, Country Manager).

Second, the challenges are best addressed when those throughout the MNE, particularly those who are recognised as being important to the business of the supplier, communicate their commitment to the code. In any case, developing true commitment to the spirit of the code may be a long-term challenge—both for the firm introducing a code and its suppliers—particularly in those areas that require managers to adopt a new world perspective.

[The MNE head of footwear sourcing] really cares very much about the code. When he was here he didn't check shoe quality, he just looked at EHS and code things (VIS 3, CSR Team Member).

Unless we can address the drivers, nothing will happen. The most rapid changes were those that required no structural changes, for example fire extinguishers. The opposite would be that managers must change their view of the world (FMNE 2, Headquarters).

b. Communicate the code and its impact

With regard to codes, we were told that employees tended to know about such activities but that they, together with managers, often do not understand the intent and requirement of the code of conduct. This is one of the primary challenges to carrying out the code. It requires explaining to managers throughout the supply chain the purpose of the code; that is, what is driving the changes the company is undertaking.

With our factories, they can do something when they focus on it. With this it was the challenge to get them to see that this was a real challenge, a permanent change in the landscape. Not just a case-by-case basis. We had to make them see, that they understood. We were really insulating them and taking the hits in the market. So it was communicating (FMNE 2, Senior Manager).

[The MNE] could give us more info on how the world is changing, with environment, health and safety, with WTO [World Trade Organisation], what is happening internationally. Also, how to fulfil labour law and, if not, what to do (CHS 6, General Manager).

The major points of interest to managers and the issues that needed to be communicated to all levels include the following:

- What the code and the CSR policy is, what it will do and what it will not do.

- Why the code is important in today's marketplace.

- What is the purpose and intent of the code in their particular location and its function.

- What is senior management's vision of and commitment to the objectives embodied in the code.

The communication process is complicated by the multiple layers that exist in both MNEs and supplier firms (some suppliers report ten or more levels within the factory and with the MNEs matrixed across regions, product lines and sports sectors as well as functional groupings). These structures, in our opinion, also pose a significant challenge to ensuring that the necessary dialogue with workers takes place.

Our factories are very hierarchical. It's a challenge to send a message down to the floor level, even when top management is already on board. A related issue is the improvement of communication and organisational structure (FMNE 3, Regional Manager).

Our research indicates there are several approaches to communicating effectively the message required by the introduction of a code of conduct. The first suggested by the interviewees is clear guidelines, standards (as will be outlined in a later section) and goals—as well as consistent views from all parts of the organisation. This last point is covered later but merits emphasis here. Various MNE managers highlighted the challenge of mixed messages. A firm implementing a code needs to project a common voice. Such clarity and consistency is necessary because suppliers may in some instances try to go around a CSR compliance officer or even a manufacturing manager, to get what are for them better—in other words, typically less costly—answers from sourcing or other managers at the MNE.

Communicate clear standards. If you say one thing, then make sure it is right. Hold off and double check (FMNE 1, Country Manager).

The factories know they can go back to headquarters and appeal, so the headquarters has to back us up, there has to be consistent support. And that requires educating our own people (FMNE 2, Senior Manager).

I don't like the term 'management system' because it sounds too theoretical. Tell them [suppliers] clearly what has to be done, and how. You have to guide them so that they are clearly aware of our materials specifications. Since 1995 we are co-operating with an environmental consultancy and they have helped tremendously (FMNE 1, EHS Manager, Headquarters).

Another suggestion we heard was that the message and lessons need to be repeated regularly at all levels, with the idea that repetition, combined with consistency, will eventually lead to some level of understanding and acceptance.

> We have found that you have to go over things again and again. Once is never enough at any level (VIS 5, CSR Manager).

> You have to keep training, constantly reinforcing the need to do these things. But at the same time you have to keep things rather positive (FMNE 2, Manufacturing Manager).

> Make sure everyone understands things the same. That is something that we do regularly. We work with the EHS teams in the factories to make sure they understand (FMNE 1, Country Manager).

> Getting the understanding all the way down through the whole hierarchy is a challenge. As long as we have a consistent and consistently repeated message, then that can help push things down (FMNE 2, Senior Manager).

Communication stretches beyond management, of course, and should reach the level of workers throughout the supply chain. Contrary to what the MNE managers expected, many—though not most—of the workers interviewed knew about the code in their particular factory and in some factories workers were even able to identify the topics covered by the code. Workers associated the code items most often with a reduction in working hours. When asked how they knew about the code, they suggested that it was through training, posting of the code at various locations in the factories, and through the distribution of cards listing code provisions.

> Posting the code is very important because we receive comments from workers that the factory is not complying. When some companies are doing training they might do it over the loudspeaker, so having it written allows workers to compare code with practice (FMNE 2, Labour Practices Inspector).

> We pass out code-of-conduct cards for all workers (VIS 6, CSR Manager).

> We attended a course done by the [supplier] CSR team, and received the little book on code (CHS 10, Line Workers).

These examples highlight an issue that becomes particularly problematic outside of the footwear sector, where many of the major brands require sole presence in the factories they contract with. In other sectors, for example apparel, a variety of buyers may be present in a single supplier factory leading to a range of codes and a diminishment of the power of any single MNE to influence actual supplier practice.

Finally, as each of the firms studied had distinct CSR compliance teams, their role in communication needs to be considered. CSR compliance teams, according to several MNE managers, are the focal point of communication efforts, dealing with a variety of stakeholders, both internal and external to the MNE, including workers, the public, suppliers and field operations, as well as senior management. They are central to the effort of presenting a consistent message and typically drive the process of compliance.

> Our headquarters role [in the CSR group] is the education of people within the organisation. Communication with the public, getting them educated on

what we are doing. Getting support from headquarters if we want to adjust orders or make some enforcement move (FMNE 2, Senior Manager).

c. Education and training in support of codes

Building understanding and changing behaviours in a company requires a well-communicated message, as well as education and training that meets the needs of various levels of the organisation and across the supply chain.

> A good set of standards is not enough. They should be accompanied by training and education of managers, supervisors and workers (THS 1, Deputy General Manager).

> Training is the number one item to make a code work (FMNE 2, Manufacturing Manager).

> Education is the key to success. Our employees—everyone has to know that this is an issue. They have to know what is the business case. What could be the PR problems, what other drivers downstream could be. We want to avoid getting legislated into doing this (FMNE 2, Headquarters).

> Just having the equipment is not enough. You must have training so you can understand [what the code requires] and equipment that will allow you to carry out your objectives and work (FMNE 3, CSR Manager, Headquarters).

We were told that training must take place at all levels, in both the MNEs and the suppliers. As the implementation of a code of conduct is particularly dependent on senior-management commitment at various points in the supply chain, an initial investment must be made in top- and middle-management training. In some cases this was done through bringing senior supplier managers back to headquarters for instruction on the code. Within those MNEs implementing codes, managers dealing with the factories must fully understand the social objectives covered by the code, the purpose of integrating these into management systems and how to do so. They must understand and support the standards and targets against which performance will be measured and be able to coach their subordinates in the same areas. It appeared, though, that training on the code for those staff not dealing with suppliers was minimal.

> In 1997 we launched a mandatory training program on [our audit framework], first of all for all employees [dealing with factories], and then for the suppliers. Standards require an interactive approach; it is not enough to create a set of good standards. It is important to educate people about them and, then, to be able to reinforce them, if necessary (FMNE 2, CSR Manager, Headquarters).

> There was a design meeting a year and a half ago and they had everybody together—there they gave an hour-and-a-half-long talk about labour issues, pay scales, safety, PVCs, and so on. The thrust was that it [the changes being produced within the MNE] was about people and how these changes would impact on them. But in terms of training, there isn't much for people who don't have contact with the factories, no training (FMNE 1, Product Designer).

> I attended nine workshops on the management system framework conducted by [a UK-based training company which conducts courses on an integrated approach to meeting code] (FMNE 2, Manufacturing Manager).

> New designers get to go to shoe school. There they do teach about labour issues (FMNE 2, Marketing Manager, Headquarters).

Again, the training methods used appeared to depend on the organisation's structure, tradition and activities. Training varied from in-house to external, using lectures, case studies or scenario building. In any case, the effectiveness of the training must be evaluated in terms of the changes in behaviours and attitudes that it produces. With regard to working with suppliers, there were variations from close involvement and monitoring of the training programme to a relatively 'hands-off' approach, perhaps providing some materials. The approach taken by the MNEs studied was to ensure that code implementation across the supply chain was preceded by some form of introduction by the MNE of the code programme to its suppliers.

> With the roll-out we had people explain specifically what each code element required (FMNE 2, Manager).

One element that was mentioned several times was the importance of making the implementation of the code 'real'. This was done through training, assisting those who impact on the success of the code to understand its role and the benefits of its implementation. The question for us, still unanswered, would be how to make this understanding possible without requiring participants to travel to the distant factories to understand implementation issues throughout the global supply chain.

> The biggest eye opener for me was coming out this way [to Asia from the corporate headquarters]. When they say that a thousand hands touch these things before they reach the customer you don't really understand that. But coming out here you see this is like a city. Changing one line affects so many people (FMNE I, Product Designer).

With regard to developing the capacity of managers within supplier factories, several training suggestions deserve mention. First, as one manager pointed out, training for local managers can be on the job. For example, it can begin by simply observing how the MNE manufacturing manager addresses the code elements during factory walkthroughs. Second, several managers suggested doing training on a thematic basis. This approach is related to the discussion on implementation discussed later in this chapter and reinforces the view by managers that attempts need to be made not to try to do too much at once but, rather, to take aboard projects in a phased manner. Finally, we also heard about the need to build cultural awareness, in particular with expatriate managers who may be less sensitive to local conditions.

> You have code training through practice. Practice means walking through the factory on a regular basis (FMNE 2, Manager).

> We hold clinics on a regular basis explaining why certain things should be done on their behalf—PPE [personal protective equipment], AIDS, food hygiene even (FMNE 2, Manager).

They have Vietnamese and Korean cultural training programmes for ex-pats and workers. We have gotten a pretty good handle on this (VIS 5, CSR Manager).

In implementing the code, the challenge was to get factories to *focus* on something. Once they are, they get it done. We are telling them: 'the marketplace has changed, consumers have changed—so, you, factory guys, have to change your attitude'. The major challenge here is education. The code can work only when factory management is on board. These guys [factory management] are technical people; they do not have management skills. They have to be educated on compensation, healthcare, environment, and so on. It's still an ongoing process (FMNE 1, Regional Manager).

Each of the factories discussed training of workers, although the actual level of training varied within the factories. In some cases, workers spent a day or two being taught about the various code elements; in others, nothing had been done and the workers had little or no knowledge about the code and its implications. In most cases, the real situation lay somewhere in between, with some workers mentioning they received training during short periods before the start of shifts or over the factory loudspeakers.

The company had to train all the workers on the code. They [the supplier] had to send us [that is, the MNE] the training plan beforehand for our review. And then all new workers have to be trained. We provide a CD-ROM that they can use (FMNE 2, Labour Practices Inspector).

They [the factory] give two days of training on EHS and code for each new employee and one day for each existing employee. They also have job-specific safety training and management training on Viet Nam culture for the ex-pat managers (FMNE 2, Manufacturing Manager).

From our experience, developing an understanding of the code appeared quite challenging—the managers and supervisors of the supplier firms, typically the ones providing the training, have only limited experience with the issues covered by the code. Similarly, many workers have little direct experience with the code either. For example, some issues such as the need for health and safety procedures would be much simpler to convey to managers and workers than other issues such as the prohibition of discrimination or the freedom of association.

Many employees don't really believe in the code. What can help is to help the supplier know how big the company [the MNE] is, why we have a code. Don't just teach the code. Teach them why we have a code (FMNE 2, CSR Manager).

In the past you used to go straight to work—now a worker is trained in factory policies, safety practices. Their rights and benefits. Most workers like the reduced hours, they want to work less but get more money (CHS 7, Line Supervisor).

I have found the code very confusing, with the Viet Nam labour law. We don't really understand. [Interviewer question: Did you receive training?] No, nothing; like the rest of the workers, I just received a copy of the written code (VIS 7, Union Head).

Assuming this last comment is true, it would make carrying out his role as head of the factory union extremely difficult. For his role is, according to him, 'to strictly follow the code and the Viet Nam labour law in terms of rights and benefits'.

Again, the role of CSR staff needs to be considered in the process of code implementation. CSR staff are responsible for a multitude of tasks including developing a communication strategy, conducting and implementing training (including development of training materials for use by suppliers, although this is sometimes done in co-operation with field operations) and monitoring (usually done in co-operation with field personnel). As is indicated by the last quote above, internal training is critical. It is needed to develop understanding of the purpose of the code and the role that CSR teams play in transforming it from mere words into something practical throughout the supply chain.

> For training we have a clear methodology. To train the CSR team staff we rely on outside experts; consultants are training on how to comply with the code. We bring the CSR people together in the regions. The CSR people themselves train the suppliers' technical managers, the same as [the MNE] is doing in other areas, like QC [quality control] and production. We have a presentation for EHS with lots of examples, and by December we hope to have one for social as well as guidelines for social area as well (FMNE 1, CSR Team Member, Headquarters).

> Some people might say [about the CSR staff of the MNE] 'what do you guys do, just sitting around, not doing anything for production'. So you need to teach them more about the company (FMNE 2, CSR Manager).

d. Internal capacity

> It is quite critical for us to build capacity of the factories, so that we can leverage resources (FMNE 3, Sourcing Manager).

Interviewees consistently highlighted the importance of increasing the capacity of both those working for the MNE and suppliers in implementing the code. At the MNE level, this in part depended on a development process, certainly related to the points we have already made about building understanding through communication and training. In one case, highlighted in the first comment below, an MNE attempted to build a core of staff located around the world that understood the goals of social responsibility and attempted to change the corporate culture and practice—yet the issue of management commitment remains central to the success of the effort.

> As part of our efforts to build CSR awareness around the world, we brought 60 to 80 people from our operations around the world to teach them sustainable business. Four times, for one week each, over a year. This changed the way many people think—we need [to think about triple-bottom-line issues] for sustainability—taking care of all three [objectives]. With environment we can demonstrate savings or profits. But it appears that's not so easy with people [issues]. With these 60 to 80 people, many want to do something, but don't know what, exactly. We brought them here to help them understand the 'what', yet have had a hard time getting their managers' managers to under-

stand how important this is. In Europe this hasn't been so much the case; we got the senior management there to move it, so it was not just a headquarters-out thing. As part of this, we provide some of the funds for workshops (FMNE 2, CSR Manager, Headquarters).

The people coming out [from the MNE headquarters] are changing. People are now more aware that cultures are different. So [the MNE] has to do training. I have seen people come out and not know what to do, how to work in the local environment (FMNE 2, Manufacturing Manager).

With respect to code implementation in a supplier factory, both MNE managers and supplier managers highlighted the importance of having managers in place who have both the willingness and the capacity to implement the code of conduct. Some of this appears to be changing. For example, managers' skills can be developed. At the same time, a number of interviewees commented that, 'you can't teach an old dog new tricks' (that is, some managers were just going to be ineffective at implementing the code).

Generally, if a supplier manager doesn't have the right attitude concerning social issues, they will have other problems [meeting audit requirements] as well, and on other items like delivering their product on time. Every time we have been involved with [problems relating to] manufacturing concerns, there were compliance problems as well (FMNE 3, CSR Manager, Headquarters).

[How do you get improvement?] Well, it really depends on a change of attitude. You depend on good management, and yes, these EHS and social responsibility ideas might be better for the factory but it depends on the managers, and they aren't in place (FMNE 2, Manufacturing Manager).

For me, to convince our managers I just look at attitude. Looking at them I can see if a manager is willing to listen or if I will have to spend too much time trying to change their attitude. If they don't want to I tell them first, if you don't follow the code we are breaking our contract with the buyer. And if we don't follow the code, [the MNE] has the right to cut orders or reduce orders. Second, I tell them this is progress of history, workers' rights, health and safety (VIS 2, CSR Manager).

There did appear to be a process of change under way, in part due to a change in the attitude of ex-pat managers working in the factories, as well as a process of learning taking place. The lesson from that appears to be the need to have effective and continual training and to encourage suppliers to select managers with the right attitude for operating under the more worker-friendly practices required by the code of conduct.

Supervisors manage workers differently now [after the introduction of the code]. In part it is due to the changes in the factory manager. Supervisors have had meetings to share good and bad practices. In the past it was just 'I am the supervisor, I am right'. But now it is more teamwork. Still there are cases of managers who do not manage in the right way (CHS 7, Workers' Representative).

Many of our factories are managed from outside [China] and the people they send in are technical people; they were not well suited to deal with this issue.

They weren't human resource-type people. We had to get them to send in
people who could understand staffing, HR, environment. And it wasn't easy
to find these people. That was true for us [at the MNE] as well; we didn't have
that experience (FMNE 2, Senior Manager).

e. The challenge of integrating acquisitions

Codes of conduct are often developed with specific organisations and their cultures in
mind. As such, the introduction of an already existing code of conduct into a new
subsidiary or acquisition can be particularly challenging. In conducting this research,
we visited one factory which had been recently acquired. We found that the supplier
and buyer faced communications difficulties which made implementing the code
difficult.

> [The new subsidiary] costing, development and production people don't sit
> down and talk, they do all the work separately. [Their new parent firm] has
> done a lot of work on code, but [the subsidiary] has some problems because
> they have their own culture. And the fit with implementing code is not so
> good. They have had some problems—groups not talking, costing is done by
> [the parent], development by [the subsidiary] (THS 1, Factory Manager).

This quote demonstrates the need to have consistency in the message being communicated. The same factory faced numerous challenges in keeping up with production, forcing it to exceed the 60-hour working week limitation being enforced in other
shoe factories.

> [At the same factory, the manager stated,] training was done by our CSR
> people—both for me and for the factory. One day for me, one or two days for
> the factory. This covered EHS, not the labour side. We don't have problems
> here with overtime, but the factory does have to use overtime, even more
> than 60 hours at times. Materials come late, some come from China, others
> from Taiwan [China], Italy and France. This can lead to problems. The labour
> law says 48 hours regular and 72 hours total maximum, paying one and a half
> for overtime, double time for Sundays and triple time for night time on
> Sundays (THS 1, Manager).

f. Costs

While a large number of managers, both supplier and MNE, argued that there is a business case for acting socially responsibly, improving the quality of working conditions
and the like, there are also costs associated with implementing codes. Such costs are
difficult to quantify, however, given their often complex nature. For example, items
such as reducing overtime combined with increased productivity or health and safety
improvements can result in fewer worker accidents.

> We just had a case of a company in China that said 'you ask us to meet your
> code and lower FOBs [free on board, cost of product to MNE on shipment from
> factory]'. We don't really sell our code results to the consumer, so there is a
> conflict, in that implementing the code has costs. We will have to pay more;

some balance is needed. We may have to increase costs (FMNE 1, Sourcing Manager, Headquarters).

There will be factories which are unhappy with this, having to implement the code and paying costs. And some companies, not just [this MNE], will say 'no, this is what we will pay'. At my last company, they did study costs; factories had costs, and we were moving to Asia to save money. So there was some discussion and to keep suppliers happy in some cases margins had to be cut. Factories will fight for something in return, including commitment for a certain purchase quantity, but in apparel this is almost impossible (FMNE 1, CSR Manager).

We don't really have any numbers on how much implementing the code costs because it is really wrapped in (CHS 10, Assistant Factory Manager).

It was clear from our discussions that there is often disagreement between suppliers and buyers about who should pay the added costs. In the areas of environment, health and safety (EHS), paying of overtime and increased wages, these costs can be substantial for firms running on tight margins. For example, ventilation systems that are used to eliminate fumes from solvents can costs tens of thousands of dollars. Suppliers understandably hope to recover from customers money spent to cover expenses they see imposed by the buyer.

We need money. The code is an investment in society. But [the MNE] didn't pay any more, so that means the costs of this come out of profits. The best way we see to deal with the costs is that we share costs. At the beginning, when we started to build this factory two years ago, there was no code. This is all added cost. The code does in some cases save money; in some cases it doesn't. For example, the Viet Nam labour law says that the minimum wage in this area is US$35 a month. They said at [the MNE] we must pay US$40. With 3,000 employees, that is an added cost of US$15,000 a month. They always pick up a higher standard. And we based our business plan on US$35. Also, [the MNE] encourages, I don't want to say forces us, to pay a bonus, whether we make a profit or not. If we make a profit we have no problem, but this is a new factory, we don't have a profit. They insist that we put this in the labour contract, that in one year we pay for 13 months. That's over US$100,000 [3,000 × US$40]! (VIS 2, Factory Manager).

We had a meeting at [another factory] and looked at how much a pair of shoes costs, using the cost sheet [the MNE] supplies, a three-page form. And we found that the cost of doing the code was one dollar a pair. With all the cost breakdowns. And [the MNE] just crossed it out. [Interviewer question: Why do you keep producing for them?] Look at the investment we have here. We need orders to pay for this, so we have no choice. Our contract with [the MNE] is on a yearly basis (VIS 3, Factory Manager).

We understand that the [MNE] code is to have better conditions for workers. But in some areas the factory could be damaged, the rentability of the enterprise could be damaged (VIS 3, General Manager).

What appears clear is that due to the close relationships that often exist for the large shoe brands, some sort of agreement is reached through the hard-nosed process of negotiation (that takes place over prices paid) regarding the costs of code-related improvements. In such situations, where both the MNEs and the factories have made considerable investment and where recent publicity has made implementing code requirements imperative, the MNEs work closely with the factories to make the code possible—essentially through dialogue. What is less clear is how this issue of cost would be addressed in other sectors where MNEs have less leverage and the suppliers are generally smaller with tighter margins.

> We were working with factories, our partners. But you have to understand, these are not our factories. And the first reaction when we laid out the code requirements was 'well, we will have to shut down'. Our approach with the factories has had to be 'OK, how much money do you have, what should be the priorities?', and from that developing a plan together. And in the beginning we had to use a lot of force. We didn't say it, but they know that we could take our business elsewhere (FMNE I, Country Manager).

> [Do you provide any assistance to the factories in dollar terms?] No, we do some free-of-charge consultancy—our fire safety specialist, for example, certainly does help factories do things right. And we have provided some EHS training here (FMNE I, Country Manager).

> I told [the MNE head of footwear sourcing] that with the code it has to be a two-way street, a two-way conversation, not one way. But there is not a 100% right, for buyer or supplier. The code has to be done, but a business needs to make money to survive (VISI 3, General Manager).

g. Local managers

The MNE codes (that feature in this study) support a 'respectful' workplace, one in which employees do not suffer physical or verbal abuse. According to interviewees, expatriate managers are often insensitive to the local culture and can be much harsher with employees than local managers—a comment made repeatedly by representatives of the MNEs, and backed up by many of the workers. The following statements provide a general outline of what we heard repeatedly in our interviews.

> There are cultural differences, not East versus West, but rather the mentality of the managers which can take a militaristic, paternalistic approach. [There are old school managers who think] 'the workers are like little kids and sometimes you have to discipline them'. Managers are very afraid of sharing power. They will argue that there isn't any other way, that in the end the workers will drive us out of business. The solution is time. The reason I am optimistic is that the paternalistic factories will lose business to those that are more enlightened. Also the countries which exported this management approach—[those where the suppliers are headquartered]—are now exporting a new generation of managers, different from the managers of the 1980s who came from a dictatorship experience (FMNE I, Regional Manufacturing Manager).

> Here Thai managers and supervisors deal with Thai workers, not the ex-pats from other Asian countries. So they feel like they can approach the managers (THS I, Worker).

To address this issue, one of the approaches being taken is the training of supplier managers; that is, building their understanding of cultural issues and the changes required in management practices under the code. MNEs are also encouraging suppliers to recruit and develop local managers.

> What is needed is training of the national managers, to help them move up the chain. With ex-pat managers [typically coming from other countries in the region], they are often locked in their ways. The goal is really to move up local managers (FMNE 2, Regional Manager).

> There were many problems at the start for the companies and the foreign managers, due to cultural difference with the local workers. Some ex-pat managers are in particular used to yelling. Things have improved a lot since before. The feedback on the training for local managers and supervisors—we give them a one-week course—is very good (FMNE 2, Manager).

> You need nationals in positions of responsibility, because some Chinese have problems working for [managers from other countries in the region]. Here they have locals up to a high level, so we have fewer worries about this [type of adverse] interaction. And this also creates an environment where people want to stay (FMNE 2, Manufacturing Manager).

> We have a problem getting the old ex-pat managers to be flexible, so we are encouraging the factories to employ more local managers. They are eager, understand local situations, operate in different ways or are willing to try new things. And this is also linked to age—local managers are younger (FMNE I, Manufacturing Manager).

Finally, several managers suggested that the ILO could play some role in developing local managers, providing training of some sort to allow them to take higher levels of responsibility in their organisations. The ILO is certainly well experienced in providing such training given its previous involvement in management training programmes. As such, this issue could be considered by its constituents.

> What you could do at the ILO is something to build up the local managers, road-show training or something like that, one week per quarter over a year (FMNE 2, Regional Manager).

4. Implementing the code in operations

In the previous two sections we considered the need to create a shared vision as well as to develop understanding and ability on the code of conduct. In this section, we examine some of the more detailed aspects associated with implementing the code into operations both at the MNE and supplier factory.

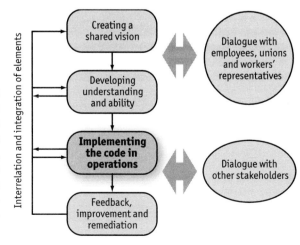

At the start it is a bit of work to implement code requirements; you have to put more effort into monitoring, partner selection. But it gets easier over time: you have some best practices in place, you set up mentors for the suppliers (FMNE 2, CSR Manager, Headquarters).

Manufacturing managers in the factories are really businessmen. Before they worried about prices and quality. They rolled out the code to us and put us through extensive training, two to three days and then a pretty hard test. At the same time, we rolled it out to the factories, starting at the top with the general managers and again training, tests even; then we had them move it down. They also had to put labour practice managers in place together with their whole supporting organisation. It was a huge job (FMNE 2, Manufacturing Manager).

Implementation of the code into the internal operations of both the MNE and supplier factory requires consideration of how to structure the department or unit charged with responsibility for managing the code. This includes determination of what role, if any, field personnel are to play in this process, the setting of rewards and objectives for those given code-of-conduct responsibilities. Furthermore, in order to gain a clearer understanding of 'how' the code is to be implemented, procedures and guidelines need to be developed either by the MNE or by the supplier factory. The following sections examine each of these issues.

a. The structure of corporate social responsibility

One of the first questions to consider when seeking to implement CSR through the supply chain is that of structure. In our review here, we consider first the overall structure of CSR management. In each of the companies visited, there were CSR departments

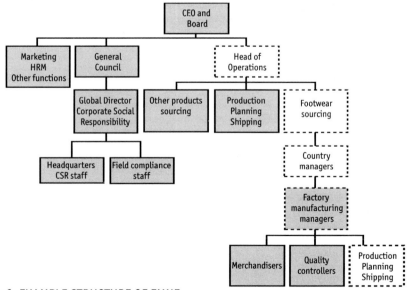

FIGURE 6 EXAMPLE STRUCTURE OF FMNE

that supported the implementation of the code. These groups grew rapidly, particularly in the two larger MNEs, with both employing several dozen CSR people based around the globe as well as in headquarters. The central components of these groups had a number of responsibilities, centred on being the primary proponents of implementing code in the organisation. These include the co-ordination of CSR/code-related initiatives within the organisation; the communication of code and CSR policy and practices to stakeholders (for example, the general public, government, civil society and others); the development of common training materials—sometimes in co-operation with operational groups; and the maintenance of the code itself, including its adjustment and improvement over time.

The structures that have emerged in order to deal with these responsibilities are varied. They represent different approaches, surrounding structures of the organisations and historical elements that impact on where the CSR responsibilities in the groups reside. For example, the structure illustrated in Figure 6 contains elements common to all three MNEs interviewed. The CSR group itself has both field and headquarters components, while footwear sourcing operates under country managers, each of whom has a number of factories reporting into their office. In this case, CSR has been, for reasons of independence, placed under the general counsel's office. In other cases we found that CSR could reside in communications—again for reasons of both history and independence—or even in manufacturing/sourcing (although the issue of independence becomes questionable here).

The companies have regional structures to some degree, with relatively large operations reporting to central offices and managers overseeing different aspects of overall corporate activities on a regional basis, including that of CSR and code implementation. For example, one buyer directly employed 650 staff in Asia, with a regional office in another Asian country supporting all operations in Asia. This office is responsible for such management functions for the region as HR, IT and so on.

In the Asian field operations in each of the companies visited, and at the factory level across the region, there is the key question of responsibility—or responsibilities—as there are many facets to implementing a code. The companies were struggling to varying degrees, or have in the recent past, with questions such as: who is responsible for developing the guidelines that back up the code? Who is responsible for auditing against code requirements? Who has to be involved in the day-to-day meeting of code requirements, for example quality control, manufacturing managers, sourcing people, CSR compliance personnel?

One finding, reviewed later in the section which addresses integration, is that with a very limited compliance team in relation to the large number of suppliers, there needs to be some role for on-site personnel or those involved in production that are in factories on a regular basis. This is particularly so given the generally large teams supporting production and quality who deal with these suppliers on a daily basis.

> The big advantage here [for implementing code] is that we have people on the ground at all times. At my last company [a large European non-sports shoe brand] we had 52 factories I was responsible for and only two or three quality assurance people travelling around to each. It is very difficult to have a code in that type of environment. Here [in his factory] I have five QAs [quality assurance people] and a manufacturing engineer, and I am here five days a week, five or six hours a day (FMNE 2, Manufacturing Manager).

FIGURE 7   EXAMPLE STRUCTURE OF FMNE SUPPLIER WITH MNE REPRESENTATION ON SITE

In general, the CSR function is still often viewed by operations managers as being largely outside mainstream business. Often, it is referred to as a service function, similar to finance and human resources in that it does not create products but creates policies and standards, and supports manufacturing. We did hear, though, that there is an increasing level of operational interaction between the CSR groups and other organisational functions.

At the field level, the MNE operations are structured around a matrix with CSR managers and staff reporting back into the CSR group at headquarters but having to work closely and in some cases in a dotted-line fashion with country managers as well as factory-level manufacturing managers. These manufacturing managers appeared in each of the factories we visited to play a crucial role in supporting compliance. With manufacturing operations and audit personnel reporting to them they were the eyes and ears of the MNE in the factories. As the on-site representative of the MNE/buyer to the supplier, they work closely with the factory managers, and can have a considerable influence over supplier operations.

> We have a new structure here. Before [a manufacturing manager] was in charge of production for all operations in the country. It was too much, so since then he handles production at [one of the company's suppliers], I handle things here. Before, development, commercialisation and production were separate organisations, with him in charge of production in the country, someone else in charge of another. Implementing code was under production. Now it is much cleaner, with me in charge here of both development/ production and code (FMNE 1, Manufacturing Manager).

It should be noted that this on-site presence is unique to the footwear industry, where the factories are very large and the relations between the MNE and supplier are close. As mentioned in the following quotes, the apparel sector is significantly different, and does not have the benefit of on-site MNE presence reinforcing the code requirements.

> In footwear you have a [MNE] manufacturing manager in each factory, and a quality controller under him, handling quality, delivery and code. In apparel it is more difficult (FMNE 1, CSR Compliance Auditor, Thailand).

> Here we have a big staff to support the manufacturing manager. Not all companies will have this (FMNE 2, Manager).

CSR officers are to varying degrees independent from the manufacturing function. When asked about this separation of responsibilities, several reasons are given: for example, a need to be independent, in order to avoid conflict of interests and a need for people with different skills sets. At the same time, some managers believe that the compliance officer, but not the central CSR group, should become a part of manufacturing—or at least that compliance officers in the field should be obliged to inform manufacturing managers on a regular basis of changes in standards and legislation. In their opinion, compliance would be within the 'main business'. Some other managers, in manufacturing, seem to be willing to accept compliance officers as part of their teams, if they come with their own budget and it would not cost the managers anything in terms of money or time of their sourcing and QC officers. According to one manager, 'In each country I could have a compliance person in my team, on the CSR budget. And, of course, this guy would need a lot of industry-specific training.'

The role of CSR staff in the field

The division of labour between compliance people and manufacturing is varied. Two examples illustrate this:

Case 1. Initial potential supplier screening and quarterly audits
When the company screens a new potential supplier, this involves not only price and quality issues, but also environmental and social issues. Therefore, EHS and social expertise is needed. Initial screening is done jointly by sourcing officers and compliance officers, sometimes together with quality control personnel, using an audit checklist to evaluate how social and environmental standards are met at the factory. If there is a problem that can be easily fixed, compliance officers may help the factory to correct any problems through training, providing the factory managers with promotional materials, or in some other fashion. If problems are corrected, the factory will get approval. Manufacturing/sourcing personnel and compliance officers work together on the regular quarterly or bi-annual auditing visits.

Case 2. New labour law in supplier country
When changes take place in labour laws within a country, the local compliance or CSR staff can play an important role. First, the country-level CSR staff will take a lead role in evaluating how the changes might affect the MNE's operations or practices in the country, or those of their suppliers. Based on this analysis, the CSR group and its compliance officers will work to educate the manufacturing staff of the company, and the supplier staff responsible for ensuring compliance with local labour laws. The manufacturing unit, working with CSR, will evaluate the financial and process effects, including timing, and work with suppliers to ensure that this is carried forward.

Supplier operations are typically highly structured and hierarchical, with ten or more levels of management and workers at the factory level. This structure may begin with a factory president, followed by a general manager over operations, a production director, then a department—for example, stitching—a department director with various sections under him (positions at this level are typically filled by men). The work in the sections would typically be broken into various lines, headed by line supervisors, and eventually the workers. It is common for there to be a number of sub-directors or managers between the workers and senior management. In factories with this type of

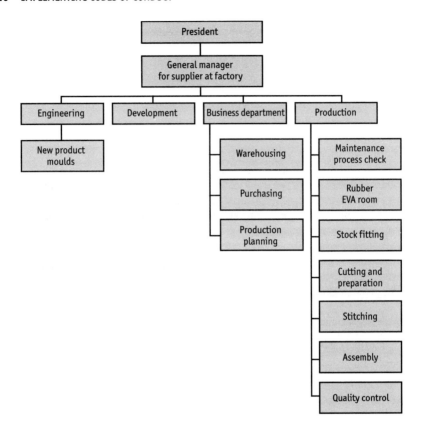

FIGURE 8 EXAMPLE STRUCTURE OF FMNE SUPPLIER

structure, there are usually people responsible for CSR and implementing the code of conduct. As was suggested by numerous managers, creating such CSR or code-related positions leads to the possibility of support staff from various areas and is an important step in implementing the code.

> The compliance manager at the factory is a crucial role, since this is the person we work with most (FMNE 2, CSR Manager).

> One of the tricks used by the factories was to have us deal with different people each time we came in to talk about code. So a very important turning point was when we got the factories to assign a permanent labour/EHS focal point. We did force them to do this (FMNE 1, Country Manager).

> We set up our programme team in 1998. We have four teams there: human rights and labour; fire safety; EHS; and manpower unit. The last one decides what kind of people we need, what their qualifications are. We will be creating new teams for our move toward lean manufacturing. There is a supervisor on the labour team, a local person, who reports to me (VIS 1, CSR Co-ordinator).

Our structure mirrors the [MNE] structure. We have fire, labour and health and safety (VIS 1, CSR Co-ordinator).

Under my authority I have 21,000 workers in six factories. In each of the factories we have three CSR people, pollution prevention, EHS and labour (CHS 8, CSR Manager).

b. Implementation at the supplier level

The implementation of codes at the supplier level is a huge undertaking when considered in its entirety. It encompasses gaining commitment and understanding, developing a plan of action for all the areas covered, and implementing each step of the plan. The following comments outline the recommendations of two managers on how to go about carrying this out.

> The first step for a new factory, just starting with a code, you have to organise a team. You need a group dedicated to this. Second, you have to make sure that everybody understands what the code means. Third, you give seminars to all the workers on the code. All the new employees have to attend a briefing on the requirements of the code. Next, we used the code guidelines and developed an action plan to meet the code. The factory develops the action plan then we [the MNE factory-level staff] review and discuss it. Then [the national-level CSR team members] review it, and if they have points then we adjust it accordingly (FMNE 1, Manufacturing Manager).

> Once we had the code we incorporated it in our business plan. Before it wasn't even in the game plan. Now we talk about things like how the food is handled. This type of thing is now a big chunk of our time, since often issues are now getting better under control (FMNE 2, Senior Manager).

The interviewees suggested that, with each of the factories, the buyer needs to develop a plan of action for how to address their shortcomings with regard to code compliance. One useful suggestion is to have the factory itself develop the initial plan, based on the findings of jointly conducted audits.

> The way we move the code-related things is to present the problems—for example a safety problem—to the factory and I let them come up with the proposed solutions. Then, if they don't have a solution that I thought about, we'll discuss it. If the factory favours a solution that we don't like, then we will put some pressure on (FMNE 2, Manufacturing Manager).

> For every single issue we have to look at what the code calls for, and then what the situation is. Then we have to come up with a plan for how to bring these things together. And we do this all with the factories. You go over the costs and the plan, adjust as you go through implementation. And we have to do this on each point in each area of the code (FMNE 1, Country Manager).

> Another challenge is to incorporate all this into the business plan of the factory. Now labour is the number one issue for discussion, since quality, delivery, price are already taken for granted. So, 50 to 80% of the evaluation process time for the factories is spent on evaluation of labour management (FMNE 1, Regional CSR Manager).

In the process of implementing a code, there is a variety of activities needed to fully support the process. Some can include the development of materials: for example, guidelines and training material. Others can include a review of the basic operations within the MNE itself, for example through the development of samples to consider how these can make complying with the code difficult or even impossible.

> We recognise the need to give support to our suppliers—we can't just give them the code—we must provide assistance. We have guidelines for EHS. We screened and monitored all the government policies on these areas, and took those that appeared most reasonable to meet for suppliers. We included those in our manual (FMNE I, EHS Manager, Headquarters).

> Our seasons have peaks and the sample teams would produce or work 24 hours a day to get these out. We had to get our headquarters to realise they couldn't make these guys put in 24 hours to get it out immediately. This may have a monetary cost but mainly it just requires better planning (FMNE 2, Senior Manager).

One element an MNE pushing for code compliance with their suppliers needs to consider is a 'rush to action'. This is because the supplier, eager to fulfil the wishes of its client, may implement approaches too quickly, without adequate consultation, in turn failing to fulfil essential requirements. This may result in the loss of goodwill between the buyer and supplier.

> Other systems, ventilation, etc., are expensive systems. They are really long-term investments. The most important investment is in your employees (CHS 9, Factory Manager).

> We do not want the factory investing in anything without my or [another MNE manager's] approval. They did so many things that didn't work out. And that [the way it is now] makes them feel good; they like that they share responsibility with us. They are unclear about standards, so they are very happy to follow our advice. And if they understand, then they will move very fast (FMNE I, Manufacturing Manager).

> You have to slow them down some of the time or they will spend huge amounts of money on projects that don't work (FMNE I, EHS Auditor).

For this reason, several managers suggested that it is necessary for the supplier to start small, to focus on policies or changes that will have maximum impact with least cost and to ensure successes from the start. One way is to address items in a sequential manner, perhaps starting with personal protection equipment (PPE) in those areas using solvent, moving on to fire safety, and so on. With the larger, more expensive changes, a longer time frame was also suggested.

> We have learned to start small, make sure you work on things that can be successful. If you try the sledgehammer approach the factories might struggle and try to do things too early [before they really understand] (FMNE I, Country Manager).

> We will focus on one thing at a time. For example, secondary containment. We will work on looking at petroleum or oil run-off, having catch bins underneath (CHS 10, Assistant Factory Manager).

Companies need to spend upwards of HK$2 million to upgrade their fire safety system, extinguishers, etc., sprinklers, alarms. We give them two years to finish. If they have difficulty then they can talk to us. We are willing to listen if they have a better solution (FMNE I, Regional EHS Manager).

It was clear throughout our visits that implementing a code at the level of the shoe factories is a large undertaking. In properly implementing a code, the MNE faces a number of questions as it seeks to guide its factory partners in complying with the code. For example, what issues should you address given the overall strategy and range of code items? Which issues are most important to the various stakeholder groups? Which ones are the most urgent and which ones have the best input/result ratio? The ranking of issues will depend on the organisation's corporate values and code of conduct; as such, some difficult implementation decisions must be taken. In our opinion, employers would benefit from increased discussion with workers on these issues as they are the primary stakeholders on whom these decisions will impact. As emphasised below, carrying out a code through the supply chain has been for these firms a long-term effort.

> The biggest gap between us and [the MNE] is time. I'm talking to you, we understand each other; but after that I have to educate my workers, and the level of education can be quite low. Some don't know left from right. [The MNE] wants things very fast, tomorrow, next week, next month. But workers don't change like that. For example, take masks. [The MNE] wanted the masks worn, and gave the factory very little time. But workers need weeks to get used to this. They didn't like it, didn't understand it. We need more time to teach, to educate (VIS 2, CSR Manager).

The need for education and co-operation between MNEs and suppliers

The implementation of a code of compliance is best accomplished through a process of open discussion and listening on the part of suppliers, buyers and workers. We believe that both suppliers and buyers would benefit greatly from increased discussions with workers. Suppliers must seek to understand the code, why it is in place, and how changes need to be carried out. Buyers need to make sure that the supplier understands what they are looking for, and should be careful to supervise what takes place. As the example outlined below indicates, this is not always an easy process. Even with close attention to detail, misunderstandings and problems, which can lead to dangerous consequences, may arise.

This factory was told before they started construction all the items that had to be in place, what EHS systems would be needed to meet the code. They already had a factory in Hanoi and it had had problems. They failed to implement system after system, in spite of being clearly discussed and with clear outlines given. In one example, they built a shallow drainage ditch or trough, eight inches by four inches, around the inside of their storage facilities, leading outside to a collection pool. So someone smoking outside could toss in their cigarette, leading a fire trail inside the building, around all four walls, and into the barrels, which could explode. The fire in the trough around all four walls would trap anyone inside. They [the supplier] were, before building this, instructed to create secondary containment throughout the facility, but failed to do so, preferring the firetrap approach. They had a wall dividing the facility into two. The trough goes under this—so a fire would too. They also failed to put needle guards and belt covers on all their stitching machines and now have to retrofit everything at a much higher cost. They are certainly going to have their orders limited until things improve. Financially, you can't, on the higher-cost items, expect them to do everything at once—but you do need time-lines (FMNE 1, CSR Manager).

We started with studies first, collecting information from the factory: policies, payment system, time recording system, things like that. From there we
focused on time recording. Before it was all hand written. We then had swipe
cards in some areas, but it was not linked to the payment system. Paper cards
were done by the supervisor, and you could put in anything. Then with swipe
cards there were problems—there weren't enough machines. People were
waiting ten minutes. Also, we had to centralise things and link it to the payroll
system. Next, we developed a handbook for the workers. There it says how
the payment system works. Before, they really had no idea; nothing could be
checked by the worker. At this point we really started with EHS; we brought
in a fire auditor from Hong Kong to see where we were. We didn't have the
staff capability in the company for this. Finally, we started doing tracking
reports for EHS and labour issues. Now we are targeting things point by point.
First fire-point labelling, then signage and so on (FMNE 1, Manufacturing
Manager).

c. Employee participation

In a number of discussions with MNE managers, it became clear that there can be more
benefit than just cost in implementing socially responsible practices and meeting the
requirements of a code. To support this view, one senior manager asserted his belief in
one of Deming's (the founder of the 'quality movement') 14 points: driving out fear.
Workers need to feel that they can participate if the organisation is going to use their
skills. While many managers voiced their support for involving workers in the production process as a means to increase productivity and quality, support for the right to
freedom of association appeared tempered by what they saw as the realities of the
workplace and local practices. With a fundamental principle of the ILO being freedom
of association, we see its observance as conversant with higher levels of employee
participation and a necessary underpinning of the right to collective bargaining.
Included in the concept of involving employees is the need to have items related to the
code in worker job descriptions and work outlines at the factory. This should also be
the case for MNE staff that have some percentage of their performance review linked to
social responsibility and code.

Our products require flexibility, so we require a more empowered worker.
Lean manufacturing is what we are pushing, and one component of that
approach is worker input. And with this we are seeing massive productivity
gains. One example: we reduced work hours 12% to get under our code
limitations, resulting in only a 5% reduction in output. Within three months
they had the same productivity. [Poorly designed] incentive programmes can
encourage workers to go slow for the first eight hours then speed up for the
final four (FMNE 1, Manufacturing Manager).

After some time for practice, we have started to have the factories put things
like PPE even in the job description, or where it is documented what is part of
the job (FMNE 2, Manager).

d. Guidelines

MNEs had a number of tools used to support their codes, explaining in more detail the meaning of what would be found in these codes. These include environmental, health and safety guidelines (including high/low recommendations on substances based on their home-country government standards) and social guidelines that address labour issues. In one case, it appeared that the health and safety guidelines were better developed, and more understandable than those in manufacturing. Labour issues appeared to be a larger challenge than implementing technical standards in areas such as toxic substances or the layout of fire extinguishers.

> We have an EHS guideline manual already in place, but will have one for the social and labour sides of the code by year end in draft form—basically saying what the code means. It will cover things like what to do in case of a strike—things they are handling on an ad hoc basis at the moment—what to do in China with extended hours, where these are legal but against the code. The code is not enough of a definition in and of itself; it's too brief (FMNE 1, Manager, Headquarters).

The above example is extremely important, however, as it highlights that discrepancies can arise between codes and local legislation. It must be remembered that a code is not a replacement for workplace working-time policies established by local law. Moreover, as was mentioned earlier, where there is an inconsistency between the code and local legislation, in many instances there is a provision expressly stating that the higher standard prevails while ensuring adherence to legislation.

> We needed a companion document that provides clearer documentation of what the audit standards mean (FMNE 1, Manufacturing Manager).

The process of developing the guidelines in the code took place in a variety of ways. For one MNE, the health and safety guidelines were largely developed by the manufacturing managers and their teams in Asia. This was done in the absence of central-office support—an approach that was seen as quite time consuming and wasteful. In another, they were developed by the CSR team, with little external involvement. Managers emphasised the need for involvement, for working closely with suppliers and field personnel to make sure that local conditions are taken into consideration.

> The EHS guidelines were developed in this team, but we would like broader ownership (FMNE 1, Manager, Headquarters).

> We have the code in 31 languages. When the first version was done, we sent it to all suppliers, who had to sign it and send it back saying they will comply. It also was raised at supplier meetings. Country managers have it in their objectives. All senior people in fact (FMNE 2, CSR Manager, Headquarters).

> Headquarters could have provided more guidance. They see it as 'yes, we must do the code' but don't provide the 'how'. It was often difficult or not applicable—since Asia does things differently than in Europe (FMNE 1, Manufacturing Manager).

The code guidelines serve as a means of maintaining consistency, allowing field personnel from the MNE to understand what the code actually means. They also provide direction for the audits that firms undertake, allowing factories to understand what they have to attain and why they might have some problems. In either case, managers emphasised that code guidelines should be understandable, and where possible graphic.

> We have the guidelines. Based on these we developed the audit forms. In this way we can do continuous improvement because we can have systematic requirements, and follow up and check against progress (FMNE 1, Compliance Manager).

> It is very important that the factories get one voice—one guy saying you have to put a fire extinguisher here, another saying put it there, and the factories said we have to know which. That is the basis of the guidelines. When you just have a code it is very general, and there is lots of space for misunderstanding. For that reason you need guidelines. We share with the companies photos, examples of best practice from other factories (FMNE 1, Country Manager).

> For the guidelines [on social and labour issues], they must be short, they must be understandable and they must be attractive (user friendly). It shouldn't be a booklet that sits on some manager's desk, but rather one that people really use. We distributed [the EHS guidelines] at a supplier meeting and it is amazing how many managers in Asia are using it to guide their organisations (FMNE 1, EHS Manager, Headquarters).

> With the code, for the public it can be very general but for the factories it has to be specific (FMNE 1, Country Manager).

In one case we also heard of the MNE developing factory-level guidelines, the translation of the code into specific elements or factory-level practices. Given the code-related issues that are specific to factories, this sounds like a reasonable approach.

> Working with the factory management we develop a shortlist of information on pay, holidays, working hours, benefits. This meets the code of conduct, but is particular to the factory. You really need to have both—the code is very general, while this [factory-specific] document is more specific. As an example, this factory puts on their form something about deductions for lunch. Other factories might not have that (FMNE 2, Manufacturing Manager).

It appeared, as mentioned earlier, that labour issues may be less clearly laid out in the code guidelines, something that would be understandable given the standardised EHS practices in developed countries—often serving as the model for practice in the developing-country factories—and the unique challenges faced with implementing labour issues, which often have to consider country-specific labour laws. Still, we heard in interviews, developing both the EHS and labour guidelines have been challenging for the MNEs.

> I got the job back in 1997 to draft a health and safety manual for the company. Headquarters made a statement about EHS but provided nothing about the way or the what of standards. So we had [a EHS expert] and some consultants. We did some TLVs [threshold limit values] of VOCs [volatile organic compounds], but we were really alone. We began, really, with environment, then got pressure and moved to health and safety, then labour. We wasted a lot of time due to the moving focus—it was not the most efficient. Since nobody

was in charge it was 'every man for himself'—or rather every factory. We could get different standards, since nobody was in charge. HQ gave no guidance so we did whatever we could (FMNE 1, Manufacturing Manager).

Having a health and safety manual finalised was a good plus. We had to develop standards, you'd agree on them with the factories and then someone would say 'this isn't good enough'. And so the factory would be upset, you'd look stupid with management. Now we have it clear. Labour issues are clear, bonded labour, minimum wage, work hours. Freedom of association is not so clear. I know that unions are not allowed. But we have various committees, for example a food committee and a workers' representatives council. Food is always an issue. You have 90% plus from the north and they want hot food. The local people, though, think that it is way too hot (FMNE 1, Manufacturing Manager).

e. Field personnel

In implementing a code of conduct, it became clear to us, again and again, that the field personnel were crucial to the success of implementing a code—as they were the ones working directly in the factories and with the supplier managers. Lack of commitment on their part would undermine implementation of a code given their purchasing power with the factories and standing on operational issues.

If CSR is not a part of the responsibilities of the manufacturing manager, and instead you have a CSR manager or representative who comes in only occasionally, it will not work (FMNE 2, Manager).

Five years ago I would have said this CSR should be for someone else, that it was not my responsibility. But they, the factories, have made real progress, so it is workable (FMNE 2, Manufacturing Manager).

Manufacturing is the main conduit of information back to the home office. The manufacturing manager in each factory is on the front line. It is a team thing that we are all tied in—we can't consider it a divide-and-conquer thing (FMNE 2, Senior Manager).

At the time we adopted the code, there was not top-level resistance but there was resistance from the country level. They were already worrying about quality and cost. For some, it was just the bad guys forcing these things, the Americans or Europeans (FMNE 3, CSR Manager, Headquarters).

I [the MNE factory-level manufacturing manager] am responsible for quality, production and CSR. It is a pretty broad level of responsibility, but as I walk through the factory I am considering many things, addressing each of these areas (FMNE 2, Manufacturing Manager).

f. Rewards and objectives

Corporate strategic plans should, to be effective, cascade through the organisation. In one of the MNEs studied, there are currently seven strategic objectives, compliance with their code of conduct being one of them. Each manager in manufacturing must reflect these objectives in his or her 'success profile', in other words his or her 'management-by-objectives' performance appraisal form. In one firm, CSR officers in the field help managers to articulate their individual objectives so that they include elements related to meeting code requirements. At this firm, social/labour and EHS issues make up 10% of an employee's evaluation in apparel and about 20% in footwear. This can be seen as substantial as 20% of the evaluation usually goes to strategic planning. As we were told, the philosophy behind this is: when it is part of their strategic plan and people's futures are tied to it, and their performance level is linked to it, they will do it.

As seen in the following quotes, there needs to be an integration of code objectives with the objectives of individual managers who can shape code compliance—taking into account the variation in challenges that may exist—if they are to support proper code implementation.

> For moving out the sustainability objectives, we have to get the language right so that people understand what you are talking about. Tie it to their strategic objective. We have to help them do this translation (FMNE 2, CSR Manager, Headquarters).

> Managers will only care about things if they are impacted by it, and if they are aware of the impact (FMNE 1, Regional CSR Manager).

> When appraising manufacturing managers on their performance on CSR, you have to evaluate their efforts [taking into consideration specific problems faced by each]. Some deal with more challenging factories than others (FMNE 2, Manager).

In the MNEs visited, managers responsible for field operations had varying percentages of their performance appraisal linked to CSR implementation.

> Twenty-five per cent of the manufacturing manager's job is officially responsibility for CSR and this feeds down the line. We have a number of people at the factories and this [CSR] is a part of all their jobs (FMNE 2, Manager).

> Twenty per cent of my performance evaluation is EHS/labour related, but these percentages don't always match reality, as this depends on the factory. I am responsible for quality, timely delivery and social responsibility (FMNE 2, Manufacturing Manager).

The linkages of rewards with objectives is of course logical—as the manager states below, making it easy for managers to do right appears to be good advice. Yet, as other managers pointed out, deciding when a manager has done a good job, and when another has not, is not easy (given that variations exist from one factory to another, as well as other responsibilities that can make focusing on CSR challenging).

> Make it the path of least resistance. Make it harder to not do right—make it easy for them to do right, so they will look for the easy way (FMNE 2, CSR Manager).

> Our internal senior production personnel have some percentage of their review for CSR and code. But I don't know who would ever recommend that they don't get the percentage. And how would you determine this? We are piloting a rating system, since we recognise that managers need to know how

they are doing. And this will impact on the factories because they are very competitive (FMNE 1, Regional CSR Manager).

It is a challenge to get management to do it. There has to be an incentive for the whole company to follow a path. I have to give incentives to the manufacturing managers [of the MNE] to do things. I say, if you move to 50% water-based cement, then I will pay you X bonus (FMNE 1, Country Manager).

The use of rewards in support of codes was not just at the MNE level. Factories also use rewards, and MNEs use rewards—including recognition and, perhaps more importantly, purchases—to support following the code; the factories themselves use rewards to encourage certain management behaviours. Finally, some factories have had to change worker pay rates, to support higher productivity levels that in turn have allowed the reduction of work hours.

Use incentives, awards, good factory ratings; it is very important for the Chinese—face. They really want to be there when you do this, so we had a meeting in Macao for all the shoe factories (FMNE 1, Country Manager).

In one factory in China, supervisors and line managers are awarded bonuses based on performance in the following areas (weights, defined for 2001): productivity, 40%; quality, 35%; compliance with code, 25% (FMNE 1, Regional CSR Manager).

Our factories have had to review their salary and bonus structures, since before it was all about reaching output levels without considering hours, use of PPE, etc. And we have had to try to get them to set this (FMNE 2, Senior Manager).

You have to change the incentive system to support efficiency and productivity, so there is a bonus system to do things efficiently in under eight hours. There was a transition when we introduced this, but it is fast (CHS 9, Factory Manager).

g. Sharing best practice

We heard from the MNEs that they have found it important to share best practices on meeting the requirements of codes, both within the MNE itself and between factories. Within the MNE, the following two comments were particularly interesting. The first concerns a regular meeting of manufacturing managers of the factory and EHS labour personnel to discuss code issues. The second concerns the use of electronic communications to share best-practice information from one location to another.

Another thing we do is within [the MNE] hold a meeting with our [manufacturing] managers in all the factories and me [EHS manager] and the labour auditor, and discuss how things are going (FMNE 1, EHS Auditor).

We have an e-mail roundtable, and we have a common e-mail; we send any suggestions there and it mails it to the whole CSR team. You can put best practices or learnings there or requests for help. And the person requesting help will be buried with suggestions (FMNE 1, CSR Manager).

The second group of comments we received highlighted the sharing of information between factories. Here we found considerable differences among the MNEs. In two MNEs, the suppliers were apparently relatively isolated, with the MNE serving as the primary link to the other factories. The first comment is representative of the limited sharing of best practice in these MNEs' factories. In another MNE, they carry out numerous activities to ensure sharing and they also benefit from light competition between the factories in implementing the code.

> We waste a lot of effort within [the MNE] because we don't share information. I am collecting pictures, but we should have common training materials, a common database of photos we can all access (FMNE 1, EHS Auditor).

> All the factories of [a large supplier group] don't share any information; it is changing a bit though (FMNE 2, Manufacturing Manager).

> Two weeks ago we organised a sharing best practices meeting which brought the Asia supplier CSR co-ordinators together. They are usually pretty junior in the supplier hierarchies, so we have to develop their power. They spent three days at a training facility we have at a factory in China, in that way we can send people out to see a real factory [as part of their training]. The companies had to pay—in the beginning they wanted to send the managers but we said 'no', we want the CSR people. This empowers them and sends a message—this [code] is important (FMNE 1, Regional EHS Manager).

> I think we [the suppliers] do a great job of communicating between factories; any factory can go and visit any other factory (FMNE 1, CSR Manager).

> [The MNE] attempts to share best practices between their factories. It is [the group of suppliers for the MNE] a big family. We even share shoe technology. If they are open to us we are open to them. In the past factories kept things to themselves, but [the MNE] has changed that. With the other brands I have not seen that (CHS 7, Manager).

The power of the 'light competition' approach was highlighted not only by the MNE, but also by the suppliers, who in particular seemed to benefit from the monthly meetings with the country manager (where code-related issues received prominent attention). Still, as the comments below indicate, such competition has to be done with care to avoid an unwillingness to share information.

> We are starting a rating system and we do let the companies [suppliers] know that this could impact their getting business in the future. There is a competition between the suppliers. OK, this factory now has a supermarket, then the others feel pressure. And there is close communication between factories; there has to be an open spirit and a balance of competition and sharing. On EHS we don't want any secrets; we just brought all the EHS managers [from the suppliers] together for that reason (FMNE 1, Country Manager).

> In Asia it is important to consider face, and the factories feel proud if you share best practice—this is true in footwear because our relationships are settled. Apparel might be harder to use some level of friendly competition (FMNE 3, CSR Compliance Officer, China).

> All companies [suppliers] should be able to benefit from our work, especially as we don't view it [that is, approaches to meeting EHS requirements] as a

competitive advantage. But the borderline is where we start to compare factories. Healthy competition is good, but must be balanced, or you won't see any sharing of information (FMNE I, Manufacturing Manager).

5. Feedback, improvement and remediation

The final aspect of code-of-conduct implementation that we heard about was the need for feedback, improvement and remediation systems. As we highlighted in the previous section, one of the key channels of feedback, particularly regarding supplier performance, is provided by information technology systems. In this section we discuss some of the systems that have been developed as well as their linkage with internal monitoring and external verification systems. Building on the need to establish objective reward systems, we examine the role of feedback and improvement both for those charged with code-of-conduct responsibilities at the MNE headquarters and those at the supplier level. Finally, we consider the issue of external reporting: an attempt by MNEs to ensure transparency of their systems.

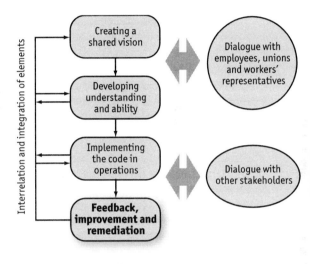

a. Information systems

What we heard from the interviewees, particularly those in the MNEs, is that companies implementing codes of conduct need to establish information and measurement systems that support a process of decision-making. Such systems need to allow the tracking of results and need to be accessible to those who make the everyday decisions. They need to be implemented within the MNE and also within the factory operations. Also the decision-making procedures need to be adapted to take into account the information available in the systems.

> You need to measure very well. So, with regard to timecards, don't rely on supervisors. Quantify where you are, so you know where the problems are. If you know you are working certain amounts past maximums, you can then push and see how much pain there is. But at the start, managers didn't know—they may be working 29 of 30 days during peak months, and they and you won't even know (FMNE I, Country Manager).

> We want information that only helps us to make decisions. Therefore we don't need too many indicators—more important is 'are they in compliance with our guidelines?', rather than 'how much water do they use?'. More important is what corrective action is needed. A top factory is one which has no corrective action requirements. If all these factories were owned by us, then we could have a large multi-variable database, but as a customer I think this is about the best that we could do (FMNE I, CSR Team Member, Headquarters).

> Sourcing, particularly in apparel, is dynamic, very dynamic. We believe that we need to orient to the corrective action lists, based on the audit system. We need to make the system simple enough that our sourcing people and stakeholders can make simple or easier decisions. Then we can decide 'do we want to get rid of them, improve them or what?' It is not just a statistical system. The guidelines are therefore important (FMNE I, CSR Team Member, Headquarters).

We heard conflicting accounts from each of the MNEs interviewed; in some cases that an information system was well developed, and from others, in the same company, that the information system addressing social, labour and EHS issues was far from useful. Generally it appears that the companies reviewed believe their information systems will at some stage require further development to be truly useful to the range of managers and staff that use the information and require it to make decisions. Each of the companies have or are developing databases under their CSR group to maintain a list of suppliers (this will be maintained by the operations/sourcing people). At one MNE they appear to have two CSR databases under development. One is directly related to the EHS guidelines already developed. In another case, a sourcing manager appears to have implemented his own database to track suppliers.

> His [the other database] is simpler. We do it in Microsoft Works at the moment, but will in the future move it to Microsoft Excel. At present it has yes/no-type entries but in the future we hope to have numeric ratings. There is still a lot of debate about that. But that is also why we are doing cross-auditing; we want to have a common understanding across Asia about what is expected. The database does not have to be that complicated, maybe a week's work, but we have a problem getting resources. Just for the guidelines they wanted HK$1,000 a page for 90 pages. Eventually we plan to put these on our intranet, rather than printing, since the companies all access our ordering site. I already have the e-mail (addresses) of all the factories (FMNE I, Regional EHS Manager).

> There is a programme called 'supplier database', which would allow us to have all data on suppliers—the code, FOB [delivery information], ongoing contracts. I know all the suppliers, and can tell you everything. It is a big problem in our company, it takes forever. For that reason in my area we just did our own mini-database (FMNE I, Sourcing Manager, Headquarters).

In terms of implementing an information system, it is necessary not just at the MNE level, but also at the factory level. One manufacturing manager in Viet Nam suggested that the following measurable items can help build awareness of CSR and code requirements: available working time and sick time; work-related visits to the clinics; worker turnover; worker satisfaction (through worker surveys) together with qualitative data on likes/dislikes. And while he suggested these systems, he also stated that most factories don't have these systems in place. One area we were told that most of the factories appear to have made considerable progress in is swipe card sign-in systems. These have been introduced so that they link to automated payroll accounting software, allowing managers to control overtime and ensure adequate payment. Also, it must be remembered that the use of worker surveys is not a sufficient replacement for full consultation and the right to collective bargaining as mandated by the ILO Conventions on fundamental worker rights.

> Our counselling system is our information system. That is how we can know if we are going to have a strike [We did a light review of the counselling system. There were around 250 suggestions or complaints filed over a three-year system, or only around 80 per year.] (VIS 7, Factory Manager).

> I think implementing the code really helps them [the suppliers] because they really had no idea how much it costs for labour. With labour costs going up they start worrying about this. But they really had no idea about unit costs (FMNE I, Manufacturing Manager).

Having consistent data was a challenge for the research team as it travelled from factory to factory. Turnover was reported in one factory at 1% a month, much higher in some, lower in others. Yet it is very difficult to compare between these figures because a variety of factors could make any such comparison like comparing 'apples to oranges'. For example, does the turnover level include people leaving before the end of their contract? Does it include those workers whose contracts are not renewed by the factory? It might be useful for the companies to come up with standardised measures of turnover, for example the percentage of contracts renewed, length-of-service average, the percentage of employees employed over one, two and three years, etc. In any case, the MNEs do appear to be working with the factories on these issues, as is indicated in the following comment.

> We had a problem getting the factories to understand why it is necessary to get information on accident rates. At first, the factories didn't really want to do this, so we did it gradually, asking for numbers of accidents causing lost working hours, then quantifying how many hours lost. Now we are going to start requiring cause-and-result reports on each accident (FMNE I, Compliance Manager).

We are concerned, however, about the fact that we heard that worker contracts were typically of short duration and consequently could cut into worker well-being. Workers consistently cited job security as one of their primary concerns. In our opinion, if workers fear for their jobs each year or so, then they are unlikely to be able to actively contribute to the proper operation of the code.

An important area where some information systematisation is under way was with regard to audit result tracking. While the MNEs conduct regular audits of the suppliers, and may from these develop detailed plans of action, the usefulness of this material is limited by its lack of inclusion in the form of an electronic database. Reports are entered in paper format, although projects are under way to have these in electronic format in the future. The following comments from MNE field staff address this issue.

> I have all the audit reports, but frankly this is an area that needs work. And we also have monthly reports from the factories (FMNE 2, CSR Manager).

> We don't share audit data, we send it to [the CSR manager quoted above]. It is up to them to use it as they like (FMNE 2, Manufacturing Manager).

> If I see something, I tell the factory and normally they fix it. But I don't usually inform the compliance people. There is no system that I use to keep track of what has to be done (FMNE 1, Manufacturing Manager).

As mentioned, each of the MNEs appears to be strengthening its databases—an effort that would have strong support from various managers who depend on information concerning code implementation and compliance issues. With these the firms should be better positioned to make decisions concerning their relations with suppliers and follow-up to things such as audits and other reviews. A similar effort at improving the information infrastructure appears to be taking place at the factory level on a case-by-case basis.

> We are just in the process of hiring a junior manager to pull all the information sources together. At present we have databases in various locations, but no worldwide database. We are also looking at some way of scoring factories, but for this we need to clarify what the stats indicate or what the numbers mean. Until we do that it is tough to do any (meaningful) rating. We don't just want a checklist, but need to better measure the impact of various factory-level practices. The apparel people do have a corporate worldwide database, but it doesn't really fit us. What databases that do exist just say things like 'has the supplier signed the checklist?' (FMNE 1, CSR Manager, Headquarters).

> We have a system to keep track of product issues we call the DPS—damn poor system. Now we are going to a new system and the CSR people have been working to ensure the audit data is included. CSR has its own database at the moment, but its data is not included [in DPS] and I am not sure it will be in the new system at the start. At the moment they do not really have a real-time system [for CSR]; what they have has limited information. Next year, in November, the new system will go online, and be linked to the SAP financial systems. Then we will be able to get all kinds of stuff (FMNE 2, CSR Manager, Headquarters).

> We have almost finalised a supplier database to keep track of problems with certain factories. It will be maintained by the operations group, and will be an open system. We can add fields as we find the need. It will cover everything, the various divisions (FMNE 1, CSR Senior Manager, Headquarters).

b. Internal monitoring

The interviewees outlined programmes of internal auditing that allow managers and others influencing the decision-making process of the organisation to know where there are problems and where improvement is called for. This could link with information systems, allowing for the tracking of results, but such tracking systems, as discussed above, are being more fully developed. The auditing process is seen as one component of an overall monitoring system that includes verification, feedback, remediation and improvement.

> One of the lessons learned is that, due to a huge number of factories, a rigid system of monitoring is needed. Now it is [our audit framework] to be replaced by [a more encompassing management framework]. Both [the audit framework] introduction and monitoring show how different organisational units can work together. [The audit] standards were developed jointly by a number of departments and external experts in public health, occupational safety and health, and so on. Monitoring is done jointly by us [in CSR], QC [quality control] and sourcing people. [Until recently the monitoring was twice a year, now quarterly. Better-performing factories remain at twice a year, as a bonus] (FMNE 1, Headquarters).

At each of the companies, initial visits are made by CSR personnel to screen potential new suppliers against the requirements of the code. Later visits are sporadic, given the large number of suppliers. At two of the MNEs, quality control inspectors do monitoring of EHS, according to their management. At the same time, there is almost always someone from the buyer in the shoe factories, given their large orders with the suppliers, so monitoring through these manufacturing personnel is more effective than relying only on the sporadic visits of CSR compliance personnel. In terms of content, the audits contain items that are intended to guide suppliers in reaching compliance with the code, ranging from EHS issues to labour practices to living conditions.

> You need to provide the company [supplier] with a definitive checklist, to let the company know what is expected of them. What we did was provide the audit checklists for both social and environment. These are much more detailed than the code, including around 70 items for the social side. If you just give them the code and say 'implement this', they couldn't do it. When a big customer requires a factory to meet a new set of requirements they have to provide guidelines (FMNE 2, Manager).

> We can pretty much use this [the auditing form/report] anywhere; maybe there are not all the elements like dorms or kitchens, but they can be used all over (FMNE 1, Manufacturing Manager).

> With our audit we look at food in the canteen, the administration of the dorms. Most of the issues in our audit framework are doing pretty well. PPE [personal protection equipment] sometimes is overlooked. I now include the audit as part of our bi-annual review of manufacturing. I still do quarterly audits and non-formal, ongoing reviews (FMNE 2, Manufacturing Manager).

Audits are carried out either by the MNE CSR field staff—EHS or labour experts—and/or the factory-level manufacturing managers, usually together with the supplier factory managers. These take place on some sort of regular basis, with decreasing frequency as suppliers demonstrate that they are in compliance and build confidence that they will remain so. Managers suggested there is a virtuous circle to improvement in the factories, that as they improve operations to be more in compliance, it frees up time for the CSR staff and manufacturing personnel to work with them (the factory management) on other issues besides meeting audit requirements.

> We started doing the internal CSR audits in 1997, once a quarter by the manufacturing manager and factory CSR manager. It takes half a day to do

and three to four days to document. The audit form is signed by the manu-facturing manager, the CSR manager and a worker representative—usually, one person picked randomly (FMNE 1, Manufacturing Manager).

In 1997 we started hearing about the code of conduct, and then we started implementing the audit framework and inspections. The manufacturing manager along with factory personnel walk through the factory and rate things. At the end the manufacturing manager and the factory management sit down and agree on findings. Then a week or so later the factory would come back with an action plan to adjust or address some of these issues. With the action plans, the factories need time to work things out, to discuss what has to be done and buy in. We conduct these on a bi-annual basis at least (FMNE 2, Manufacturing Manager).

As the factories move up the curve [better understand audit systems], it frees up more time for our people to do more upstream stuff—we don't have to check monthly, but quarterly. So we can spend time on training, and then on pilot activities. Footwear staff [of the MNE] can start to train EHS staff in apparel, or to train supplier staff. Time recording or getting companies to do their own measurement and feedback means we don't have to do the auditing (FMNE 1, Regional CSR Manager).

For the apparel side, the EHS and labour audit systems should be integrated. In footwear, we will most probably have separate reports and systems because we have strong groups working on EHS. All monitoring will be by CSR staff (FMNE 2, CSR Manager).

We heard different levels of usefulness concerning the audit results—in some cases managers suggested that these serve as a plan of action for improvement; in others that they really constitute just a quick checklist of items. We were also concerned that the brevity of these audits might not provide management with adequate information to make informed decisions. Nevertheless, most managers emphasised their importance in enforcing compliance.

We use the [MNE] audit form to keep track of our progress. We send the 'code tracking issues' to [the MNE] on a monthly basis. We don't do quality pro-gramme tracking, [the MNE] does this. Every factory gets the report and sits down with [the country manager of the MNE] who gets everyone together. In fact, the factories work quite heavily together (CHS 10, Assistant Factory Man-ager).

Based on the EHS guidelines we have developed an audit system, including the tools to develop an action plan of corrective steps. For EHS we have a complete system—the scoring system is nearly finalised (FMNE 1, CSR Man-ager).

The audit inspections should change little from one inspection to the next, since these are just check marks, not really for inspection (FMNE 2, Manufac-turing Manager).

We don't track audit results that closely. As a factory does well, we check them less often even. We do this quarterly or bi-annually, for apparel less than for footwear. And the inspections are done either by QC [quality control] or compliance or both (FMNE 1, CSR Manager).

An important shift that appears to be taking place in two of the MNEs was the move from a compliance or an 'end result' focus in audits to more of a management systems approach. Both of these MNEs suggested that the need was to get away from policing and enforcement, serving more as advisors. As such, the framework being put forward by these firms is targeted at more systematic management issues.

> With footwear we are working much closer with managers to help improve the management skills. We are trying to move ourselves away from policemen to being advisers. It is better to check and advise than to police and enforce. But in apparel we are a long way from that. If you think of the move from auditing to a fully integrated management system supporting our code, then we are much further down the curve on apparel (FMNE 1, Regional CSR Manager).

> Our management systems framework takes into account support systems and processes, versus the audit framework, which is more focused on EHS and social objectives. They [CSR] now have three consultants that will help suppliers do [implement] the framework. Our external auditors just basically do checking to see whether the EHS and social objectives are being met (FMNE 2, Headquarters).

> The audit framework is very end-result focused. My job is to make sure that they don't even use certain substances [that would violate the requirements of the framework]. The audit framework is an evaluation tool, while the management systems framework is the system that operationalises it (FMNE 2, Headquarters).

c. Verification

The process of verifying compliance with a code of conduct varies from company to company, and within companies, in a variety of ways. The MNE managers interviewed recognised that the monitoring systems they have in place need to be improved particularly in the area of building trust. This recognition appeared to stem from increased scrutiny and criticisms by workers, students, the media and NGO organisations. The central tenet of these groups is that stakeholder engagement is an essential aspect of the verification process which aims to ensure that the firm and its supply chain are acting in a socially responsible manner. Some interviewees stated that this recognition was a recent change.

> We were slow to public disclosure. We appeared threatened. In reality this was not the case. We were not as clear in explaining why we are and what we are trying to achieve. We wanted to be perfect (FMNE 2, Headquarters).

> People don't trust us. We need to explain to people, we need to get external monitoring going, the [NGO initiative] we just joined. The most important for us [from a management perspective] is self-study and monitoring. But for outside, they want confirmation (FMNE 2, CSR Manager, Headquarters).

The MNEs are attempting a variety of approaches to boost transparency and to build trust against a backdrop of media, NGO and student criticism. These include allowing student groups and certain NGOs targeted access (usually at the country level), providing access to academics to carry out studies, and even providing access to research programmes (such as this research project, it can be assumed). The primary means of verification appears to be the use of third-party independent monitors that report to the firm and use the MNEs' own CSR personnel to carry out reviews.

> We have decided to hire our own staff for compliance and build up our own team, rather than go for third-party checking. In this way we can have strategic impact—by developing the team and fulfilling objectives (FMNE I, CSR Manager, Headquarters).

In the view of several managers, the best approach to improving monitoring is to improve the governmental enforcement of national labour laws. This is, according to these managers, particularly true when you get away from the large centralised operations present in the sports shoe sector and consider other sectors, such as apparel and retail, where verification is particularly challenging due to the large number of suppliers and lack of dominant buying relationships. It was also suggested, in discussions with trade unionists and members of workers' organisations, that empowerment of workers would provide a better approach to monitoring, allowing the workers to police their employers themselves. In this view, the most effective means of verification is a fully empowered and accredited trade union present in the workplace.

As the quotations below highlight, inspection by either internal MNE staff or external, third-party auditors needs to be carefully considered to ensure both reliability and validity. Reliability refers to the need to ensure that the results of an inspection will be applicable from one day to the next—and therefore perhaps calling for, as suggested here, random monitoring which would assist in not allowing factories to undertake surface-level improvements in preparation for an audit and go back to less compliant ways afterwards. Validity refers to the need to provide independent data to those stakeholders with which the firm is attempting to be transparent.

> The code doesn't solve the problem. Neither does monitoring—I know that [a professional auditing firm] can be easily tricked. One third of the factories are still playing games. Monitoring is not effective. What's needed is attitude and also compliance with national laws where we source (FMNE 2, CSR Manager).

> Monitoring needs to be random. You might pop in any time, without announcement (FMNE 2, CSR Manager, Headquarters).

d. Feedback and improvement

In the interviews we conducted with managers, they suggested that systems are needed to provide feedback to people whose actions or decisions determine the results of code implementation. Workers need to know how they are performing. It is for that reason that many of the factories visited provide continuous updates on how the production operation is performing with regard to the current day's production targets. In the same manner, interviewees suggested that managers need to know whether they are meeting social responsibility objectives: for example, a firm's objectives for reducing workplace accidents or a supplier's performance against the objectives they have agreed to in a buyer's code of conduct. In our view, increased dialogue, in particular the empowerment of workers through supporting freedom of association, would lead to less of a top-down approach to the implementation of codes as direct worker feedback could be used to assist in determining the best way to implement the code particularly with respect to the training needs of workers.

> In the States and Europe they measure things like downtime and absentee rates, linking social issues with productivity concerns. Four years ago we didn't see many programmes that really measured these things, or many that did it systematically (FMNE 2, CSR Manager).

> We overreached, defensively, at first. Yet with time we learned to be transparent. But what you should ask other companies is 'what obligations do you feel?' We are under [consumer pressure], so we use it; we are transparent and we show the challenges. And this is the only way to get feedback and learn (FMNE 2, CSR Manager, Headquarters).

As mentioned previously, the objectives associated with code implementation need to be linked in some way with rewards, so that continuous improvement is encouraged. When considering the findings of the monitoring and information systems, firms need to address some problems immediately. For example, firms must have zero tolerance for forced labour. In other cases, firms may need to ensure that steps are in place to improve the support given to those responsible for implementing the code, for example by addressing insufficient understanding of the code by line supervisors through increased training.

Based on our review of the various companies and their codes, we would suggest that feedback is an element that is interlinked with all other elements of the management systems in place. Feedback is needed on CSR audits, both for the factories and the MNE managers who work with the factories. Individual managers require feedback on their own contributions toward supporting the corporate code of conduct. Importantly, there is still room for improvement in feedback systems. There were suggestions that were specifically made, for example, concerning the establishment of baselines—a common practice with metrics. The second suggested the provision of training to suppliers so that they can understand and implement feedback systems in their own operations.

> We should have set some measurements at the start, so that we had a baseline to compare against. We would then by now have a good benchmark, so we could measure the results of our interventions. But we didn't (FMNE 2, Manufacturing Manager).

> We are creating a workshop that helps participants create metrics and measurement systems. We think that systematising things, knowing how we are doing, is crucial (FMNE I, CSR Manager, Headquarters).

Finally, one of the MNEs held regular country-level meetings for managers from all their factories, where code issues received prominent consideration. Although mentioned earlier, the importance of such an approach, that is, one based on providing feedback for this MNE and its suppliers, merits further mention here.

> There are around eight high-level meetings a year chaired by our country manager. All the senior managers from the suppliers are there and even

managers from Korea. There I can get messages across very clearly through my presentation. The country manager, the planning manager, the production manager, EHS compliance, the labour auditor are all there. We use graphs and charts to get things across clearly, and that is a powerful way, in front of all the other factories, to get them to understand the code. These meetings were one of the best ways we used to get the code across. It demonstrates to the factories the country manager's support. And he will really put a factory on the spot if they haven't done much or need to make progress (FMNE 1, Compliance Manager).

The monthly forum [with the MNE country manager and other supplier factory managers] is a real incentive, since no manager here wants to lose face. [The country manager] chairs the meetings and these can help us move things. They, the managers, will see what needs to be done; [the country manager] will make it clear how important things are, and code issues are very important there (FMNE 1, Manufacturing Manager).

The monthly meeting was an important thing for building support for doing code [with the suppliers] (FMNE 1, Manufacturing Manager).

In the monthly meeting they cover production, quality and code. And there you can really lose face. This month we are going to get hit—we have big problems getting the water-based adhesives to work and so we are using too many solvents (VIS 3, CSR Team Member).

In terms of where to target initiatives and improvement, several managers made suggestions. These included working within the audit framework, then moving suppliers up toward more difficult targets; for example, targeting those manufacturers who have the capacity to promote new initiatives and in general targeting initiatives that have the greatest effect for the least cost.

Our audit framework is very basic, not very specific. The items there provide a good start, and some of our more advanced sites can now target the OSHA standards (FMNE 3, Manager, Headquarters).

For new [code-related] initiatives we go with the vendors we have the longest-term relationships with. They are willing to work with us. Global manufacturing has to be integrated because we have to support those manufacturers who do try (FMNE 2, Headquarters).

We target the items that give the biggest impact for the least cost. And as soon as companies [suppliers] realise that they can save money, then they are willing to use the technology (FMNE 2, Headquarters).

In terms of the tools available to encourage improvement, purchasing is an obvious tool. It has to be used on a limited basis, however, because a perception of unfairness can taint the relationship between the supplier and MNE. At the same time, when developing an information system at the factory level, the benefit rather than the danger of such a system needs to be emphasised.

I have seen where [the MNE country manager] cut an order by 200,000 pairs when we caught a factory working on Sunday. And it really made them sit up and take notice. And of course he brought it up in the monthly meeting. It's not a thing to do lightly, but it is effective (FMNE 1, CSR Manager).

You need to develop a system where the factory can feel free to report without people being afraid of being penalised. In that case, you would need a system of improvement to address the cause, not to punish those involved (FMNE I, CSR Manager).

The means of implementing improvement at the factory level is often dependent on those working at the factory level. This would include members of the quality teams or the manufacturing manager himself. To the degree possible, the comment that the factory management be held responsible would appear appropriate and is supported by our findings. The use of digital cameras to document improvements, particularly in the area of EHS but also with regard to living and eating facilities, could prove useful to other firms.

We are planning on using the quality team to also do the follow-up on improvement action plans. Their approach is very similar and systematic (FMNE I, CSR Manager).

I made [the factory manager] responsible for implementing the code. And he was very reluctant but I said 'there is a lot of money to be spent here, and you have to be involved'. Now he is happy because the results are positive (FMNE I, Manufacturing Manager).

One company [a supplier factory] will install some emergency showers. I will then send out photos to all the other factories, which gives the factory management face. The others will then try to find something they can do to get recognition. But you have to find some balance, so they don't just hop from project to project, trying to outdo each other but forgetting their past efforts. One way is we will focus on one area, for example secondary containment, and all factories will work on this for one month. There we encourage the exchange of information between the factories (FMNE I, EHS Auditor).

The digital camera is one of my most important tools. We send pictures of good plug installations, good safety covers, best practices and worst practices (FMNE I, EHS Auditor).

Finally, the comments of one manager were particularly insightful. He suggested that there is a hierarchy of activities and goals, with quality, delivery or price being paramount, while other issues such as compliance with the code are further down the list. In times of crisis, these goals would take precedence, while code initiatives would be put off until a later date.

We are having quality problems at the moment, so when this happens the code initiatives fall by the wayside. Systems in place continue but new initiatives are out of the question. It is all part of the quality management system. Once you get management working well, you have more time (FMNE I, Manufacturing Manager).

Progress and growing commitment to improvement in code-of-conduct compliance were themes that were continuously heard in our discussions with MNE and supplier managers.

e. Other reporting

There were other forms of reporting that were presented by the MNEs in support of transparency and feedback. These included written reports, discussed in the first two comments presented below, as well as some other important approaches. For example, one firm provides data on monitoring over the Internet, while each of the firms has public relations efforts and outreach programmes to improve dialogue with their stakeholders. This is further reviewed in the next section.

> We are developing a structure for a social and environment report as a complement to our annual financial report. We're currently working out the table of contents, on filling out the things that our stakeholders will be interested in. They will be particularly interested in the code, how we will support and monitor compliance. We need a data-gathering system that allows us to get all needed information and indicators from the supply chain. We recognise the need for sustainable reporting, and for transparency (FMNE I, CSR Manager, Headquarters).

> We must be consistent, with a global reporting structure. We hope to move it toward quantitative information with time. In 2000, though, it will still be qualitative. So in 2001 we will have more specific accurate reports for our stakeholders (FMNE I, CSR Manager, Headquarters).

6. Interrelation, integration and dialogue

Interrelation and integration of elements

a. Interrelation and integration

In our review, it appeared that the elements that compose the MNEs' management systems for implementing a code never exist in isolation. Each of the elements reinforces and has an impact on another so that changes in one element feed back into the others in either a virtuous or vicious circle effect. The starting point, we heard, is the setting of a corporate or organisational vision with regard to social responsibility: for example, 'where do we want to go?' The answer to this question—which as we were told by one MNE can result in a very different vision for the firm, as presented below—has driven the evolution of the other components.

> In seeking to become the 'best company' rather than just the best sports product company, we have to get more tightly coupled

with our suppliers. We embrace the concept that supply chain employees are [our] employees (FMNE 2, CSR Manager, Headquarters).

Several important decisions appear to have evolved from an ad hoc process, presented in the first comment below, to increasingly (in each of the MNEs), albeit to varying degrees, an integrated, comprehensive or systematic approach. Examples of some of these decisions include the training required, measurement and reward systems, the nature of their relationships with suppliers and the roles of staff.

> We weren't really doing this at the start due to the media, but as much due to conscience. Various individuals were doing initiatives because they believed it just was right (FMNE 1, Country Manager).

> Quality doesn't start at the end, it starts at the beginning. So our QCs [quality control inspectors for MNE] are getting training on integrating quality. And I think the code is the same: don't take care of problems when they occur, make it so they don't occur. With garments or footwear, one reject is a loss of money, so prevent them from the beginning (FMNE 1, Quality Control Manager).

> Eventually we will head toward a comprehensive approach. There are four pillars of factory performance in the future: 1) delivery—are they able to get things out on time? 2) are they meeting quality requirements? 3) compliance with code and 4) financial performance and stability. For the moment there are islands in the company, concerned with each, that need to work closer together. We are already doing this with EHS, which is hand in hand with quality. The social area can be improved and will be in the mid-term. Long term, quality control and code of conduct will be together. At the moment this is very theoretical (FMNE 1, CSR Team Member, Headquarters).

Some elements in the framework we have used to describe the code implementation process are clearly dependent on other elements. For example, while feedback is listed after that of integrating and implementing code into the establishment of reward systems, such a reward system would require accurate information systems that can provide inputs into remuneration or purchasing decisions. The comments below highlight the importance of management systems in maintaining a code of conduct, and how such systems are one means of reducing the burden of compliance monitoring.

> The reality is, once you have things in place it really is not such a big deal. Once you have done the training and policies are in, it is something that just runs (FMNE 2, Manager).

> I am responsible for training national staff for all the company's Viet Nam factories. We are going to train all the managers on an integrated approach, quality, production and environment and social responsibility (FMNE 2, Manufacturing Manager).

> What we are basically doing is pushing ISO 9000-type systems without calling for the certification—because we have little faith in the certification procedures in Asia. If we require certification today from our factories, tomorrow they all will be certified. So we push the factories on their implementation systems (FMNE 1, Country Manager).

> I [as manufacturing manager] am trying to get a consistency in terms of quality, and so there should be no increased focus on standards at different points or circumstances. And that applies to CSR and environment as well (FMNE 2, Manufacturing Manager).

> The easiest way to maintain things is to have a good management system in place (THS 1, Manager).

In taking these interrelations into account, firms have been adjusting the guidelines they provide to factories, moving from just presenting the code and enforcing a standard audit form to actually supporting systems needed to comply with the code.

> [The management framework] is not just a checklist, like [the audit framework]. It is a management system that gives suppliers a list of practices that they have to document on request. Stages of [the management framework] introduction will include inventory, cross-training and implementation of new standards that cover social and environmental issues. [This management framework] is more systematic and more centralised than the former approach. It is also much broader; it will probably cover up to 40 topics (Various inputs, FMNE 2, Headquarters).

> Both the code and our management systems are important. The code is simple and clear; it gets across what we are trying to achieve. But strict adherence to the letter of the code is not going to get you there. I have never seen a case of a factory that works [at implementing code] and doesn't have a [management] system (FMNE 1, Regional Manufacturing Manager).

It is clear that when considering the systems approach in the implementation of a code there is a need to consider all participants and their role in complying with the code, rather than just placing full responsibility on the shoulders of the CSR group. In our review, managers at both MNEs and suppliers argued that to properly implement a code the supporting responsibilities had to be integrated into the job description of various staff members—particularly those at the factory level.

> [The code] requirements have to be everybody's responsibility, but you need leaders and experts (FMNE 2, CSR Manager, Headquarters).

> I spend 80 or 90% of my time in the factory and of that 40% is work on implementing the code. It has been as high as 60 or 70%. I have people handling the daily work, but lean manufacturing is closely linked with meeting the code. You couldn't have lean without having code and safety and health under control. That would lead to waste (FMNE 1, Manufacturing Manager).

> We [the supplier] have two full-time CSR people, but there are so many people involved, fire teams, other people all doing code-related work or as part of their regular job (CHS 10, Assistant Factory Manager).

One point of concern—causing a debate—was the degree of responsibility that should be held by quality control inspectors. Two reasons for this debate were cited: first, it was said that quality control (QC) personnel needed to focus on priorities, for example, delivery and specification/quality levels of product. There was concern that having to worry about code items would interfere with these. Second, it was pointed out that supporting a code required specific skills, particularly in the labour area. In any case, at least two of the MNEs are placing some degree of responsibility on the shoulders of QCs.

> One thing I have already requested is that the QCs [MNE quality control inspectors] be trained in the code. They have been 'informed'. The code will probably be one of our responsibilities in the technical group [a responsibility that was, at the time of research, still being debated by the MNE management]. This is a big debate, but because of my time [in another large MNE] I guess it doesn't seem like a debate—I think it is my job, to do my present work and implement the code (FMNE 1, Quality Control Manager).

> Next year the quality control people will have—possibly—a greater role in implementing code. EHS is easier than labour, you need special skills for that and auditing timecards can be time consuming. EHS is really not a great deal of extra work (FMNE 1, CSR Compliance Auditor, Thailand).

It should be noted that when these discussions took place, they mixed apparel QC with footwear QC. We were told that with a large number of apparel suppliers, the QC people are often the only MNE staff that visit the suppliers on a regular basis. In the shoe factories, MNE manufacturing managers are often present on a daily basis and can handle a large degree of the supporting functions related to the code.

The role of a CSR unit in this integrated approach appears to be quite central, yet still under development. As the manager in the first quote mentions, the CSR compliance personnel are to some degree moving away from being inspectors or enforcers toward becoming facilitators. They may be the ones who convene meetings, support initiatives and provide guidance. But increasingly it is the rest of the organisation that implements the code on a daily basis.

> Before, five years ago, CSR was not at all integrated. Now apparel and footwear are starting to integrate sustainability into their operations—not just by CSR enforcing the code. And it is not just about compliance, which sounds like end-of-the-line checking (FMNE 2, Headquarters).

> The effort must be multi-disciplinary and while CSR may convene a meeting all the others must be buying in. We make decisions collaboratively [on CSR issues] (FMNE 2, Operations Manager, Headquarters).

The shift from implementing a code of conduct through a separate enforcement organisation to integration within the firm is not easy. According to the managers interviewed, it requires changing people's attitudes and views about what their priorities are. It requires developing skills in the factories with regional personnel as well. As mentioned below, it is not something that is done overnight.

> Integration is not something that happens overnight. It has not moved through our entire organisation, but it has to be done step by step (FMNE 2, Regional Manager).

> We think this will get to the point where we don't have to bring this up; we would not have to be there telling them 'watch this, do that'. So that it is just included—a profile we present and they are things that will be present (FMNE 2, Senior Manager).

Combining lean manufacturing with implementing codes of conduct

One MNE told us that it realised it could no longer compete solely on the basis of cost because the prices for sports shoes are 'non-inflationary' and will not grow over time. The only option, it felt, was to compete on quality, yet higher product quality requires new operational approaches. For this reason, it has begun the introduction of 'lean manufacturing', an organisational approach to increased flexibility in supply chains. Lean manufacturing entails a tight coupling between buyers and suppliers, increased co-ordination due to reduced inventories and shorter lead times, and a need for the increased flow of information.

Lean manufacturing, based as it is on eliminating disruptions in the supply chain, requires higher labour quality and a lower turnover of workers. The MNE is trying to achieve these two labour objectives by:

- Providing the suppliers' employees with multi-skills training
- Increasing workers' involvement
- Rethinking the compensation strategy for the workers in its supply chain
- Improving and reinforcing its labour standards throughout the supply chain

The MNE has recently performed pilot tests of lean production, introducing the approach at some of its supply factories through a multi-stage process, first hiring consultants to help train its field managers and then helping them to provide training for factory employees, and, second, wholesale training for tier-one (product) as well as key tier-two (material) suppliers, including four weeks of classroom time and practical follow-up.

The introduction of the lean production system was initially planned for up to one year. However, the successful results were achieved after only six months. This was done because of higher-quality factory managers and workers in those locations chosen for pilot tests and due to the beneficial combination of 'lean manufacturing' training and the introduction and training on the code of conduct.

As a result of this pilot test, turnover decreased, a cleaner and safer work environment was created, and productivity increased by up to 100%. The success of this test is attributed, in part, to the fact that it combined the MNE's code of conduct and lean manufacturing efforts. According to one sourcing manager, '[the code] is an investment in people to make lean manufacturing successful', and the code and lean manufacturing send the same message, that workers and their opinions are important.

In the view of one manager, it might take three to five years to make factories truly 'lean'. On the other hand, the results were much better than they had expected. The pilot tests showed that the introduction of lean manufacturing leads to lower turnover, in some cases 50% of the pre-lean manufacturing levels. The MNE managers attribute lower turnover to the benefits of the systems/lean manufacturing approach they are undertaking, together with the resultant worker empowerment and reinforcement of code requirements. The managers suggested that workers, having seen the factory's productivity and working conditions improve, decided that their current jobs were worth keeping because they might have a better future by staying there.

It should be noted, however, that some critics of the lean manufacturing approach call attention to the fact that central to the implementation of lean production is the need for JIT delivery and low inventories. This means that suppliers must be able to customise a product, produce an order or shift production quickly from one model to another on the production line and deliver the end product to the buyer within a tight time-frame. Thus, in order to satisfy customer demands in terms of quality, design and time-frames and still meet code-of-conduct requirements, there needs to be close co-ordination between the supplier and the buyer. As Levy (1997: 96) points out, this is difficult and time-consuming. Furthermore, it is not always feasible for low-cost vendors to incorporate engineering or volume changes quickly. Therefore MNEs pursuing a lean production approach need to exercise care and recognise the potential flow-on effect this could have on code-of-conduct issues. The globalisation of supply chains has led to increased flexibility for MNEs based, in part, on arm's-length relationships with their suppliers. This flexibility is enriched through lean manufacturing with supplier factories having to develop the capacity to respond to the increasing demands being placed on them.

Attitude is long-term. This can assure that if we pull out, it will not be easy to change things back to the past. Codes do not change attitudes. Things can be changed through changing management attitudes, not through a piece of paper on the wall (FMNE 3, CSR Manager).

b. Some implications of codes for functions

Each of the areas covered thus far has implications for people throughout the organisations studied. In this section we review the impact of implementing the code on several different groups—CSR, purchasing, manufacturing and quality, and human resources—as well as product design and development processes. We will also consider the implications of codes and the issues they address with respect to government and the potential for multi-company co-operation.

i. Role of CSR groups

At each of the companies visited the CSR function is the primary organisational force driving CSR and code implementation within the company. CSR groups are typically responsible for developing guidelines, training materials, initiating new programmes, ensuring cohesiveness across regions and sectors, and communicating with stakeholders such as students, international organisations, and regulatory/governmental bodies in their home countries. They 'manage' the code, update it and make sure the code is integrated in company strategy. In the field, CSR groups work to ensure compliance with codes, inspecting new factories and to a large degree inspecting existing suppliers. EHS management is in some cases incorporated under the responsibilities for monitoring the quality control inspectors. However, distribution of this responsibility appears to be in flux with some CSR field personnel changing roles to serve in an advisory fashion (both to the MNE manufacturing people and the supplier factory). Concomitantly, the MNE manufacturing and quality personnel (at the country level) are undertaking more of a 'watchdog' role.

> EHS is a line management function, not a CSR function at the country and factory level. We in CSR are a service function to develop guidelines, train, look over the process. When you look at it in that way it is much simpler. We check, are free to give feedback to factories, give them the time to fix things, come up with plans, get more input on changes and approaches—before I report back to my management. In that way, I work as a middleman, keeping them [the factories] on my side. I have to be the good guy, able to work with them. And if it is needed, then the country management can come down on them (FMNE 1, CSR Manager).

> Everyone on our team can provide consulting support to our suppliers. We have great experience with health and safety. We have [a CSR expert in China] who is an expert on social and legal issues (FMNE 2, CSR Staff, Headquarters).

At the country level, CSR compliance staff appeared to work closely with manufacturing/production personnel at the firms studied; these areas are a primary means of introducing needed changes and enforcing the code requirements. In each company, though, some tensions between these groups were reported. In some instances, CSR personnel were viewed as watchdogs; as such they were seen as complicating or inter-fering in the already challenging job of purchasing and manufacturing. Is it possible to avoid such tensions? According to one sourcing manager, when asked 'What needs to be done to avoid tensions in the field?', replied, 'One has to define standards, and make them the same in each country. As soon as we had done it, the conflicts started to end.'

> There is a bit of an 'us' and 'them' relationship between CSR staff and country managers. We have had to look at what role people feel. We have had some issues with CSR staff being too aggressive, and we need to better train our own team on how to work with managers (FMNE I, CSR Staff Member, Headquarters).

> You want to maintain a separation between compliance and manufacturing people. We want compliance people to have independence of judgement. This work also takes a different type of person; you need people that have knowledge about the delicacy to deal with the issues involved. Not just a buyer who can rationally call for the lowest price at the highest quality (FMNE I, CSR Staff Member, Headquarters).

As mentioned earlier, one of the recommendations of managers interviewed was that each supplier appoints personnel that are responsible for implementing the code, so that responsibility is clearly vested in one individual or group. This person should, we were told, serve as a focal point of the compliance efforts in the factory and, as such, needs to have some degree of power. We sensed in our meetings that the degree of power of the supplier CSR staff varied greatly, perhaps reflecting varying commitment to code as well.

> Things really depend on the CSR manager, the general manager is too busy. He lets me carry out everything. In other factories the CSR manager has to listen to the factory manager, and isn't given full control. I would recommend that at the start, before implementing CSR, you have to find a qualified, experienced CSR man (CHS 8, CSR Manager).

> If we are going to do business with [the MNE], then we are going to have to do their code, said my boss, so we have to send a guy with strength and ambition (CHS 8, CSR Manager).

The future of CSR groups, it would appear, is to continue to become more of the MNE's and supplier's internal consultants, guiding efforts, ensuring consistency and providing materials and tools. The recommendation appears valid that firms should avoid the development of original material when already developed quality material exists. Certainly, the firms we reviewed had spent enormous amounts of time developing guidelines, audit forms, concepts and the like. Over time, it appears likely that these types of material will be available on the Internet or in other accessible forms to sup-pliers or contractors.

> In the future [this company] will not need [a CSR] group to control its global supply chain. We will not be managing suppliers' systems, they will be man-aging their systems, and we will put our energy into other parts of business . . . The same as manufacturing was taken out [of the company many years before], so will the compliance component (FMNE I, Senior Manager, Head-quarters).

Plagiarise good practice and the code and anything else you can get from a good company (FMNE 2, CSR Manager, Headquarters).

ii. Purchasing and the selection of suppliers

Purchasing decisions in MNEs take place through a matrix of interaction between the product managers in charge of specific sectors, the sourcing managers for segments, for example sports shoes or apparel, and the country managers responsible for factories. In this process, the question traditionally of concern to those determining sourcing was: Can the supplier deliver the product as specified, at the delivery date agreed and for the price contracted? Quality, delivery and cost have increasingly been joined, we were told, by code capacity in the purchase decision. The power of purchasing appeared essential to getting compliance.

> Without our purchasing power, it [implementing the code] is almost impossible (FMNE I, Country Manager).

> We always have the power of the 'shot across the bow'—to wake up companies that don't take it seriously. We didn't have to use that that much but we knew it was there (FMNE 2, Senior Manager).

Supply chain management and manufacturing is, from what we found, primarily the responsibility of the operations groups and their sourcing managers, as well as country managers reporting into these operations departments. The breakdown is by sector—footwear, apparel and sporting gear, and equipment. In the footwear area, MNEs have, for the most part, a stable group of suppliers, some of whom have long-term and well-established relationships with the buyers.

> We value strategic partnerships, and particularly in footwear we have long-term relationships. You understand each other, there is trust, ways of working with one another are understood, you can work out problems (FMNE 2, Headquarters).

In those cases where the buyer is looking at new suppliers, then the decision to buy is typically preceded by an audit, either by the buying firm/MNE itself, or by a third-party auditor. If it passes this review and is found to comply at an acceptable level with the company's code, then the purchasing/sourcing group is free to choose the supplier. In this process, managers suggested that not only company practices but company location are crucial. Some countries will, several managers suggested, be more trouble in the long run in terms of compliance problems than they are worth in terms of cost savings.

> We evaluate our buyers, the people working for me, not so much by code. We have lead time, quality, etc. The code is on the side of the CSR team. We filter first, the code is a prerequisite, and then we worry about other issues. Audits are then done on a regular basis. Our quality controllers are also trained in code issues, so when they do QC checks they also check code items (FMNE I, Sourcing Manager, Headquarters).

> Country assessment and selection is key. Countries have to meet your screen, 'can you do business in a country, can you work there?' It [not going into a

low-cost country because it does not meet requirements] may cost more in the short term but long term it may save your reputation (FMNE 2, CSR Manager, Headquarters).

There was a recent case where one of our competitors was awarded the contract because we were not willing to lie. I applaud our company for taking this stand (FMNE 2, Operations Manager, Headquarters).

In those situations where you don't have the power of a large MNE or sole-buyer status, then it comes down to choosing the right vendors. You would have to judge, when you ask them to do something, will they be willing to do it (FMNE 2, Manufacturing Manager, Viet Nam).

The above comments were addressed to managers who, for the most part, had responsibility not only for footwear but for apparel as well. In footwear, with its long-term relationships, future potential purchases are the lever for compliance. In various cases, we heard from managers who had experienced, from both the supplier and the buyer perspective, the use of this lever to encourage better compliance with the codes of conduct.

This [potential future purchases] is the main lever for getting compliance. The suppliers know this, and it is quite powerful. In the last two years we have terminated five [apparel] suppliers. We can have more impact on companies where we are still engaged. If the company won't let us in, if they wouldn't let us audit, then we would have no choice but to end the relationship. To pull out of a footwear supplier would be very expensive, though, and has never happened—the time we have done it were all apparel suppliers. The [several dozen] shoe factories [we are working with on code]—one can say they are all moving forward and we have a closer relationship (FMNE 1, Sourcing Manager, Headquarters).

The code limits are minimum requirements, and in those cases where a supplier is falling short then we work with them to get them back within the standards. Termination is not a common thing due to code violations—it has never happened with footwear and only [a handful of] times in other areas, with suppliers failing on code also falling short for other factors [quality, cost]. At the same time, quality and cost are the driving factors (FMNE 1, Sourcing Manager, Headquarters).

Supplier factories also purchase the materials needed to manufacture the products. In those cases, the MNE/buyer may need to work closely with the supplier, to ensure that it follows code objectives, for example, through the purchasing of more expensive water-based adhesives.

It is a tough sell to a purchasing guy to convince them to buy an adhesive at seven [dollars] a kilo, when they currently buy at two and a half. You need to demonstrate other benefits, higher efficiency, that kind of thing. But still there is a lot of resistance due to institutionally entrenched beliefs and interests. When there is a cost benefit, then we can just get them to go ahead with it. In other cases, you just have to tell them, 'listen, from now on no more use of this substance or that' (FMNE 2, Headquarters).

Finally, given that purchasing is a primary lever for enforcing the code, there is a need for feedback between the monitoring systems and the purchasing system—in spite of attempts to demonstrate the business case to suppliers for acting responsibly and complying with the code. What is required is a commitment by the sourcing group to sacrifice one priority for another. For example, the factory in question may be the lowest-cost and highest-quality producer but still be repeatedly violating code requirements concerning use of personal protection equipment.

> We also need the support from the rest of the organisation, for example, from purchasing. If you fail an audit, then you need to have them lose an order (FMNE 2, CSR Manager).

> No company really cares about the rating on the [labour/EHS audits], they care about orders (FMNE 2, Manufacturing Manager).

iii. Human resource management

It is interesting that, in spite of the fact that many of the issues addressed by the codes concern labour and human resource issues, the human resource department of MNEs were almost entirely absent in the actual development or implementation of the codes or their guidelines. There seemed to be a separation of what were viewed as internal human resource issues to the MNE and external human resource issues relating to the supply chain.

> HRM is not heavily involved in the CSR/code-of-conduct process; rather they are operating only within the boundaries of the company itself. They may comment on the guidelines being developed concerning the code, but that is about it (FMNE 3, CSR Manager, Headquarters).

> We are developing a labour manual for suppliers. We probably have an internal manual, but haven't paid much attention to it. We have kept a line between labour issues internally and labour issues externally. HRM will help us recruit staff, but developing labour standards for suppliers—on that I would rely more on people outside. In terms of HRM doing things across the supply chain—there is nothing (FMNE 2, CSR Manager, Headquarters).

> In developing the social guidelines to support our code within the factories, human resources was not really involved. They don't see that they have any role for things beyond the company border. Perhaps they will review the document at the end (FMNE I, CSR Staff Member, Headquarters).

It was clear that the human resource management roles of various parties elsewhere in the MNEs, as well as within the supplier organisations, needed to take on greater responsibility in this area. Manufacturing managers told us that in many cases their own handling of HR issues takes up the majority of their time, whereas before they were mainly concerned with production numbers, quality and delivery dates. Similarly, the factory management itself was forced, by the codes and greater pressure from the MNEs, to become more familiar with human resource management, hiring personnel to address this function, creating labour practice teams and training managers in how to be more responsive to local or human resource issues.

iv. Manufacturing and quality

The role of MNE manufacturing personnel in the footwear supplier factories is largely settled. Repeatedly, we heard how manufacturing managers from MNEs have the responsibility at the factory level to implement codes and to work with suppliers to make sure that the code is supported (for example, see the third comment in the quotes below). Yet, even there, there was dissent or reticence. The first two comments below illustrate this, with the first supporting the view that CSR at the factory level is the manufacturing personnel's responsibility, and the second (from the same company) calling for manpower from the CSR group to support code compliance.

> They created a new division under the head of CSR, and it was they who carried the ball on CSR, who had the vision and understood the goals. They might be the drivers of studies and initiatives. Still, it is our responsibility [in footwear manufacturing] to make sure that it happens. If someone is in a factory we try to drive it home that it [CSR issues and compliance] is their responsibility. We have to move it out. We may face one hundred initiatives, and we have to evaluate these on the bottom-line impact. The responsibility of my team was to make sure that we made spec in all its aspects (FMNE 2, Manager Operations, Headquarters).

> If you have good communication and top-management buy-in, then it [implementation of CSR] will work. But for me to support your programmes better, then the head of CSR should put a body in my area. There is a disconnect, which needs to be overcome by communication (FMNE 2, Manufacturing Manager, Headquarters).

> Country managers are in a tough position, with 25% of their performance target on implementing code. This is a triple bottom line for them—volume, delivery and code. And these can be in conflict (FMNE 2, CSR Team Member, Headquarters).

A larger issue of discussion, typically in the apparel operations of the companies, was the role of the quality control inspectors with regard to compliance monitoring. Here, particularly in one company, we heard again and again about the debate of whether people should be held to some degree responsible for the code, as well as other items of quality and delivery. To us it appears that, given the immense number of factories supplying these firms, this expansion of roles would be an important step in ensuring compliance.

> We have not resolved the debate about the degree of involvement we need to have from the QC people (FMNE 1, Regional CSR Manager).

> For the time being, managing compliance with the code of conduct and quality control have been purposely separated. Compliance people prepare corrective action plans; we think the QC people should go on QC checks and also take these with them, to check the way things are headed. The synergy would be if QC people were trained in code compliance, then they could do a full package, both in pre-evaluation and follow-up. The QC taking this responsibility is limited by their workload; they have too much to do (FMNE 1, CSR Team Member, Headquarters).

> For involving the QC people it is really a time issue. They have to worry about 'is this shirt the right colour?' Country managers do have to worry about

complying with the code, and hopefully this will trickle down to the QC people (FMNE I, CSR Manager, Headquarters).

v. Product design and development

One area related to manufacturing needs that needs to be considered is product design. The improvement of working conditions—for example the elimination of toxic substances—does not only begin in the factory; it can also start with the designer in headquarters. In the same way, requests for samples can have an impact on working hours by creating the requirement for excessive overtime. CSR and following the code, therefore, have implications that must always be considered in their broader context, not only by the CSR personnel but other managers as well. This reality indicates the need to educate and involve a wide range of participants in code compliance efforts.

> My group has four targets: eliminate waste; eliminate harmful substances; develop closed-loop business models; and sustainable growth. These have an impact on many areas, and will lead to designers having to ask a whole new set of questions. With regard to sustainable growth, we have to consider 'how do our new ways of doing things impact on our business practices and success?' For example, we created a clean, fully recyclable product—and it would have faced duties of 48%, versus 20% for the shoe it would replace. So we would have to change legislation [to make the product economically viable]. Also, we are looking at the business issues facing companies that we want following our practices—how do we help them. What are the disincentives to acting right? What can we do to challenge them? (FMNE 2, Manager, Headquarters).

> Our long-range goal is to redefine quality (for designers) as also including the environment. If you go to a designer they have little or no control over social issues—who you source from, how they work, etc. But with environmental issues it is easier; designers can know their impact. We take it for granted that the CSR group has taken care of the code and social issues. Your designers don't worry about that (FMNE 2, Manager Headquarters).

As outlined in the example above, while managers have been attempting to redefine the notion of quality to incorporate the environment, they have considered that designers have little control over social issues. However, our research in other cases indicated that the work of designers can impact on factory production and hence on social issues. Therefore, it would be reasonable to also include social issues when addressing the issue of quality.

c. Role of government

Regarding the issue of higher customs duties, legislation can block a firm's attempts to act responsibly or follow its code. Many of the MNE managers interviewed emphasised the importance of building good relations with national governments in their suppliers' countries.

> You have to get the government on board, because they control a lot. If you want to effect real change for the masses then you have to get the government to support things (FMNE 2, Regional Manager).

> We have been co-operating on EHS with all the other companies, but the government has not been so helpful. They want to be paid for attending, paid for sharing government standards. And since we want to influence changes in law their attendance would be important. And we want this co-operation to be wider than just the MNEs (FMNE 1, Country Manager).

> There is less tension between manufacturing and CSR people if the demands of CSR officers are backed by domestic government requirements and legislation (FMNE 2, CSR Manager, Headquarters).

For each of the companies reviewed, domestic labour law provides a 'floor' for their code; in other words, the company requires compliance with domestic labour law or the code of conduct, typically whichever is higher. This highlights an important recurring theme in this research: codes of conduct cannot be considered in a vacuum. They are supplementary not only to domestic law but also to international requirements or duties. Consequently, codes of conduct can be an important vehicle for the implementation of domestic law.

> When I started they gave me two things, the code and the Viet Nam labour law. We ask factories to follow whichever is higher. For example, the Viet Nam labour code doesn't mention the minimum age, but our code does (FMNE 2, Labour Practices Inspector).

> The code is a way of communicating the Viet Nam law; it puts it in a simple way for workers to understand (VIS 5, Workers' Representative).

> Local government limits overtime to 200 hours a year from a base of 48 hours a week. And we follow the law. We are closed on Sundays, except for maintenance. We have had informal discussions to increase the overtime limits, and workers are supportive about this (FMNE 2, Manager).

> Our policy is that we follow the laws on the books, and if those laws aren't good then we will work to get the law changed. As an example, we have been discussing with the government about changing the law on physically challenged workers [disabled workers]. Presently they have mandated limited working hours, and we think that if they are capable of working the same hours, then we think they should be allowed to—since it would support hiring them. We have 60 or 70 in one of our factories (FMNE 2, Regional Manager).

Perhaps the point that was mentioned most often with regard to domestic governments was not so much the need to create new labour laws, but rather the need to enforce the domestic laws already on the books.

> The other question is how do we get other non-branded companies or suppliers to move forward—not to pass the buck? But to what degree is that our responsibility? And for that you have to get government involved (FMNE 2, Regional Manager).

> The government needs to clarify standards and laws. The laws are often quite good, but the enforcement can be done better (FMNE 1, Country Manager).

> The codes help us [the government], because, although our national law is good, we can't have inspectors everywhere all the time. [The local government is carrying out inspections at both state-owned and private factories,

but the staff is not adequate to cover the large number of factories] (Local Government Labour Official, China).

At the same time, as one manager pointed out, such calls for enforcement may seem ironic, given the reluctance in most circumstances of firms to encourage government regulation.

> Calling for the government to just carry out their laws is a bit hypocritical,because we are always pushing for government to stay out of our way. And then when there are problems we ask them to step in. I think we have to be able to carry out our own standards and for that you must dedicate the resources. It requires resources (FMNE I, Country Manager).

One of the greatest challenges firms face, with regard to local government, is the establishment of reliable standards. As is pointed out in the comments below, this is in

---

The role of multinationals and domestic labour law

Two approaches demonstrate the role of MNEs in the development and training of both local supplier staff and government officials on issues concerning labour law. One of the things we found when we interviewed managers in Asia was that the MNEs, operating under domestic labour law, have to: (a) ensure by themselves the implementation of law by their suppliers, as enforcement mechanisms are weak; and (b) work with government to change domestic labour law to better fit the reality of the local 'working world'. We consider each of these in turn.

The large brand-name companies are held accountable—by their consumers—for certain areas of concern such as child labour, overtime limitation and fair payment for overtime. Yet it is not these companies but rather their suppliers who would presumably be committing any infraction. The rules the MNEs often enforce with suppliers, through their codes, are over and above local labour law, reflecting better the values of their home country. With weak enforcement capacities at the domestic government level, MNEs are having to develop the skills of their own staff to carry out compliance with their code—a type of enforcement typically (in the US or Europe) carried out by local government labour inspectors.

The MNEs/buyers also have to support suppliers' efforts to develop the skills of their compliance personnel so that they understand the requirements and their implications for practice, and have the knowledge and power to make needed changes. Supporting legislation or laws require both the capacity of those governed to understand what these laws imply for their own actions and the mechanisms to ensure that the laws are followed. In a way, the companies are taking on both responsibilities.

The second issue relates to the role of MNEs in informing the domestic government about what they face in their sector. According to those we interviewed, governments often have taken labour law from industrialised countries and adopted it as is. Sometimes this is good, they told us; other times it does not fit the reality of what local firms face in their own economic and environmental circumstances. MNEs that operate in many different countries under different legal requirements may find that they have to take a role of developing understanding with the government/labour representatives to modify domestic labour law to meet certain business realities. As an example, in Viet Nam the law limits the work hours of disabled personnel and requires that they get paid the same wages as other personnel for fewer hours worked. The MNE would like to see their suppliers employ more disabled workers—for whatever reason, conscience or public relations. Yet the supplier firms are unwilling to do so, since these staff cost more per hour worked than other non-physically challenged personnel. In the end, the domestic law only hurts those it is meant to help. The MNE has been working with local government officials to get them to develop exceptions to the law in the case of those physically challenged employees who can work the same number of hours as other staff, as long as their circumstances are taken into account. For instance, those with an artificial leg may need a position that allows them to sit for most of the day, yet have no problem working the same hours.

terms of both standards creation—not only of a standard but a workable standard—and consistency; for example, through the limitation of exceptions.

> Governments need to come up with standardised regulations. We get regional, national standards—if they would just come up with a common standard it would be very helpful. One example is with environmental issues. Before, I did the environmental impact assessment. For the national level for acceptable noise levels outside the factory it was 85 decibels, but for the city they asked for 65 decibels. They need to enforce their standards, but on a slow, step-by-step basis. And some laws are too strict—40 hours a week is the maximum with 36 hours a month overtime . . . but nobody sticks to this, so it serves no purpose (FMNE 1, Compliance Manager).

> Another thing we face is regional exceptions. Companies would say 'hey, we got this piece of paper', but we eventually convince them [to stick to the requirements of the code] (FMNE 1, Country Manager).

d. Multi-company projects

The implications of codes also stretch beyond firms and their supply chains to other companies in the sector or operating in the same supplier countries. We heard from a number of managers that the MNEs should not compete on labour issues, that there should be some universally accepted norms and standards. Worker representatives have similarly argued that even though guidelines exist for firms such as the OECD guidelines, there remain inconsistencies between international codes. They stress that there is a need to fill this deficit in international regulations to ensure that firms are not able to benefit from unfair competition based on inadequate labour standards.

There appeared to be a growing realisation among the companies that it was an initial mistake to face the social problems on their own. Some companies have developed partnerships with other companies and other stakeholders to develop technologies, share information and make compliance easier. Such partnerships could possibly give the companies a better understanding of unions, civil society and labour issues. Yet, as the comments presented below indicate, such co-operation does not occur naturally.

> Partnerships are important. To people here at [the MNE], this culture is very individualistic. We did our code, relied on closely tied consultants or experts, and we have now tried [a multi-company initiative—which had some problems]. But we have learned from the process. And while we do not usually deal with competitors, the [initiative] has [several of our big competitors] as well (FMNE 2, CSR Manager, Headquarters).

> We aren't doing much with the [other MNE] located next door; maybe the supplier management [which produces for both companies] can do something to share best practices. But my working with the [other MNE] people is not part of my job (FMNE 2, Manufacturing Manager).

> Our guidelines on EHS are confidential. We have debated whether to share it widely, even with competitors. But each time we have shared things nothing has come back (FMNE 1, CSR Team Member, Headquarters).

> Even with the [multiple-firm initiative developed under the auspices of an NGO] thing, there were very different levels of progress; things didn't move at all times. There were lulls of three or four months. You need to keep the communication channels open to help us and the others understand (FMNE 2, Regional Manager).

In spite of the challenges of getting fierce competitors—both buyers and suppliers—to work together, a number of managers suggested that this would be very beneficial. In each of the producing countries, as well as at the corporate headquarters of the firms, managers indicated reasons for co-operation.

> In many cases we develop a technology but we need all the others in the industry to move it along to make it a standard. We have to remember that this is bigger than me and bigger than the company, so we have to move it along and support it (FMNE 2, Headquarters).

> We find that what is good for us is often good for the industry. Being green doesn't always benefit you in dollar terms, so there is no real reason not to share practices with competitors (FMNE 2, Headquarters).

Areas of possible co-operation stretched from working together to eliminate dangerous solvents from the production process, to developing a standard code of conduct for the factories to jointly develop a common interpretation of local labour laws. For example:

- **Water-based substances**

  > We held a conference in Bangkok where we showed how water- or detergent-based processes can be as effective as petroleum-based solvents. We were afraid of legal challenges and lawsuits from working with other firms, anti-competition stuff, but it was OK (FMNE 2, CSR Manager).

- **Low-volume businesses**

  > With those companies where you have only 10% of the business you would hope CSR would be a common ground (FMNE 2, Manager).

- **A common code of conduct**

  > If you took the top five suppliers it would end up with about 65% of the market. And there is very little difference between our codes. We could probably work out the differences (FMNE 1, Regional Manufacturing Manager).

- **Interpreting local law**

  > Factories are really complaining about the different interpretations of local regulations. Each company then comes with its own checklist. This is certainly one area where there is opportunity for improvement; we could work much more together. But I don't know how we can do it (CHS 7, Department Manager).

Role of the ILO

Numerous managers in the companies we interviewed also called for more exchange of information within the sector and asked if the ILO could serve as a forum for discussion. Some managers also suggested that the ILO should consider coming up with its own global code of conduct. These issues are obviously within the domain of the ILO's Governing Body to determine.

> There could be an important role for the ILO in facilitating co-operation between the MNEs in improving working conditions. If you get companies involved and make it easier for them to work together, then the [large American and European brand MNEs] might be willing to work with you (FMNE 2, Regional Manager).

e. Dialogue

In the interviews conducted in doing this research, we heard that maintaining an ongoing dialogue with stakeholders was a key element to the design, implementation and management of codes of conduct. Generally, we were told that the greater the inclusiveness of stakeholder communication, the more effective the programme for management of the code. Within the footwear sector, we found the highest levels of engagement of both internal and external stakeholders, which in many cases were formalised in forums, roundtables and other activities that allowed for the sharing of experiences and concerns. Such stakeholder engagement reportedly assisted greatly in establishing a shared vision, understanding and ability, integration of social performance commitments into overall operations, and a system for feedback and remediation.

In large part, the evolution of stakeholder dialogue in the footwear sector was driven by historical developments, which has allowed for the longest period of engagement among the three sectors of this study. Over time, MNEs in the footwear sector have made a significant shift to include the participation of external stakeholders in debating the agenda for labour, social and ethical performance standards. Internal communication with workers and their representatives is particularly developed when considering the fact that footwear MNEs place code-of-conduct or compliance managers directly within some supplier factories. This provides an avenue for almost immediate feedback regarding concerns within the workplace. It also puts the MNE that much closer to hearing the concerns of local stakeholders such as the community in which the supplier is based. Regarding external stakeholders, comparatively, footwear MNEs again have had the longest time to interact with players such as the media, NGOs and other advocacy groups, which continue to exert pressure on the behaviour of MNEs across the board. Further, some of the footwear MNEs interviewed had actively engaged with broader stakeholders such as investors and financial institutions, a number of which are calling for increased attention to labour, social and ethical standards.

V
Review of the apparel sector

1. Background

The apparel industry is one of the world's largest employers with over eight million workers globally (Sajhau 2000). It is often recognised as a stepping-stone to industrialisation as garments may initially be produced in the home and then, with the influx of minimal capital, produced in factories. Apparel production is labour-intensive, requiring few skills, and those that are required can be learned on the job. The industry is considered low-tech, as technological advancements have come to the industry slowly, primarily by way of specific aspects of production, such as computer-assisted design, computer-assisted grading and marking, and computerised cutting. For this reason, apparel production may be found in developed and developing economies alike. Generally, as economies become more industrialised and wage pressures increase the apparel industry declines in importance and countries focus on developing more sophisticated industries such as electronics, computers and automobiles. Still, given the employment and economic gains provided by a vibrant apparel industry, organised labour and domestic manufacturers seek to maintain a domestic hold on the industry, mainly by adopting a protective system of tariffs and quotas.

The resulting trade legislation in conjunction with the global search for the lowest wages has driven the location of apparel manufacturing throughout the world. Consequently, we will examine apparel manufacturing from a global standpoint with particular emphasis on production in developing economies such as China and India, which in addition to having the largest world populations have significant apparel production industries and have much to gain and lose, respectively, from impending trade legislation. The US, which is the largest importer and consumer of apparel products, and which was until the 1950s the leading apparel producer, will also be considered. Additionally, we will discuss other countries that have a keen interest in the forces that affect the industry. Finally, we will offer some thoughts as to the future of the global apparel industry.

a. Outsourcing

'Beginning with the move from the relatively high-wage unionised northeast to the low-wage non-unionised south in the 1920s and 1930s, US apparel manufacturers have for a long time relocated production in search of cheaper labour' (Bonacich and Appelbaum 2000: 54). Labour intensity, relatively low productivity growth and easily learned skills have made the apparel industry in industrialised countries particularly vulnerable to competition from low-labour-cost countries as reflected in statistics showing that, by 1996, imports had come to account for almost 60% of the US and UK apparel markets (Doehringer *et al.* 1998: 3). By the end of the decade nearly 75% of all US apparel imports came from East Asia (Doehringer *et al.* 1998: 3). In the 1980s and 1990s, due primarily to trade legislation and rising wages, apparel production spread to other parts of Asia, notably China. Today, seemingly simple garments such as the coat pictured in Figure 9 may be composed of parts produced around the world.

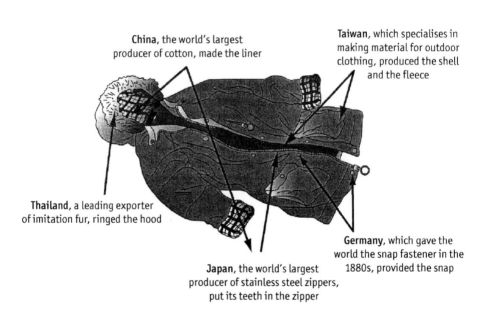

China, the world's largest producer of cotton, made the liner

Taiwan, which specialises in making material for outdoor clothing, produced the shell and the fleece

Thailand, a leading exporter of imitation fur, ringed the hood

Germany, which gave the world the snap fastener in the 1880s, provided the snap

Japan, the world's largest producer of stainless steel zippers, put its teeth in the zipper

FIGURE 9 COUNTRY OF ORIGIN: EXAMPLE

Source: The Industry Standard

By 1991, combined production in Hong Kong and Taiwan, China, the Republic of Korea and the People's Republic of China accounted for more than 40% of United States apparel imports. As wages began to rise, particularly in Hong Kong, China, the Republic of Korea and Taiwan, China, entrepreneurs from these areas began to move apparel production into other areas. By 2002 this figure had fallen to just under 25% due in large part to the growth of imports from Mexico and Central America.

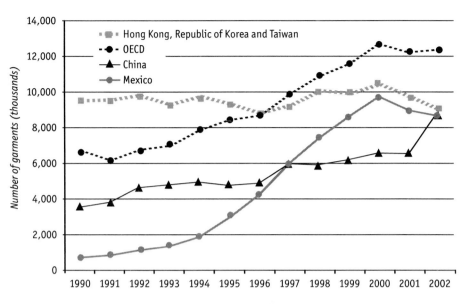

FIGURE 10 TOTAL US IMPORTS OF TEXTILES AND APPAREL, 1990–2002

Source: US Department of Commerce, The Office of Textiles and Apparel

b. Production process

As global sourcing in the apparel sector has evolved, so has the complexity of the supply chain. For example, in Mexico and China it is typical to find garment-producing companies that are Hong Kong or Taiwanese subsidiaries. While actual garment manufacturing is contracted out to developing-world producers, branded apparel and private-label enterprises are responsible for the marketing, merchandising and distribution of products. The following supply chain example (Figure 11) provides an idea of the actors involved in apparel production.

At the mill level, materials such as fabrics, zippers, threads, trims and buttons are manufactured and sold to apparel firms or their contractors. Contractors take orders from branded apparel and private-label MNEs and produce to their specifications. Generally contractors assemble garments by way of original equipment manufacturing (OEM) production, also called full-package production, for which the contractor takes complete charge of the entire production process from the purchase of textiles to the manufacture of apparel. Sometimes, more technologically advanced contractors will have original design manufacturing (ODM) capabilities, meaning that they can design as well as produce garments. Then, contractors often subcontract production to additional factories or sometimes to homeworkers. MNEs based in Europe or the US may not be able to identify all of the enterprises producing garments, or parts of garments under their brand names, leading to complications in monitoring good labour practices.

Apparel manufacturing is a two-step process involving the pre-assembly of garments and garment assembly (Abernathy *et al.* 2002: 133). In pre-assembly are the areas of

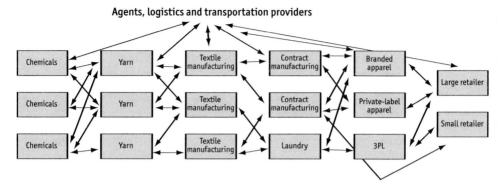

3PL = third-party logistics

FIGURE 11   APPAREL SUPPLY CHAIN

Source: Johnson 2002: 4

design, marker-making, spreading and cutting operations.[35] Most innovations in production and information technology are taking place at this level, which can be more readily automated. For example in the area of design, computer-aided design systems (CAD) now contribute to over 40% of design used in apparel manufacturing today (Abernathy *et al.* 2002: 9). This is opposed to haute couture or hand-designed apparel, which represents the smallest amount of garment production (Abernathy *et al.* 2002: 133). Once a garment is designed a marker is made for the pattern. Then the cloth is spread out on a table, and finally it is cut into a pattern that is ready for sewing. The manufacturing processing map (Figure 12) provided to us by apparel supplier GS 1 based in Guatemala shows the manufacturing process in detail.

The second process in apparel manufacturing is sewing or assembly,[36] which is characterised by the progressive bundle system (PBS), a production operation system which has been in place since the 1930s and is still dominant today (Abernathy *et al.* 2002: 171). Once cutting is complete the pieces are removed in stacks, inspected and arranged in bundles for sewing. The bundle is then given to a worker, who typically performs one sewing task on each garment in the bundle. Once the worker's task is complete, the bundle is passed on to the next worker for continued sewing and further inspection. Machines are laid out in such a manner as to speed up the passing of bins of garment bundles from worker to worker. After sewing the garment is ironed, re-inspected, hung, packaged and shipped.

In addition to the PBS system, there are at least two other assembly processes utilised in apparel production: first is a unit production system (UPS), which is essentially a

---

35   Often these tasks are held by men, especially marker-making and cutting, which use heavy equipment. Men are also often employed as iron masters and in buttonholing and fixing. According to Sajhau, men make up about 26% of global apparel workers (Sajhau 2000: 23).

36   It is estimated that two-thirds of all workers in the apparel industry are employed in the sewing process, and of these almost 75% are women (Sajhau 2000: 24).

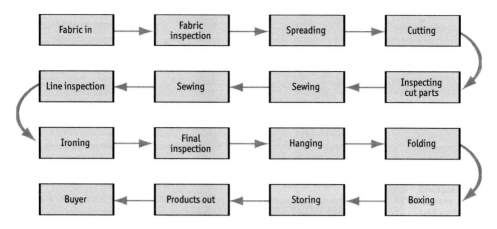

FIGURE 12 GARMENT MANUFACTURING PROCESS (IN-FACTORY)

mechanical conveyor system that transports work automatically from one station to the next. While rapid and efficient, the UPS system is very expensive to install and due to the nature of heavy equipment involved, difficult to modify; hence it is less prevalent in factory operations. The second system is called a modular production system and involves grouping work around like tasks, such as the assembly of a sleeve. Tasks are assigned to teams of workers, or members of a module, and these teams work together to produce part or all of a garment. Benefits of this assembly process include shorter work-in-progress times as team members are trained to perform more than one task so that they may step in and help rather than allow work-in-progress build-up, and a modular-based compensation system, affording workers pay based on production of the group.

c. Production costs

Factory-based production costs vary between companies and location of the factory. In the apparel sector in China, for firms that purchase their own fabric, material costs make up about two-thirds of production while labour and overhead account for about one-sixth each of overhead costs. For apparel firms that use fabric supplied by their customers, labour costs usually account for 30 to 40% of total costs, overhead expenses usually run between 40 and 50% of total costs, and thread, needles, buttons, zippers and other supplies make up the remaining 10% (Gu 1999: 22). Firms in India report the same general trends, with material costs accounting for 60 to 70% of production overhead, labour roughly 15% and fabrication and processing accounting for the other 15% (Vijaybaskar 2002: 66). When the full extension of the supply chain is taken into account, the cost structure of the industry breaks down as follows (Table 7).

Cost components	Percentage
Retail shop profits and other costs (personnel, rent, administration and advertising)	50
Brand profit, overhead and promotion	25
Material costs and factory profits	13
Transportation/taxes/import costs	11
Factory workers' wages	1
Retail price	100

TABLE 7 COST STRUCTURE OF THE APPAREL INDUSTRY

Source: Vijaybaskar 2002: 51

d. Just-in-time (JIT)

Enterprises in the competitive apparel market are finding that, in addition to keeping costs down, it is increasingly necessary to be flexible in response to constantly changing demands. Fashion changes rapidly, which in turn affects the entire production process. Consumers are demanding a wider variety of products at lower costs available on an around-the-clock basis. In order to respond to this demand, enterprises have adapted their production methods and systems of organising work and managing stock. Retailers have adopted lean retailing systems by which they can rapidly respond to consumer demands. Information technology (IT) gains such as bar coding systems allow retailers to track sales on a real-time basis. Electronic data interchange (EDI) allows retailers to convey this information to their suppliers. Suppliers therefore must be ready to fill and refill orders several times in a season, often within two to three weeks from order to delivery. This JIT delivery system means that retailers need to hold fewer inventories and, subsequently, inventory management risk has been shifted to the supplier/contractor. For the supplier, forecasting has become even more difficult and he or she must therefore operate JIT production in order to meet retailer demand. This may mean holding more finished goods on hand and therefore increasing costs or employing a casual labour force perhaps either by subcontracting or by overworking employees during the high season, and then laying them off or underworking employees during the low season. Hence the onus for JIT production may fall back on the workers who absorb the risk by working either too much or not at all. Lean retailing coupled with the tariff preferences currently available to Mexican and Latin American suppliers has affected sourcing decisions.

e. Worker base

At the end of this section are tables of data collected by researchers from apparel factories visited in Honduras, Guatemala, Thailand and Sri Lanka. Data could not, given the limitations of the research, be independently verified. In all countries, workers were predominantly female, with Thailand and Sri Lanka factories both employing over 80% female employees. In all factories labour turnover was fairly high, ranging from 2 to 10% per month, with the exception of one factory in Guatemala that reported maintaining 50% of its workers for over ten years. Wage systems and minimum compensation varied widely between factories and countries. Workers in all countries worked on average 60 hours a week including overtime, spread over a six-day week. All factories except one reported being subject to one or more codes, with the range being anywhere from one to ten different codes for a single factory. Factory ownership was often foreign, though over half of the factories visited in Sri Lanka and Thailand were locally owned.

f. Trade legislation

With offshore production and textile imports increasing, countries such as the US have sought legal measures to protect the domestic apparel market. Four general waves of trade legislation can be observed. The Multifiber Arrangement/Agreement (MFA) was introduced in 1974. The MFA provided for bilateral agreements between trading nations that would regulate trade in apparel and textiles by means of an elaborate quota system. One of the effects of quotas has been to disperse apparel production throughout the world as US companies have sought new sources of production in countries where quotas are unfilled or nonexistent (Bonacich and Applebaum 2000: 57). As a result of the MFA, India and the Philippines became important apparel suppliers. The MFA expired at the end of 1994 but its provisions will be phased out gradually and are due to end in 2004 under the Interim Agreement on Textiles and Clothing.[37]

The quota system organised under the MFA gave rise to garment-based export economies in many Asian countries that had no tradition of garment exports. Essentially, as a result of quota restrictions, Asian countries that had used up their own quotas, such as Hong Kong, China, and Taiwan, China, established manufacturing platforms in other Asian countries, which were not in a position to fully utilise the available quota (Joshi 2002: 2). Countries such as Bangladesh, India, Pakistan, Nepal and Sri Lanka experienced a tremendous rise in employment in the apparel sector in the past 20 years due in large part to quota agreements. As the MFA is due to expire at the end of 2004 there is a great deal of apprehension at this time among these countries concerning the possible loss of jobs and incomes in the sector. Similarly, not only the quantity of jobs is under threat but also the quality of employment, as price competitiveness places pressure on wage costs.

Another major development in global sourcing arose from the 1985 bilateral agreements between the US and the Caribbean Basin countries. The '807a' sourcing agreement, part of the Caribbean Basin Initiative (CBI), sought to liberalise quotas on garments made from fabrics produced and cut in the US, and was a means to protect the US textile industry. As a result, Caribbean Basin countries began to rise in importance as apparel exporters. CBI production rose from 4% of apparel imports into the US in 1991 to 11% by 1997 (Abernathy *et al.* 2002: 234).

---

37   For more information on the Interim Agreement on Textiles and Clothing please refer to the WTO website: www.wto.org.

Finally, the North American Free Trade Agreement (NAFTA) is widely attributed to the monumental rise of the importance of Mexico as a supplier to the US apparel market. In 1998 the Mexico/CBI block surpassed the Asian 'Big Four' (China, Hong Kong [China], the Republic of Korea and Taiwan [China]) for the first time in value of shipments to the US. By 1999 the Mexico/CBI block accounted for US$16.7 billion of imports to the United States market versus US$16 billion for the Asian 'Big Four' (Abernathy *et al.* 2002: 234).

g. The apparel sector in 2005

Some experts such as Abernathy *et al.* (2002) from the Harvard Center for Textile and Apparel Research (HCTAR) argue that this view of global sourcing as being influenced by comparative factor costs, exchange rate fluctuations and quota and tariff legislation is 'old news' and does not take into account the 'new news' affecting industry sourcing decisions. Key to this 'new news' is the lean retailing model described earlier (Abernathy *et al.* 2002: 4). With retailers demanding rapid replenishment on a greater variety of products, proximity of supplier to retailer is assuming greater importance. Indeed, the costs and time involved[38] in shipping from supplier to retailer are changing the nature of sourcing.

Mexico and the CBI countries compete with China to be the dominant supplier region to the United States of America. Additional data suggest that as Japan and Europe adopt lean retailing models, sourcing may well become more regionalised with Eastern Europe and North Africa supplying Europe and proximate Asian sources supplying Japan (Abernathy *et al.* 2002: 20). The future of the apparel industry is likely to be influenced by the growth of internal retail markets, as 'the growth in income levels and domestic consumption in China and Mexico will focus these major producers on their own markets' (Gu 1999; Stiglitz 2000, cited in Abernathy *et al.* 2002: 20). As leading retailers relocate globally they may well find incentives to establish and support local supplier networks.

The information displayed in Table 8 was provided by factory management, and was not independently verified.

---

38 Case evidence collected by Abernathy *et al.* (2002: 9) suggests that lead times from suppliers in Mexico or the CBI to US retailers may range from four to nine weeks while retailers sourcing from China face seven to sixteen weeks or more.

	Honduras 1	Honduras 2	Honduras 3
Staff composition	60% female, 40% female	65% female, 35% male	60% female, 40% male
Average number of employees	3,000	6,000	2,000
Labour turnover	7% per month	100%, reducing to 60%	8% per month
Wage system and average monthly wage (AMW)	average = minimum × 1.6, and many achieve 2× minimum wage	US$50 per week (a good worker gets about 50% higher than minimum wage); piece rate	US$4.57 per day
Maximum working hours per day/annual leave	44 hours/week	60 hours per week; overtime is voluntary	44 hours per week, but paid for 48 (thus 7th day is free); 60 hours max.
Number of codes	5	8	n/a
Company type	United States-owned	United States-owned	Taiwan-Chinese-owned

US$1 was approximately equal to 16.52 lempiras at the time of this research.

TABLE 8   APPAREL FACTORIES VISITED IN HONDURAS, GUATEMALA, THAILAND AND SRI LANKA *(continued over)*

	Guatemala 1	Guatemala 2	Guatemala 3	Guatemala 4	Guatemala 5
Staff composition	60% female, 40% male; Average age 25–40	62% female, 38% male	60% female, 40% male	55% female, 45% male; 60% from rural areas	70% female, 30% male
Average number of employees	760	2,000	2,200	10,000	3,000
Labour turnover	N/A	5% (3.5% per month)	6% per month	57%	Low turnover with >50% of workers working >10 years
Wage system and average monthly wage (AMW)	Minimum wage is US$117.54 overtime paid per hour; incentive bonus based on co-operation, courtesy, collaboration and dedication; bonuses also for production line	Total average wage is US$243.67	Minimum wage, plus production bonus	Incentives based on quality and efficiency per line Average salary: US$215	Minimum wage plus bonus
Maximum working hours per day/annual leave	6 hours per day, 1.5 hours voluntary overtime	2 hours overtime per day	8 hours per day, 1.5 hours voluntary overtime	Maximum 60 hours per week	8 hours/day + 2hrs O/T + Sundays when needed
Number of codes	1	4–5	n/a	2	7
Company type	Korean-owned	Korean-owned	Korean-owned	Guatemalan family-owned	Chinese-owned

US$1 was approximately equal to 6.97 quetzals at the time of this research.

TABLE 8 (from previous page; continued opposite)

	Thailand 1	Thailand 2	Thailand 3	Thailand 4	Thailand 5
Staff composition	95% female; 100% of supervisors are female	82% female, 18% male	85% female, 15% male	80% female, 20% male	80% female, 20% male
Average number of employees	200+	150–180, + 200 at branch	724	350	700
Labour turnover	Turnover fluctuates between 1 and 5%/mth	10–15%	10 workers per month	3% per month	2–3%
Wage system and average monthly wage (AMW)	Workers paid daily wage, generally the basic wage of US$3.84. Bonuses are paid if target exceeded	Grading system: A, B, C, D plus piece rate and attendance bonuses—unless there are emergencies, where it resorts to daily rate. Min. US$3.84/day	Minimum wage for unskilled workers, piece rate for skilled	Minimum wage, piece rate	Daily: minimum wage for 8 hours Target: higher than minimum wage, depending on skill
Maximum working hours per day/annual leave	8 hours/day, 6 days/week	8 hours/day + 2 hrs O/T, 6 days per week, sometimes more depending on production	Usually 11–12 hours/day; sometimes 60hrs+/wk	60 hours/week	8 hours per day; no O/T
Number of codes	3	10	6	3	6 buyers
Company type	Thai-owned	Thai family-owned	Korean-owned	Chinese-owned	Thai-owned

US$1 was approximately equal to 42.97 baht at the time of this research.

TABLE 8 *(from previous page; continued over)*

	Sri Lanka 1	Sri Lanka 2	Sri Lanka 3	Sri Lanka 4	Sri Lanka 5
Staff composition	84% female, 16% male	85% female, 15% male	80% female, 20% male	78% female, 22% male	82% female, 18% male
Average number of employees	870	2,000	1,000	950	2,300
Labour turnover	5%	8–10%	5–6%/month	10%/month	2.47%/year
Wage system and average monthly wage (AMW)	Minimum US$30.44, scale based on skills, attendance bonuses, hardship allowance; trainees US$28.38/mth	Minimum wage plus skill bonus	Minimum wage plus bonuses including bonus for no leave taken	Machine ops: US$32.77–46.44; new recruits US$25.80 + attendance bonus; service bonus US$2.58/year	Between US$34.67 for trainee and US$69.40 for skilled operator, US$5.16/mth attendance bonus, bonus also if no leave taken
Maximum working hours per day/annual leave	60 hours/week	57.5 hours/week, 7.45 am to 6.45 pm	60 hours/week	10–12 hours/day, 5 days per week, sometimes Saturday depending on schedule	8.30 am–6.30 pm, 45 mins compulsory overtime, 5 days per week
Number of codes	5	3	3	8	5
Company type	Taiwanese-owned	Sri Lankan-owned	Indian owner, Hong Kong-based	Sri Lankan-owned	Sri Lankan-owned

US$1 was approximately equal to 96.89 rupees at the time of this research.

TABLE 8 *(from previous page)*

2. Creating a shared vision

In the previous section we discussed the background to the apparel sector with particular emphasis on the nature of production and the role that production practices, such as JIT or lean production, increasingly play in this sector. Against that backdrop, the following sections provide details of our findings regarding the process of code-of-conduct implementation among apparel MNES (AMNEs) and their suppliers.

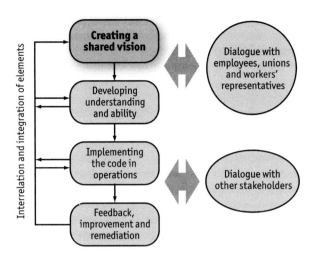

a. Top-management commitment

As in the other sectors studied, one of the most critical elements of the transformation of the principles in a code of conduct into practice is top-management commitment. Top-management commitment, we were told, is almost always a decisive determining factor in both the creation and the implementation of a supplier code of conduct within the AMNES interviewed. AMNE managers reported that the decision to implement a code came from the chairperson. In addition, however, we heard that commitment within the top management of key divisions or departments also plays a crucial role. This reflects the often wide implications (and corresponding departmental duties) of code creation and implementation. One American AMNE reports, for example, that 'The decision to implement a compliance programme stemmed from the Chairman, Sourcing and Legal (departments)' (AMNE 2). In some cases the initial push has come from other areas of management. In AMNE 6, the production manager asked the owner if he could do something about compliance. At AMNE 3, it was the director of store planning that initially drove the CSR process. While these latter examples show that the drive for the introduction of a code of conduct may emanate from an internal champion further down the hierarchical chain, the need for broad-based commitment emanating from the top should not be underestimated. Without it, the implementation of a code of conduct is likely to stagnate due to lack of resources or simply opposition to a process often requiring shifts in management priorities as well as the introduction of new management systems. In fact, our research suggests that given the sometimes complex internal politics of large MNES, with sometimes conflicting interests between divisions, the role of senior management in setting priorities is vital if a CSR programme is to have any authority.

> The CEO drove the process [at AMNE 10]. This is very important and a huge benefit. Everyone knows that it is a given. Middle management has different

priorities, so there is a natural tension. I am amazed at how much time members of senior management would spend on these issues. It is very important that senior management gets involved in the discussion especially when it comes to the threat of 'we can close down your business' and standing by it. Our licensing business may be just a small part of the business but still there are royalties involved (AMNE 10, Director CSR).

At the factory level, the influence of the buyers, that is, the apparel MNEs, is clearly the main determinant of the adoption of a compliance programme. But it is not the only determinant, and top-management commitment at this level also plays an important role. As one leading NGO pointed out,

In terms of the factories, [. . .] it is basically about the owner and whether he or she cares. There is a need for an internal champion. Management attitude is very important (NGO 2, Director).

It is also important to recognise that management decisions are not made in a vacuum; rather they are often influenced by market or industry developments. One American-based trade union organisation regards codes as a product of external pressures, and sees their shape and substance as part of a 'continuum' representing different goals and degrees of credibility.

Codes are part of a continuum—a response to public pressure. We see codes as corporate responses to this public pressure. In some cases the corporate responses are a PR exercise; in other cases measures have been introduced by the companies to address problems and in some cases, by good will (U 7).

A key determinant of where a company lies on such a 'continuum' is the level of commitment to the code found in its top management. This level of commitment is seen not merely at the rhetorical level, where it is common for senior management to espouse support for the code. Rather the most important indicator of a company's level of commitment is in the resources that senior management devotes to the programme.

It takes more time and effort to do this [compliance]. Key things: you need presence, follow-up and people who know the management system (an understanding of payroll, piecework rates, quality). At the corporate level, if senior management walks the talk and demonstrates they will hold the line, it's OK. You need the resources, money and time (AMNE 10, Vice President Apparel).

We just cannot get the support we need. We do our own systems support, finance and budgeting. We need support for just some of the daily things like dialling into the network. We have just introduced off-line forms that can be completed so that the people only need to be connected for as long as it takes to send the form. Those little upgrades mean the world for the team (AMNE 4, Vice President CSR).

The role of top-management commitment may also present a threat to code implementation in firms with established compliance programmes that are the target of merger and acquisition activity. In late 2002, for example, a large European retailer was acquired and, months later, the new management terminated the company's code programme and withdrew the firm from the Ethical Trading Initiative.

b. Making the business case

In developing support for the use of codes, business people throughout the value chain, from the AMNE to the agents to the manufacturers, all referred to the 'business case' as a strong influence. Essentially the 'business case', as outlined in the chapter dealing with footwear, is that companies will benefit financially from code compliance, either by boosting productivity, attracting new customers, retaining existing customers or by avoiding penalties such as cancelled orders, government fines or litigation costs. Given that managers at both the AMNE and supplier factories are operating in a competitive business environment, the emergence of the business case for CSR is not surprising.

It is important not to misconstrue the business case at the level of the AMNE as a proactive marketing strategy absent extenuating circumstances. Although social compliance programmes may indeed produce long-term financial benefits by reducing staff turnover, improving quality and boosting productivity, the initial investment in training and compliance management can be cost. As one AMNE remarks, regardless of whether the compliance programme produces financial benefits, 'this was something [that the company] had to do' (AMNE 3). For both the AMNEs and suppliers, the introduction of a code of conduct or sourcing principles is increasingly becoming a 'normal' part of doing business.

In most cases AMNEs are reacting to external sociopolitical pressures. These pressures have in turn been translated into financial pressures as sales are impacted by customers applying purchasing conditions related to labour issues. In some instances, financial pressures have arisen out of litigation costs. Other costs can be imposed by brand damage. While brand-related costs are sometimes intangible, given the heavily brand-reliant nature of the industry, such costs can nevertheless be large and valuable. Indeed, brand image is crucial in the modern world of the 'virtual firm' where all production is outsourced and the core firm is essentially limited to design, value chain management and brand promotion. Therefore a business case does emerge, in so far as AMNEs seek to avoid the additional costs imposed by external pressure groups, especially damage to brand image.

The supplier level is often removed from the sort of sociopolitical pressures that the AMNEs face. Yet many of the direct costs of compliance are borne at this level. Managers at a supplier factory in Thailand, for example, objected to various costs imposed by compliance management, while noting that positive benefits to the bottom line are difficult to see.

> When they come in, they [auditors] affect production. Auditing doesn't improve the bottom line. In my opinion, it is something that we have to follow but in terms of productivity, it doesn't affect it a lot . . . Maybe the code has helped us have less labour problems but not with productivity (THS 6, Manager).

An operations controller adds, 'Quality is probably better but there is nothing measurable or concrete' (THS 7, Operations Control). A Thai production manager acknowledges the costs of code compliance, but also believes that meeting code requirements will have positive long-term effects on the rest of the production process.

> Our biggest investment has been because of code compliance. It is connected to each other. If there is a bottleneck in production it feeds into working hours, increased overheads and reduced profits. So we need breakthrough

> action. In the long term, there will be benefits to the factory. In the short
> term, it has reduced our margins but in the long term it is an investment. The
> investment that I am talking about is the new stores building we are putting
> up, renovations, new machinery and painting (THS 4, Production Manager).

Despite cost complaints and the varying degrees of support for the business case, emphasis on bottom-line impact remains an integral part of the AMNEs' dialogue with their supply chains. This argument is one that we heard reinforced through others active in the code implementation process, including some leading audit certification bodies.

> It is important to make the bottom line case at different points throughout the
> supply chain (TPA 2, Director).

The business case for the manufacturers and other subordinate members of the supply chain is directly related to the purchasing conditionalities imposed by the client AMNE. Clearly for the suppliers, the cornerstone of the business case is the possibility that lack of compliance will lead AMNEs to cancel their business. One operations controller from a supplier in Thailand succinctly put it, 'You have to change or you won't get orders'. As Liu Kaiming of The Institute of Contemporary Observation in China observed:

> It's the MNEs' orders that compelled the role of the code of conduct in
> improving the working conditions and workers' rights, so in order to get the
> MNEs' orders, the factories would like to improve the working conditions and
> workers' living environment, decrease the overtime work and increase the
> standard of wage according to the code of conduct (E 4).

At a Sri Lankan factory, a manager explains that there was resistance to the buyers' codes at first, but then it became clear that future orders would be directly tied to compliance.

> [We] First heard of codes in 1994 with the O 8 code. We first fought with the
> buyers. Then AMNE 4 came. Then O 5. They all gave their procedures. There
> was nothing we could do. The director explained the need for codes. He
> linked it to the difficulty of getting orders from buyers. To get up to standard
> took us two years (SLS 1, Production Manager).

Thus the business case for suppliers is a straightforward 'carrot and stick' approach. Lack of compliance leads to fewer or no orders, while compliance may lead to further orders, possibly more than usual. As AMNE 3 explains, 'We threatened to move our production and pointed out that we were happy to work with facilities that wanted to improve. It really was about the factory's attitude and support.' AMNE 4 echoes this point, observing that the business case attached to code implementation was important in bringing about a change in the attitudes of business people in China.

> There have been changes in China. For example, increased awareness of
> codes of compliance. From the beginning, the businessman or factory owner
> did not have awareness that this was important for their business. Now they
> know it is if they want to do business with big brands like FMNE 2, AMNE 1 and
> AMNE 4; [now] they are more willing to do things, for example, health and
> safety (AMNE 4, Director Codes of Conduct).

An advocacy active in this area reaffirms this approach, observing that: 'The way to do this was to first let the factory know that they had to do this to get business and then, if they implemented the code, they could use it to get more business [Hence the competitive advantage linked to codes] (TPA 1, Director).

It is important to also point out that the 'carrot' in this approach is not merely orders, but *good* orders; that is, from customers who are willing to pay good prices and who pay invoices promptly. This is an important distinction, especially in difficult economic times and in developing countries which are often plagued with bad debt and late payments. Time is money and late payments can trim or even eliminate the operating margins of small producers. These issues are very important to the finances of small and medium-sized enterprises (SMEs) that make up the majority of the apparel industry supply chain. Thus, the opportunity to sell to global brands with a healthy cash flow is an attractive incentive. As AMNE 3 notes, 'Management [at the supplier] is generally co-operative [. . .] We [at the MNE] pay fairly generously and always on time. Thus, we are regarded as a bread and butter type of buyer.'

As code implementation spreads through the industry, proactive members of the supply chain are not necessarily waiting for AMNE initiatives. In one or two cases, members of the supply chain are developing CSR programmes on their own initiative. This is particularly clear among agents. Several agents have taken action because they could see the emergence of a strong business case for compliance programmes. 'At [Agent 1], it was our own internal initiative', reports Agent 1. 'The key people knew it was something gaining a higher profile and we wanted to give our customers greater confidence.' 'It is a condition of doing business today', Agent 1 adds, 'Today everybody has codes'. Agent 1 goes on to assert that, 'Frankly, it is a competitive advantage.'

To some extent, agents are responding to the same sociopolitical pressures as the large MNEs. Agent 3, for example, was subject to litigation costs as a result of labour practices in Saipan. Agent 3 explains that, 'Basically the driver [for forming a compliance team] was Saipan, as Agent 3 was a defendant in the action there and thus decided to set up a compliance team.' Agent 1 makes a similar point, observing that, 'The motivation was our clients and customers but the biggest driver was country of origin. The speciality group didn't believe it would be serious but once our clients got caught [in the Saipan situation], we had to do something.' Now, Agent 1 points out, business is clearly tied to meeting certain expectations. 'I think we are different [from competitors] in the fact that my team controls the issuance of contracts. We have an approved factory list and only those approved can be used.'

The findings suggest that the 'business case', the attempt to retain or increase orders while avoiding punitive costs, has filtered down through the apparel industry supply base, from AMNEs, to agents and ultimately to factories. AMNEs are making the argument for the necessity of compliance with a code of conduct to their suppliers and are using the explicit threat to cancel orders if suppliers do not comply. Members of the supply chain are following the initiatives of the AMNE and in rare cases are also demonstrating independent initiatives. Finally, code compliance is beginning to be seen as a competitive advantage or, at least, as an emerging industry norm.

3. Developing understanding and ability

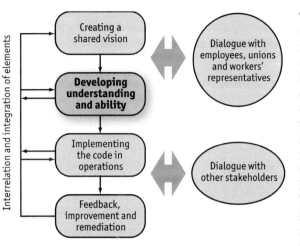

The process of developing understanding and ability is onerous, requiring time and an investment of resources. In some ways, it is an extension of the commitment demonstrated to the code-of-conduct implementation process by those at the very top of an organisation. What we heard repeatedly throughout the interviews was that commitment to the established social policy objectives can be evidenced through investment in building understanding, communicating, training and building internal capacity. This applies both to the internal capacity of the AMNE staff as well as to others in the supply chain. The following paragraphs outline some of the suggestions provided by interviewees on how understanding and ability may be developed.

a. Make compliance a priority with all components of the supply chain

As noted above, the AMNEs interviewed are working to make code compliance a priority for all members of the supply chain. An important part of this process is communicating the business case and the consequences of non-compliance. But AMNEs are also taking additional steps to convey a sense of priority among suppliers, including numerous training sessions, special legal compliance education, and a focus on internal capabilities for compliance management. Yet, as with any significant new development in industry, this is not necessarily an easy or flawless process for many AMNEs and their suppliers. As one AMNE points out, 'It was difficult. Most of these factories we had been using for years and then all of a sudden we turned around and said, "we care about this"' (AMNE 3).

The first phase of nearly all AMNE code implementation programmes is to address code-of-conduct issues at their first-tier suppliers. At the time this report was researched, for example, AMNE 3 only conducted CSR programmes with its first-tier suppliers. This is a natural place for compliance programmes to begin. Yet early indications suggest that, as CSR programmes mature, they will extend deeper into the supply chain, and begin to govern CSR conditions at more subordinate levels of the supply chain. AMNE 3, for example, indicates that, 'The goal for the future is to monitor in the dye houses and fabric suppliers' (AMNE 3). Some AMNEs have either already begun implementing codes for subcontractors or have simply forbidden certain suppliers from contracting out work. In some instances, suppliers must apply for approval from the MNE before subcontracting work; a practice which is incidentally not uncommon in quality control programmes.

> We cannot use subcontractors for AMNE 4, but can for the other companies. AMNE 4 has tighter standards than the others. They emphasise human rights and health and safety more than the other customers (GS 2, Director).

There are also early indications that, as AMNEs attempt to implement their codes of conduct at deeper levels in the supply chain, they will be enlisting their first-tier suppliers to provide support.

> We applied to AMNE 4 to subcontract for any given processes. AMNE 4 has to certify them [subcontractors] but they still come under our umbrella and are our responsibility. If there is a problem, AMNE 4 copies me and I ensure that there is follow-up. We have about seven to eight subcontractors, mostly for sewing (HS 1, Manager).

> We have four factories and four plants which we can use for RMNE 7, Agent 2 and AMNE 9. The auditor audits these factories. Reports are given for both our factory and the subcontracting factories. I receive orders from management to see if everything is under control in these factories. I will now have some support because a new person has been hired. I went to two factories last week and I will go again next week (GS 4, Compliance Officer).

b. Communicating the code and its impact

One of the principal means of communicating the code is to issue it to suppliers and require that they post it in accessible locations for the workers and management to read. This practice is fairly common among AMNEs. In some factories that we visited there were as many as six codes of conduct posted throughout the factory premises.

> Codes were given to us in 1999 and 2000 to post on our walls by RMNE 3, AMNE 1, AMNE 10, O 8 and O 9 (THS 7, Operations Controller).

All of the AMNEs interviewed have taken obvious steps to facilitate communication with supplier employees by, for example, having the codes translated into local languages. Similar to other AMNEs, AMNE 4 notes that, 'We require our code to be posted in the local language in the factory' (AMNE 4). This last code requirement is an interesting one as it highlights the fact that, in some instances, the local language may not be the spoken language in the factory. This is something that we witnessed in our research. In Guatemala for example, there were some migrant workers who spoke a different dialect from those from the local area.

In addition to posting codes, local factory management, at least at some locations, hold regular meetings with employees to communicate the code. At a supplier in Thailand, for example,

> We have a management meeting each week to communicate to the workers and teach them. There is a department manager who communicates directly to the workers. You cannot expect 100% results. The group managers tell things directly to the employees and the section heads at the same time (THS 7, Operations Control).

Yet simply posting a code and communicating its existence to workers appear to be insufficient. An NGO active in this field insists that this is not enough: 'Workers don't even know what a code is. The language is heavy. Workers don't understand it. Codes get translated in the United States and local usage is ignored. No specific protections to workers are offered' (TPA 3). Furthermore, the practice of posting codes in the local language is also inconsistent, with some employee groups reporting that there is no code visible in their factory, or at least not in their local language. A trade unionist in Sri Lanka points out, 'Workers have no idea. Codes are in personnel managers' offices where they have no access' (U 8). A Cambodian union official echoed this observation, saying that, 'The code is not always posted in factories. In some instances it isn't even translated into Khmer' (U 3).

Clearly code communication, both at the supplier level and the AMNE level, is highly dependent on broader training activities. Interviews suggest that, although there is some work being done in this area, it is by no means a straightforward process. Agent 3 in China explains, 'The difficulty was how to communicate [the code] to everybody. We didn't work this out. There were a lot of inconsistencies' (Agent 3). A Thai manager echoes this frustration with how to communicate the code: 'FMNE 2 came and asked if the workers knew the code but didn't suggest how to tell them about it' (THS 5, HR and EHS officer). A Sri Lankan HR manager indicates they are taking some steps to communicate existing factory rules, but recognises that much more needs to be done in terms of promoting buyer codes: 'Employees are told of [factory] rules at the stage of interview. At the time of recruitment, workers are given a handbook [of factory rules]. I suppose much more can be done to educate them' (SLS 6, HR Manager). To a significant degree, the training and communication process is a learning process for both the trainers and the trainees, with some firms initiating compliance programmes on the back of little training, and then following up when problem areas become apparent. As Agent 1 in China says of its experience, 'We trained other senior QCs on a part-time basis.' Agent 1 wanted to see first how well the programme takes.

It is important to note that cultural and language barriers often exist between management and workers within apparel factories. While clearly not an insurmountable obstacle, it does provide a natural impediment to communication, including communication of code issues. The language barrier is a product of several fundamental trends in the apparel industry. One is that manufacturers from more developed east Asian economies (for example, the Republic of Korea) have expanded their production bases into lower-labour-cost countries (and/or countries with under-utilised MFA quotas). This has resulted in expatriate management at numerous factories in parts of South-East and South Asia, as well as Latin America. Another factor contributing to the language barrier is the increasing predominance of migrant labour within this sector, something that we saw in almost all of the countries we visited; these labour groups typically come from poorer provinces and can be entirely composed of ethno-linguistic groups that are different from those of management and the location of the factory. In China, for example, many of the production bases on the east and south-east coasts rely heavily on workers from inland provinces with separate linguistic traditions. As a result, communication often occurs via an interpreter, and this can be problematic. In addition to linguistic problems there can also be cross-cultural issues. In many factories in Cambodia, for example, the managers tend to be Chinese, which leads to both linguistic as well as cultural misunderstandings with the local Khmer workforce. The Chinese management is not unaware of these difficulties and therefore makes a special point of hiring local staff. There are some supplier factory owners, however, who are cognisant of these challenges and realise the importance of effective communication within an organisation. 'If we operate in Cambodia', says one Chinese director of a Cambodian factory, 'we think it is better to have a local staff' (CAS 1, Director). At that particular Cambodian factory, all staff are local, except the director who is Chinese.

Challenges associated with code communication are not, however, only felt on the supplier's side of the supply chain. As AMNE 2 explains, 'Education and bringing up awareness internally is the biggest challenge. I don't think that people in my company understand that there are international standards. Suppliers are more educated than internal staff'. MNEs themselves are employing various strategies to communicate the code to their own employees not necessarily directly involved in the code-of-conduct implementation process. A common tool for some MNEs to communicate the code is to publish it internally on the company's intranet. AMNE 3 indicates that information about the compliance programme is included in the company newsletter and eventually the company intends to publish it on the Internet. The communication process also focuses on the downstream side of the supply chain, namely retailers. Firms are taking action to communicate the code to retailers, including the front-line employees of retailers who must handle questions from consumers. AMNE 3, for example, indicates that it meets with store staff to tell them what to tell customers when they ask about social accountability issues.

c. Education and training in support of the code

The communication of the code of conduct is probably most effectively achieved during the education and training processes in which many firms in the apparel sector are engaged. The central objective of these education and training programmes is to build understanding, ability and capacity. We were told that the introduction of training programmes has occurred at various levels of the supply chain including AMNE management (especially AMNE field personnel), third-party auditors, supplier- (or factory-) level management and, to a more limited extent, factory workers. The training is conducted primarily by AMNEs, but also by agents, NGOs, third-party auditors and certification organisations involved in this arena. The forum for the training varies from national conferences and international conferences to on-site factory and country-specific programmes. It should be noted that not all AMNEs offer this type of training nor are all suppliers given the opportunity to attend such training.

> There is no training from the compliance officers that is given to us. They only do the interviews and audits (HS 2, Director).

> I have not had any training in codes. All I know is just what I have learned over the years (HS 4, Compliance Officer).

A common practice is for MNEs that are less experienced, less committed or simply under-resourced in implementing their code of conduct to free-ride on training conducted by other MNEs.

> I don't know if they (suppliers) have training on compliance issues. However, it usually isn't a problem because someone else, a competitor with a compliance programme, has already trained them (AMNE 2).

It must be remembered that this type of free-riding would not be possible without an enabling mechanism, namely, the increasingly generic content of codes. Notwithstanding this practice, pioneers in this field insist that conducting their own training, on their own standards, with their own people, is important. The rationale for such an approach, they say, is that suppliers are better equipped to understand the culture and the values of the MNE buyer.

The following sections highlight some of the main aspects of the training that is conducted based on what we heard through our interviews.

d. Who attends training conferences?

A number of AMNEs interviewed stated that they offered training opportunities for managers on their codes of conduct. Supplier managers who reported attending such conferences or workshops, as they are sometimes called, substantiated this. The training conferences for supplier management are typically attended by senior management, either general managers, or managers in charge of HR or health and safety. Describing a two day training session conducted by AMNE 1, a Thai HR manager says, 'The HR assistant manager, the EHS officer, all line leaders and managers attended' (THS 1, HR Manager). An assistant manager notes that training sessions are 'mostly attended by the personnel manager and the person in charge of safety' (THS 3, Assistant Manager). It is important to point out that we were told that there has been a change in the attendees of training conferences. Originally it was only the most senior directors or managers who attended the conferences as they were viewed as a 'high-level' opportunity to impress the AMNE buyer and potentially might lead to increased business. Unfortunately, this did not yield the best results as upper management was rarely responsible for directly operationalising the practices advocated by the AMNE. Trial and error, lack of tangible and long-lasting change and the passage of time as well as learning by both the AMNE and supplier factory managers, has led to a noticeable change in attendees. We were told that the current trend is for AMNEs to insist that only those directly responsible for code implementation attend the training conferences. Notwithstanding this, most AMNEs believe that it is still important for upper-level factory management to understand the objectives of the training conferences, to be supportive and to empower their managers to make the necessary changes.

e. Benefits of the conferences for supplier management

National and international conferences provide special opportunities for the suppliers to discuss common challenges and share success stories. The general manager from a supplier in Cambodia, for example, illustrates this point regarding a regional conference held in Singapore: 'AMNE 7 organised a seminar on compliance issues in Singapore. It really helped us because we now know what is happening in other factories, with other labour laws' (CAS 2, Deputy GM). The typical programme at one of these training sessions is described by a manager from a supplier in Thailand:

> I have attended other training courses conducted by the buyers such as FMNE 2 and AMNE 1. The training covered their code of conduct. It was done at a hotel with people from other factories too. There were about 60 or 70 of us.

There were three speakers, one was the auditor and two were from Hong Kong. The buyer says what topic will be covered or what the objective is and the company decides who should attend. There is usually a combination of a presentation and a working group of about ten people to discuss a case and then present our findings (THS 5, HR and EHS Officer, Supplier).

One of the things that we heard repeatedly from those charged with implementing the code at the supplier factory was how much they valued receiving advice from the MNE compliance officers. In some instances this advice extended to encompassing such issues as where cheaper raw materials, for example, adhesives or factory machinery that still met the requirements of the code of conduct, could be obtained. This type of advice is what we would describe as 'win–win' advice. The supplier factory wins twice because it cuts costs and at the same time is able to meet the buyer's code requirements without having to increase expenditure.

Conferences as part of a continuous improvement programme (CIP)

It is becoming clear that these training programmes are continuing to evolve. The AMNEs organising the programmes appear to be doing so as a regular feature of ongoing business, rather than merely as one-off events to launch a new code. 'There have been a number of workshops in the past one and a half years', an operations controller in Thailand reports, 'AMNE 1 has done one two years in a row as has AMNE 10 and O 10. Agent 1 is also doing training. There have been about ten to fifteen workshops and NGO 1 encourages or requires our people to attend' (THS 7, Operations Control).

Conferences present opportunities for the AMNE

These events provide the MNE with an opportunity to send head-office staff to meet directly with a number of suppliers, to introduce new issues, address common concerns, and provide training exercises based on the actual experiences of suppliers. An operations controller for a Thailand supplier describes the events he attended: 'Usually the workshop is a one-day workshop looking at things like hiring practices, HR and EHS. There are different modules, problems discussed and case-study examples of things like PPE' (THS 7, Operations Control).

Some conferences can be more substantial, particularly with regard to the training delivered by AMNEs to their own compliance field staff. AMNE 4 describes the functioning of its large regional and global conferences which are held for the MNE's own field personnel:

> We have a regional or global conference each year. All compliance officers meet in one place. There are now two and the next one will be held in China in July. The team from head office may give new policies, business updates, etc. The head-office person briefs on new happenings, shareholder interests, organisational developments and share in training. For example, last year we did training on interview skills during a three- to five-day conference. We have a team meeting every two weeks where we talk about cases, problems encountered or experienced in the field. Alignment is the most important thing. We have a code, guidelines and laws. We give case scenarios, for example code conflict with law with respect to ages 14 or 16. It has to be the stricter one (AMNE 4, China).

Issues raised during training

The nature of the training often indicates the types of issue being faced by compliance managers. Agent 1 in China, for example, indicates the value of auditors with experience, and the potential dangers of corruption in the compliance management process:

> We have a training programme for auditors. Most have been with us since 1994. I hold their hand and do audits in the field with them. It is good to have people who have worked with the company for a longer period of time to be sure they won't take money (as in bribes) and they already have exposure to what the client's needs are (Agent 1).

A more common issue mentioned in interviews is knowledge of local labour laws. A third-party auditor in Cambodia indicates that in addition to training managers on the buyers' codes of conduct, it also focuses on local labour law. A local labour organisation supports this focus, observing that, 'There is a need for managers to understand the law—in contrast to unions, who get enough training on this' (U 3, Cambodia). AMNE 4, in China, also focuses on training suppliers in local labour laws, but includes workers as well as managers in its training programmes.

Training also plays a crucial role in developing broader compliance management skills. The very nature of the subject, which includes a multitude of potential issues and conditions, requires the ability to 'think outside the box' in certain circumstances. Agent 3 in China highlights this point by emphasising the use of personal judgement in addition to legalistic rules: 'We have a manual for the internal team but I don't recommend that our people go by the book. Often you have to judge things on a case-by-case issue.'

Gaps in training

Despite existing efforts, interviews suggest that some gaps remain. An HR manager for a supplier in Thailand complained that, 'No training is provided by the buyers on their code' (THS 6, HR Manager). Another manager for a supplier in Thailand explained, 'AMNE 4 and RMNE 3 have codes. They first introduced them around 1997/1998 and gave us a copy but they don't give you any training. They tell us they have an office here and we can call them' (THS 6, Health and Safety Manager). In other cases, even where there has been substantial training, the quality or effectiveness of the training comes into question. In Turkey, for example, despite the fact that managers have attended training sessions conducted by their AMNE buyers, as well as having conducted their own training sessions, many of the factories are still struggling to meet the required health and safety standards. In particular, confusion persists over workers' rights and details of code compliance addressing such rights.

Training of workers

While the regional conferences and the sharing of experiences across borders is welcomed by most, there remains a need for local programmes to address country-specific issues, as well as to allow accessibility for personnel other than senior managers, who may not have similar opportunities to travel. Concerning this last point and supporting what we noted earlier in this section, an operations controller for a supplier in Thailand observes that:

The trend in the beginning was to send more sales [people] and factory owners. I thought it was good because support should come from the top. But nowadays you send those closest to the action. The problem is that when the workshop is held abroad, you cannot send the real people, those in the front line (THS 7, Operations Control).

AMNE 3 agrees, emphasising that 'the next step is worker training' (AMNE 3). Other AMNEs are also recognising this and in some cases shifting the focus of training from management to front-line employees. AMNE 4 explains that past training for managers has opened the door for a greater focus on front-line employees. 'Most factory managers are participating in workshops and training such as those organised by NGO 1 and NGO 2 and that is why, from working closely with vendors and factory management in the past, we are moving to working with workers' (AMNE 4). Thus, it appears that while training of managers is a key first step, it is also necessary to include workers as the training programmes develop further. In a few instances, the training of workers is already taking place under the supplier factory's own initiative, although typically this training is provided by supplier factories at the instigation of the AMNE (that is, the buyers). A Thai operation, for example, explains its various programmes for training workers on the role of AMNE codes in this process:

> We have training about once per month for about 150 workers in things like product quality, first aid. We try to do it ourselves. All workers attend the training. For new workers we have a 20- to-30 minute induction programme. We explain the company rules, background and our buyer list. We use the buyers' codes and Thai law. For working hours and product safety, I talked to the personnel manager and gave a handbook with Thai legal requirements. I looked at all the codes and tried to understand them, to see the critical points and where there was conflict with the codes (THS 3, Assistant Manager).

In another example from Thailand, the HR and EHS officer explains that paid annual training is held for the workers, during which MNE code issues are explained to the workers:

> An all-worker meeting is held once a year. We talk about the code or Five-S [a factory improvement methodology]. Workers are paid to attend this meeting and I am the one who talks to the workers. I present the code, emphasise the issue of pregnant women, overtime and talk about things based on the code and on Thai law (THS 5, HR and EHS officer).

The training of workers has also demonstrated some imaginative and innovative techniques for communicating code content. In a Cambodian factory the code of conduct is given as an ID card in Khmer to workers [U 1]. Worker training can, however, present obstacles not found at other levels. One obstacle in particular is the general education level of workers. With the apparel industry employing relatively unskilled labour in less-developed countries (LDCs), it is not uncommon for workers to have only a minimal education. This can mean, for instance, that workers may not be literate; thus, written codes have little meaning. As a supplier in Guatemala explains:

> The system is a bit different here because we are in the Red Zone of Guatemala. The poorest people live in the areas close to the factory. It affects the factory. We consistently have to raise awareness as the workers have low

educational levels, and are more practical. The approximate primary educa-tion is of between one and four years of schooling (GS 2, Personnel Manager).

In such a situation, thought needs to be given to the development of appropriate training for these workers. In Honduras we were told of a supplier factory hiring a local mime troupe to perform for workers and translate some of the principles of the code into something visual that the workers could relate to.

Internal capacity: other approaches

In addition to training activities, AMNEs are actively working, in co-operation with suppliers and agents, to develop an internal capacity for compliance management in the form of set procedures and processes, both at the international (that is, the AMNE) level as well as the local supplier level, to ensure the sustainability of improvements. In many ways the capacity development process is very similar to the quality development process with which most AMNEs and their suppliers are already familiar. One MNE explains the multi-faceted work of its officer in charge of developing supplier capabil-ity:

> She took [NGO 7's forms] and created assessment forms that were sent out to suppliers with the idea of them undertaking assessments themselves. She worked with the production department to inform them what was going on. Feedback was given to factories verbally and written. Initially, a one-page letter was sent to suppliers explaining the programme, what it would do and what date it would commence (AMNE 3).

This function at AMNE 3 is representative of the work going on in other AMNEs. The development of internal capacity at the MNE level typically involves the creation of a new corporate department with special responsibilities for CSR issues. The 'CSR depart-ment' can vary in name across the industry, but the functions are normally the same. The CSR department can also vary in its position within the firm. These departments can be found in corporate HR, legal, public relations (PR), purchasing or marketing. As the importance of the CSR issue to the apparel industry increases, the CSR departments are increasingly autonomous corporate units with increasing oversight authority over other corporate operations. AMNE 2, for example, explains developments in its CSR department:

> The [CSR] Department is now responsible for the strategic planning and new business development department (15 people) where all new business initia-tives and ideas begin. That is to say that the cross-functional approach is not unique to compliance. In essence, this approach involves choosing the people and allocating resources, developing a project plan and milestones according to a deadline imposed by the chairman (AMNE 2).

Some manufacturers are benefiting from the capabilities acquired during the ISO certification process. In this way, they are expanding existing functions, such as quality control. Speaking of code implementation, a Thai manager explains, 'I do this as part of our ISO and how to improve the quality of the factory—not because buyers ask me to. ISO didn't suggest it either but an initial ISO consultant suggested certain procedures to improve quality and one was a meeting with workers' (THS 5, HR and EHS Officer).

Other factories are incorporating buyers' codes into their own factory handbooks. Thus, code implementation builds on, and further develops, the firm's existing human resource apparatus. A Sri Lankan compliance manager explains this process at his factory: 'We have printed a book in Sinhala which are the guidelines for working in this factory, pay, overtime, discipline procedures. We regularly update our rules accordingly if we get a new buyer' (SLS I, Compliance Manager).

f. Costs

The question of who bears the costs of training on code-of-conduct issues is an important one, demonstrating the commitment of both the AMNE and supplier factories. In some instances the AMNEs are subsidising suppliers' training programmes. AMNE 3, for instance, assists financially in the training programmes conducted by suppliers and it also offers to pay for the necessary infrastructure improvements (e.g. lighting, fire extinguishers) if the supplier itself cannot afford to pay (AMNE 3). Since factories typically supply to more than one MNE, AMNE 3 has been attempting to establish a cost-sharing scheme among other AMNEs for special training of personnel at suppliers.

> All factories have worker committees to educate workers on issues such as sexual harassment. The problem is that it is expensive. Sometimes in the factories we only represent between 10 and 40% of production. Thus we need to use our network to leverage and encourage participation in the training programme. We are currently looking for someone to pay for half of the worker education programme which we estimate will cost US$10,000 per factory (AMNE 3).

However, cost sharing is not always a simply achieved objective. We heard that some less well-known AMNEs are reluctant to collaborate with other better-known brands for fear of having the spotlight drawn to them by activists. Others simply do not have the budgets to match those of bigger, more ambitious training programmes that might be attempted by larger AMNEs.

Another way that the costs of training are being subsidised at the factory level is by some of the AMNEs providing factories with suitable training materials free of cost. For example, some AMNEs are preparing code-related educational material that factory management can give to its workers. A supplier in Thailand reports that one of their buyers provides the company with leaflets regarding the code of conduct, which the supplier in turn distributes to its workers (THS 5, HR Manager). Similar to this process, but further down the value chain, governments and industry associations can absorb some common costs by providing assistance in the form of both direct financial grants as well as key technical assistance in training. This type of activity is seen both at the MNE level, with MNE home-country governments offering assistance, and the supplier level, with manufacturing-country governments offering training.

> It is about educating manufacturers, workers and contractors. With assistance from the United States of America Department of Labor and the Garment Industry Development Corporation, we are providing training at the contractor level on how to run a more efficient business. We are looking at possibly getting OSHA to provide training in health and safety (AMNE 3).

Government inspectors do free training here for fire evacuation and safety. This is done in the factory (THS 4, Production Manager).

4. Implementing the code in operations

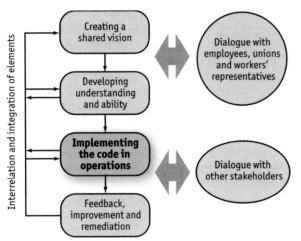

a. The structure of CSR

A precursor to the implementation of a code of conduct in any organisation is the determination of organisational structure. This includes the assignment of responsibilities for certain tasks among divisions, departments and managers within the organisation. The organisational structure will generally be guided by the company's goals and strategies (something we discussed earlier in this chapter). There is no one-size-fits-all model in determining which structure to adopt; rather, factors such as budget, size of the team and existing structure of the organisation will be key determinants.

An organisational chart provides a visible representation for the particular structure adopted by an organisation. The ability of an organisation to function efficiently depends on its authority structure; in other words, the hierarchy that exists and is reflected in the organisational chart (Daft 1995: 12). We heard that deciding to whom the compliance department should report is a difficult decision for many companies. All of the AMNE representatives interviewed regarded this as an important decision that has resounding implications for the effectiveness of the compliance programme, however. Key factors of consideration include independence of the department, history and culture of the organisation. In most cases reporting was to the legal department/ general counsel's office. But in some instances the compliance department reported into sourcing/supply chain management or human resources.

> Structurally, our programme looks indirect but I have huge influence because the head of supply chain is everyone's boss. If she wants something done, it's done (AMNE 7, Compliance Director).

In the AMNEs interviewed there were various ways that responsibility for the code were assigned. However, in all cases there were people specifically tasked with code responsibilities. When questioned why, a typical response was, 'There is greater recognition that this is a full-time position. That it requires a professional competency that we need to have as a company. Clearly it isn't something that a person can do part-time' (AMNE 7, Compliance Director). In some cases, these responsibilities were regarded as complementary processes to wider CSR initiatives being undertaken by an organisation; in other cases, separate compliance departments were established specifically with responsibility for the code. As could be expected, our research showed significant differences in the approaches adopted by small and large MNEs.

> There is no unit. I have complete responsibility for code issues (AMNE 2, CSR Manager).

> We have gone from a team of 125 people to 105 people but our reductions happened at headquarters, not in the field (AMNE 4, VP CSR).

In AMNE 2, AMNE 3 and AMNE 8 (among the smaller MNEs interviewed), the 'unit' consisted essentially of one person based at headquarters who was given responsibility for ensuring that communication, training, auditing and monitoring took place. Each of these organisations, however, expressed different motivations for the structures that they had adopted. In AMNE 2 the structure was reflective of their relatively small supply base, which consisted of approximately 20 suppliers based in China and 20 suppliers based in the US as well as their close and long-standing relationship with these suppliers. The manager pointed out that, 'The way I get any work done is by organising teams of co-workers. For each of the three areas that I'm responsible for (labour standards, community outreach and general CSR), I have a team . . . While none of these people reports to me, we address issues together, and individuals often work on projects to move the entire effort forward' (AMNE 2, CSR Manager). This team-based structure is depicted in Figure 13.

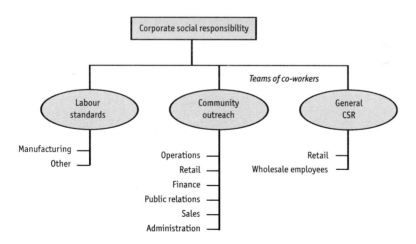

FIGURE 13 CSR TEAM-BASED STRUCTURE, AMNE 2

AMNE 3 explained that it had just embarked on establishing a programme associated with code implementation and it envisaged that a larger unit would be created in the future. AMNE 8, on the other hand, chose to rely predominantly on external auditors, hence the lack of a need for a large unit based at headquarters.

My team consists of three auditors in Asia [two in apparel and licensing, one in footwear in China], one auditor in Europe, one in Africa and one in the Dominican Republic who focuses on community investment for workers and worker education. We use external auditors mainly (AMNE 8, Director, Compliance).

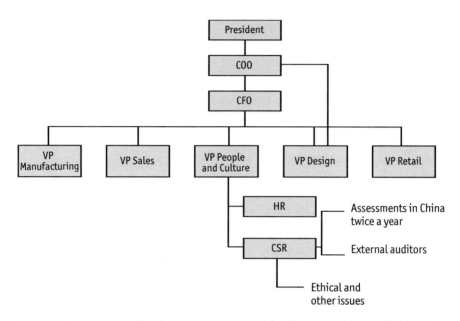

FIGURE 14 ORGANISATIONAL STRUCTURE AMNE 2 WITH SMALL SUPPLIER BASE

However, each of these smaller AMNE managers stressed the role that other functional departments played in assisting them with their day-to-day functions. It is worthwhile noting here, as it demonstrates how structure influences operations.

In contrast to the approach outlined above, each of the larger AMNEs had committed substantial resources, employing between 10 and 100 people based either at headquarters or throughout the world, tasked specifically with code-of-conduct responsibilities. Due to the size of their operations, these AMNEs tend to have the advantage of having regional offices undertaking important corporate activities such as buying/purchasing, quality, IT and HR, and providing useful support functions for the compliance staff.

There are ten people in the United Kingdom and two are co-ordinators, four in Shanghai, three in Hong Kong [China], and one in Bangkok (AMNE 8, Compliance Manager).

We have a code of conduct office in each region Asia Pacific, Southern Europe, Middle East and Africa, the Americas and a global code-of-conduct manager (AMNE 7, Production Manager).

Responsibilities of compliance groups typically include the development of an overall company vision with regard to the code, adjustments to the code to reflect new priorities or objectives, the establishment of global policies and processes including information systems and budgets, external stakeholder engagement, education internally of staff on the code of conduct and externally of supplier factory workers and managers. The division of responsibilities between field personnel and headquarters personnel varied from one AMNE to another but, in general, we heard that the staff in the field were responsible for conducting audits while staff at headquarters were responsible for analysing the information contained in the audits, as well as setting policy and procedures regarding the overall compliance process. To illustrate this point, we have provided the following example (Figure 15), based on elements common to all the larger AMNE firms.

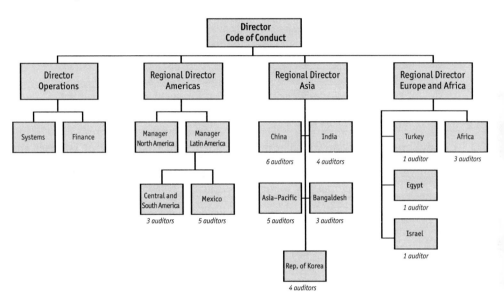

FIGURE 15 CSR STRUCTURE: APPAREL MNE

In this example, the important role of the regions can clearly be seen. The designation of authority and the assignment of tasks to the regional offices were regarded as necessary conditions for an effective compliance programme by all of the larger AMNEs. This quote by AMNE 7 illustrates the point clearly.

> There are inherent tensions between the regions and headquarters. Therefore if you take away too much responsibility from them, it takes away too much from regional ownership of the issues. We want to keep the code of conduct embedded in operations. I want it embedded just like the other functions. This is progress. I don't want it to go the other way. To me, this is how CSR should look no matter what the issue—but we aren't there yet (AMNE 7, Regional Director).

b. Field personnel

Field personnel play an important role in connecting the CSR departments of AMNE headquarters to actual operations in supplier factories. Indeed field personnel are an integral component for any proper functioning MNE CSR programme. Typically, as outlined above, AMNE CSR departments consist of field and headquarters components, with some degree of regional structure. The following example, taken from AMNE 4, shows the nature of responsibilities allocated to regional office staff.

> We have Compliance Administration staff who communicate with the business partners. They schedule the monitors' visits and send the violations list to factories. They follow up and do changes to the [IT] system to say that this is an approved vendor. The monitor then monitors the factories in their region. The numbers vary according to geography. They have to do thorough audits and have precision when entering the results. A monitor can be upgraded to a higher grade depending on the type of job that they are doing. A higher grade generally supervises someone and usually has one country of responsibility or a smaller region. They filter some issues. The manager is then more responsible for managing and less for monitoring. They deal with escalated issues and figure out approaches and how to deal with them. They develop teams, hire, train and motivate them (AMNE 4, Vice President).

The allocation of these types of responsibility to regional offices is based on the view that these offices are better equipped to provide the appropriate cultural context, language competence and the social sense necessary to address code-of-conduct issues. In fact, when business pressures forced cutbacks in staffing at AMNE 4, these were undertaken at the headquarters level of the compliance department, a move the vice president believed was better for the department as a whole.

> We focused on layoffs on headquarters and kept our resources on the ground intact. Now we have more work done in the field and this works well because now we do things that the field thinks will work out rather than cooking up a scheme at headquarters and rolling it out (AMNE 4, Vice President, Compliance).

It should be noted that, unlike the footwear sector, AMNEs generally did not tend to have dedicated, on-site presence within the supplier factories, except for one supplier factory that we visited in Guatemala. Due to the size and strategic importance of this supplier, AMNE 7 has a sizeable team based within the factory premises itself.

> We have ten people here. There is an administrator and two process leaders to manage the production and to ensure that the labour requirements are followed, including the code of conduct and the contact between headquarters and the client. There are two production administration people who assist on administration, three quality auditors, and one temporary worker assisting in administration. I work on pricing, customs and logistics (AMNE 7, Process Leader).

AMNE 7 regards this factory as one of its more impressive performers on code-of-conduct issues due to the presence of its team on the ground.

> We have dealt with GS 3 directly as opposed to with third parties and this has worked for us. In GS 3 there has been an evolutionary growth because they

have had to learn and we have worked with them to solve problems (GS 3, Process Leader).

While it is not practical for AMNEs to physically have a presence in all of their supplier factories, there is a lesson that can be learned from the experience of AMNE 7. By working with suppliers, by assisting them directly and growing with them rather than simply adopting a policing approach, there is a greater opportunity to ensure compliance with codes of conduct. The step by AMNEs to increase their presence on the ground, in the regions and within their countries of operation, is useful toward ensuring code compliance.

As AMNEs deploy CSR field personnel, they have come to recognise that having effective field personnel requires an investment in full-time positions with a suitable level of professional competence. Indeed the emergence of full-time, competent field personnel can serve as an indicator of a more developed CSR programme. However, it should be noted that only a few of the AMNEs interviewed regard compliance officers in the field as professionals. Those that did not, we heard, had difficulty in retaining staff.

> We have dedicated more full-time resources and have located more resources in the field, because there is greater recognition that this is a full-time position. It requires a professional competency that we need to have as a company. Clearly it isn't something that a quality person can do part time. Also there has been a recognition that we cannot have people located just in head office. We need the cultural context, the language competency and the social sense (AMNE 7, Director, Global Code).

Given the nature of apparel sourcing, this necessarily means a globally diverse spread of field personnel reporting back to a headquarters office that is typically located in the United States or Europe. This situation presents challenges for managing the flow of information as well as maintaining a consistently applied global standard or code of conduct.

> I report to the VP for CSR. There is myself and two regional heads. In total, there are four people in Operations who have been with us at HQ for about two years. We face some challenges because we are a global organisation. We are the only corporate function in headquarters but with our team spread throughout the world. Getting information back into headquarters is a challenge (AMNE 4, Senior Director CSR).

The biggest challenge according to AMNE managers located at headquarters is trying to get the field personnel to be on 'the same page', taking into account cultural differences and language skills.

> The comprehension levels differ and we need to simplify things and understand the realities of field personnel, for example the taking of a laptop into the field as I am doing on this trip to China so that I can understand their reality. They are all day in the field and then have to spend four hours on paperwork with suddenly the connection cutting off. We need tools that are simple to use and deal with the complexity of creating global policies and still have the flexibility to respond to fact-specific situations (AMNE 4, Senior Director CSR).

Given that it is the field representatives that interact at the so-called 'coal face', that directly deal with workers and managers at the supplier level, resources need to be invested in order to ensure not only the retention of high-quality staff but also the flow of information from field personnel back to headquarters. The issue of information flow is addressed later in this chapter.

c. Implementation at the supplier level

The implementation of codes at the supplier level is a complex function requiring several different activities simultaneously. These multiple activities are described throughout this book and include the functions of communication, training, auditing and the development and implementation of corrective action plans (CAPs). This section explains the way some suppliers are organising management to direct these CSR tasks.

It has been observed that leading AMNEs are developing corporate CSR departments to manage issues of CSR globally throughout their supply chains. At the supplier level, the implementation of CSR programmes also requires specific tasks to be assigned to specific managers. The emergence of formal, if not yet fully developed, compliance management systems within supplier companies is a significant sign of the impact of AMNE codes. As one of the experts who participated in the research suggests, 'The strongest indicator that code implementation is robust is the development of internal management systems within the supplier factory—or, at least, the inchoate formation of such a system' (E 1).

Since suppliers are typically small to medium-sized enterprises, managers at the supplier level may be assigned multiple responsibilities. Thus, we were told that the manager in charge of compliance at the supplier level may have other duties. Typically the responsibility for code implementation is assigned to the head of the HR department, although in some rare cases there may be dedicated compliance officers. As has been outlined, a few of the supplier factories that we interviewed have taken a proactive approach to the issue of codes of conduct and compliance generally and have assigned responsibility for such matters to a particular individual. In most instances, however, the establishment of such a role has resulted from the suggestions of MNE field personnel or training. The role of the CSR management at the supplier level often involves co-ordination with other departments such as production.

> The compliance programme comes under the personnel department. The personnel department has four groups: social security; health, labour issues and day care; control of salaries; regulations (GS 1).

> We have production people such as the production manager and the chief mechanic, human resources and safety. HR is responsible for hiring, firing and looking at worker rights. They have to communicate issues with production and supervisors. Production is responsible for everything because HR goes to them with the problem, the same as the safety managers. The team meets once a month and it reports to the president. The meetings are recorded (HS 1, Manager).

The duties of the compliance officer at the supplier level typically entail maintaining factory standards in accordance with code requirements, and implementing CAPs. As the duties of the compliance officer become integrated into the day-to-day management of factories, CSR programmes also become more fully implemented on a regular basis.

> The compliance officer has been working for more than one year. The following changes have been made: record-keeping for health and safety and checklist for health and safety (GS 2, Director).

> [My responsibilities as compliance officer include:] Beginning of day: check conditions for health and safety aspects, attending clients, helping the personnel manager, helping employees, for example regarding suggestions, going around the factory with the AMNE 4 Compliance Officer (approximately every one to two months) (GS 2, Compliance Officer).

> I brief auditors, look after wages, make sure timecards and payroll are correct, look at the severance process, review personnel history, and am responsible for general supervision of the plant looking at things like exits, hallways, first-aid kits, unsafe action by workers, external areas, and general cleanliness of things such as toilets. I prepare confidential interviews in any parts of the plant or outside. I actually conduct interviews with the workers to sound out what is going on, or just to have general information. I will ask them about their supervisors, about the Korean management and their work colleagues. I do these interviews twice a month with about 30 employees. I also prepare training materials, guidelines, handbooks, and give information regarding the legal processes and announcements. I co-ordinate first aid and evacuation training, as well as training in the use of chemicals and the use of health and safety equipment. I conduct meetings with pregnant and nursing mothers and I must also provide service to clients, such as reports (GS 4, Compliance Officer).

> I am responsible for administrative issues and compliance. I report directly to the general manager. My most important responsibility to me and my boss is compliance. I am president of the committee on health and safety in both plants. I am in charge of security at all of the plants, for example I look at exits, the safety of people, good working environments and food. I deal with security personnel, the maintenance department and make sure that things like the electricity panels are OK and that all of the signals work. I make sure that all of the documentation is in order; I look at production and complaints (HS 4, Compliance Officer).

d. Conflicts between codes and local law

This section notes one of the more general issues related to implementation at the supplier level, namely the issue of conflicts or inconsistencies between code standards and the legal standards of the country where manufacturing is taking place. This issue was discussed in Chapter II. At the heart of the conflict rests the conundrum faced by managers who may be uncertain as to which standard to apply. Furthermore, they may view standards in codes as foreign and non-applicable in their own operating environments. A manager from a Thai supplier notes, for example, inconsistencies in overtime requirements:

> The code that was established by a buyer in the US, doesn't always work here. Do you know the story about the tree that is transplanted? Sometimes it is true that a tree that grows well in the US might not grow so well here. For example, overtime. Thai law allows 36 hours while codes allow 12 hours. And some codes allow an excess of hours over the peak period if we tell the brands that we want extra time. In non-peak periods, we don't work overtime (THS 6, Manager).

This overtime example indicates a general problem of implementation at the supplier level when there are inconsistencies among the various MNE codes and between the various codes and local labour law. Arguably there can be advantages to a more important role for local law; a role which would include better defined standards, monitoring and enforcement. Apart from the codes' influence on suppliers, codes are also raising new questions about the role of local labour law enforcement. As a production manager from a factory in Thailand observes:

> There needs to be more enforcement of the law. I think that both the code and the law should be there. The government should get involved more. If we get a code from the US or the UK, they look at similar labour rights from those countries but culturally in Thailand it is different. It must go hand in hand for these bodies to bring it to world-class standards (THS 4, Production Manager).

Laws in Thailand

Thai labour law and the perception of economic reality by factory management often prevent the implementation/adoption of voluntary labour standards. For instance, the Thai Labour Protection Act of 1998 permits up to 36 hours of overtime per week, while voluntary labour standards advocate 12 hours of overtime. Member factories of the Thai Garment Manufacturers Association face the dilemma of short order periods and fluctuating demand for their products. On the other hand, workers' rights advocates argue that the present Thai daily minimum wage does not cover the living expenses of workers. Factory workers sometimes live in substandard conditions in an effort to send a small portion of their earnings home. Thai workers do not support a reduction in working hours, since they supplement their income through overtime pay. Many workers will even protest or change workplaces in an effort to gain overtime pay. Conflicting labour standards, a low minimum daily wage and the dire financial needs of workers often result in adverse working conditions for employees in the garment industry (E 4).

Local law enforcement versus MNE codes

The emphasis on a greater role for local law enforcement is shared by some labour organisations. A trade union representative, for instance, argues that governments, ultimately, must play a greater role in the local implementation of labour standards. '[MNE monitors] aren't in the factories every day. They aren't conscious. They screw up for a variety of reasons. In contrast, governments at least are subject to recall' (U 7). Yet arguments for greater host-government involvement must recognise the environment of weak government institutions that exists in most developing countries. The reason MNE codes arose in the first place was precisely because there was little or no domestic government enforcement of adequate labour and EHS standards in the host countries (even though these laws often exist on paper).

Role of national labour law

Code provisions may include requirements that suppliers conform to: (a) international labour standards, (b) national labour laws, or (c) 'free-standing' code provisions that do not directly incorporate international or national law but rather establish new standards. The leading instance of a free-standing provision is the 60-hour limit found in most corporate codes.

As to matters other than such bright-line, free-standing rules, our research team heard that CSR personnel most often turn to national labour law, which provides the most specific and comprehensive set of rules that can be taken 'off the shelf' for ready application.

> Our goal is to cite local law, except in cases where the code is stricter, because local law provides specificity (RMNE 3, Director Corporate Compliance).

In some cases, reliance on local labour law also eases the 'problem of legitimacy' created when outside monitors purport to impose legal standards on local actors—CSR personnel can simply admonish factory managers to 'follow the law of the land'.

> Following the law of the land is incorporated in our code and gives us most of what we need. There are some countries where factory managers are insulted by our inspections. It's easier if we can tell them we're just following the rules promulgated by their own government (Agent 3, General Manager).

There are two interesting aspects in the CSR personnel's reliance on local law. First, outside observers of the CSR process often assume that MNEs are applying either a highly privatised code of conduct or a universal code of international labour rights (promulgated and legitimated by the ILO). In fact, CSR staff generally seemed to understand that the bulk of rules for which they examine supplier compliance are rules of sovereign national law. Second, even the CSR personnel's apparent emphasis on enforcement of local law may be misleading. When pressed on the question during field interviews, ground-level monitors acknowledged that the actual baseline standard they apply is in fact the actual existing practices of the suppliers.

Reliance on local law raises the question of where CSR personnel obtain their information regarding such laws. A number of MNE representatives interviewed use a privately developed database on national labour laws, access to which is granted upon paying a fee. Others rely on manuals created by managers or purchase legal treatises available in local markets.

> The buyers did not discuss Thai labour law with me. I learned it from a book that can be bought locally and I discussed it with the personnel manager. I know it well; it's not too complicated (THS 8, Manager).

The creation of a database on national labour laws reflects the importance of national labour law as an ostensible baseline for compliance. It also demonstrates that initiatives by private industry can serve the function of 'harmonising' interpretation of national law—a function that has eluded academic, judicial and international organisational efforts (E 1).

Corruption and institutional weakness in LDCs

The weak institutional environment of many production countries (that is, where suppliers are located) is one wherein local laws do not necessarily cover ILO fundamental labour rights and EHS issues. And in countries where local laws *do* cover these rights and issues, these laws are not necessarily enforced in any meaningful way. There are numerous factors contributing to this institutional weakness, but a prominent issue worth highlighting is the role of corruption. As production in the apparel industry has shifted to countries with lower labour costs, it has also located itself in countries with high levels of perceived corruption (see Figure 16 below).

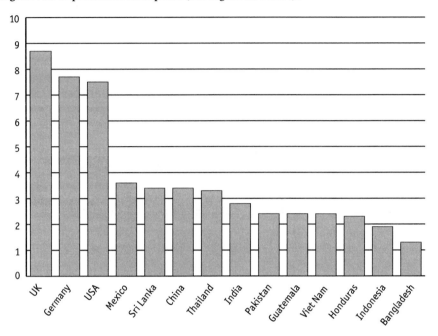

10 = very low perceived corruption, 0 = very high perceived corruption

FIGURE 16 PERCEIVED LEVEL OF CORRUPTION IN SELECTED APPAREL-
MANUFACTURING COUNTRIES AND APPAREL MNE HOME COUNTRIES

Source: Transparency International, 2003

Problems related to corruption were mentioned in several of the interviews we conducted. The problem of corruption manifests itself in perceptions that government inspectors are taking bribes to not enforce particular regulations, or that joint ventures between government and industry may create conflicts of interest that prevent government from fully enforcing labour regulations.

> Corruption is rampant and labour inspection is not real. Government partakes in concealment—in making the problem go away . . . Code of conduct is not enough because the labour ministry still needs to check. Yet, the ministry is corrupt or does not understand payroll, accounting, etc. . . . Some factories are joint ventures with the top government ministries, leading to problems upholding workers' rights and quota allocation (U 2, Cambodia).

> It is frustrating to see [the labour inspector's] role in relation to labour con-
> flicts. Far from being impartial, they go in to persuade workers to accept what
> the employer wants. Falsification of records is common. There are insuffi-
> cient finances and skill, and corruption is a problem (U 4, Guatemala Co-ordi-
> nator).

> The culture of impunity affects customs requirements which are non-compet-
> itive, arbitrary and subject to corruption as well as transport. Until the gov-
> ernment shows commitment to the rule of law, it will be at a disadvantage
> (NGO 4, Guatemala).

> National law should look after this but in most cases, including Sri Lanka, the
> real situation is that the national bodies when they come to inspect the
> factories are surprised and there is also corruption (THS 4, Production Man-
> ager).

The issue of corruption also includes accounting malpractices in the private sector intended to circumvent local government reporting requirements. As the 2002 Enron and Arthur Andersen scandal in the United States clearly demonstrates, even in highly developed countries, government watchdog agencies cannot always ensure that accounting malpractice does not occur. In developing countries, which typically lack the resources and experienced personnel to maintain large and sophisticated auditing and oversight bureaucracies, the opportunities for abuse are that much more pro-nounced.

> Double record-keeping is common in Sri Lanka. The abuse is because of the
> overtime legislation. The law is not clear. They are now asking for an increase
> to 70 hours per month (NGO 9, Sri Lanka).

In addition to corruption (and sometimes related to it) many developing countries simply do not have the resources to fund well-functioning bureaucracies. Thus, it is not clear how effective government labour inspectors are, even in those countries that have such inspectors. In Thailand, for example, management and labour representatives provide mixed feedback regarding labour inspectors. The manager of a supplier observes that, 'The local ministry labour inspector comes in once a year.' A union representative on the other hand observes that 'There has never been an inspector in my nine years of working in the factory' (U 6, Thailand).

Another aspect of institutional weakness in developing countries can be insuf-ficiently developed labour laws. In many developing countries, there simply are no laws addressing certain labour conditions. An EHS officer for a supplier in Thailand, for example, points out, 'The law [in Thailand] doesn't require factories to keep records or to submit a report on EHS. It depends on what the manager decides' (THS I, EHS Sup-plier). At another extreme, some apparel manufacturing countries may be developing labour laws that are not conducive to the full expression of key labour rights, such as the freedom of association. In Cambodia, for instance, there are complaints from employer and labour groups that recent developments in labour law have served to undermine union effectiveness:

> A labour law was passed in 1997. It was a time bomb—the biggest landmine
> in Cambodia. One by one the unions came in and they started blowing up,
> one by one. There are so many provisions in the labour law that the unions
> can blow up one by one (IA I).

MNEs as 'police': Privatising the enforcement of labour standards

It is within this context of institutional weakness in developing countries that apparel MNEs were originally pressured to take action to ensure that certain labour standards were being met within their value chains. Interviews with MNE agents indicate that some of the MNEs see their role as a 'policeman of last resort', compensating for institutional weakness in the apparel manufacturing countries.

> We have become the policeman of last resort. We enforce the laws that the countries don't want to enforce. The countries should enforce the laws or the WTO should play a higher role (Agent 1).

> Local law is not enforced. If it were then we wouldn't have to do this [monitoring] (Agent 2).

> The law in Thailand is very good but we don't have time to enforce it. It all comes down to one person but it should be the government inspector (Agent 1).

At least some labour groups in the apparel manufacturing countries acknowledge this 'policeman' role, noting that the MNEs' compliance management programmes are often far more effective and stringent than some countries' own labour laws. In Cambodia, for example, a trade association observes that, 'codes of conduct are principles, but if you look at the details of the audit forms, their compliance requirements are ten times harder than our labour law' (IA 1).

A mixed approach

While acknowledging the effectiveness of MNE codes, critics still have concerns about what is seen as the privatisation of labour law. Clearly codes have been successful in areas where local law enforcement has failed or been inadequate. Yet, long term, as the production countries develop their institutional capacity, many of the functions of code compliance management may shift to local governments. A leading trade union argues that at least some of the investment going into code compliance management should be directed instead towards increasing the capacity of production-country governments to enforce international labour standards:

> Codes are a tool—one tool in the toolbox. The competitive pressures on companies in the market are such that there have to be rules. The privatisation of the labour relations process is dangerous. Codes have opened up a window to give opportunities where we wouldn't have had them otherwise, but how much money would have been better spent on upgrading the ministries? (U 7).

As local-government capacity develops over time, the future of implementing labour standards at the supplier level may rest on a combination of both industry initiatives and local government initiatives. However, since MNEs will remain answerable to their key stakeholders, in particular concerned customer groups, it is unlikely that the MNE's role in implementing labour standards will ever disappear altogether, regardless of how well-developed local government institutions become.

e. Employee participation

Role of workers' committees and the question of unions

A debated but fundamental question about employee participation is exactly what is the purpose or role of workers in the management structure. A representative for AMNE 9 believes that, 'If worker and management communication can be improved, there won't be any need for compliance because they will do it themselves' (AMNE 9). This suggests that the primary role for workers' committees and other forms of employee participation is to improve communication between workers and management. Yet, as interview feedback on the role of unions suggests, there are additional questions about the role of workers in policy formation and code implementation. These questions address whether or not management and workers have the same set of priorities or interests and, if not, how these divergent interests might be resolved through a worker–management negotiation process. Simply stated, if conflicts exist between a management view and worker view, then merely facilitating communication will be insufficient unless 'facilitating communication' is taken to mean organising a structural or formal negotiation process.

A manager from Sri Lanka indicates that if a union were to form at his factory, he would take a minimalist approach to worker rights, sticking strictly to mandatory legal rights. He would do this as part of an anticipated struggle with the union (that is, it is his opening bargaining position). Significantly for this study, he notes customer pressure as a reason why such a negotiation process, or struggle, would be unhelpful.

> People talk about unions and all that. If there is a union, I will stick to the minimum accounting—to what the law says that I should give them, if I have to sit and fight with them. My customer doesn't have time for that (SLS 3, HR Manager).

Other interviews in Sri Lanka question the politicisation of unions, and the creation of deadlocks in a power struggle between management and unions that undermines both worker and management aspirations.

> Unions in Sri Lanka have a political agenda. They put a spoke in management. It results in workers and unions both not getting anywhere (SLS 3, HR Manager).

> The most important thing with unions and workers is to have confidence and not give false promises. Think about welfare issues, issues other than just wages for workers. It depends on your management style. It requires a personal investment on the part of management (SLS 4, Manager).

These concerns about the politicisation of unions reflect the particular situation in Sri Lanka where industries other than apparel have a more substantial history of organised labour. It may also be the case in other countries with a similar history with regard to labour organising. In countries with less experience with organised labour, the question of unions is rarely raised by management. In some cases this is due to the small size of apparel suppliers; in other cases simply because there is no history of unions in the apparel industry, or similar industries, in the given country.

> We are a small factory and thus have not had a need for unions (THS 6, Manager).

> There is no union here and workers were never asked to join or form one. No factories have unions in this area. I am not sure if the workers know what a union is (THS 4, HR Manager).

Confusion about the role of the right to freedom of association and collective bargaining and exactly how to implement a union remain common in many of the countries where supplier factories are located. Interviews in Turkey, for example, suggest that almost all of the factories were struggling to meet the requirements associated with the right to freedom of association and collective bargaining. In a number of instances, confusion regarding the meaning of freedom of association emerged. For instance, managers were uncertain whether the right meant that workers had to be organised in their factories or merely whether they were able to organise if they wished.

It is also worth noting that the demographic make-up of workers in the apparel industry may have some bearing on the formation of unions. Typically apparel factories, such as footwear factories, employ mainly women, often below the age of 25. In some countries, such as China, the workers may also be internal migrants of an ethnic or linguistic minority in the factory location. Even where governments support the right to freedom of association, all of these demographic factors can undermine the ability of workers to know about and/or exercise their right to freedom of association.

Given the concerns of some supplier managers about the role of unions and the lack of experience with freedom of association in some countries, there remains an important question. If unions do not exist, can the goals reflected in AMNE codes be achieved and what alternative avenues exist for workers to express their right to organise? Furthermore, where unions do exist, what role do they play in the code-of-conduct implementation process?

Worker perspective

Interviews conducted with union officials suggest that the union sees its role as a check on management power: 'Unions need to build substantive relationships with management to hold them accountable' (U 9). The role of unions as advocates of management accountability may be complementary to the role of AMNEs as auditors. While the AMNE auditors have the advantage of an outside perspective and knowledge of industry 'best practices', union officials have the advantage of direct inside knowledge and continuous engagement with both workers and management. The advantages unions can bring to the auditing process alone would be helpful in overcoming lingering questions of credibility surrounding AMNE compliance efforts. As a Thai union remarks, 'From the surface, the outsiders may see that [factory managers] have a good relationship [with the workers] but in reality [factory managers] say yes but don't do anything' (U 6).

Yet union officials note the concerns of management, observing that, 'management most fears a change in the power relationship' (U 9). This sentiment can also be found in the comments of a Sri Lankan manager quoted in the previous section. Indeed, the acknowledgement of a power relationship between the two groups cuts to the core of the debate about unions. It also acknowledges that the core issue is not so much a question of 'communication' between workers and management, so much as it is a question of 'negotiation'. As a Thai union observes, 'If the issue causes the factory to lose benefits, it takes a long time to negotiate' (U 6). Thus, the role of unions and arguably the role of employee participation in code compliance is in negotiating working conditions and holding management accountable to its commitments (not least of which being its code commitments to buyers).

It is important to note that when one speaks about power relationships in supplier factories, it is necessary to include the role of AMNEs and their agents in the overall picture. While shifts in the power relationship between workers and managers at the factory level are possible, the role of the AMNE as the ultimate source of power in the industry remains a constant. It is the degree of AMNE influence over its suppliers that first sparked controversy over supplier labour standards and ultimately leads AMNEs to implement code compliance programmes. Keeping this in mind, the position of AMNEs on the role of unions and of employee participation in code compliance management is highly significant. Interviews suggest, however, a high degree of ambiguity among AMNEs in their support for unions. AMNE 2, for example, says, 'Our approach to freedom of association is to say that it will be applied "where permitted by law". We do it [uphold freedom of association] domestically [in the US] because the laws here are much stricter' (AMNE 2). Yet this approach stands in contrast to numerous other code standards such as minimum age of employment, overtime wages, use of PPE and general EHS requirements. In those areas, code requirements are often far higher than local law requirements. Indeed, AMNEs have in a number of instances instituted code standards that exceed legal requirements in supplier countries particularly on such principles as working hours and minimum age.[39] This is a direct result of complaints that supplier countries lacked adequate labour laws or enforcement capabilities. Yet when it comes to the issue of freedom of association, AMNEs typically break from this practice.

In China, AMNE 4 notes that, 'We do not force or encourage the factory to set up a union. It is the factory's choice and workers need to have the freedom to join or not' (AMNE 4). While this is an unambiguous policy, the question of whether or not the workers really do 'have the freedom to join or not' arises. Clearly the most obvious proof that workers have the freedom to join is if a union exists. As long as unions do *not* exist, however, there will be lingering doubts among some critics. Especially as long as most manufacturing countries continue to have relatively low enforcement of international labour rights. This produces an awkward position for AMNEs who have yet to clearly resolve their position on the subject. As AMNE 4 acknowledges, 'Things haven't moved beyond us wondering how much we should get involved with unions.' This challenge is especially pronounced in countries that have little experience with independent labour unions. AMNE 3 observes this situation in China:

> We talk with those in the industry and probably some unions but not in China. I personally have not come across many unionised factories nor union members. I don't think it is common for people to be union members. We have 4,000 to 5,000 factories in China. If anything, workers don't understand what a union is about (AMNE 3).

---

39   See Chapter II for more details on code-of-conduct principles and legislative requirements.

In attempting to resolve this issue, some AMNEs have advocated and assisted in union formation, at least in limited cases. NGO 2 notes an AMNE 9 test case in China wherein AMNE 9 worked directly with one of its suppliers to set up a union.

> AMNE 9 did a test case in helping set up a union in a factory. All workers were involved in the election and 13 people were elected to form a union. However, the challenge was that no one knew how to hold a meeting, etc. for this to get off the ground. So they gave training. This sort of thing can work but it must be in a factory where the existing union co-operates (NGO 2).

As noted above, in many of the factories visited, unions were non-existent. However, in many instances worker organisations existed in the form of worker committees, which, many would argue, are not legitimate worker organisations. Further, given the environment in which numerous AMNEs are operating (e.g. in countries where the right to freedom of association and collective bargaining is not necessarily fully supported), AMNE compliance staff have begun exploring other avenues for workers to have a voice. It should be noted that these avenues in some cases are being established as an alternative to the establishment of trade unions and, for this reason, opinion is divided on the part of workers' groups as to whether the establishment of worker committees is a 'first step' that can be taken in order for workers to fully exercise their rights in the future.

Organisation of workers' committees

Employee participation in the implementation of codes is a necessary component for the long-term success of compliance management. Employees provide a key source of feedback regarding working conditions and (along with management) are one of the principal targets of training and education regarding EHS issues such as the use of PPE. In an environment where there is a noticeable absence of trade union organisations, a key tool of implementing codes within the organisation at the manufacturer (that is, supplier) level has been the creation of workers' committees to facilitate dialogue between workers and management. Workers' committees provide management with feedback about workers' concerns. They may also provide workers with a forum within which to learn about new management initiatives in, for example, the area of EHS. Through workers' committees, some AMNEs and supplier managers have been able to communicate new code compliance initiatives to the wider population of workers, via their worker representatives.

The challenge with workers' committees, however, rests with their electoral processes. Typically, the way that AMNE compliance officers advocate the establishment of such committees is through the election of representatives from the factory floor or of the heads of manufacturing lines. It is envisaged that workers participating in such committee work would do so during company hours and be paid for their participation. As we saw, this is not always the case. In some factories we visited, the committees meet on a more ad hoc basis but, in the more developed factories, committee meetings were scheduled on a regular basis. A supplier factory in Thailand, for example, has a workers' committee, which consists mainly of workers and meets quarterly. While doing work for the committee, members are paid at a rate equivalent to their daily work rate. The members of the committee were selected by the workers through a general election;

the election was based on the suggestions of the Thai Ministry of Labour (THS 5, HR and EHS Officer). In a Sri Lankan supplier factory, on the other hand, the workers' committee meets once a month and members of the committee are representatives from each production line—the secretary of the committee is a machine operator (SL 2, HR Manager).

> All senior managers have to meet with the welfare committee: one person from each production line and each division, approximately 30 in total. The representatives tend to be on the factory floor. There is an open-door policy. There is a hierarchical difference but they are more comfortable than those in the East (SLS 3, HR Manager).

> Even within the AMNE, worker committees have been established. Within AMNE 3 itself three worker committees have been established for workers to send in their complaints. A recent complaint related to it being too cold in the distribution department (AMNE 3).

> Most meetings are not held frequently. It depends on the issue. There is a monthly welfare committee meeting that the HR manager attends (THS 4, HR Manager).

> The workers' committee writes if it has any questions. A recent complaint/request was for a free lunch (SLS 2, Personnel Manager).

Lack of workers' committees

Some suppliers, however, have not organised a workers' committee, opting instead for alternatives, such as EHS committees which include employees selected by management. In other cases, representatives may be selected by staff to help facilitate communication, but do not necessarily have a direct role in policy formation. The issue of selection is an important one to consider if these committees are put forth as examples of 'worker organisations'. A further finding is simply that some managers are not sure what committees exist in their factories, or how they are chosen, which suggests a low-profile role for these committees.

> Not within our current programme do we have working committees for health and safety (RMNE 3).

> There is no union or workers' committee but there is a committee appointed by staff to disseminate information (Worker Interview).

> We have a welfare committee which is the same structure as the EHS committee. I am not sure how it is chosen though (THS 1, HR Manager).

> I think we have a welfare committee but I am not sure who is on it (THS 6, Manager).

Given the controversy regarding the establishment of workers' committees in that they are seen by some as a means of blocking or removing incentives for more effective means of worker representation such as the establishment of trade unions, it is difficult to draw concrete conclusions regarding their absence.

Additional forums for workers

There have been a number of other approaches that have been adopted by supplier factories either at their own instigation or at the suggestion of AMNE compliance officers in an effort to engage managers and workers in dialogue. One of the most interesting examples that we saw while conducting our interviews was that of a Sri Lankan supplier who organises regular feedback sessions with each section of the factory. Reflecting both the typical demographic of apparel employees (that is, young single women) and Sri Lankan family culture, the same Sri Lankan factory organises an annual feedback session with the workers' parents. In this particular factory we were told that these feedback sessions led to a reduction in labour turnover and worker grievances as management implemented changes suggested by workers and their families during these sessions.

> Hold discussions once a month with three people: production assistance, supervisor, worker representatives (nine people—machine operators and helpers) to discuss problems (SLS 1, Production Manager).

> There is no workers' committee but weekly meetings are held in each section. Also there is a parents' get-together once a year where the MD asks them their questions and hears their grievances (SLS 8, Director).

There have been many developments into alternative forums for engaging workers in key decisions within the workplace. These have included 'quality circles' that originated in Japan in the 1970s, to the large 'works councils' movement prevalent in Europe. Originally focusing on such issues as quality control and quality management, such forums may prove effective in implementing the labour, social and ethical standards embraced by CSR and codes. While not the subject of this book, much remains to be done in exploring the dynamics of such worker forums. Our research suggests that the ILO is an appropriate entity in which to conduct further research and analyse developments.

Use of suggestion boxes

A common feature of employee participation programmes that we heard of is the use of a 'suggestion box' which allows employees to provide anonymous feedback to management. In some cases the suggestion box was implemented on the supplier's own initiative; in others, the suggestion box was the idea of agents or the AMNE. The key determinant of the usefulness of the suggestion box is who reads the suggestions and how they are handled. Interviews suggest that when senior management or HR management is involved directly in the feedback process, there is more opportunity for communication and implementation of suggestions.

> We also have a suggestion box. We only put this out a month ago and so far there have been no suggestions. Agent 1 asked us to put it there (THS 6, Manager).

> The owner opens the suggestion box letters and not us. He doesn't tell us what is in the letters. I have heard that some have complained about how the supervisor treats them, that they are too tough. In this case the owner will talk to the supervisor and ask them to be better. I initiated the suggestion box myself about one year ago (THS 2, Assistant Manager).

Open-door policies

Another feature of employee participation that was cited in interviews is the use of 'open-door' policies at some supplier factories. As one Sri Lankan HR manager observes, 'We have an open culture here. There are 17 people in HR and at least five to seven are available each day' (SLS 5, HR Manager). This is reflected in the comments of another Sri Lankan supplier:

> I am open to having workers come to talk to me. My door is always open on Fridays but I have no set schedule. Workers can also come and see the factory manager if they have a problem. If they do have a problem usually they first inform their supervisor who then tells the section head in charge, then the production manager and then the factory manager (SLS 6, HR Manager).

While open-door policies can be a useful supplement to other employee participation programmes—to the degree that doors are truly 'open' and the power distance relationship is such that workers would see management as approachable—there are significant shortcomings that should be considered. Principal among these is that there is no anonymity and little confidentiality for employees going to see a senior manager; if a line worker sees a senior manager to complain about a section manager, it will be clear to all parties concerned which worker has complained. In the absence of additional support mechanisms, the efficacy of an open-door policy can be limited.

5. Feedback, improvement and remediation

a. Information systems

As in other areas of supply chain management, information technology (IT) plays an important role in code compliance management. The need for information systems that allow the tracking of results and enable the decision-making process was mentioned by all apparel MNE interviewees, echoing comments by FMNE managers. Repeatedly AMNE managers stressed that these systems need to be designed, implemented and utilised in such a manner that the information contained in the system is incorporated into decision-making processes. However, as we heard, many of these steps have posed a

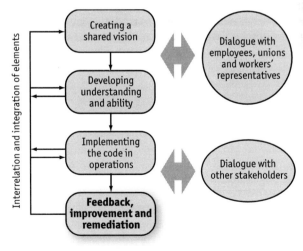

challenge to some companies. In contrast to the brands, our interviews revealed, not surprisingly, that supplier factories tend to rely less on IT and more on informal discussion, that is, on interpersonal relationships, as well as paper record-keeping in some instances. This is reflective of the small to medium scale of industries involved in production, their sophistication and their budgets, although there were some larger suppliers with sophisticated IT systems designed to assist in the management process. These systems are predominantly used to record business statistics, keep track of production results (including productivity and accident rates) and to undertake online bidding, a necessity to compete in the global marketplace.

Evolution of IT systems

IT systems to manage internal and external compliance audits and to track results have evolved alongside the compliance management process itself. However, as AMNE 9 points out,

> Systems strategy is generally poor in this industry. There was rapid growth in the 1980s with international expansion. Therefore our systems were always an afterthought, not well thought out and no strategy. After eight years, they became more of a barrier and a major issue (AMNE 9, Chief Technology Officer).

This evolution is often the result of demand-driven pressures for information by those within the MNE itself. In fact, in some instances the development of IT systems for compliance has been the result of competitive pressures on sourcing/purchasing departments as well as efforts to streamline the overall supply chain management process. AMNE 7 supports the view that systems development is often an afterthought.

> We have recently been talking to other footwear and apparel brands and many of them are installing new ERP [environmental resource planning] systems. This is a major undertaking. The purpose is to integrate order management and invoicing and to track deliveries. We are all beginning to roll this out. A number of them are using SAP systems. I have been talking to FMNE 2 and AMNE 9. But a database is not always the first thing on your agenda (AMNE 7, Director, Codes of Conduct).

The ad hoc development of IT systems in support of compliance is reflected in the variety of systems currently being utilised by firms. Some interviewees have created systems based on well-known platforms such as Oracle, SAP and Access. For a number of reasons including cost and complexity, others are relying on Excel spreadsheets and more manual approaches, for example in the tracking of audits. This can lead to a number of problems including the inability to generate useful information and the cumbersome process of manually inputting information into various documents. As a consequence, we heard that it was difficult to ensure important decisions were made on the basis of the information that was being collected. Notwithstanding the room for improvement, all interviewees regarded their systems as indispensable tools.

> We have a code-of-conduct database on which the actual assessment form can be found. It is some kind of customised Oracle database but it is difficult to change and make it do what we want. Originally it was seen as a static archive but now we need to track certain things and have resorted to manual Excel sheets. Next year, we need to push for a major overhaul (AMNE 7, Director, Codes of Conduct).

What we have here is an Access database that through a cumbersome manual process takes information from our Lotus Notes databases and uploads it to Access (AMNE 4, Compliance Officer).

We are currently using an Excel spreadsheet where we record information of our suppliers and their regulation details (AMNE 8, Compliance Co-ordinator).

Our database is web-based. First it was an Access database, then we had a software company create a web-based system. Now we have historical information. It has been incredible. I can't imagine being without it (AMNE 10, Compliance Director).

Coverage and consistency

Most MNEs have developed systems to track the audits of their suppliers and to help manage the follow-up audit process. One of the difficulties associated with this relates to the global reach of many MNE supply chains. Due to the disparate location of compliance staff and auditors, it is often a challenge to ensure consistency in terms of data gathering and reach of the system itself. This can lead to the situation where information is only collected regionally with limited scope for cross-referencing on a global basis.

Within each region we are tracking this information but we need to do it globally. We track the basic performance measures but these are only gross measures. What we really want to know is how these suppliers are doing. We need to look at people, process and priority and identify our high business and high people suppliers and we need to see our risk with these (AMNE 7, CSR Manager).

We tried to run a report region by region but it did not reflect what the real issue was. The reports we tried to run just did not tell us enough. For example, with minimum wage is it an issue of trainees or just minimum wage? Nuance issues like freedom of association and discrimination are more difficult to get across but all these problems are out there and people are making judgement calls (AMNE 4, Compliance Officer).

The physical distances between field staff and headquarters as well as the need to rely on poorly developed or ineffectual telecommunications systems further complicate accurate data collection. Consequently, we were told that auditors and administrators might find themselves working off-line, inputting information into a system which, by the time it reaches headquarters, is already out of date.

There are challenges with respect to where the inspections take place. The information is currently added off-line but with the new system we want to allow real-time updates (AMNE 9, Chief Technology Officer).

I would say that we input about 12 (audit results) per month. We have no plans to go live with the system. In an ideal world we would have an Oracle database but that costs money and takes time (AMNE 8, Compliance Co-ordinator).

Furthermore, the ability to control information input into the system and ensure consistency of language and terminology, we were told, is directly correlated with the number of people inputting data. The larger the number of people involved, the more the problems of language and misunderstanding become an issue.

> The system was originally designed in a smaller world. Examples of problems include the search capacity. It is difficult to find the database entry of the audit if you take over the factory from someone else. Also there are issues of not understanding what is the real issue, access speed and double documents (AMNE 4, Compliance Officer).

> The challenges with compliance are retrieving data and making it into a common language and the need for subjective responsiveness ratings (AMNE 10, Senior Manager).

Those responsible for the system at headquarters are then faced with the challenge of having to ensure that the system accurately reflects the status quo on a global basis. This means that the issue of replication and synthesis of information from regional databases into global databases is extremely important. Yet, as the quotes below show, this is often the greatest challenge for these systems managers.

> There are problems with replication and synthesis of the database and also it is not a relational database and therefore sorting and reporting is not there. There are challenges in making it work both real time and off-line as it is dependent upon phone connections. Also, from experience we know that information has to be confidential. There is a challenge then in making things real time, say, when a worker has a complaint that has to be noted and investigated. The issue becomes how to treat this complaint until it is investigated because until then it is just an allegation (AMNE 9, Chief Technology Officer).

> The replication process occurs three or four times a day. Within 24 hours we hope that all databases are synchronised. In some countries it may take them up to half an hour. Each pop-up may take five to ten minutes. People will spend a couple of hours each night just making entries (AMNE 4, CSR Manager).

The responses

Some AMNEs have attempted to resolve the issue of consistency of information by creating 'drop-down' text fields for auditors and field staff to utilise in inputting information. The advantage of such texts rests not only with conformity of information gathered and ease of comparability of reports generated but also can lead to reduced effort required in inputting the information. This is an important consideration given the challenges that were mentioned with telecommunications systems. However, interviewees were keen to stress that drop-down boxes should be utilised only in limited circumstances as their advantages are often outweighed by their disadvantages, namely the lack of detail and clarity regarding a particular situation. Where possible, most firms seem to use a combination of drop-down field texts as well as open text fields. Training is then provided on the terminology to be used in the open text fields to ensure consistency.

There are a series of categories and first phrases to choose from and then there is an open field where you type in all the issues found. Over the last few years we have worked to get people to do more in the open field. It is tough to have a template because the situations vary. We don't know enough. We are to some degree out there on our own. What information should we capture? How? (AMNE 4, Manager CSR).

Other solutions include granting limited access to the system, giving only those in compliance or CSR departments the ability to input information and those at head-quarters the ability to change information once it has been input.

> We hold our factory database close within the department so nobody apart from compliance or legal has access. Even individuals only have access to the country in which they monitor because there is sensitive information (AMNE 4, Compliance Manager).

> We have a code-of-conduct database where all assessments and guidelines can be found. It is accessible only to code-of-conduct people (AMNE 7, Compliance Director).

> Access is given to myself (compliance director), auditors and the apparel department; basically anyone in *my* world (AMNE 10, Compliance Director).

Determining, however, just who should have access is difficult and is dependent on the way that CSR or code of conduct responsibilities have been allocated within an organisation. We were told that, while compliance personnel may have access to the compliance database, their access to the purchasing or sourcing database may be limited, resulting in islands of important information that are not necessarily shared between departments.

> Our current system is an Access database; however, it is not supported by our company generally so therefore it is kept separate from the public drives (AMNE 8, Compliance Co-ordinator).

> We have a database-sourcing matrix for both our brands. Our system does not accept a contractor without a specific code. It lists the sourcing manager. You cannot issue a contract without approval . . . It is not a code of conduct matter. It is just for sourcing (AMNE 7, Sourcing Manager).

> Every brand was doing something different. There were islands of information . . . At the moment we can still see where the purchase orders are raised but they are on different systems. Right now the code-of-conduct database is decoupled from sourcing and purchasing. They can look at both but there is no direct linkage. In the future we want two-way communication, that is, a unified system. This is not easy to do because purchase orders are placed through agents and factories subcontract to other companies (AMNE 9, Chief Technology Officer).

One pioneering AMNE is attempting to deal with the above-mentioned challenges, recognising the need to integrate compliance into overall company processes. AMNE 9 is in process of designing and creating a generic holistic system that will link compliance with other functional departments. Their objective in this exercise has not been to create profit but rather to develop a tool to solve an industry-wide problem. It is hoped that this system will allow firms, among other things, to better co-ordinate the activities between purchasing and compliance departments, to plan audits, better assess supplier factory risk and to track the results of corrective action plans (CAPs).

> The basic requirement of this industry is a multi-dimensional product. Most ERP packages have a single product but in this industry you need room to work through the entire supply chain at different levels. For example, you have 10,000 pairs of shoes and you need to refill an order for one pair of shoes, of a particular design and style, in a size three and a half. Other industries create individual items. SAP had to rewrite its entire R3 suites. There were other practices too, such as the way we allocate short product to customers that they had to take into account . . . One frustration is that people don't like to write software. We tried to convince other factories to write software but we couldn't convince them and that's why we decided to build a system. We are building it so that it might have value to other companies (AMNE 9, Chief Technology Officer).

Many of the interviewees reported that the solution to the problems associated with their existing systems rests in the investment of more resources: both financial and staffing. However, such an investment is costly and, as AMNE 7 indicated above, is not always the highest priority for an organisation—particularly for supplier factories. The current trend, however, appears to be for AMNEs to develop their systems while simultaneously encouraging their suppliers to develop a better information infrastructure. Analysis of the results of this encouragement remains a matter for future study.

b. Internal monitoring: internal factory audits

The effect of buyers' codes and buyers' audits on suppliers appears to be their increased management of code issues. The more proactive among suppliers are taking measures to ensure they pass buyer audits. In addition, the involvement of suppliers in the CAP creation and implementation process appears to be further supporting the development of compliance management skills and practices among manufacturers.

> We evaluate ourselves and hold a meeting every Friday and give ourselves a score. The self-evaluation is based on the codes. We started the self-evaluation because of all the AMNE 1 comments, which were true. On the computer, for example, AMNE 1's compliance officer showed 20 people dying in China because of electricity problems (THS 1, HR Manager).

> We have a daily meeting for 15 minutes but the weekly group meeting lasts half an hour to an hour. A group consists of one production line. The short meetings are more like a reminder. The real meeting is separate from the 15-minute daily meetings which inform workers of anything they need to do, problems with garments, PPE and needle guards, etc. Weekly meeting—top management and line management—is work oriented and discusses things like compliance, safety, production and food. Monthly meetings—whole factory—talk about things like quality of life. All the workers meet with the manager and HR. It gets broken down into different groups. The owner discusses things like how to plan savings, prevent danger, and family planning (THS 7, Operations Control).

As compliance management skills develop there is also an increasingly formal and professional approach within the factories to managing EHS and labour issues. This is significant given that many of the manufacturers in the apparel industry are SMEs, which, especially in developing countries, often lack such formal management systems.

> We have a EHS committee in the factory as per Thai law. We have 11 people. One president, four supervisors, five operating workers and one EHS officer. It meets once a month. People from each of the departments discuss the problems of accidents and PPE—why workers don't want to use masks and gloves [. . .] There is a monthly welfare committee meeting that the HR manager attends (THS 1, HR Manager).

Many of the management approaches developed in the factories are based on the MNE recommendations provided during audits, the development of CAPs and general training. It is important to emphasise, however, that MNEs are not describing in detail how factories should manage compliance issues. Rather, it is the factories themselves who are learning by doing and developing compliance management systems on their own.

> I got a lot of evaluations, audit forms and books from FMNE 2 and AMNE 1 and summarised them to a six-page checklist for each factory and came up with my own CAPs. We started doing our own audits (THS 4, Production Manager).

> We are still working on our EHS records [. . .] I am making up our records based on the lectures I attended and have also asked my friend (THS 6, EHS Officer).

A key feature of developing internal monitoring capacity is the specialised training of managers. Numerous interviews suggest the emergence of EHS managers within factories. These managers benefit both from MNE interaction as well as from local government-sponsored training programmes, where available.

> The EHS officer was trained for 30 days and is at what is known as the professional level. We have six EHS people in this factory: one at the professional level and five at the supervisor level. They are trained by the Ministry of Labour (THS 2, Owner).

Despite the emergence of specially trained EHS managers, these managers are not necessarily serving as *dedicated* EHS officers; that is, their EHS responsibilities are not their only responsibilities. Having various operational managers trained in EHS duties can help to spread knowledge of EHS issues and practices throughout the factory. Also, in SMEs with limited management staff, it is commonplace for managers to wear 'more than one hat' (that is, serve in more than one capacity). These things said, however, there may be problems associated with the lack of a full-time dedicated EHS officer, especially during peak operating conditions when operational duties may distract a manager from his or her EHS duties. In a worst-case scenario, titles such as 'EHS officer' may be distributed in a superficial 'window dressing' way to a manager who already has full-time responsibilities. It is more likely, however, that a dedicated EHS manager whose job evaluation is based *primarily* on EHS functions will properly manage these issues.

Illustrating the above point, the owner of a supplier in Thailand says, 'Both myself and the assistant manager go on the [code compliance] audits. The EHS officer doesn't go with the auditor very often as this person reports to me.' When asked, wouldn't it be helpful for the EHS officer to also accompany the auditor, the owner replies, 'Yes, but he doesn't because he is the supervisor of the washing department and it takes up too much of his time to do this, especially in peak season when there are many audits' (THS 2, Owner).

c. Verification: External factory audits

The practice of conducting code compliance audits on suppliers appears to be widespread and increasingly commonplace among AMNEs. These audits are 'external' in that representatives external to the supplier factory itself conduct them. They should be distinguished from third-party audits, which are discussed later in this section. Supplier interviews suggest that looking at code compliance issues is becoming a standard function of any factory visit by a buyer, or buyer representative to a supplier factory. In the experience of an HR manager from a Thai factory, for example, 'Any buyer who comes in, focuses on worker EHS' (THS 6).

There is, however, no evidence that all factories in the supply chain are being audited. Excluded factories can include subcontractors and component manufacturers. Agent 3, for example, acknowledges, 'We audit the actual manufactures but not components or trim' (Agent 3).

Methodology of the external audit

The audit process of MNE and third parties typically includes three main aspects: a physical inspection (or factory 'walk-through'), a documentation inspection and interviews with workers. Throughout the process, factory management is consulted, questioned and given feedback. A Thai factory owner explains the process at his plant: 'there is an introductory meeting followed by a tour of the factory. They ask for documentation such as timecards, payroll and factory rules' (THS 2, Owner). Another Thai manager finds the same procedure at his factory: 'normally they do a documentation check first, walk through the factory and interview' (THS 7, Operations Control).

Typically, external audits are conducted by one to two auditors depending on the size of the factory. When working in teams of two or more, the auditors will normally divide the various tasks (physical inspection, documentation and interviews), assigning specialists in each area to carry out the function. Agent 3 describes its audit office: 'we have a team of 15 people that has a dual role—both clerical and operational.' It is out of this team of 15 people that Agent 3 will send auditors, one or two at a time, to individual factories. Agent 3 goes on to point out the three main objectives of the audit. 'In doing audits there are three things to consider: findings, CAPs and time frames.' The section below looks at the methodology of the audit process itself, the process by which findings are produced. This process is explained by examining in turn each step in the process, the physical inspection, the documentation inspection and the interviews. CAPs, which include time-frames for remediation, are examined on pages 217-19.

The time required to conduct a factory audit varies in relation to who is doing the auditing (which determines the thoroughness of the audit and how many members of the audit team there are) and the size of the facilities being audited. Interviews with auditors suggest an average of around two labour days per audit. According to AMNE 7, the audit takes 'one full day with two auditors or two days for a larger factory that produces for major brands'. Agent 1 says, 'The documents are prepared and the compliance audit takes a minimum of two days.' AMNE 4 states that, 'The audits take two man days including transportation.' This time frame is echoed by Agent 3 who says, 'The audits take two man days in a factory.' It is the general impression of ILO researchers, however, that MNE managers and auditors may be exaggerating the time spent on audits. Certainly the impression of factory management is that audits are conducted in not between one to two days, rather between half to one day.

> An audit takes half a day. They walk around, interview managers and some workers, see the payroll (THS 6, Manager).

> It depends on the brand—half to one day is the longest (HS 3, HR Manager).

> The audits take about half a day, about four to six hours (S 7, Operations Control).

A key to compliance auditing is the quantification and specification of the sometimes subjective or otherwise generalised criteria found in a code of conduct. As Chapter II explains more fully, detailed auditing guidelines form a key part of the auditing process. RMNE 7, for example, says, 'We have a procedures document, about 60 pages long, talking about things such as sample size, communication, employee interview, etc.'. The goal of these guidelines is to specify both the methodology of the audit and *objective* criteria by which to judge non-compliance. Significantly, however, only some factories ever receive a copy of the auditing guidelines from the MNE. For those factories that do not, this may undermine their ability to meet code standards. A possible explanation for this is the proprietary nature of MNE guidelines, which some MNEs treat as a confidential internal document. In any case, we were told by some AMNEs that it should not be too difficult for the factories to 'reverse engineer' the guidelines based on observance of audits and audit feedback. Nonetheless, we think it might be more helpful to give all the factories a copy of such guidelines, as we were told code-of-conduct issues are not considered to be competitive issues.

The 'walk-through' or physical inspection of the factory is one of the three key parts of an audit. The physical inspection is used to examine such items as: emergency exits, sanitary conditions in toilet and dining facilities, the use of PPE among workers on the shop floor, and safety guards on machinery, among other things. Typically the auditor is accompanied by a factory manager (either EHS or HR manager, or sometimes senior management/owner) during the tour through the factory. During the walk-through the auditor may point out items of concern that may or may not be violations of the code.

> They make some comments and observations but do not necessarily record every violation. During the walk-through they have interaction on how to improve. Sometimes the auditor gives me a test to see how I check fire equipment. At the end of the audit day there is a briefing (THS 7, Operations Control).

> I did the factory walk-through with the auditor; they marked non-compliant things and then we talked on how to improve (THS 6, EHS Officer).

> During the walk-through it will be the HR person that accompanies the auditor and the EHS officer or sometimes the compliance manager and the EHS officer (THS 7, Operations Control).

Separate from the physical inspection is an audit of documentation relating to, among other things, payroll, employee records and EHS-related documentation. Due to the large number of employees at a typical apparel factory, the documentation audit is confined to a relatively small random sample. In the case of follow-up audits, the sample may not be random; rather, it may focus specifically on records that raised the suspicion of the auditor during a previous audit.

> From the documentation check, it will be auditor, the HR person and her assistant who are involved. The auditor looks at the employee records, salary, timecards and makes copies—a page or two go in the report (THS 7, Operations Control).

Interviews suggest, however, that auditors do not always include all documentation in their inspections. As one EHS officer for a factory in Thailand reports, 'The EHS inspector did not ask for a report or any documentation—just did a visual inspection. The auditors only ask for product reports and not for EHS records' (THS 6).

The third key facet of the audit process is worker interviews. This stage in the audit allows workers to provide direct feedback about conditions within the factory. Such employee feedback is important for supplementing and corroborating the physical inspection, documentation and interviews with management. Inconsistencies between worker interviews and other facets of the audit can lead to a more in-depth audit of the facilities. In addition to providing a 'check' for other aspects of the audit, worker interviews are important in that they allow workers to provide critical feedback and raise issues that may have been overlooked by auditors.

> We have an interview with 12 workers. If they give questionable answers we take another 12. The interview is conducted outside of management. The workers are chosen randomly, from all departments and we use local people to do the interview (Agent 1).

Each AMNE has its own interview methodology. Depending on the methodology, workers are either chosen at random, or based on certain characteristics. These characteristics can include: gender, ethnic group, length of time with the company, position (e.g. line supervisor or worker), production area or youthful appearance. In addition, auditors may choose specific employees whose timecards or personnel records raise questions.

In some cases, factory management appears to be actively involved in selecting workers for interviews. An HR manager in Thailand explains that, 'Some buyers allow me to pick out the workers because they don't want to interrupt the production process' (THS 3, HR Manager). In Sri Lanka, a factory worker observed that, 'When workers are interviewed, the managers choose the workers and tell them what to say.' Such practices may undermine or eliminate the employee's sense of confidentiality during the interview. The result can be less than candid replies from workers about conditions within the factory.

Auditor interviews with workers can be further complicated by other sociocultural factors—for example, gender ethnicity and language—which lead to communication barriers. These factors lead to an increased risk of employees either saying nothing at all, or simply saying what they think they are *supposed* to say, as opposed to what they actually think or know about factory conditions. This situation undermines the reliability of fact-gathering by the auditors.

AMNEs are trying to overcome these sociocultural factors that can inhibit worker interviews. Accordingly, some auditors are taking more innovative approaches to put workers at ease during interviews, to improve communication and to maximise assurance that there will be no retribution from management for criticising operational practices. These approaches include, for example, the practice of Agent 1 referred to above, of using local people to conduct the interviews. Auditing specialists such as NGO 9 have emphasised the need to use interviewers who share similar demographic characteristics as the workers being interviewed (e.g. ethnicity, gender, age, etc.). Agent 1 also recognises the benefits of matching the gender of interviewers to inter-viewees, claiming that, 'Women talking to women, you can get more truth.' Ensuring confidentiality during the interview, as well as the selection process, is also a key ingredient to assuring workers that they can speak freely and critically of factory operations. The quotes below from an AMNE and a factory manager indicate these various approaches to worker interviews:

> There is this strange scenario in China where workers don't talk a lot so we try to break the barriers. The interviews are all conducted in a separate room. There is an equal split of male and female compliance officers. Sometimes individual interviews are conducted, sometimes group interviews (AMNE 4).

> The interviews take place in a meeting room on site. The HR manager requests for the employee to go to be interviewed but the auditor doesn't allow [the HR manager] to be in that room or near that area (THS 7, Operations Control).

In addition to the factors highlighted above, there is a further factor that may sometimes impede a worker's candidness during an interview. Without sufficient assurance to the contrary, a worker may also believe that, by reporting incidents of non-compliance, she is jeopardising her own job, as well as the jobs of her colleagues, by risking the cancellation of orders and the consequential closure of the factory. This belief can be supported by two practices of which workers may be aware. The first is publicised incidents of factories failing compliance audits and subsequently being dropped from major buyers' supply chains. The second is an explanation of the audit process from factory management, which may portray the audit as a test to be passed or else orders will be cancelled and jobs lost. This situation cuts to the core of the whole practice of auditing: if there are no sanctions for non-compliance, then auditing has little real meaning or material impact. However, if orders are cut to a non-compliant factory, the factory may be forced to shut down, and the now unemployed workers are likely to be worse off than before. Clearly this is a dilemma, but one that appears to be increasingly addressed by buyers and auditors. As discussed in Section 5.b above, there is an increasing emphasis on dialogue and remediation in the compliance process. Auditing is still seen as a test, but one which increasingly highlights opportunities for improvement, rather than grounds for the termination of orders.

Note also that the issue of whether factory management should communicate with workers on the fact that audits will be held is open to criticism from a number of perspectives. If management does not explain the meaning and potential consequences of the audit, they can be criticised for not communicating with the workers. If, on the other hand, management explains exactly what the auditors are doing and the consequences of non-compliance, then management may be criticised for 'priming' workers to give the 'correct' answers to auditors' questions.

Preliminary audits

In addition to auditing existing suppliers, some AMNEs are also conducting preliminary audits of *potential* suppliers. This code compliance pre-evaluation appears to be becoming an integrated part of the initial supplier selection process in a number of pioneering AMNES. As AMNE 5 explains, 'An introductory visit is carried out and an evaluation report is conducted. It looks at price, capacity, quality and other brands the factory is supplying to, in addition to the code' (AMNE 5). This experience is also reported by suppliers. In Cambodia, for example, a manufacturer says, 'AMNE 7 did a check of facilities, labour compliance, etc., *before* any orders were placed' (CAS 2, Deputy GM, emphasis added). AMNE 7 confirms that this is a standard policy applied to all potential suppliers. 'For new factories we require compliance before any orders would be placed' (AMNE 7). However, AMNE 7 does not conduct pre-approval audits for indirectly sourced goods. '[For indirect sourcing] there is no pre-approval as it is too difficult' (AMNE 7). As auditing and code compliance becomes more mainstream, the focus of compliance management may shift more towards preliminary audits. Factories having ongoing business with code companies have a higher awareness of, and compliance with, code issues. As a result the risk profile of suppliers shifts such that it is new suppliers, or suppliers without a long history of supplying to the major brands, that represent the greatest risk of non-compliance. In AMNE 4's experience,

> Most violations occur with new factories that haven't worked for us before. This is revealed in the pre-evaluation. They pay below minimum wage. Often they don't even know about minimum wage. And they always hold up part of the workers' wages as 'savings' (AMNE 4).

In addition, another key factor supporting a shift towards preliminary audits relates to the internal corporate politics of the AMNE. Simply put, it is far easier for MNE CSR managers to exclude a new supplier from the supply chain than it is to eliminate an existing supplier, since the latter would be more likely to spark conflicts with operations or purchasing departments within the AMNE.

Use of third-party auditors

A significant feature of emerging compliance management programmes is the use of third-party auditors. Most MNEs in the apparel industry are now contracting auditing work out to various types of third-party auditors for at least some of their suppliers. An important feature of third-party auditing is the added margin of credibility it provides to external stakeholders. As AMNE 3 acknowledges, 'We needed to have independent verification for people on the outside.' However, the issue of credibility is not the only factor influencing the use of external auditors. In addition to the issue of credibility, the choice between using third parties or in-house staff appears to be based on the particular requirements of the factory location—as well as the internal capabilities of the MNE. In other words it is a question of feasibility. But it is also a question, at least indirectly, of cost, since third-party auditors are usually more expensive than in-house auditors. As a result of these factors, in many instances both in-house and third-party auditors are used, depending on the circumstances of the AMNE and the factory being audited. AMNE 3 and AMNE 7, for example, both use a mixture of in-house audit teams and external parties:

> Forty per cent is done in-house and 60% by third party. The procedures are identical. We currently have two multi-country, third-party auditors, one focusing on an individual country and another one coming on stream. They are [TPA 3, TPA 1, O 3 and TPA 6], which is specific to Guangzhou. O 8 is currently getting up to speed. We established a pilot programme with O 3 (AMNE 3).

> AMNE 3 has its own audit for factories and we also use third-party audits. The determination of in-house audit or third-party audit is based on the location. In-house is done in the US, China and Taiwan [China]. In other countries we use third parties. In China we also do third-party audits (AMNE 3).

> It was decided to have a bi-programme. On direct sourcing we decided to have our own people to go into factories. On indirect sourcing we saw that it was too big and needed external people (AMNE 7).

When deciding on which external auditor to use, again factors such as local capacity often play a decisive role. Those firms that are emerging as leading players in social auditing still have significant gaps in their capacity in certain countries. As a result, MNEs typically will use several different external auditors. AMNE 7, for instance, uses at least three different external auditors, the choice of which is based on their relative capacities in a given country.

Some interviews suggest a perceived quality difference between in-house and external auditors, with a preference for the former. It is the perception of MNE staff that the MNE in-house auditors provide a higher-quality audit. Suppliers echo this sentiment, often indicating that the in-house auditors usually have far more experience in the industry and are thus better suited not only in recognising processes within the factory, but also in recommending practical solutions. The general perception that emerges is that in-house auditors are seen more as an extension of the MNE's supplier development functions (which include, for example, issues of quality) while external auditors come across more as policing agents.

> The buyer auditors have real practical experience. They have been in factories before, worked in production or even hold a degree in labour law. The third-party auditors seem very young, like fresh college graduates as if they have an accounting degree as opposed to management or operations. Thus they go by the book (THS 7, Operations Control).

> Buyer auditors are more experienced while third-party auditors are by the book. They don't look beyond their checklist but it also depends on the individual auditor. The third-party monitor acts like a policeman. As if it is

> more like a fault-finding mission. Buyer auditors are more helpful. They come and help us resolve our problems such as with EHS equipment; they gave us a list of sellers. They are more like a mentor (THS 7, HR Manager).

Despite this perceived difference in the quality of the auditors, there does not appear to be any objection from agents or manufacturers to the *principle* of third-party auditing. Indeed, in some instances, these parties may themselves recommend the use of third-party auditors. As Agent 1 declares:

> Today everybody has codes but their expectations for enforcement are different. We always tell them to get an independent third party to monitor us because we in effect are their employee (Agent 1).

MNEs, on the other hand, may have some fundamental reservations about third-party auditing. Principal among these is the issue of control. MNEs must check the work of third-party monitors in a way that would not be necessary for in-house monitors.

Autonomy of CSR departments and the auditing function: a conflict of interest?

In any auditing or verification programme, whether financial or social, efforts must be made to avoid conflicts of interest, and even the appearance of conflicts of interest. Following the Enron and Arthur Andersen scandals in the United States in the early 2000s, it is widely understood that there is a potential for conflicts of interest between auditing departments (whether internal or external) and other departments within a firm. A key challenge therefore is providing auditors with a sufficient degree of autonomy, such that they may accurately report, as per the auditing guidelines, without fear of penalty. For external auditors, this means that any other business of the auditing firm with the client does not act to influence audit results. For internal auditors, this means that the corporate management of the MNE provide the internal CSR department with sufficient autonomy in relation to the business operations units (e.g. purchasing or merchandising). Providing the right mix of integration and autonomy is a challenge. As AMNE 2 observes, 'There is a level of independence that monitoring must have, even though you need it integrated, and this is a challenge' (AMNE 2). Indeed some critics in organised labour question the entire concept of using private, for-profit, auditors to verify a compliance programme.

> The lessons of Enron are the same here [with codes]. The idea that you will have someone paid from the company and auditing it . . . A conflict of interest exists. Internal monitors look at the private business of the company. At the end of the day they are interested in the bottom line, not meeting the standards. For this reason, public laws are required (U 8).

Frequency of audits and follow-up audits

The AMNEs interviewed tend to audit their entire supply base every one to two years; typically in a two-year cycle, half of the supply base will be audited the first year and the second half the second year. Of those factories being audited, reports indicate that they are being audited at least once per year, by at least one of their major clients. In some cases they are being audited much more frequently by multiple buyers. The common frequency of visits reported by suppliers, MNEs and agents was quarterly.

> We get audited three or four times per year (CAS 2, Deputy General Manager).

> We conduct audits in China, Taiwan [China], Philippines and Indonesia every three to four months. We also audit in Thailand, Malaysia, the Republic of Korea, Hong Kong [China], Macao, Sri Lanka and India (Agent 3).

> Audits are conducted at least once a year per buyer but exactly how many times, I cannot tell you (THS 3, Assistant Manager).

> AMNE 1 audit us about once every two to three months. They came in about two years ago with a low-volume order. AMNE 4 comes here more often, sometimes even once a month. They started here about five years ago (THS 5, HR and EHS Officer).

A crucial part of the auditing process is the corrective action plan (CAP), discussed in more detail in Section 5.d. As part of the auditing process, opportunities for improvement are identified and factories are given a defined period of time to make the necessary improvements. Therefore an important aspect of auditing is the 'follow-up' audit, designed to measure compliance or progress made towards compliance. As TPA 6 in Cambodia explains, 'We do an initial report and visit 60 days later to see how they are doing and whether there are new issues.' From the perspective of an HR manager at a factory in Sri Lanka, continuous periodic follow-up is an integral part of the auditing process: 'Brands undertake factory evaluation and constantly follow up (approximately three months later)' (SLS 6). AMNE 4 adds a more nuanced understanding to the frequency of follow-up audits. The firm acknowledges that the frequency of the follow-up depends on the particular non-compliant practice identified during the initial audit.

> Two evaluations are carried out as well as one follow-up each year, for all factories. The follow-up depends on the issue identified. For example, if it is a health and safety problem, the follow-up visit will be conducted in a relatively short period of time. If it is a wages or overtime issue, it will be scheduled further out (AMNE 4).

The relatively high frequency of follow-up audits puts an emphasis on the auditing process as more of a continuous improvement process rather than a mere policing action. As discussed in Section 5.d below, the audit process is increasingly becoming a development process rather than a pass or fail testing procedure. This is reflected in views held by suppliers about follow-up audits:

> AMNE 10 did some of the first audits. There were about eight or nine of them done by [TPA 6]. We saw more of a continuous improvement with these audits. The audits were like follow-up audits. They gave back comments and checked if we followed through or not (THS 7, Operations Control).

Of possible concern to the industry is the issue of overlapping audits. While some factories in the supply chain may not be the subject of any audits, others are the subject of numerous and overlapping audits, typically by firms with similar if not identical code standards.

> Auditors come in every two to three months for AMNE 4 and RMNE 3 and occasionally O 16, usually from the importers too such as Agent 1 and other third-party auditors like [TPA 6] and [TPA 3]. There are a lot of people here. It's just like a market here (THS 6, Manager).

> One brand comes once a quarter. Last month five brands came in. On average, though, one brand comes in once a quarter (THS 3, HR Manager).

Another area of concern is the quality of the follow-up audits. Our research indicates that the quality of the follow-up audits can vary significantly. Of special concern are low-quality follow-up audits wherein 'proof' of compliance can be as simple as a faxed letter or photo from the supplier which purports to show that corrective action has been taken. Such 'evidence' is often inadequate, particularly when it comes to less tangible issues such as the right to freedom of association or discrimination.

Announced versus unannounced audits

Factory audits vary in whether they are announced (the factory receives prior notification of an upcoming audit) or unannounced (a surprise audit with no prior notification). Announced audits are sometimes criticised because they allow the subject factory to make 'temporary fixes' to operating conditions for the period of the audit. Some key aspects of EHS, for instance, are particularly susceptible to temporary fixes. Unlocking emergency exits, removing obstructions from passageways and fire-fighting equipment, and reminding workers to use PPE, are all examples of 'quick fixes' that may be employed to meet code compliance. However, to the extent to which these beneficial alterations fail to become regular factory practice, the use of announced audits fails to promote code compliance.

> Brands don't tell unions that they are coming but management tells the workers. They don't inform the workers directly but if you see a supervisor running around, cleaning things up, you can figure out that there is an audit (U 6).

> We are told about the audits about one month in advance. Normally, if the auditors are from abroad we will have at least two weeks' notice but if they are local, from the company, then one week. During our weekly meeting, we make an announcement. All the managers are told and we expect them to go back and tell the section chiefs and employees so that everybody knows. We expect them to co-operate, to make the place nice to see visually. We also want them to understand and consistently act according to the code (THS 7, Operations Control).

Despite their inherent weaknesses, announced audits may still play an important role in compliance management. They may, for example, be useful for factories new to the supply chain and receiving their first audit. Agent 1 indicates that, as a rule, 'the first audit is always announced' (Agent 1). Since many of the factories new to compliance management are particularly susceptible to failing a surprise audit, we were told by some AMNEs that it may be beneficial to ease them into the process with announced audits at first, to be subsequently followed by unannounced audits. This accords with the view of auditing as a learning/development process rather than a policing process (see Section 5.d below). As the observation below indicates, this step-by-step approach appears to be the situation with at least some factories:

> Previously we would get one to two weeks' notice in advance of an audit but now they are surprise visits because we have developed enough. I would tell the workers an audit was coming up via the PA system. I would tell them to inform them, to keep things tidy and general details about who was coming and why (THS 5, HR and EHS Officer).

However, a number of AMNEs pointed out that, in order to assure that compliance is an ongoing reality within factories, rather than only a temporary feature during an audit, unannounced or surprise audits must play some role in the auditing process. As an assistant manager for a Thai factory indicates, this is the practice for at least some buyers with at least some of their supplier factories: 'Sometimes they come here with their merchandiser or sales team and they go and look around. She then marks us and give us points even if the audit is not scheduled' (THS 3, Assistant Manager). However, a leading certification organisation insists that the practice of announced audits remains a controversial issue for some buyers: 'The only way that spot checks are done is with NGO 6. Some buyers, however, don't allow this and we have to give 24 hours' notice. This is a touchy issue' (TPA 3).

The current trend in announced versus unannounced audits suggests that initial audits are almost always announced and, as factories develop their ability to comply with code standards, the audits begin to become increasingly unannounced. This pattern conforms to findings elsewhere in this book that suggest the entire auditing and compliance management process is not intended as a strict 'comply or die' programme. Rather, this pattern of beginning with announced audits and later moving towards unannounced audits conforms to the model of compliance management as a long-term development programme.

Timing of audits

The timing of audits can influence certain findings. For example, we were told that, in the middle of the fourth-quarter rush, there may be blockages in the hallway created by extra inventory. Since the lack of compliance is only temporary (lasting a matter of days), some factory managers, and indeed some buyers, do not always consider it a serious issue.

> Last month AMNE 4 audited us and said that the factory was packed. They gave us a corrective action order asking us to find a storeroom to keep our products. But sometimes when the goods are shipped, the factory is empty and if the auditors come a day later, they wouldn't tell us to get a storeroom (THS 6, Manager).

> There is limited space during peak seasons and things come out of the lines but it's not a serious issue for the buyers (THS 3, HR Manager).

This attitude is understandable; however it remains flawed. Specifics of code compliance, especially those relating to EHS, are like seatbelts in a car: to gain the desired safety benefit, you need to employ them all of the time and not just most of the time. If specific standards, such as clear hallways and exit ways are necessary for fire safety, then they are necessary every day of the year, and not just *most* days of the year. There is no law of nature that says a fire or other health hazard cannot occur the few times a year that the factory is not in compliance.

This situation emphasises the ongoing need to generate deeper understanding among suppliers of the purpose of certain standards, as well as the need for buyers and auditors to consider seasonality issues when conducting auditing. Rather than avoiding audits during the busy high seasons, that is probably when they are needed the most. If a supplier is capable of maintaining compliance during peak operating conditions, then it is more likely it will remain in compliance during the less stressful off-peak periods.

Need for uniform standards, conflicts among standards and sharing of information among suppliers

From our research, it is clear that most AMNE codes have many principles in common and address many of the same substantive issues. As a supplier from Guatemala remarks, 'Most guidelines and requirements are the same. There are maybe 5 to 7% of differences' (GS 2, Personnel Manager). AMNE 2 echoes this point, following a study of other industry codes: 'The benchmarking analysis exercise told us that essentially all codes look the same at the end of the day' (AMNE 2). Even though there are strong similarities between codes, there are some people who still contend that there are grounds for consolidating codes into fewer, broader-based industry codes. One US supplier contends that the sheer number of codes can lead to confusion at the supplier level:

> I think the code of conduct is a good thing to have. I just wish we had every customer with one code. Now we have code-of-conduct battles—who can make a bigger poster. There is hardly any difference between them, only the logo. You end up with so many posters on the wall that the workers don't read them (USS 5, Compliance Officer).

However, what must be remembered is that the similarity between codes does not mean all codes are identical, nor does it mean that the auditing rules of each AMNE are identical. Indeed they are not and these inconsistencies can lead to confusion, frustration and obstacles for suppliers.

> It is not so much that the codes are different, but that the unwritten things keep changing. Each brand claims to have the best code. Some focus on factory safety such as health and safety. This can happen without justification. I have a corporate safety manager in Pennsylvania. OMNE I requires us to train 20% of workers in first aid but, I ask you, what rule book does this come from? Also, with fire extinguisher training, supervisors and mechanics get training here, but I do not want all our operators having training. We can't match it up to US international standards. We are constantly in correspondence with the brands. We back up our positions. A lot of times they will agree with us. This is noted in the file and we go through the same thing the following year on the next audit (HS I, Manager).

The inconsistencies at the detailed level of compliance management are recognised by some AMNEs although they are perceived as being minor in nature. For example, the director of AMNE 7's code of conduct observes:

The code itself does not need fine-tuning because this is exactly what we are doing. When we say freedom of association or working hours, we need to know how this translates into practice. Most companies, NGOs and monitors think that codes are 95% consistent and in agreement in language. What we need to know now is how does this play out at the factory level. We need transparency (AMNE 7).

The interviews suggest a need for uniform standards throughout the apparel industry, including both the standards of conduct in the codes themselves as well as the standards or methodology of the auditing process. Greater uniformity of standards would better facilitate communication and sharing of information between purchasing firms within the industry. It would also reduce occasional conflicts between standards that can result in confusion or redundant measures at the manufacturer level. As Agent I explains:

We need some sort of harmonisation in terms of standards. They [the factories] are bombarded with different audits. We need to join hands and start to get serious about helping the factories. We need one core organisation that researched the law and offered training programmes to compliance managers. Then everybody would be dancing to the same tune (Agent I).

This view appears to have support among a cross-section of AMNEs as well as labour advocacy groups. A leading US certification body observes that, 'At present, the goal is to make sure that within the monitoring industry there are enough standards' and goes on to argue that, 'There needs to be more standardisation, something akin to CPA [certified public accountant]' (TPA 3). AMNE 2 shares a similar viewpoint, saying that, 'Something that would be wonderful would be to get industry partnership. In apparel retail everything is proprietary but this isn't about the product anymore.' Yet one apparent obstacle, or perceived obstacle, to industry partnership on this issue is the question of anti-trust compliance. Several interviews mention compliance with US anti-trust laws as a significant impediment to intra-industry information sharing. As NGO 2 observes:

An FMNE 2-based representative in China suggested a common database for disapproval with the idea being to loosen up resources so that companies would then be free to explore other relational approaches. They suggested that we could fund the database and members could contribute. The problem is anti-trust issues in the US (NGO 2).

As a result what we saw was that the practice of information sharing about specific factories between buyers remains largely inconsistent, intermittent and informal. There is virtually no sharing of information at the headquarters level of the AMNE (apart from meetings at conferences, etc.); rather, what limited and informal sharing there is takes place at the level of AMNE field representatives. An AMNE 4 field representative, for example, says that he and other AMNE representatives 'regularly meet, discuss and share experiences'; nevertheless he admits, 'I don't tell my management about this because legal would not allow it.' AMNE 4 goes on to emphasise the informality and inconsistency of information sharing, explaining that, 'I have met informally with AMNE I and RMNE 3. At this moment we still don't share factory information. It isn't shared between sections in AMNE 4 either. This is a matter for our director.' Meanwhile a representative from AMNE 1, which is subject to a different legal environment, says, 'Sure, I tell FMNE 2 and AMNE 4. Why not?' These statements all reflect a low-level confusion about whether anti-trust laws would preclude co-operation in the area of supplier labour standards. Some have argued that the legal departments of the AMNEs have to date been too cautious in their approach to this subject. They point to other industry standards such as QS9000 for the United States auto industry and state that these illustrate that there is room for co-operation on standard setting within an industry that does not amount to illicit collusion.

Despite the hesitance instilled by anti-trust concerns, there are some nascent acts of industry co-operation that suggest that uniform management of standards may emerge in the future. AMNE 5, for instance, indicates that 'Compliance teams for FMNE 2, AMNE 4 and AMNE 5 meet to discuss differing standards in an effort to reduce confusion'. NGOs and others can play a significant facilitating role in this process. As AMNE 7 explains,

> In relation to communication with other brands, NGO 2 has set up a buyers' compliance group which meets in Hong Kong (China) about four to six times per year to discuss issues relating to compliance in China primarily. We talk about issues we have in common, how we can leverage and how we can think creatively to create training programmes. This is very useful. We also pick up the phones and talk to each other. For example, if a factory has been failed by one brand and [our company] comes in and assesses it and it passes, we call to find out why. In this example the previous failure was due to a subcontractor (AMNE 7).

Co-operation of this nature is beneficial for all in this industry, particularly for those AMNEs that are serious about developing effective compliance programmes. As such, we would hope to continue to see more examples of similar co-operation in years to come.

d. Feedback, improvement and remediation

Feedback

The auditing process has opened entirely new relationships in the dialogue between manufacturers and buyers, and, in limited situations, between workers and factory management as well as workers and AMNE management. Interviews suggest that feedback is growing in both the frequency of communications and the depth of issues discussed. In some cases the audit process and the buyers' new purchasing conditions have enhanced the negotiating position of organised labour in the apparel sector. As a union representative in Cambodia explains, 'Some factories are very afraid of buyers and therefore to threaten to contact them is a "big stick" ' (U 3). Thus, as critics accurately point out, while audits in and of themselves may not catch every questionable practice, the position of buyers as enforcers of new labour practices can empower local unions. A representative from another union in Cambodia highlights the importance of the buyers' new position, saying that, 'Buyers play an important role in getting conditions to improve. They [the unions] threaten them with letters and calls to the US and the ILO' (U 1).

This development in the dialogue process, however, does not necessarily suggest any increased hostility in labour management negotiations. On the contrary, apart from some extreme and early examples of factory closings, failure to comply with codes is increasingly being met with more progressive remediation practices according to some people we interviewed. Audits are increasingly envisioned by AMNE representatives to be about long-term supplier development, and less about short-term policing. According to NGO 2, this is a welcome evolution in auditing practice, which should yield more results over time.

> Once a face becomes familiar, they [the auditor] get more information. Auditing cannot be viewed as an end itself. Once it is viewed as a relationship, where you can negotiate advances over time and there are communication efforts, a business relationship, then changes can be made (NGO 2).

'Comply or die' versus remediation

This long-term development method is necessary to overcome a stark 'comply or die' approach that can actually be counterproductive. The 'comply or die' approach is the idea that factories will be eliminated from a supply chain if they fail to meet code standards during even a single inspection. As a Thai manufacturer explains, 'RMNE 3 was first. The people came from [TPA 6] in Thailand to give us a grade and said that we could go ahead with production. If they didn't, they just said that we will drop you' (THS 7, Operations Control).

A strict approach to compliance as advocated by some groups is one that suggests that even a single audit failure can lead to termination. AMNE compliance managers and directors point out that such an approach can be problematic in a world where many suppliers would not pass a thorough audit on every principle encompassed by a code of conduct. As AMNE 2 points out, 'There is a need and a want for us to be more preventative. In reality, almost no facility will comply 100% with a compliance programme.' As discussed above, the auditing process is a learning process, and the detailed practices covered by the codes are sometimes complex, new or different from those that manufacturers may be accustomed to. If the manufacturers are left with no flexibility in this learning process (that is, room to learn from their mistakes), they will be under greater pressure to try to undermine the auditing process by cheating or bribing. Indeed this pressure to meet compliance may even trickle down from management to the workers. As the owner of a supplier in Thailand explains, 'The worker knows that the auditors are from the buyers and they know that compliance will happen' (THS 2, Owner). A Sri Lankan factory manager explains the relationship between continuing business and code compliance to the factory's workforce: 'We explain to workers that

Adapted from the website of one MNE

Some workers' advocates have requested that we never pull our business from a supplier factory. If we do, they argue, the loss of our business may cost factory workers their jobs. However, if garment manufacturers believed that our business was guaranteed—that we would never pull out regardless of conditions in their factories—we would send a very mixed message about our commitment to enforcing our code.

Others think we should leave as soon as we determine a supplier is not in compliance with our code. We often wrestle with this dilemma. Although there are no easy answers, we have concluded that resolution depends not just on strict application of established rules but must also be flexible enough to take into account the specific facts and circumstances involved. In most cases, we would prefer to work with a supplier factory to improve over time rather than terminate business with them.

the company may lose orders unless we comply with buyers' requirements' (SLS 3, HR Manager).

In this way workers may come to understand the consequences of non-compliance. Thus too stark a regime, one in which non-compliance can lead rather abruptly to factory closing, also creates pressure among the workers to cover up non-compliance for fear of losing their jobs. A prominent Thai labour organisation recognises this competitive pressure on workers, highlighting the potential for manufacturing MNEs to close factories and move to alternative locations in the case of negative reports.

> Codes have had a negative impact. They are labelled as a customer demand. The workers are not allowed to tell the facts because they are already threatened. The company will change the issue of trade union to better working relations. There needs to be a global initiative from letting MNEs move from one place to another. There needs to be a tie up of the global rules (NGO 8).

In this way, a 'comply or die' regime can actually dissuade workers from reporting non-compliance issues. Rather than correcting issues of non-compliance, under such a strict regime, they may actually be driven further 'underground'.

Of course, while too stark a regime causes problems, too weak a regime fails to encourage reform. Elimination from the supply chain is the ultimate punishment, but increasingly it is seen as a last resort, and one that follows numerous opportunities for corrective action. Both AMNE 7 and AMNE 3, for example, have developed a 'three strikes' audit programme that requires a supplier to fail three audits before being eliminated from the supply chain. In addition, the elimination of suppliers is treated as an extreme measure and is handled in most cases by corporate management rather than regional management. AMNE 3 reports that,

> They [corporate HQ] make the final decision with respect to terminating factories. The regional offices can make recommendations but the final decision comes from [corporate HQ]. This keeps it consistent and apart from the business (RMNE 3).

Another pioneering practice is the development of factory rankings, such that factories are not subject to a stark 'pass or fail' grade, but instead are given a ranking. Agent 2 explains: 'We rank factories A, B and C by looking at: manufacture in same place, worker conditions—safety, water supply, legal practices—beating, shouting, forced labour' (Agent 2). This is a process that may become more widely adopted in the industry. AMNE 4, for example, indicates that 'At the moment the factories are not ranked but a system is currently being developed.' The system AMNE 4 is developing, 'ranks the factories "high–medium–low" ' and the goal of AMNE 4's remediation is to upgrade the firms over time: 'The idea is to bring 10% of the low intensity up to medium and so on.' This ranking system allows both suppliers and buyers to gauge a factory's development towards greater compliance or towards greater non-compliance. This allows all parties a more transparent look at how a factory is progressing, and helps to avoid the sudden shocks of a strict pass/fail approach. In addition, to the extent that this grading is transparent and made available to current and potential employees, workers may use it to base their decision on whether to work for a particular factory or not. Workers seeing a long downward trend in a factory's scores may also have some forewarning of the factory's possible closure.

While a balanced approach is necessary to avoid the problems of a strict 'comply or die' approach, the fundamental power of buyers is their ability to eliminate suppliers from the global supply chain. Under certain circumstances, for instance where factories make no progress over time towards meeting acceptable labour practices, the elimination of the supplier must go ahead if codes are to have any real force and MNEs are to demonstrate their genuine commitment to their code.

Use of corrective action plans (CAPs)

A key component of remediation programmes as an ongoing supplier development process is the use of a CAP. The formation of the CAP can vary somewhat across the industry, but a typical process involves both the buyer and the manufacturer agreeing on a CAP through dialogue. A CAP includes specific recommendations on what practices need to be changed and how these problems should be addressed by the supplier. As AMNE 5 says, 'We give [the factories] suggestions and recommendations on how to meet our requirements.' An important feature of a CAP is the inclusion not only of specific practices to improve, but also a time frame within which these improvements must be made. The CAP then forms the basis of subsequent audits, which seek to ensure that agreed improvements were met within the agreed time-frame. Agent 1 explains the basic concept of a CAP:

> We have a follow-up assessment for compliance. A CAP, formed by the assessor, auditor and factory, together with the time-span for correction, is given. There is a week to reach agreement on the plan and then a signed acceptance of it is sent back to us. The guideline is centralised. Normally the auditor deals with factory management or the CEO. The general time-span is 30 days—60 days—90 days (Agent 1).

The joint creation of the CAP can take the form of splitting the CAP into two parts: (1) those things that require improvement; and (2) the means by which they will be improved. AMNE 4, for example, employs this type of co-operation with manufacturers to arrive at a joint plan.

> The problem rests with corrective action. Now there is a two-way commitment: Areas For Improvement [AFI] and a Facility Improvement Plan [FIP]. We determine the AFI—as opposed to looking for problems—and we ask the factory to determine an FIP. We give them a minimum of 30 days to improve. Merchandising can threaten not to give further orders (AMNE 4).

Interviews with manufacturers indicate a high degree of involvement in the formation of CAPs. This can be helpful in allowing suppliers flexibility and creativity in finding solutions, while at the same time operating within the code prescriptions of buyers. The resulting relationship is one wherein buyers establish the rules and goals and suppliers establish the factory-specific actions to meet compliance.

> I go around with the auditor. We inspect together and point out what is wrong. Afterwards we have to do the corrective actions. I prepare the CAP and how to make the corrections based on both what the auditor says and ourselves (THS 5, HR and EHS Officer).

> AMNE 4 said that we had to pay minimum wage and so we changed our system but AMNE 4 didn't help with this. I did this myself (THS 6, HR Manager).

> FMNE 2 does the audit and we have to prepare the corrective action plan and send it back to them. Then another audit is scheduled (THS 3, HR Manager).

> The corrective action plan is mostly done by EHS officers and the HR person but sometimes they CC [carbon copy] me (THS 1, HR Manager).

> Sometimes the feedback is verbal and sometimes it is written. We make the CAP. We have to tell them how long we need to improve. What they ask, we answer. If some things aren't clear, we ask them to please explain. We never disagree with the auditor (THS 2, Owner).

> If there is a long list, the auditor lists the non-compliance [issues or areas] and allows us time to fill in the CAP and when we can do it (THS 5, HR and EHS Officer).

However, it should be noted that this involvement does not occur across the board. In some of the supplier factories visited, factory managements' role in the CAP was limited to agreeing to time-frames specified by the AMNE representative. AMNEs that have adopted a more 'policing' type of model with regard to compliance exhibited this type of approach.

The use of CAPs as an integral part of auditing can create a continuous improvement process focused on long-term supplier development, rather than short-term pass–fail checks. This is a sentiment expressed by AMNEs as well as suppliers. A Thai operations controller observes:

> By having periodic audits, it causes us to increase our focus on [compliance]. RMNE 3 is extremely strict. There is increased pressure on management and employees. They look at things like the total number of toilets, environmental certificates, 57.5 hours, leaking taps. But they give us time to improve and give assistance to address issues [in CAPs] (UKS 2, HR Manager).

CAPs as negotiable

It is in the development of CAPs that code compliance auditing moves from general principles to concrete, detailed implementation. As in the implementation of any specific programme, there can be some negotiable issues, usually relating to time-frame, but occasionally relating to feasibility or alternative standards. A Thai HR manager at a supplier says, for example, 'When AMNE 4 came in and said the workers had to rent rooms, we negotiated on the time.' The manager goes on to point out other negotiable issues: 'Overtime is negotiable. For example with FMNE 2, we asked them if we could follow Thai law. Workers must sign up for voluntary overtime. This is the case for the other buyers too' (THS 6). Negotiations can occur not only with the creation of CAPs but also with the findings of audit reports. The comments of an operations controller in Thailand illustrate this point.

> We will look at the report and if there is something that we disagree with, we negotiate it. Sometimes the auditor speaks with the workers and doesn't put the complaint in the audit report but goes back and tells the buyer (THS 7, Operations Control).

Negotiation in the CAP and reporting process allows a useful degree of flexibility; however, care must be exercised to ensure that negotiations for alternative time-frames or means of compliance do not degenerate into negotiating an allowance to avoid compliance. In the following comment, an AMNE 4 representative indicates the frustration that can arise from manufacturers trying to 'negotiate' their way out of meeting compliance.

> The commitment by the factory is often less but brands are not happy with this. For example, I called a meeting with the general manager, compliance officers, etc. Many excuses are given for being late. I listened to their story and then discussed whether there was a first visit, follow-up, discussion. I give them copies of factory improvements—assist the factory to meet standards (AMNE 4).

The auditing process as a consulting process: benefits to manufacturers

As noted above, the auditing process is increasingly seen as a part of the wider supplier development process by many AMNEs. Supplier development is the process by which buyers provide advice and consulting to suppliers, as an investment, to help improve, among other things, their productivity and quality. This is typically in the form of detailed practical suggestions on everything from organising factory workflows to better systems of storage to IT solutions. The introduction of code compliance management in the 1990s has extended the range of topics on which some AMNEs now advise their suppliers, to include labour and EHS issues. There remains, however, a tremendous amount of overlap between these different aspects of supplier development. At the very least, the practice of sending factory inspectors and providing practical advice is identical to earlier quality and productivity development practices. The HR manager of a Thai supplier notes the practical immediate benefit of such code compliance-related advice: 'Buyer auditors . . . help us resolve our problems such as with EHS equipment, they gave us a list of sellers. They are more like a mentor.' The manager goes on to say that, from his perspective, code compliance is very much a part of a supplier development process: 'It is more or less the same for different brands. I don't feel that the buyer comes like a policeman but they come to help to improve' (THS 7, HR Manager). Multiple supplier interviews observe that, through the CSR auditing process, the buyers provide the suppliers with new concepts and ideas about how to better manage certain functions:

> The buyer auditors give us a fresh outlook. They give you points on things you do not pick up because you grow accustomed to it. It is like a wake-up call to us. For example, electrical wiring: we are accustomed to taking short cuts. Now we walk around with the EHS officer and take pictures of things that are wrong and send them out just like the buyers trained us. Basically, the pictures were sent out to our department heads to show them what to look for (THS 7, Operations Control).

> The positive thing is that it [auditor advice] has helped us look at things differently . . . Changes have been like night and day. No exits, no ventilation and also they [the workers] just work overtime continuously for two to three days in a row. This doesn't happen here. People are aware of it here (SLS 3, HR Manager).

Indeed, from the interviews it is clear that as suppliers grow accustomed to the auditing process and increasingly see it as another aspect of their development, they also begin to develop higher expectations of support from the process.

> It is better if the auditors had a more in-depth study but it would have to be a one-week study and not just a few hours' audit. They would need to do a workflow analysis. Normally FMNE 2 does this. They come back very often. Sometimes on the production side they come back once a week. They are giving lots of support. They will not interfere though with the factory processes. They mainly focus on the code. They have set training systems and procedures to educate the people (THS 4, Production Manager).

It must be noted that a principal part of the advice provided via the auditing process concerns compliance with local labour laws. This is a challenging process since, as discussed in Section 4.b, many developing countries lack an effective legal and enforcement infrastructure. Local labour laws are often weaker than the standards embodied in codes and in some cases local labour laws regarding particular practices simply do not exist. This situation is typically combined with weak enforcement mechanisms and relatively high rates of corruption among government officials. The result is that many factory owners and managers are under no great pressure either to be aware of local labour laws or to abide by them. Thus a role of auditors has been training local managers about their countries' own laws and how they relate to code compliance. As a TPA 6 auditor says of factory managers in Cambodia, 'In my experience, managers don't understand how to relate labour law to the buyer's code.' Indeed, our research suggests that many auditors themselves do not have a firm understanding of the local law in many LDCs; in large part this is the result of the weak legal environment and lack of government transparency. There have been some attempts to add more transparency to the situation; for example, NGO 2 has developed a database of the labour laws of many producer countries available to subscribers for a fee. While the ILO does provide access to similar information through its website, managers interviewed stated that they found the BSR database to be more useful for information pertaining to enterprise-level practice. Despite the confusion about local labour laws, AMNE training and audit programmes appear to be developing at least some new awareness of local labour laws among suppliers. As AMNE 4 observes, 'In terms of [suppliers'] knowledge of their own local labour laws, this has increased' (AMNE 4).

Another, sometimes overlooked, aspect of supplier development is the relation of other initiatives that complement compliance management. Agent 3, for example, says, 'I push better time management to increase productivity and decrease costs. Not every factory has the capacity as we work from small to large factories.' The development of better productivity at the manufacturer level can have indirect knock-on effects for compliance management. It is not uncommon, for instance, for factory managers to see simple cost avoidance as the principal means of decreasing costs and achieving or increasing profitability in an otherwise low-margin part of the value chain. In principle, factory managers may tend to avoid obvious costs such as higher salaries, better EHS infrastructure, food and housing. A result of this is a constant downward pressure on wages and necessary EHS infrastructure. By helping factory managers to identify alternative approaches to decreasing costs and increasing productivity (such as improved time management, workflow, purchasing, financing, etc.), buyers and agents provide indirect support for better code compliance.

e. Other reporting

Dialogue with NGOs

In addition to audit reports and corporate CSR reports, a significant part of MNEs' public dialogue is between the firms and NGOs. This dialogue process with NGOs provides vital feedback to MNEs, not least because NGOs are often the chief critics of current and or former MNE labour standards. NGOs are also important links in a communication chain between MNEs and concerned members of the public, particularly in the important North American and European markets. Dialogue with NGOs may help MNEs better understand areas that may require more attention and methodologies that may need to be changed, supplemented or reinforced. NGO 2, for example, is an NGO with associations with industry. It seeks to facilitate dialogue between MNEs as well as dialogue between MNEs and NGOs. NGO 2's functions include moderating meetings between MNEs and NGOs, as was done in China in 2001 for AMNE 1. The purpose of that meeting was to provide AMNE 1 with critical feedback on its 2000 CSR Report. A NGO 2 representative recalls the meeting, observing that,

> It was useful because some of the things said in the meeting surprised them. They were surprised to hear that the NGOs said that they should try different approaches and not just focus on the number of audits. AMNE 1 requested this and we will do another one in the US. The NGOs that were there included NGO 13, O 3 and O 4 (NGO 2).

From what AMNE managers told us, this networking and dialogue function has also been helpful for the CSR managers within MNEs, to quickly come up to speed on best practices and the top concerns in the industry. At AMNE 3, for example, one of its CSR managers spent the first six months on the job learning by talking to other companies and NGOs in the NGO 2 network. Yet clearly the relationship between AMNEs and NGOs varies across a spectrum from critical-but-co-operative to acrimonious. Indications of the latter type are found in the comments of a representative from AMNE 2, who feels that 'NGOs are only out to get you. They are not partners. The media are in the same boat.' At RMNE 3, a representative in China observes that 'We don't have a directive to engage positively with NGOs.'

Public reporting

Perhaps the highest-profile form of communication with stakeholders is the emerging practice among some MNEs of publishing annual CSR reports. These public reports, in part due to their novelty, often serve as a launching pad for further dialogue. Much of this dialogue is concerned with the content and structure of the reports and in turn this feeds back into the auditing and compliance management mechanisms.

> The key issue is how they report their codes, for example, AMNE 1's first report for 2000 was a tentative attempt to put in black and white how they wanted to monitor. Their 2001 report is far more specific. There was more information than from anyone else that we've seen. They gave a full list of the number of factories in the country monitored, and the number dropped. They are setting a new industry standard as far as reporting goes. We asked if they would list their supplier factories. They said there were no ideological

reasons as to why not, and are working on it. The difference is really a cultural one (NGO 4).

In respect to the role of voluntary public reporting and the important role of transparency, a high-profile legal case that recently settled in the US is worth noting. In *Nike v. Kasky*, filed in 1998 by a US resident, Nike was accused of fraud under a California consumer protection law for allegedly making false claims in a public relations campaign. The claims in question relate to Nike's response to criticisms by human rights groups regarding working conditions in Nike contractor facilities overseas.

The details of the legal arguments are complex, and not the focus of this book. In brief, Nike argued that the communications made by its executives, including letters to newspapers, athletic directors and others, were protected forms of commercial speech under the Constitution of the United States of America. Since the issue of its labour practices had become a matter of widespread public attention, Nike argued that it was entitled to participate in the debate about its labour practices without fear of legal retribution. However, the California Supreme Court disagreed, and ruled that Nike's statements about factory conditions constituted 'false advertising' within the meaning of the California law.

One important consequence of this legal case in the context of issues dealt with by this research is that Nike decided not to issue its Sustainability Report for 2003. After the filing of many legal briefs by various MNEs and employer groups, the United States Supreme Court agreed to review the decision of the California Court. It was hoped that this ruling would clarify the definition of protected corporate speech. Civil-society organisations were concerned that the ruling would lower the standard for truth in advertising, and reduce transparency. Unfortunately, there was an out-of-court settlement reached by Nike and Kasky, and thus this issue remains unresolved.

Sustainability reporting: the details

Sustainability or social reporting is still a relatively new concept for many companies. Indeed, lack of consensus exists regarding the nature of such reporting including the degree of depth, indicators and data to be supplied. As such it was not surprising that few of the companies interviewed for this research produce sustainability reports. Those that did varied greatly in style, content and level of detail, adopting both traditional and progressive reporting elements. Common features included the provision of:

- A 'Summary of Annual Performance'—providing ease in presentation of complex issues and enabling comparison with performance in previous years
- Details regarding where goods, supplies and product content were purchased—adding perspective regarding the global reach of the MNE
- Specific measurable criteria for ranking and scoring suppliers—demonstrating a practical approach to the selection of business partners

In some cases even sensitive business information was included, such as specific areas of non-compliance discovered in factory audits, as well as the number of employee terminations. Further innovative elements such as sections referencing legal labour issues and the level of transparency were also incorporated in some of the reports.

In the MNEs interviewed, one clearly stood out as cutting edge with regard to sustainability reporting. We heard from managers that, while there has been a steep learning curve regarding the content and presentation of their report, the feedback from external stakeholders was instrumental in guiding development of the most recent version of the report. Now, this MNE provides far greater detail than in its first report, including things such as the number of factories audited, the number of factories per country and the specific product lines of each factory. Further, each factory is identified as a main contractor or as a subcontractor. Such detailed information provides a more accurate picture of the actual global supply chain and sourcing system. Beyond auditing, the MNE includes detailed information regarding the training it provides, along with useful case studies on the impacts and effectiveness of training.

A detailed explanation of the system for ranking suppliers could lead to greater transparency and information sharing. Providing the specific number of supplier relationships terminated for violations of code principles could seem to demonstrate a greater commitment to social responsibility and the provisions of their code of conduct.* We heard from the MNE itself that they find the factors for termination useful in designing future training programmes and screening suppliers. A similar comment was made by NGOs who found that this information allowed them to participate more fully in the multi-stakeholder dialogue offered by the MNE, as well as assist in a grass-roots advocacy role.

However, as this MNE acknowledges, along with other managers interviewed, these are only the first steps, with additional content and subject matter required to be identified and incorporated. As sustainability reporting is very much in its infancy, it is natural to expect the progressive inclusion of additional information, content and detail based on lessons learned and the collective experience of MNEs in the field.

* This should be considered in the context of discussions regarding the termination of relationships with suppliers dealt with earlier in this chapter.

6. Interrelation, integration and dialogue

Interrelation and integration of elements

Feedback, improvement and remediation

Implementing the code in operations

Developing understanding and ability

Creating a shared vision

Dialogue with other stakeholders

Dialogue with employees, unions and workers' representatives

a. Interrelation and integration

Large AMNEs, like all large firms, have complex internal politics marked by differences in interests, priorities and incentives. The actions of the firm will, to a large extent, be determined by these internal politics. Thus the position of a company's CSR management in the larger corporate governance structure is important to the outcome of CSR programmes in the field as we outlined in Section 4.a. As Agent 1 observes, 'The challenge rests with the gap between production, sourcing and compliance' (Agent 1). Therefore it is important to integrate compliance management with other mission-critical functions of the firm, and establish mechanisms for resolving conflicts between these function areas. As AMNE 7's CSR manager explains:

> We want to keep the code of conduct embedded in operations. I want it embedded just like the other functions. This is progress. I don't want it to go the other way. To me, this is how CSR should look no matter what the issue—but we aren't there yet (AMNE 7, Director CSR).

One possible approach is to integrate compliance, sourcing and production within a single management group. The Vice President for Production at AMNE 4, for example, argues this point:

> Compliance, corporate sourcing and production are all separate. I have never understood why. This invites dissent. Corporate sourcing should have production and compliance beneath it. It should have consistent criteria because compliance does not have the final word and there is a tremendous risk for us to go on record (AMNE 4, Vice President Production).

Integration of the three functions provides some advantages in terms of sharing of information, better integration of compliance functions with day-to-day supply chain management, and increased alignment of priorities between the different function areas. The key problem with such a close-knit integration, however, according to AMNEs interviewed, appears to be the undermining of the compliance function's independence. It is inherent in the compliance management process that there will be conflicts, at least in priorities if not basic principles, between compliance and sourcing and production.

Furthermore, there will almost certainly be conflicts between the incentive structure and targets of sourcing and production with the targets of compliance. If compliance is made a sub-group of the larger supply chain management function, it will have difficulty implementing its programme when conflicts arise with sourcing or production. For this reason, a certain degree of independence from the operational side of the firm is required. In several companies (including AMNE 4), compliance finds this independence or autonomy in the corporate legal department. As an indirect corporate office, the legal department of any firm offers a degree of independence. Furthermore, legal departments, by the nature of their function within a firm, often enjoy both a high degree of authority as well as direct access to senior management.

> [The labour compliance group] makes decisions on a day-to-day basis. I report to the General Counsel. If I were advising other companies, I think it's a model that they should think about. It's important when we do have a disagreement with sourcing, particularly for our team [. . .] These governance issues are more important. This is an integral part of our structure. I report to someone who is higher than the head of Sourcing. If we need to go toe-to-toe, we can (AMNE 4, Vice President CSR).

> My department has moved around the company. For two years we were in supply chain. This was critical because we were part of the organisation. Now I am in legal. I am more independent. I chose to be placed there earlier this year. The way I see it, now Compliance is a department that could reside anywhere. Legal is independent and we have gone through different phases. It is good to have a degree of independence (AMNE 10, Director CSR).

> We placed compliance [in legal] where it has the most independence from operations so that the output can be done without concern from that person's job. Human resources in our company doesn't have that broad based a compliance as it does in other companies. If the supply chain group resisted terminating, I would get involved. So would the CEO but, to date, supply chain has been very supportive (AMNE 10, General Counsel).

A method of integrating the CSR function into the strategic leadership of a firm's value chain management is the formation of cross-departmental management teams. AMNE 7, for example, uses this approach as shown in Figure 17.

As AMNE 7's director of CSR management explains, 'There is a worldwide supply chain leadership team comprised of the Senior VP, code of conduct team, sourcing strategy, director of demand-driven replenishment and logistics.' A similar cross-departmental strategy team is employed at AMNE 4:

> The legal strategy committee is made up of the general counsel, head of communications, head of sourcing, head of supply chain, a board member, the chief administrative officer and me. It looks at the key ethical sourcing issues and evaluates what efforts will be undertaken when (AMNE 4, Vice President CSR).

Apart from formal corporate governance structures, it is worthwhile to observe that large AMNEs are subject to their own internal politics, which are often characterised by informal connections throughout the organisation. As a result, the ability of CSR personnel to engage effectively in compliance management depends in part on the receptiveness of personnel in other departments to the principles and ideals of CSR. It

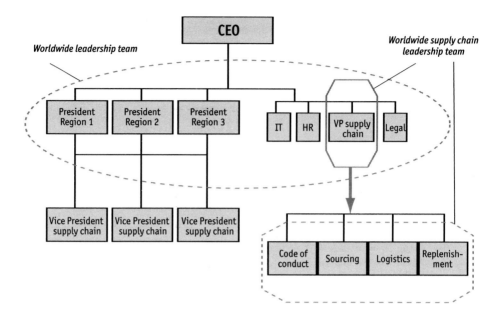

FIGURE 17 CODE IMPLEMENTATION MANAGEMENT TEAMS

also depends on the CSR manager's ability to develop and make effective use of informal personal connections. These abilities are crucial to making the best use of the 'dotted lines' in any corporate organisational chart. Ultimately, as in other functions in a company, the ability to motivate and inspire people in other departments is essential to the success of a CSR manager.

> Auditors will now report to me largely because of personal reasons. Reporting in sourcing organisations was getting artificial. Now they have a dotted line to me. It will change and be direct. I was an independent piece and they were part of 'production'. I have done it for a few years. Now we are integrated into operations enough (AMNE 10, Director).

With multiple corporate departments engaged in various aspects of managing and implementing code compliance, internal communication between the departments is a key success factor. In AMNE 2, for example, the company has a clear outline of how CSR compliance decisions are communicated to key departments.

> We have a tiered communication approach in AMNE 2 so that those that are most affected hear about things first. In the case of compliance, those in logistics, for example, must hear about it before HR. Then it will be the production offices and agents and finally it will be rolled out to all the associates (AMNE 2).

b. Dialogue

The importance of dialogue in the code implementation process in the apparel sector has been highlighted throughout this chapter. It should be noted that our research was complemented by academic thought supporting the need for stakeholder engagement in developing effective code-of-conduct implementation programmes. Several leading academics including Dara O'Rourke have stated that the systems for CSR and code implementation should be evaluated according to a number of criteria, including legitimacy. A commonly asked question is, 'Are key stakeholders involved in all stages of standard setting, monitoring and enforcement?' (O'Rourke 2003).

Within the apparel sector our research indicated that awareness is developing regarding the need for both internal and external dialogue with stakeholders. AMNEs interviewed appear to recognise the need for active engagement and ongoing dialogue with stakeholders as a fundamental element to the establishment of a shared vision, understanding and ability, integration of social performance commitments, and systems for feedback and remediation. However, our interviews revealed that engagement of internal stakeholders, such as workers, unions and workers' representatives, was more advanced than the dialogue with external stakeholders. While we found it difficult to ascertain one causal factor for this situation, the most commonly cited reason was linked to the distrust that some AMNEs had for certain journalists and activists based on the exposés conducted in the mid-1990s.

Generally, it appears that dialogue with stakeholders within the apparel sector is a developing phenomenon. While not as advanced as the mechanisms for engagement as those in the footwear sector, AMNEs are making efforts in outreach to both internal and external stakeholders. Throughout this book, references are made to such engagements, though it is worth mentioning recent developments again. For example, AMNEs acknowledged their need to develop and communicate an effective message on the code of conduct not only internally but also externally with their key stakeholders. Further, some AMNEs have clearly seen that the challenges that face them in expanding internal capacity to design, implement and manage CSR and code commitments would be significantly reduced through dialogue with stakeholders. Importantly, many AMNEs are starting to more formally engage with stakeholder dialogue, which is a positive trend in this sector. Nevertheless, in order for genuine dialogue to occur there must be a level of transparency which as yet does not appear to exist to a great degree in the apparel sector.

c. Some implications of codes for functions

Codes of conduct and their supporting management systems are increasingly becoming a common feature of leading apparel brands worldwide. This development has several implications for multiple corporate functions. The key feature of well-functioning compliance management systems is that they are appropriately integrated into the company and not simply added on. This means that CSR management, in order to operate effectively, must integrate itself or have close relations with numerous functional areas within the firm. These functional areas include: purchasing, human resource management, and manufacturing and quality control.

i. Role of CSR groups

In discussing issues of structure of CSR and integration in Section 4.a we also mentioned some of the responsibilities of the CSR or compliance department. At its core, the role of this department is to drive the code-of-conduct implementation process. We heard that the introduction of a CSR department in many companies has been a relatively new phenomenon, leaving these departments free to evolve in ways that best fit specific company cultures and practices.

> Nobody else was doing this stuff. This was radical. We just evolved. We created checklists, gave presentations and it became part of our business agenda. It started in footwear. Basically we created over time a culture with the footwear team and they started saying human rights. This reflected that we had made it part of their culture. We then moved to apparel (AMNE 9, Vice President Compliance).

CSR department staff have the central role in the implementation of code process. Typically, they are responsible for drafting and updating the code, integrating it into the operations of the company, establishing specific programmes including conducting audits, providing training and communicating both internally and externally on code-of-conduct issues. As AMNE 4 points out, '[The labour compliance group] makes decisions on a day-to-day basis' (AMNE 4, Vice President CSR). In short, they are responsible for managing the code. This includes ensuring that there is global consistency in terms of their implementation approach.

> Global consistency is important to us because we are a decentralised business . . . Therefore it's important to have shared business planning and annual operations planning with the other units (AMNE 7, Director CSR).

In most of the MNEs interviewed there was recognition of the importance of CSR groups working with other functional departments, and in some companies, such as AMNE 3, this is reflected in the role of the compliance department. In fact, in this particular company the approach of the CSR group for apparel differs from that for footwear.

> We realised that we need to do several things similar for apparel but also some things differently. We needed to create a culture within the team. One part is to establish a common set of systems and accuracy but even this is not sufficient unless they see it in the teams. Therefore ensuring that sourcing people travel with the compliance teams is important. We need to make it live for them—and you can only do this by sharing with them what it looks like. We also need to deal with middlemen, namely trading agents (AMNE 9, Vice President CSR).

From this comment we can see that the role of the compliance department includes the education and development of staff from other functional departments.

ii. Purchasing and selection of suppliers

An important implication of CSR management for purchasing and supplier selection appears to be a further streamlining of MNE supplier bases. As was observed by one of the experts, 'In general, the implementation of compliance systems encourages the narrowing of the vendor and contractor base' (E I). To be clear, purchasing departments across multiple industries have a tendency to perform periodic reduction exercises to reduce the number of suppliers in their supply base. While having multiple suppliers provides any firm with reduced risk and greater price competitiveness, these advantages can be satisfied with a relatively small critical mass of suppliers; beyond such a critical mass, the management of a large supply base begins to impose costs on the MNE. Therefore reductions in AMNE supply bases cannot be completely attributed to CSR management. Nonetheless, CSR management appears to be playing a role. As the costs of CSR management, particularly supplier audits, increases proportionately with the number of suppliers, these costs may add an additional incentive for AMNEs and their agents to reduce their supplier base. As Agent 3 notes, 'We aimed to do 450 [audits] from the beginning but after starting compliance we scaled it down to 150 for both compliance and commercial reasons. We also cut down on the number of vendors.'

Note that with product volumes in the industry remaining steady or increasing, the reduction in the total number of suppliers for AMNEs also implies an increase in the volume production of each individual supplier. Thus CSR management may play a catalytic role in encouraging consolidation at the supplier level.

iii. Human resource management

The implications for wage levels in factories remain an open issue. Some aspects of CSR management, such as ending pay discrimination between men and women, may have a marginal impact on wage rates in factories. And certainly where factories are currently, or have in the past, been paying below minimum wage or not providing overtime pay, code compliance programmes may make noticeable and significant differences in workers' wages. However, the fundamental cost pressures of the industry, combined with the entry-level nature of many of the jobs in the factories, does not suggest that wage levels will rise significantly, in the absence of changes in minimum-wage laws in the countries of manufacture.

> The question of reforms in the brands' pricing policies, in order to allow the factories to pay higher or living wages, must be an industry-wide initiative— although there are instances of factories that have improved productivity sufficiently to absorb these kinds of cost (AMNE 4, Vice President CSR).

> It's the Wal-Mart mentality: customers want price, price, price . . . Our challenge is price . . . We're getting less for a unit today than ten years ago (USS 5, Safety Manager).

> The big buyers, like AMNE 4, simply state a non-negotiable price. For the smaller companies, [brands/buyers] price is negotiable (USS 4, Owner).

Another potential implication of CSR programmes is the development of unions at the factory level and, therefore, the need for the human resource departments of the factories to develop constructive and co-operative relations with such unions.

iv. Manufacturing and quality

Many of the CSR issues in the apparel industry can be traced to the circumstances of the manufacturing process outlined at the beginning of this chapter. The speed of the production process is a root cause of many compliance issues.

> Compliance officers recognise that two elements of the supply chain structure have particularly acute effects on the capacity of factory managers to achieve compliance—short production deadlines and price competition. Compliance systems nonetheless tend to repress these topics, in light of the business pressures that produce the underlying structural problems (E 1).

This is a point that is being recognised by at least some within the industry. The VP for CSR at AMNE 4, for example, realises that effective CSR management necessarily has implications for the manufacturing process.

> Production from the start affects compliance, in both pricing and production schedules. It's not ill-intent on the part of production [managers]. It's just a problem of not thinking about the effects on compliance . . . I need to educate merchandise about unnecessary speed in the turnaround process—so it would be a good thing for me to meet formally with marketing and design, but it hasn't happened yet (AMNE 4, Vice President CSR).

v. Role of government and intergovernmental organisations

An implication of CSR programmes has been an increasing interest in the role of government and/or intergovernmental organisations in the regulation of code compliance. This is a natural consequence of the search for industry-wide standards and consistency in implementation. The global nature of the apparel industry, however, suggests obstacles for regulating code compliance efforts from any one national government. As a result there have been suggestions that the ILO undertake the role of global regulator of code-of-conduct activities. One of the experts noted that several managers proposed that all or part of the compliance task be turned over to a sovereign international organisation such as the ILO. These managers suggested that the ILO could overcome the problems of (a) duplication, (b) legitimacy and (c) competence (E 1).

> There are too many conflicting rules and, equally important, too many conflicting remedial orders for the suppliers to fulfil [. . .] We'll get better results if the compliance programmes were more uniform and were stronger. The ILO should carry this out (Agent 3).

> We need a credible independent monitor looking at all factories, like the ILO or Department of Labor. It must have the capacity for not just policing but for remedies and worker training (AMNE 4).

> There's a need for governmental involvement—by the ILO or by domestic agencies—to make the private efforts stick (AMNE 3, Senior Manager Corporate Compliance).

While governmental action within an intergovernmental organisation such as the ILO might be a helpful contribution, it is worth noting that national government action may also provide a sufficient catalyst. The key markets of the US and the EU carry enough influence in the industry such that code compliance regulation within one or both of these markets would be likely to be sufficient to set a global standard. Given this fact, there are some who argue that, in addition to the ILO, the OECD and the WTO may also be appropriate forums for establishing a global CSR governance structure.

vi. Role of agents

Another implication of CSR management may be a changing role for agents. Agents play a key role in facilitating the manufacturing process. They are often the ones who decide what gets produced where. They are the key middlemen in the value chain who connect MNEs to factories. As a result they have, in many cases, even more influence over factories than do individual MNEs. It is at the agent level that many CSR functions, such as auditing and standardising codes, could be concentrated. Already, agents are increasingly falling into the role of code compliance managers as MNEs make such actions a requirement for further orders.

> One of our strategies is to shift to Agent 1, which can exert more leverage than
> AMNE 3 alone, because Agent 1 is sourcing for other companies as well as AMNE
> 3 from any given factory or vendor (AMNE 3, Vice President Sourcing).

However, it must be remembered that not all AMNEs use agents. In fact, our interviews suggest that, as competitive pressures increase, companies are absorbing the roles traditionally played by agents with the hope of increasing their margins. This would of course bring them closer to their supply chain and potentially enable them to exercise greater leverage; this issue is explored in greater depth in the retail section of this book.

VI
Review of the retail sector

1. Background

The retail sector is a US$3 trillion market. The top five global retailers alone had sales of US$1 trillion in 2002. The retail sector has evolved into a global maze of sourcing and production channels for the myriad consumer goods demanded primarily by consumers in industrialised economies. Characterised by fierce competition, global consolidation, transnational expansion and new channels of distribution, the retail sector is dominated by global players which include department stores, mass merchandisers, clothing retailers, speciality retailers, convenience stores, grocery stores, drug stores, home-furnishing retailers, consumer electronics retailers, Internet retailers, catalogue and mail-order companies. Of note is the fact that competitors in the retail sector often share any number of the literally thousands of global supplier factories in low-wage developing economies which are contracted for production.

This section focuses on retailers that carry both 'hardlines' (which include appliances, consumer electronics, home furnishings, house and garden wares and jewellery, among others) and 'softlines' (also called consumer non-durables, such as apparel, footwear and accessories), in particular department stores, which are historically important to the development of retail, and mass merchandisers, which presently dominate the sector. In this sector hardlines are frequently no-name or store-brand products delineated only by a country-of-origin sticker; as such, tracing the supply chain in order to examine working conditions at the factory level may be difficult if not impossible.

a. Outsourcing

Driven by low-price directives, retailers have continued scouring the globe to find suppliers of low-cost merchandise such as gifts, furniture and consumer electronics. This trend has fuelled a global economic network where retailers, brand-name manufacturers and trading companies set up decentralised production networks in exporting countries with low labour costs, generally located in the developing world. Production is carried out to the specifications of retailers and designers by a tiered network of contractors that make finished goods for foreign buyers (Gereffi 1999: 2). Increasingly, production of products for the retail sector is taking place in China. 'In 2001 total worldwide goods procured from China came to US$10 billion—more than 70% of which came from Guangdong province—and the figure is expected to reach US$12 billion in 2002' (Sito 2002).

b. Retail buying operations

In operating terms, major retailers often utilise buying offices or agents to facilitate purchasing, with some companies maintaining buying offices all over the world. Some retailers we interviewed cited having 30 or more international buying offices in such cities as Hong Kong, Kathmandu, Mexico City and elsewhere. Buyers from these offices generally have responsibilities for certain lines such as apparel, toys, or sporting goods, and enter into contracts with suppliers[40] to purchase produced or finished goods that will then be sold by the retailer. Where copyrighted products are in question, such as toys based on film characters, buyers must usually first go through a licensee who will then contract with an agent for production, or directly with a supplier. Excerpted below are comments from a buyer on how sourcing decisions are made:

> When looking for suppliers and products I look at marketability. A product has to sell. There needs to be a solid supply structure. The factory and supplier have to be able to deliver quantities throughout the season and price is very important in this competitive marketplace. The whole focus of our business is the customer. The 'what' and the 'when'. Our second focus is on service, the way we handle the orders from our customers; and our third one is on price (AMNE 8).

We were told that buyers tend to use criteria such as speed, flexibility, quality and particularly price in sourcing decisions. China, for example, has an abundant supply of low-cost labour.

When buyers do not go directly to suppliers, agents are employed most often by small to medium-sized retailers and occasionally by larger chains. Agents are often residents of the country in which the retailer is sourcing (Glock and Kunz 2002: 281) and usually represent a group of factories or vendors. Typically agents are knowledgeable about 'trade laws, language, culture, and production capabilities of the manufacturers they represent' (Glock and Kunz 2002: 281). Working with agents has two aspects: first, the use of agents may obscure information on the supplier for the retailer implying that the retailer may have little knowledge of who produces products or how they are made; second, whenever an agent is involved margins are unclear and it is quite possible that the middleman is squeezing his or her profit from further down the supply chain. Simply, the lower the price the agent offers the higher the margin he or she makes. The result is that agents are often cited as furthering the 'race to the bottom'.[41] Generally

40   The term supplier generally refers to a person with whom the retailer has contact. This person may represent one factory, or a group of factories under the umbrella of one supplier name. Suppliers may also be referred to as contractors, so-named for the production agreements signed between retailer and supplier. Suppliers are also called vendors for the role they have in selling to the retailer.

41   The race-to-the-bottom argument is that competition between countries can lead to a rapid dismantling of their national regulatory systems, with negative impact on the protection of labour standards.

the agent contracts business out to a supplier who will engage a factory that will often subcontract production to another factory and in some cases homeworkers. These market dynamics lead to concerns regarding workplace conditions such as long work hours and low wages as some suppliers and agents seek to cut costs wherever and however feasible.

c. Production process

Retailers under competitive pressure to deliver the right product at the right price have entered into global buying practices involving multiple tiers of actors in which speed of delivery and low-cost production are of paramount importance. From the supplier's standpoint this competitive pressure starts early, for in order to obtain retailer business, supplier factories often enter into a competitive bidding process, often via the Internet, knowing that contracts will probably be awarded based on how inexpensively they can produce. Online enterprises such as the Worldwide Retail Exchange (WWRE) and the Global Net Exchange (GNX) facilitate supplier bidding by holding online auctions initiated by the retailer. Usually a retailer will describe products he or she is seeking and suppliers have a certain time-window in which to submit their bids. Globally, competition is stiff among suppliers vying for business and it is common for factories to agree to fulfil orders under terms that could strain the production process. These strains may be attributed to three factors. First is the issue of seasonal demand: high season from a factory standpoint usually runs from April to December. As retailers have shifted focus from long-term forecasting to rapid-response electronic data interchange (EDI) technologies, they not only provide less lead time to the factories when placing orders, they require refill orders during the season. This makes it difficult for a factory manager to predict accurately the size of the workforce needed and the amount of time required to fulfil contractual obligations. In short, it impedes effective production planning and can lead to what is referred to as the 'bullwhip effect' on supply chains (see Figure 18).

The bullwhip effect is the result of both material and information delays in a supply chain, as well as feedback loops in the decision-making process. Because of delays, those further down the line, such as suppliers, tend to react to information well after it has been a reflection of market reality. It can result in overtime, as firms underestimate the workforce needed to complete an order, or alternatively, in layoffs as demand falls.

Second, retailer loyalty to a supplier is often limited to one or two seasons depending on products produced, as discussed by this retail executive:

> I am sure you have heard about churn rate and we have a huge churn. The world is ever driving the phenomenon as it chases a reduction in price. The movement is to the East. We want to have long-term relationships but we are not impervious to commercial pressures. September 11th, China and the WTO have forced changes upon us. We are compelled to go other places. We don't naturally look for other suppliers but occasionally we get kicked there (AMNE 8, Director CSR).

> Even though I said we have churn, this isn't the case across the board. We have some suppliers with whom we have worked for 10 to 15 years. We have greater churn in hardware and gifts because we don't repeat lines. For example, we may sell a golf set one year, and we may even sell it the following

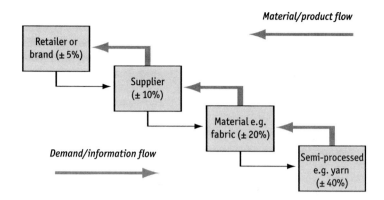

FIGURE 18 'BULLWHIP EFFECT': ORDER FLUCTUATION AMPLIFICATION IN SUPPLY CHAINS

Source: Adapted from Mason-Jones and Towil 2000

year but you will never get a third season because there is pressure to sell another product (UKS 4, Director CSR).

Third, suppliers who are aware that this may be at best a one- or two-time order may accept orders from a multitude of retailers in order to ensure the viability of their operations. One retailer noted that they like to maintain factory leverage of between 10 and 15% as, that way, 'the factory is not too reliant on us, and we are not too reliant on them' (RMNE 8). Once again, the pressure to carry out all of these orders simultaneously can strain factory operations to the point of compromising or even breaking good labour practices that are emphasised by code-of-conduct compliance requirements.

d. Factory operations

Factories producing hardlines for retailers can vary in size from small, averaging anywhere from 40 to 150 workers; medium, from 150 to 300 workers; and large, from 300 up to 1,000 or more workers. Generally factories are organised along functional lines to fit specific manufacturing needs. Most work requires unskilled labour, though some operations, particularly when handling metal or cutting devices, require skilled labour. It is difficult to generalise about the nature of production and factory operations for all product lines, as there are a multitude of factors influencing the factory processes. In general, production plants set up machines and processes in the manner most efficient to produce a completed item. The idea is that a product flows in a straight line, minimising delays. To illustrate this point and some of the challenges associated with social compliance and production, we consider one of the processes typically involved in the production of a retail product, namely, final assembly.

An interesting example is the assembly of a kitchenware gift basket that may be shipped ready-for-sale to a major retailer in the US. Within one supplier factory one worker might be in charge of taking a ready-made basket, passing it to another employee who adds pre-fabricated cutlery and then passes it to another employee who adds completed ceramic dishes who then passes it on to another worker who inputs glassware, and so on until the basket reaches the point in the assembly line where a worker shrink-wraps the entire gift basket and places it on a conveyor belt. This conveyor belt takes the basket to the shipping department where it will be placed in a container along with thousands of other gift baskets to be transported to an agent who will then ship the goods, in time for the holiday season, to the retailer in the US or Europe.

In this seemingly clear process what is unclear is who supplied the baskets, the cutlery, the glasses and the ceramic dishes for assembly. Probing further backwards along the supply chain one could ask the question, 'Who made the metal for the cutlery and the plastic for the handles?' And more importantly, 'Under what conditions were all these items made?' Certainly a retailer can scrutinise the assembly factory easily enough, for it is a known entity. However, as one moves further down the supply chain it becomes much more difficult to identify subcontracting factories, much less audit them for compliance to codes of conduct for good labour practice or even quality. One executive reported that the global retailer for whom he worked has 32 different business units in 50 countries, 200,000 licensees and indirect relationships with 10,000 factories in 100 countries. Given the sheer size of this retail supply network, the challenge of auditing factories so as to ensure compliance with labour, social or ethical obligations is a daunting task.

e. Worker base

The information we gained from our site visits included the fact that the retail suppliers in Thailand comprise a workforce with a significant percentage of male workers. In all but one factory, at least 20% of the workforce was male, with one firm possessing a ratio of 14 men to 1 woman. By contrast, though consistent with the other sectors addressed in this book, female workers overwhelmingly staffed the supplier facilities in China. Regarding the distinction between an average Thai factory of several hundred workers versus a much larger Chinese factory of thousands of workers, the retail sector in China did not have the same overwhelming size disparity that was found in the apparel sector. Similar to China, supplier factories in Thailand included joint ventures as well as 100% locally owned public companies. Further, the observation that wages in Thailand were on average higher than those in China may contribute to the relocation of factories to China.

f. Distribution and logistics

Once produced, goods are ready for shipment. In the past shipping expenses were absorbed by the supplier but increasingly retailers are paying some or all transportation costs in order to better control both the flow of merchandise and its costs (Levy 1997: 320). Generally, retail goods arrive directly from a supplier to a retail store distribution centre. Retail distribution centres were pioneered by Wal-Mart in the 1970s in order to control the costs of product distribution to its rural stores.[42] Innovative

---

42   In effect Wal-Mart decided to perform its own distribution function (Levy 1997: 316).

distribution-centre technologies created by Wal-Mart and widely employed by many retailers today include cross-docking and electronic data interchange. Cross-docking occurs when incoming shipments are unloaded at one bay and, in the case of merchandise that has been shipped ready for sale, are sent by a high-tech system of laser-guided conveyor belts to another bay to be shipped out the same day (Tuck 2002: 2).

Cross-docking is essentially what differentiates a distribution centre from a warehouse; with cross-docking, merchandise is not stored but transferred out immediately, thus reducing costs of warehousing or storing goods. Other goods that require further processing, such as repackaging and delivery, remain at the distribution centre for a longer period of time; yet this may still be less time than at a warehouse where goods may be stored for weeks or even months before they are put on the store floor.

Larger retailers generally utilise distribution centres and while these centres have resulted in lower inventory and logistics costs (Levy 1997: 316) they may be too expensive to maintain for smaller and medium-sized retailers with fewer outlets. According to Michael Levy and Barton Weitz in their book, *Retailing Management* (1998: 321), these retailers may choose to work with third-party logistics companies that facilitate the transfer of goods from supplier to retailer. Such independently owned companies include transportation companies that facilitate the movement of merchandise, warehousing companies hired by either retailers or suppliers to store goods until ready for sale, freight forwarders which act as goods consolidators, combining small shipments from a number of shippers or vendors into large shipments that can be moved more cheaply, and integrated third-party logistics services which may combine two or more of the above services in a 'one-stop shopping' approach.

g. Issues in retailing

Business and economic decisions are generally driven by cost and quality and often have an indirect impact on the workplace conditions in supplier factories. For example, regarding inventory control, whenever possible, rather than holding inventory, retailers prefer to receive new shipments within a selling season. Called 'lean retailing', retailers now push the onus of inventory control backwards onto the supply chain. It is suppliers that must manage flexibility requirements demanded by retailers. Regarding transportation, if it is the supplier who determines the mode of transportation then the cost is added directly to the cost of the goods. Thus retailers may end up paying more than they would have otherwise for products (Tuck 2002: 5). Some retailers address this problem by mapping out transportation routes and pre-selecting proven transport companies and presenting these solutions at the time they contract business with the supplier.

Quality is an important issue in this sector. One of the reasons retailers have such a vast number of suppliers is because, in addition to seeking low prices, they are looking for quality production, a search that may take them to many factories around the globe. Subsequently the only way forward is to streamline the supply chain. As one retailer remarked during our interview,

> We also moved to key business items and therefore we are ordering larger quantities. I feel that we could exercise leverage like this. Larger quantities mean fewer skewers. An order quantity a year ago was about 14,000 pieces

and now it is for 70,000 to 100,000 pieces so a factory can get a good run. But it is not just about a large initial order. We need a strategy for repeat orders. We have a transparent up-front communication strategy with our suppliers and if we see the life-cycle of a product category ending we let them know (RMNE 3, Vice President Sourcing).

h. Streamlining the supply chain

Our research indicated that the retail sector recognises that it can greatly benefit from the streamlining of its supply chain, as has been initiated with some success in the footwear sector. Streamlining is advantageous to the retailer from a cost perspective as fewer suppliers mean lower costs. From a supplier point of view, it is much easier to plan production around orders from a handful of key retail clients for control of overheads, and quality control. From a social perspective, continuity of orders over time is one way to positively impact good labour practices. The fewer factories a retailer has to work with the easier it may be to monitor and verify effective implementation of labour and code-of-conduct requirements.

The question 'How to streamline the supply chain?' remains. The answer, not surprisingly, lies in technology. Clay Parnell, a principal with Kurt Salmon Associates, says that the best way retailers and manufacturers can collaborate towards success is by 'collaborative planning, forecasting and replenishment (CPFR)'. The goal of CPFR is to 'utilise improved process and enabling technology to allow partners not only to share sales and forecast information but also to view and act jointly upon exception situations' (Parnell 2000: 1). Indeed, retail leaders such as Wal-Mart and Sears, among others, are committing major resources to inventory management and tracking systems. They view forecasting technologies as vital tools to help them predict sales and manage inventories in bad as well as good economic climates.

In addition to technology, retailers are already placing huge bets on the potential buying power of developing economies, particularly China. Wal-Mart, Carrefour, Metro and 7-11 have already set up shops in China. They hope to capitalise on the increasing buying power of this nation of 1.2 billion. While for the moment the disposable income of this vast nation is relatively low, United States exports to China continue to increase. With China's accession to the WTO, this amount is expected to grow exponentially into the future. Finally, perhaps as retailers are establishing stores in the backyard of their suppliers, this will offer a greater incentive to solidify and streamline supplier relationships. All these developments affect the manner by which MNEs in the retail sector approach management in CSR and the labour, social and ethical commitments embodied in their codes of conduct.

The information in the following table (Table 9) was provided by factory management, and was not independently verified.

Staff composition	80% female, av. age 30 yrs	14:1 male–female ratio, segregated jobs, female administration	35% male, av. age 32–35; 90% from north-east	90% female, av. age circa 25 yrs, segregation by sex, 95% are locals, not migrants	66% male, 34% female (female av. age 25–30 yrs), s'visors: 37 male, 21 female; mgrs: 9 male, 5 female; clerical: 17 male, 25 female; most production workers from north-east
Average number of employees	650	2,800 in auto seat factory, 2,100 in auto body factory	640	300	640
Labour turnover	1–2% p.a., av. tenure 9–10 years	1.5% p.a., av. tenure 5–10 years	1% p.a., av. tenure 4 years	circa 15% p.a., av. tenure 3 years	10% p.a., av. tenure 5 years
Wage system and average monthly wage (AMW)	Basic + bonus depending on individual and company; US$186.30 per month	US$5.82/day average, without O/T. One annual bonus of 2.6 month's pay/year. Pay is in top third of companies	Mainly time-rate, with a little piece rate. Av. rate US$4.31/day. Bonus of 1.3 month's pay once a year. Also a performance bonus. Pay is in top 20% of companies	US$3.19/day average rate: US$0.23 for meals, + bonus. After 3 years, get 15 days' wages, and 3 days on top of this for each successive year. Monthly attendance allowance of US$4.66, and gold chain. For extended good attendance US$34.93 for 1st year, US$163.10 for 6 years + 15 days' bonus. 30 workers received this last year	US$197.95–209.59 per month base pay. + O/T and bonuses (1–3 months annually depending on profits). Hard-working allowance per section. Attendance bonus of US$46.58 per year
Maximum working hours per day/annual leave	70 hours per week (trying to reduce)	84 hours per week	9 hours/day, 6 days/wk (56 hours/wk) + av. of 2 hours O/T /day	<60 hours per week	54 hours/wk, 36 hours O/T max. (av. 84 hrs/wk)
Number of codes in factory and start dates	4+ 1997	12 Various dates starting 1972	5+ 1992	1, 1999	2
Company type	Japanese-owned joint venture, 75% Japanese, 25% Thai company. VP, MD, Production Manager, and Sales Manager are Japanese	100% Thai public company, which also has 15 joint ventures, accounting for around 50% of total output	Joint venture with Taiwanese, 69% Taiwanese, 31% Thai HQ in Taiwan, China	100% Taiwanese-owned family firm	Private company, joint venture with Japanese partner owning 49%

TABLE 9 RETAIL FACTORIES VISITED IN CHINA AND THAILAND *(continued over)*

	China 1	China 2	China 3	China 4	China 5
Staff composition	>90% female, from island provinces	90% female, aged 18–26, from island provinces	52% male, aged 18+, from island provinces	90% female, from island provinces	80% female, av. age 21, from island provinces
Average number of employees	2,000	300 peak, now 240	2,993	1,500	300 peak
Labour turnover	6–48% p.a.	20–30% p.a.	46% p.a.	<10% p.a. in factory, double that in other 2 factories	120% p.a.
Wage system and average monthly wage (AMW)	Piece-rate system, workers experienced, hired locally; US$90.61	Time-based pay, individual bonuses; US$66.45–72.49 per month	75% time-based, 25% piece rate, bonuses based on efficiency, and company profit (rare); minimum wage at least	Time-based w. performance bonuses; US$48.33 in low season, US$72.49 in high season	US$60.41–72.49
Maximum working hours per day/annual leave	US$90.75 per month. Minimum wage at least	8 hours per day, max. 2 hrs overtime per week		8 hours/day and Sat overtime 36 hours/month overtime max.	0 hours per week, overtime in busy season (not more than 20 hours/wk)
Number of codes in factory and start dates	5+, circa 1990	5	2, September 2001 and early 2002	4, 1998/1999	4, starting 1997
Company type	Family, husband and wife chair	Owner-managed, HKK-based	Public co. based in Taiwan, China. 40 Taiwanese managers work here	Private company with 3 partners (not family)	Private company, owner-manager, HQ in HKK with 30 employees

TABLE 9 *(from previous page)*

2. Creating a shared vision

As with the footwear and apparel sectors, the creation of a shared vision around the code of conduct, its implementation and, more broadly speaking, the CSR programme as a whole, was a starting point for the retail MNEs interviewed. In light of this, in this section we examine the important role that top-management commitment plays in this process at both the MNE and supplier level. We then go on to consider the nature of the business case regarding compliance programmes in the retail sector.

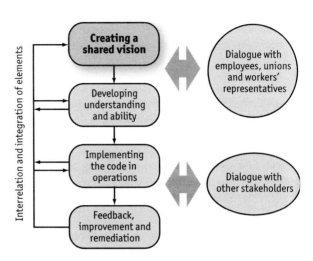

a. Top-management commitment

An obvious first stage in the development of a code-of-conduct or compliance programme is the creation of the code. In this, the retail industry has benefited from the examples of first movers in other sectors such as footwear and apparel, as well as input from NGOs and the Conventions and guidelines of the ILO.

> The NGO 3 wrote the code for us. We worked for one year together to find the right words. In drafting our code we looked at ILO Conventions and regulations. We didn't look at other codes because we were confident in NGO 3 (RMNE I, Administrative Manager).

> The Benchmarks used were the ILO provisions, early developments of the apparel industry partnership as well as looking at efforts of AMNE 3 and a handful of other companies (RMNE 3).

For some retail MNEs (RMNEs), the creation of a supplier code of conduct was an extension and modification of existing internal codes or values statements. In a sense, this task represents the updating of older value statements to deal with the modern realities of CSR and global supply chain management.

> The CEO said that this issue is included in the policy of RMNE 2. It is part of the values and politics of the company. We already had a value and mission statement written over 10, almost 15, years ago and one of the points covered the issue of social responsibility. You have to remember that this September will mark the 40th anniversary of RMNE 2's establishment. However, our values were made for internal use only. So we had to adapt it and work out what it meant (RMNE 2, Global Sourcing Manager).

RMNEs with more experience in CSR management have sometimes updated their codes to reflect lessons learned. RMNE I, for example, felt that its code should distinguish between those criteria that were minimum requirements for doing business and those items that were aspirational goals.

> Our new code was already written. Because the first was not good enough, we decided to change our code. We had more experience and knew what was important. We worked with a lawyer to change the code. The biggest change is that we decided to have two parts. The first deals with the most important criteria which must be adhered to and the second sets out our goals. The biggest change was on the issue of wages and the living wage. [We have two parts because] we know from experience that it is not possible to demand all the things at the same time (RMNE 1, Administrative Manager).

Once the code has been created, as in other sectors researched, we heard that top-management commitment plays an important role in the development of a shared vision regarding the code implementation programme. The overall role of the CEO and the board in firms is to identify industry trends and broad strategic goals. Instigating a programme to implement a code of conduct often falls within this function. Thus, as other firms within the retail industry or in similar industries adopt codes of conduct, and as NGOs make their concerns felt in the boardroom, we heard that top management in some RMNEs has reacted accordingly.

However, we were told that often the initial moves towards management of code-of-conduct issues are taken by senior management in corporate management functions (for example legal, PR or communications, HR) or operational divisions (for example, purchasing, logistics, marketing). At RMNE 1, for example, the corporate communications department played a pioneering role in the firm's move towards compliance management:

> Our chiefs, particularly those in communication, were convinced we had something to do. We heard what happened with FMNE 2, OMNE 6 and AMNE 4. Also, at this time it was the beginning of the campaigns by NGO 3 in France (RMNE 1, Administrative Manager).

Within RMNE 2, the pioneering move came from the top management of operational divisions, such as purchasing, that had direct experience with conditions in supplier factories.

> We started this approach in 1996 or 1997, because we wanted to write a [code] to define a position of RMNE 2 concerning the position of child labour. This was just before the World Cup and we were a sponsor. It was also around the time of the campaigns of NGO 3 and the FMNE 2 exposé. It was an operative decision, not from the CEO but from operational experience with our suppliers. Suppliers were asking many questions of us. The first ideas came from the RMNE 2 Foundation and our sourcing team (RMNE 2, Global Sourcing Manager).

These pioneering actions at the operational level indicate that code-of-conduct-related market pressures, such as brand protection, are being felt at the concrete level of day-to-day business within the firm rather than merely at the broader strategic level of the board in many instances. The experience of early movers in the retail sector suggests that senior management of operational divisions should not necessarily wait for CEO and board leadership on the issue of compliance management. Rather, in some cases divisional managers may be in a position to take the initiative, and subsequently seek support from the board for their activities.

> We had a team of people including myself as the admin manager, the manager of the textile department, imports manager, the director of communication and the director of bazaar. We met, brainstormed and decided to make a training programme on our code. At the beginning we had no special budget to do this. This only came after. The board of directors approved the budget for training and this was organised by our communication team. We have a training school for our buyers and all employees, generally run by HR. This is where our induction programme is done and it is where we did our training programme (RMNE I, Administrative Manager).

While the initiation of code-of-conduct activities may take place at the level of divisional or departmental management, we heard that such activities are unlikely to be translated into ongoing concrete programmes without the support of the CEO. The role of the CEO must be to continually stress the priorities of the firm, including its commitments to CSR management, which includes issues encompassed by the code of conduct. Accordingly, it is the role of the CEO to break 'log jams' in the corporate governance hierarchy—that is, to ensure that the execution of code goals is not blocked by divisional or departmental managers with divergent interests.

> [Compliance] is something that doesn't bring anything into the business, it covers you. Unfortunately for me, one of the buying directors in our business was anti this process, and the new buying director has question marks too. He controls our Far East offices, so our commitment to ethical trading is under review. The CEO believes that it has to be something that exists but the question as to what form it will exist in needs to be reviewed (RMNE IO, Ethical Trading Manager).

CEO and board-level commitment is especially necessary given the complex nature of large RMNEs whose management hierarchy is often characterised by pyramids within pyramids. Thus, as some RMNEs pointed out, divisional managers who are non-co-operative with code-of-conduct initiatives can effectively undermine such initiatives by not enforcing them throughout their division or 'pyramid of control'. However, while CEO leadership can play an important role in aligning the priorities of all divisional management, it is still important for compliance managers to actively 'sell' the compliance programme to key divisional managers, as well as other important stakeholders, such as suppliers. Without the buy-in of these key divisional managers and the management of the RMNE's main suppliers, the effectiveness of the code of conduct or compliance programme will be undermined. Thus, while CEO commitment is necessary, it is often not sufficient.

> We didn't sell our programme properly in the business. I think you need to sell it to everybody and you need to think about whom it's going to affect: buying, merchandising and quality assurance. I think that buying is most important because they are the ones that have cheque books. Here we had communication at the board level and we expected it to cascade down. But I don't think that that's what you should do, you have to do it yourself. You need to have communication externally as well. You need to tell your supply base what you're going to do. In our instance we wrote a letter. We gave them the code and we told them that we were going to audit. We also listed the

costs. It went down like a red flag and we got much negative feedback and they were also hassling the buyers. Buyers knew, but the trading director didn't know about this and it didn't cascade to the team so they were in an uproar. At the end of the day, we had a proposal which was accepted by the board of directors, by our chairman and the CEO, but it didn't cascade down (RMNE 10, Ethical Trading Manager).

While CEO and board-level commitment is important in setting up a compliance programme, it is absolutely crucial in maintaining it. Management of code-of-conduct issues in a global marketplace may result in occasional conflicts between short-term commercial priorities and the long-term, broader CSR strategy of the firm. Successful code management requires the board to demonstrate solid commitment to the overall CSR programme. Without this commitment, the compliance programme would almost certainly be whittled away by periodic challenges from operational divisions. Creating a strong foundation of commitment, however, sends a message to operational divisions that the company's commitment to its code guidelines is genuine and not open for debate. This will encourage a faster mainstreaming and integration of the programme into the firm's day-to-day operations.

[Our] Consumer Products [department] makes the requirements for review of working hours for Thailand, Malaysia and Singapore. Singapore just slightly exceeded the requirements. Thus, Consumer Products asked for a review because, they said, they would lose business there without an increase in working hours. They presented their information to the board. The board didn't even have to vote. It just reached a general consensus not to increase the hours (RMNE 3).

At the supplier level

Top-management commitment at the supplier level plays a key role in meeting the code requirements of RMNE customers. Code implementation activities at the supplier level can range from mere window-dressing efforts to genuine and active commitment to factory improvement. Where a supplier lies on this range is often determined by the commitment of its top management to the principles embodied in RMNE codes. In UKS 1 a shift from the low end of this spectrum to the high end was caused by a change in ownership and thus in top management. We heard that the new owners of the supplier took a more genuine interest in complying with buyers' codes.

I report in to the CEO. It was with the [new management] take-over that my job title also changed at the same time. Basically this was to reflect that social compliance was not going to be just a general policy on the wall but rather that there was a genuine commitment to it (UKS 1, Compliance Executive).

This shift in CEO commitment in UKS 1 reflects essentially a shift in the ownership structure. Within supplier firms that maintain the same management, however, such a shift can also occur. In UKS 3, for example, senior management came to realise that compliance management was not a niche area of the retailing industry, or a management fad engaged in by one or two select customers. Rather, UKS 3's management realised that a more fundamental shift in how the industry operates was taking place, and that to be competitive in such an industry suppliers would need to make a strategic shift in their approach to compliance management. The result of this shift in strategy by the supplier's senior management was a new, more effective approach to compliance; that is, code-of-conduct management within the supplier's operations.

> In the last eight months there has been a big change with our management. Before it was a case of people saying, for example, if RMNE 6 demand it then we will do it but if others do not, then we will not. Now the Chief Executive and the light sewing division manager realise that social compliance is not going away. The attitudes have changed and I have support from the very top. Now it is not a case of having RMNE 6, RMNE 3 or AMNE 4 require it. We realise that if we are serious about exporting to the US market, as is one of our aims, then we need to do this as a matter of course (UKS 3, Compliance Manager).

Since many suppliers to RMNEs are small to medium-sized enterprises (SMEs) with flatter management structures, CEOs often play a more hands-on role in code implementation than in the other sectors studied. The ongoing support of the CEO to code-of-conduct implementation plays an important role in creating effective management systems at the factory level.

> I have the commitment of the main board of directors and the CEO. The CEO sits at the end of this office and at the end of the corridor is the quality and engineering solutions head. On Fridays, when the sales figures come out, because of the need for a break, the CEO will often come to see me. He will ask me things like 'where are we at, what are we doing'. He is fully focused, he has a handle on moral issues and also is an astute businessman (UKS 2, Head of CSR).

In many small suppliers that we interviewed the cost of meeting code requirements was a particular concern. Top-management commitment is crucial at this level for allocating sometimes-scarce resources towards factory improvements. Without senior management support, the effectiveness of supplier-level code implementation efforts will be greatly reduced.

> The commitment of top management makes it easier for me to implement the codes. For example, if we want to buy some equipment for improvement, we get support from the top management. The boss trusts me to be responsible for all this. We don't have any mechanism for a formal review at the end of each year, but the boss is checking this all the time (CHS 1, Logistics Manager).

> Top-management support makes a big difference. For example, two years ago I came back from China and while the chief executive and MD were sympathetic to me they were concerned about us potentially not having enough business because we might cost ourselves out of the game. They pointed out that we needed to be realistic about our achievements (UKS 3, Compliance Manager).

b. Making the business case

Protection of brand value

In the highly competitive world of retailing, brand image adds a substantial amount of value to a typical RMNE. Brand image helps to forge lasting relationships with customers which is important in a low-margin industry that relies on repeat purchases and lifetime customer loyalty. As in other industries, as RMNEs introduce their code-of-conduct programmes they are often pressed to put them into a business context. The most direct contribution of code-of-conduct programmes to the retail industry's bottom line is in the protection of brand value.

> As we have rolled out the programme initially and to our business partners, there was not the global concern. The more difficult aspect of our education programme has been why they should be concerned about this issue. Therefore we have resorted to bringing it down to the business level—protection of the brand, what the philosophy is (RMNE 3).

For retail firms, brand image translates into sales. Thus when brand image is damaged, sales suffer. As a result, the importance of a programme on code-of-conduct issues is sometimes difficult to discern when it is functioning well (and protecting brand value). RMNEs interviewed were keen to point out that the business contribution of a compliance programme becomes relatively clear, however, in those firms where such a programme does not exist or plays no significant role.

> RMNE 6 had suffered poor sales directly because of a television exposé. At that time they realised that they need to protect their own brand. They appointed a manager, and called in the chief executives of RMNE 6's top 13 suppliers and announced that they were introducing a project on social compliance and that they would issue their general sourcing principles. RMNE 6 stated that they expected buy-in from all the suppliers (UKS 3, Compliance Manager).

The principal threat to brand image in the retail industry is 'bad press'. Negative media coverage, especially exposés on poor labour conditions in supplier plants, can produce significant damage to brand image and, consequently, sales—matters to which all RMNEs interviewed were particularly sensitive.

> The major US retailers are dreadfully exposed to bad press. Many organisations target retailers like AMNE 9, FMNE 2, O 9, RMNE 4 and AMNE 4. Last year AMNE 4 and FMNE 2 were hit in [a large Asian apparel factory] by a television exposé. As a result there is increased consciousness with US retailers (UKS 3, Compliance Manager).

> Production will only be stopped in certain situations [where] we would have no control over our quality or over the environmental and ethical issues. Much of this is driven by media attention and we cannot afford to take risks (RMNE 9, Group Company Secretary).

While RMNEs work to protect their valuable brands, we heard that in some cases suppliers have recognised the importance of their brand and are adopting code compliance as means to boost their own images *vis-à-vis* customers. As a Thai supplier to RMNE explains, 'We have to have the customer codes. It's better for the image' (THS 14, Production Manager).

Suppliers' business case: necessary to sell to buyers

The business case for suppliers is relatively straightforward: if they do not comply with the codes of RMNEs, then they will get no orders from those customers. Thus compliance for suppliers has simply become a base cost of doing business. As the comments below reveal, a growing number of suppliers are not being given the option of opting out of compliance programmes.

> Our CEO attended the RMNE 6 presentation where he was told that this was a mandatory term of business (UKS 4, Ethical and Quality Manager).

> I don't like talking about compliance with the law. You need a deterrent in business terms. And in business terms the deterrent is lack of orders, not a labour inspector (UKS 2, Head of CSR).

Accordingly, the RMNEs interviewed have increasingly been making their codes of conduct an integral part of the purchase order process.

> We attach this document [the code] to all our orders. It goes to all our suppliers. It has to be signed by the suppliers in order for them to do business with us. It could be the international merchandisers or the liaison merchandisers who show the code to the suppliers (RMNE I, Administrative Manager).

> The [code] forms a contract with local suppliers. Without this document signed, commercial negotiations cannot begin. So the [code] is given by merchandising (RMNE 2, Global Sourcing Manager).

This new requirement encompassing code-of-conduct issues in selling to RMNEs presents suppliers with another criterion which they may use to distinguish themselves from their competitors. As is discussed throughout this book, compliance with MNE codes is often not a case of full compliance or no compliance; rather, there are various degrees of compliance. The greater the supplier's capability to consistently meet and maintain code requirements, the more that supplier has to offer a RMNE. Where other factors such as cost and terms of delivery are equivalent, the supplier's management of code issues may be a decisive factor in winning additional business from a RMNE.

Suppliers' business case: improvement of management systems

A common argument for the business case of code implementation in many industries is the positive impact of improved labour conditions on worker productivity. As in other industries, there was some evidence for this in the case of suppliers to the retail industry that were interviewed.

> For example, RMNE 6 has had one of its suppliers in Morocco conduct literacy classes for all of its employees which then spread to all of the other suppliers doing the same. Basically in Morocco, 65% at least of women are literate and many of them are over the age of 25. RMNE 6 found at the end of 1999 that one factory was giving literacy training which was linked to the government so basically all that supplier had to do was to provide a facility. This supplier then shared this information with the rest of the benchmarking group and informed them that by providing literacy classes he had increased productivity by 15%, because the workers could now read and write the instruc-

tions. Consequently all the other suppliers decided to follow suit (RMNE 6, Central Co-ordinator, Ethical Issues).

What is perhaps far more interesting in the retail industry, however, is how some suppliers view poor labour conditions as a symptom of much deeper problems in productivity management. This view is particularly applicable to the issue of long working hours. According to this perspective, we heard that the question being asked is not so much, 'how can better labour conditions improve productivity?' Rather, it is, 'how can improved productivity produce better labour conditions?' The fundamental problem in factories with poor labour conditions is being perceived as a problem with productivity in some cases. Thus, by drawing attention to improving labour conditions in a factory, the hope of some RMNEs is to simultaneously address the productivity issue. RMNEs regard a solution to the productivity issue as producing benefits for the workers as well as profits for the supplier firm and it is this point that they are emphasising with their suppliers. The compliance manager from UKS 3 explains this approach in UKS 3's factories.

> By increasing productivity I knew that we could bump up earnings, decrease the need for longer hours, hire less people and add profits to the bottom line. Therefore, there would be no real cost to compliance. My conclusion was that we needed a productivity programme. We had to look at line balancing and supporting the factory. We needed to ensure that patterns, trims and fabrics were at the factory on time. This was an internal problem with our purchasers. We also had to look at our operating methods and set targets for improved efficiency. The results were that the RMNE 6 unit went from an efficiency of 45 to between 70 and 72. Approximately one third of the factory produces for RMNE 6 and in that facility there is no perceived cost for compliance. The other two thirds of the factory are now panning out the whole process (UKS 3, Compliance Manager).

The focus on code compliance at the supplier level can add broad knock-on effects for management systems in general. Managing productivity, inventory, quality and human resources are all impacted by efforts to improve labour conditions in the supplier factory. Thus there is a view among some suppliers that investing in code compliance represents a long-term investment in better-quality management systems.

> We should encourage people to follow the code and recognise the importance of the reasons for the code. If you look at ten years ago when factories implemented TQM or TQC, some manufacturers said we do not need that. As long as you have quality or competitive prices then you don't need that. I see code of conduct the same as TQM. Without this you will lose business (CHS 3, Admin Manager).

3. Developing understanding and ability

Following the creation and establishment of a code of conduct and
a common vision regarding its
meaning and implications for
business are the important steps
associated with developing understanding and ability of all who are
involved directly and indirectly in
its implementation. In this section
we explore the ways in which
RMNEs communicate their code to
their suppliers and what degree of
leverage they have over what in
many cases is a vast supply base.
We also examine in detail the
associated education and training
that takes place and the important
roles that workers play.

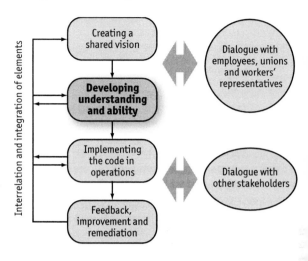

a. Making compliance a priority with all components of the supply chain

A vital role of the CSR department is to establish systems and processes for the communication of the code throughout the MNE so that all MNE employees
and managers in the supply chain understand the meaning and purpose of the code. In
this section we examine the various methods used to achieve this goal.

Communicating the code to suppliers

We heard that, in order to be effective, communication of the code must be a continuous process of reinforcing the RMNE's commitment. In general it begins with the first
contacts between the RMNE and any new supplier.

> RMNE 10 has an induction programme, and ethical trading is covered in there
> through a broad statement. We state the concept of it and we mention that
> we have a dedicated department. It is part of our portfolio issues. It forms part
> of our responsibility in terms of conceptual holistic terms, but not in terms of
> specific terms (RMNE 10, HR Director).

Some RMNEs find they are benefiting from the prior propagation of codes in the
footwear and apparel industries. As a result of the increasingly widespread use of
codes, many suppliers in the retail sector were already aware of codes prior to being
informed directly by the RMNE. As the compliance manager for supplier UKS 3 observed,
'Globally, the movers and shakers within factories all know about social compliance.'
This mainstreaming effect of code compliance programmes somewhat eases the RMNE's

job of introducing the CSR codes. Suppliers are at least familiar with the concept and, in most cases, the content of the codes. Indeed some suppliers in this sector have actually approached the RMNE asking for its code.

> We have raised more and more awareness with our suppliers but in many instances it is our suppliers who are saying to us, 'what are you doing about this?' and they want guidance from us on this issue because of increasing pressure that's being placed on them (RMNE 9, Group Company Secretary).

Nonetheless, from our interviews it seems that there are some areas where RMNEs may not be doing enough to communicate their code to suppliers. Familiarity with the concept among suppliers may lead some RMNEs to complacence. The attitude of an administrative manager at RMNE 1 reflects an unproductive approach to communicating that particular firm's code of conduct.

> We do not ask suppliers to put the code on the wall. It has not been translated into other languages and even if it was most of the workers do not read Chinese. And finally, this code is just one of many. The purpose of all the codes is similar. If suppliers have a lot of buyers saying the same thing then hopefully more of it will come into their heads (RMNE 1, Administrative Manager).

An effective approach to code-of-conduct implementation includes consistent communication of the code, not only to create an awareness of the code, but also a sense of priority. A particularly constructive means of code communication is the development of training programmes for factory management. Some suppliers such as UKS 2 have adopted a systematic approach to developing training programmes with their subcontractors.

> For existing suppliers, it's easy, because we are in those factories all the time. So what we simply did was that we ran training sessions within the UK over a period of half a day in the RMNE 6 standards and how to apply those standards. The people who attended were any senior-level people with procurement or working knowledge with suppliers. The only people that were left out of this training were our offshore people. Now we have gradually been prioritising this training to our existing supply base offshore by country. So for instance, we have already carried out the training in Morocco. Basically the decision to focus on which country was made by just picking those regions with the main bulk of our business, that is, it was a financial decision (UKS 2, Head of CSR).

Moving beyond training programmes is the holding of meetings between managers of an RMNE and its suppliers on code-of-conduct issues. In the case of RMNE 6, the result has been a constructive team effort to arrive at solutions that impact the entire supply chain due to the drive of the RMNE. Of all the RMNEs interviewed, this approach appeared to be the most ingrained and developmental.

> One of the first things that I was asked to do was to attend meetings with [RMNE 6 personnel] and from then on I basically had a crash course. We conducted six weekly meetings. At first the top 13 suppliers that attended these meetings would sit down and think about what we were going to talk about. Today these meetings are more structured. We talk about things such

as training, audit companies' attitudes and standard of work (UKS 1, Compliance Executive).

It is interesting to note that RMNEs tend to expect large MNE suppliers of branded products to ensure their own compliance programmes. As a result, many have focused on suppliers of private-label or store brands, often referred to as 'own brands' (as they are the own brands of the RMNE), as well as 'no-brand' products.

> Basically, I looked at how we get to produce these branded products, but not the big name brands—these I put to one side because I knew they would manage their own compliance (RMNE 7).

Leverage over the supply chain

RMNE compliance managers stressed that rapid churn of their supply base and low off-take of a supplier's total output are issues that affect their ability to make their code a priority with suppliers. Concerning low off-take, RMNE 1 explained, 'When RMNE 1 does a social audit in the factory it cannot impose changes because the turnover for us is not enough and we do not have the power. How can we be stronger?' (RMNE 1, Administrative Manager). A contributing factor to the question of off-take may be the nature of the goods with which retailers deal. Hardlines, in particular, were cited as a product category in which retailers often do not claim a large percentage of any given supplier's production, as reflected in the comments made by Agent 1: '[Compliance management] is simple if you control 100%, then it is easy. [However] in hardlines to be 3% in a factory is a huge deal.' Rapid churn of the supply base may also undermine an RMNE's ability to communicate the code and make the code a priority for the supplier. It has been seen in practice in other sectors studied that both communication and making the code a priority is achieved through an extended relationship between the MNE customer and the supplier. In the case of RMNEs that switch suppliers often, it may be difficult to establish the type of business relationship required to effectively communicate the code and establish it as a priority for the supplier.

> Our decision on sourcing is very important. First of all it always depends on price. The code and our programme makes a difference for us in working with suppliers because we cannot guarantee orders year after year and yet are asking for changes. Today we are looking for solutions to this challenge but it is tough (RMNE 1, Administrative Manager).

Of course the opposite, a low churn rate, may have the effect of helping to communicate the code and establish code compliance as a priority within the supplier. Further studies on this need to be conducted before firm conclusions can be reached.

> We rarely jump from one supplier to another, so when you ask me a question about non-directly owned factories, this is what I want to remind you. We tend to go into a supply base and to develop it into our supply chain for long-term partnership reasons. This is important because we have a, well, not really joint venture in Morocco, but we have three factories there, which have worked with us for as long as I can remember. This is important because you need to have a stable relationship and full leverage (UKS 2, Head of CSR).

Distinction between hardlines and softlines

Another unique aspect of the retail industry is the distinction between hardlines and softlines. Several interviews suggest that the challenges of communicating a CSR programme are different for each of these product lines. Supply chains for hardlines in particular are mentioned as presenting obstacles. As Agent 1 argues, 'It is a huge challenge. In softlines we began ten years ago. In hardlines it is different, except for certain lines.'

This challenge is also reflective of the complexity of the supply chain that is typically found in hardline products. Repeatedly, RMNE managers stressed that it was more difficult to ascertain exactly who was the producer of a particular hardline product and consequently who should be held accountable for the implementation of a code of conduct. For this reason, most retailers interviewed have opted to commence the code implementation process with their softline suppliers with a view to expanding to hardline suppliers in the future.

b. Communicating the code and its impact

Communicating the code to workers

One of the primary stakeholders of CSR programmes are the workers which the programmes are intended to support. It is crucial therefore that RMNEs take appropriate measures to communicate the code and its intention to workers in supplier factories, particularly if workers have not been involved in its creation. From our interviews it appears that this need for communicating to workers is often underestimated by both suppliers and RMNEs. A representative from a supplier in the UK, a supplier which in turn sources product from developing countries, expressed the belief that, 'I do not think that workers need training on social compliance . . . I don't think that there is a workforce that is looking for more training' (UKS 3, Compliance Manager). Yet such views fail to recognise the low level of basic abilities, such as literacy, among many unskilled factory workers in developing countries. In many instances, illiterate workers have no understanding of their basic rights under the law or MNE code provisions. Innumeracy among workers, to take another example, undermines their ability to judge the accuracy of their pay. These issues both complicate the communication of codes and point to the need for increased efforts to communicate effectively with workers.

The most commonly cited means of communicating codes and code provisions to workers was via factory induction programmes. It is both reasonable and desirable that workers are introduced to MNE codes at the very outset of their employment; thus induction programmes can provide an opportune time for communicating the code. Some firms, however, pointed out the risk in adopting such an approach as the meaning of the code and its provisions may be lost among the wide variety of factory rules and job-related instruction that occurs during a typical induction programme. As many of the firms interviewed supplied products to more than one RMNE, we heard that they tended not to include coverage of each individual RMNE code in the induction programme but rather provided a broad overview of the common elements of all applicable codes. In many instances these broad elements were translated into generic company rules and procedures. While communication of the code during induction programmes is necessary and appropriate, the evidence from our interviews suggests that it is not sufficient and should be supplemented by subsequent and ongoing means of communication, particularly of elements not included within the induction programme.

> First there is an orientation course which covers company policy, rules and regulations, tasks. It lasts half a day and includes code training. We tell them about ISO quality and importance of customer satisfaction (THS 13, Manager).

> We have an induction programme of one day's duration which encompasses: the rules and regulations of the company, policy of the company, that is the production policy, occupational safety and health, benefits, meals—three per day, dormitories. We also discuss guiding principles [based on MNE codes]. We don't give a copy but just read them, and they are also posted on the board. We propagate the system through a public address every week (THS 14, HR Manager).

> Workers are aware of what code of conduct is because of the induction programme (CHS 1, Chairman).

> To ensure that workers are aware of their rights, all this is explained to newcomers as part of the induction programme given by personnel. And once or twice a month we explain about their rights. This is normally done workshop by workshop. The last one was last week. It is carried out by the personnel department, and is done for all the workers in the workshop (CHS 1, Logistics Manager).

> There is an induction programme which covers rules and regulations, working time, welfare benefits, logistics, food and canteen, dormitories, and safety inside the factory, fire-fighting. This kind of training is held from four to six pm. Sometimes they have training for new regulations within this format. She is paid for this training session. The training is done in three sessions of two hours each, that is, over a period of three weeks (CHS 1, Personnel Manager).

> Workers know about code as it is on the board in the factory. We also give some training. Managerial staff will read the articles of the codes to the workers during the induction period. This is done by personnel staff in the workshop. They read each code to the workers. We also teach fire prevention to the workers (CHS 2, Quality Supervisor).

Improved induction programmes

Standard induction programmes may be improved with more focused training on code provisions and, where available, presentations from workers' representatives and/or local government labour officials. Additionally, special attention could be paid to assessing workers' comprehension of the issues being explained. A supplier in China takes a useful approach by interviewing workers after their induction programme to see if they understand the code and its application to their job.

> There are lectures on rules and regulations in the factory, codes, policies and principles about the government, labour law, trade union rules, etc. New-

comers this month received one day's training on all this. People from different departments come and give lectures, for example, the Trade Union—the workers' representative will give the lecture. For fire prevention, that department will come and talk to them. I train them in the factory rules and regulations. The lecture is followed by an interview, that is, a questionnaire to see if they remember it. We train the code, and the assistant to the director gives an oral examination after the lecture. An example of a question: if you work overtime, how much should you be paid? (CHS 2, Personnel Manager).

Challenge of communicating with illiterate workers

According to managers interviewed, it is always desirable to issue workers with their own personal copies of key documents, such as codes and other important job-related information (for example, pay rates, bonus schemes, overtime regulations). We heard of many different ways to provide workers with copies of codes of conduct.

> A pocket-sized version of our code is distributed to workers (RMNE 3).

> Each worker has a card with a code, an ID card—when workers start they get this. The supervisor reminds them. There are codes all over the factory (THS 12, Manager).

Both RMNE and supplier managers stated that efforts to provide workers with personal copies of written information can be helpful. As we touched on above, a major obstacle to communicating codes through written documents, however, is the high proportion of illiteracy among unskilled labourers in developing countries. We heard that illiteracy is especially prevalent among the young women who typically make up the workforce in many factories, especially softlines. Apart from literacy training programmes (note example in Section 2.b), the only apparent means of overcoming this challenge is via oral communication. However, managers in supplier factories undertaking such communication felt that it was important to complement oral communication with some means of testing comprehension in an effort to gauge how well workers understood the communication that had taken place.

> We train workers on the code and factory rules in the beginning, usually in the first month. In the beginning we sent the written documents to them but found that it was difficult to get them to understand because they could hardly read. So we have now changed to verbal training and test them orally (CHS 3, Production Manager).

Challenge of measuring worker comprehension of codes

Indeed the extent of workers' comprehension of codes and specific code provisions is an area of debate. Factory managers often reported that workers are aware of codes. From our interviews we heard that the common practice is for codes to be displayed on the walls of factories and mentioned during induction programmes and regular announcements.

> Most workers know what codes are (CHS 2, Personnel Manager).

> Workers know what code is because we put code on the notice boards in the workshops. When workers first come, we explain the code to them and we tell them that more customers will want us to meet code and that we will be audited on this (CHS 5, Production Manager).

> We believe they understand. Supervisors also inform them about the code. Once a month, supervisors will talk about key issues: production, safety, etc. At the beginning the supervisor talks about code. This company follows the law already (THS 9, Personnel Manager).

While it may well be that workers are aware of codes, in most instances from our interviews the extent of this awareness was not at all clear. Do they understand the difference between RMNE codes and other factory regulations? Do they understand specific provisions of codes? Do they understand the implications of those provisions? What is of importance is whether or not workers understand basic code principles, such as those addressing freedom of association, limits on work hours or overtime pay requirements.

> Workers don't understand codes of conduct. What I think is that it is important that workers can see the impact of these things physically. When it comes to code of conduct in implementation, I am a firm believer of good induction training for all employees, including concepts of fair trade and the explanation of what codes of conduct are so that when employees see these things on the wall they understand (UKS 2, Head of CSR).

Need for more-developed approaches to communicating with workers

Some RMNEs recognised that code communication can be improved through a greater focus on communicating the code to factory workers. Few RMNEs had actually undertaken such an approach as part of their implementation process although some highlighted this as a goal for the future development of their compliance management programmes.

> [One of our key programmes is] education: for licensees, vendors and manufacturers, factories and workers. We want to expand on worker education as this has been limited to date (RMNE 3).

> I encourage managers to start an education programme [for workers]. Hopefully we will have to sit down at one stage and do one of these programmes with the management and the workers to allay the management fears [about freedom of association] because they are all terrified. But at the end of the day I want to do the training in conjunction with managers. Right now, my training is aimed at middle managers, for example, the China workshop, and so the training for workers and managers is a target for next year, sometime after April (RMNE 6, Central Co-ordinator, Ethical Issues).

Demographics of workers

The demographic profile of workers in developing-country suppliers to RMNEs provides insights to the challenges of code communication. In many countries, factories producing both hardlines and softlines are often staffed by migrant labour. Factory workers, especially in softlines, tend to be young (below the age of 25) women.

> There are now 2,000 workers from inland provinces such as Hebei, Hunan and Sichuan. Over 90% of workers are migrant women (CHS 1, Chairman).

> They come from Northern provinces and are mainly women: 90% between 18 and 26 years of age (CHS 2, Director).

> Eighty per cent of workers are female, mainly migrant workers (CHS 5, Production Manager).

> There are 1,500 workers, of which 70% are female and 30% male. They come from all over, from 65 provinces (THS 14, Director).

Since many workers are female migrants, they often live in dormitories owned by and located near the factories where they work.

> Migrant workers come from a range of provinces inland. Most of them, nearly 100%, come from inland. About 80% live in dormitories and 20% in their own houses with their family (CHS 3, Production Manager).

> The average age of workers is 23. Seventy per cent are female and 30% male (CHS 3, Production Manager).

Many workers in this sector work only for a limited period of time and then return to their region or country of origin. However, supplier managers reported that there are significant numbers of workers settling in the areas where they work, raising important questions regarding infrastructure and services in the factory vicinity.

> Workers live in this area. Some workers migrated from other areas but got married here and stay. That was at the beginning of the factory. There used to have dormitories at the beginning of the company, but now the workers have family here and live around here. Sixty per cent of workers came from the north east [poorest and black in colour]. Workers from these areas don't like to work hard (THS 9, Personnel Director).

> In China 80% of workers live in. Most are from peasant farms in the north. For some the main aim is to secure employment and to build a better life. It used to be that they would do this for some months and then go back home and marry. Now many stay and make a new life in the south as there are more prospects there, it is more western and there is more employment (UKS 3, Compliance Manager).

c. Education and training in support of the code

An important aspect of compliance management is providing training to key stakeholders on the provisions of corporate codes and their implications for specific day-to-day operations. Many RMNEs offer various degrees of training in support of their code. From our interviews it is clear that the focus of the training varies in terms of the recipients of the training and the topics covered. Many, such as RMNE 7 and RMNE 10, take a broad approach.

The roll-out took place intensely and extensively. We did training in Europe and Latin America of vendors, factories and RMNE 7 staff (RMNE 7).

I did a series of presentations to all in the head office and externally to colleagues and call centres, retailers, and to our suppliers on RMNE 10's values and ethical trading. Basically I explained what and why. I did this last year to about 2,500 people. We have also developed our ethical trading intranet which needs development. It is accessed by 2,200 people in head office and there are about 7,000 terminals if you include stores, our national distribution centres and our auditors in the field. Two people are working on this net. We also have our magazine which goes to all employees and includes articles on what we do. Basically we are bringing it home to people. The ethical trading group was involved in the first comic relief in 1999 and there were two pages on how our factory produced things (RMNE 10, Ethical Trading Manager).

Training within the RMNEs in some instances extends downstream to the retail storefront. As CSR issues begin to overlap with customer service issues, it becomes increasingly important for front-line sales personnel to be able to address consumer concerns at the point of purchase.

I am in charge of communication with stores. My idea is to explain what we do because more and more customers and NGOs are asking our store employees. It is dangerous for us if our employees do not answer. I am planning on training them this year. Last year we sent an information leaflet to management in each of our stores telling them about our programme (RMNE 1, Communications Manager).

A key focal group of RMNE training are the purchasing officers (or 'buyers') of the RMNE. These managers, who often have direct relationships with suppliers, are trained on the provisions of the code and the implications it has for their job. Some RMNEs also provide their buyers with training on the broader conditions of life in LDCs, which serve as challenges for LDC-based suppliers.

In 1999 our international buyers (numbering 60) received training. It took two years to get to this point. We had outside people assist in the training, including one person from the NGO 3, one person who spoke about geopolitics [a consultant] and one from an NGO who talked about action against hunger. The training was conducted over two days. We told our buyers that we wanted to go to our suppliers to see what the conditions were, that we had to try to improve the work conditions and see if there was child labour (RMNE 1, Administrative Manager).

I have implemented a training programme for our buyers—that takes one day. For other people I do a half-day training programme. It is not mandatory. Only those who want to know about it attend. So far, I have trained all the international buyers and some French buyers. In total about 200 people. We have approximately 55,000 employees just in France including our store employees (RMNE 1, Administrative Manager).

It is notable that in the training programme of RMNE 1 described above, *all* of the international buyers had received training despite the fact that the training programme was *not* mandatory. This perhaps reflects the interest of buyers in some firms in the actual implications of the code on their work. Indeed it is sometimes through buyers that RMNEs train suppliers in compliance management. This training explains to suppliers the expectations of the MNE's code and the implications this has for factory management. Training at the supplier management level also includes details of the MNE's approach to auditing. This training is intended to give suppliers a fair understanding of what is expected of them and how they might reasonably meet these expectations.

> Our merchandising department introduces our social responsibility programme to our suppliers. At the beginning of the relationship we explain the [code]. We have a guy based in Hong Kong who is in charge of production of suppliers [who does the CSR training]. He used to do just quality but he now also does [code compliance] audits. He was trained. We spent one or two days there to train him. The main problem for us is to explain things to be near to reality. We need to know the regulations, laws etc. (RMNE 2, Global Sourcing Manager).

> I meet with my top 15 supply chain managers in the UK every six to eight weeks. [. . .] I have to explain to these people that there is no commercial edge to this because, even if the smallest business suffers, everyone is going to have a damaged edge. We have a very confident team of social compliance experts now. My next ten suppliers are learning from this team. I use keynote speakers from my top 15 and this second group meets every three months. Some of them even have to fly in because they tend to be large offshore businesses with head offices in either Hong Kong [China], Turkey or Austria, but they are still big enough to warrant treatment from the bottom of the pack. We have only started this group in the last six months. There is an agenda and minutes of the meeting are kept. For example, the group will be a totally level group and we will circulate the chair (RMNE 6, Supply Chain Compliance Manager).

RMNEs often benefit from the training programmes of other RMNEs as well as AMNEs and FMNEs. While the code provisions of these MNEs are often similar, it is noted by suppliers that different MNEs often emphasise different elements of their codes in their training. This overlapping of training at the supplier level can result in a beneficial externality for all other MNEs' code programmes.

> Workshops were held by FMNE 2, AMNE 4, OMNE 5 and RMNE 3. AMNE 4 was about environmental protection, working hours, wages and, most importantly, safety. They taught how to maintain safety in the workshops. The workshops are normally one day long, or sometimes they can be up to five days of training, for example FMNE 2 on the same topics as above. The workshops are held in other factories, hotels, etc. The purpose of this training is to explain their codes and how to implement them. It is better to have individual company training. Although there is not much difference between companies, they may have different ideology and emphasis. For example, AMNE 4 places more emphasis on environmental protection while FMNE 2 concentrates more on wages calculation (CHS 1, Logistics Manager).

In some instances we heard of suppliers that are subject to only one RMNE code, and thus training from that individual RMNE may play an important role in influencing conditions there. Such training may also 'set the stage' for the supplier's future relations with other RMNEs, and the supplier may come to see code compliance programmes as standard operating procedure for large RMNEs.

> Apart from RMNE 6 and the working groups we have, no other brands have given us assistance. The only contact that we have had outside of the audit is if I have contacted them. I have met with AMNE 4 in Hong Kong [China] and Sri Lanka and the RMNE 3 people. Most of our training though has been from RMNE 6 (UKS 3, Compliance Manager).

RMNEs that were in more advanced stages of their code implementation process stated that they often included country-wide workshops for the management of supplier factories. These workshops, we were told, not only allow RMNEs to provide training on code compliance, but also allow managers from different factories to discuss common challenges, and share best practices, in meeting code requirements.

> In the last two and a half to three years, RMNE 6 has increased awareness and has developed local benchmarking groups in places such as Morocco, Sri Lanka, Indonesia, Turkey, Egypt, India and Viet Nam. These benchmarking groups are basically local suppliers working together to share information. They have also created country-specific one-day workshops with a view to building the capacity of local managers. There have been four so far in China and these have been conducted in Cantonese or Mandarin (RMNE 6, Central Co-ordinator, Ethical Issues).

Formal training programmes for suppliers help them to prepare for the subsequent stages of auditing and corrective action. For those suppliers, or their personnel, who do not benefit from formal training programmes, auditing seems to play the role of a front-line training programme where suppliers enter into a 'learn by doing' process.

> I didn't get any formal training [from the brands], but since I came here various auditors come and they check what I know about the details of their codes, so this has been a learning experience for me (CHS 2, Personnel Manager).

d. Training of workers in code compliance

Training of workers in code compliance issues is often scant in the retail sector. Some training programmes do exist, for example during induction programmes, but these are often insufficient to develop any sustained or developed understanding of code issues and their implication for workers' day-to-day activities.

> There is no need for training. It is at production meetings regarding new orders that all workers get to know what customers need regarding quality and production. When newcomers arrive they get to know what their rights and responsibilities are, that is, through the induction programme (CHS 1, Chairman).

Where suppliers have provided workers with training, it was often on job skills and basic factory safety practices. While this is important, it does not substantially develop the workers' understanding of the code and its various provisions.

> We provide workers with some training. Design work may need some higher education, and if workers have more education, we can promote them. They can learn easier. We provide training on rules and regulations, then safety, then basic task skills, then on-the-job training regarding tasks by the team leader. Training on rules and regulations is about one hour on induction. Safety training is also one hour. For each subject we give an hour (CHS 5, Production Manager).

To effectively train workers on code compliance issues, there needs to be more focus on a periodic basis, rather than merely during one-off induction sessions. The following example provided by a supplier in Thailand provides an indication of a more ingrained approach to the training of workers.

> An induction programme was used for workers in the past and is used now. This is an orientation and we then follow up with supervisors of each section—giving them information and discussing the rules and regulations with them. We do this the first time we recruit and then do follow up. Orientation takes one day. Training is done on an ad hoc basis. It covers general information and safety and ISO. For example, rules and regulations and how to be with other workers. The personnel officer will go round and see that workers understand and do the right thing. It is difficult to convince workers to wear PPE. We try to explain to the workers about hazardous issues and every year we have a Health & Safety week to bring them greater awareness. We put posters up to show workers, and FMNE 1 also [provides] posters (THS 9, Personnel Manager).

The importance of worker training lies in the ability of empowered and trained workers to act as an internal check on code compliance. Workers who are aware of their rights and who feel confident those rights will be respected are perhaps the best means for ensuring compliance in every facet of factory operations. It is the workers who are ultimately on the front line of the manufacturing process and it is they who will be in the best position to provide feedback on code compliance issues.

> In some cases factories are teaching themselves and, also at the auditor level, we are holding the factories' hands which is why we have put out sample documents. But you are right, auditing isn't always working and therefore we now need to educate the worker to see if they can push the factories (RMNE 7).

e. Costs

The costs of compliance management are a prominent concern of both RMNEs and their suppliers. At the supplier level there is particular concern about the costs of compliance, though this concern can vary significantly from factory to factory, depending on the financial strength of the supplier as well as the amount of corrective action required to meet minimum code standards. A supplier from China, for example, reported few problems from a cost perspective when meeting code conditions: 'We have not yet met any big challenges in implementation changes as normally what is suggested is something we can do fairly easily or not at big cost' (CHS 1, Logistics Manager). The same supplier, however, also noted that the redundant processes of managing compliance with multiple codes adds unwelcome costs: 'It is difficult to have several auditors from different companies—it makes our costs higher. So this is not so good' (CHS 1, Chairman). Other suppliers complained of the costs associated with meeting code standards, yet clearly recognised the overall benefits to the workers in their factories.

> The code has had the effect of: avoiding chemicals hazardous to workers' health, changing chemicals—for example water-based glue, reducing lead content in the production process. If there are better environmental and working conditions then the workers are happier. The disadvantages are that it is costly to implement the code (THS 9, Managing Director).

Indeed, for the management of suppliers that genuinely want to improve working conditions and wages, cost was often cited as a major obstacle. These suppliers pointed out what they saw as a fundamental contradiction in the MNEs' programmes: namely, that while CSR management stressed improvements to meet code standards, the same MNE's operational management (purchasing, sales) was continually applying downward pressure on price. Ultimately this perceived contradiction would come to a head at the supplier level; here suppliers felt their margins were being squeezed by the need to meet MNE price demands and squeezed yet further by the need to meet the MNE code requirements. We heard that suppliers saw that their only way out of this 'lower income and higher cost' trap was to implement innovative productivity solutions. Productivity improvements, however, are dependent in part on the industry; for softlines in particular, managers reported having only modest productivity improvements.

> The negative thing with the code is the cost. The company really wants to make good things for the workers but normally the salespeople are not related to the people doing the auditing. They always want a better price from us while code-of-conduct people ask us to pay better. This is a challenge for us. How can we make both departments happy? The only thing we see is the cost. If we can achieve productivity and efficiency then maybe we can offset some of the admin costs (CHS 3, Administrative Manager).

> Until we can increase wages and reduce working hours we're going in under the CSR banner, but in reality it's about brand protection. The only way to change this is for brands to absorb cost (UKS 2, Head of CSR).

For the RMNEs, the principal costs of compliance management are usually the audits, particularly as there tends to be a greater reliance on more expensive external audits than in other sectors. Most RMNEs bear some or all the costs of audits, or at least initial audits. There was some reported divergence between the practice of UK- and US-based MNEs, however. In the US it was reportedly more common for the RMNEs to pay for the costs of factory audits, while in the UK it was reportedly the reverse, with suppliers picking up the bulk of the cost. A third-party auditor serving RMNEs on both sides of the Atlantic observed, 'In the United Kingdom, vendors pay for the programme in contrast with the US where retailers pay' (TPA 4, Business Development Manager). In terms of cost sharing between RMNEs and suppliers, RMNEs have also devised incentive programmes regarding the costs of audits. Several RMNEs reportedly bear the cost of audits only when suppliers pass the audit. Again, TPA 4 observed that, for example, 'RMNE 6 suppliers have incentives for factories—if they fail an audit, they must pay'.

RMNE 9 has a similar procedure. The Group Company Secretary for RMNE 9 explains that: 'For the initial audit, RMNE 9 pays. It also pays for all of the schedule audits. However, if a company fails an audit and there needs to be a re-audit, then the supplier is accountable' (RMNE 9, Group Company Secretary).

An important background factor influencing both the suppliers' and RMNEs' perception of compliance cost is the inherent comparison to the costs of pre-code operations. Such comparisons, however, may discount illegally externalised costs, such as suppliers that may not have paid the legal minimum wage, or met legal fire, safety and environmental guidelines. Certainly it is true that illegal activity can often be the source of considerable short-term cost savings; but the cost structure of illegal activity is hardly the basis of comparison for a legitimate factory participating in the global value chain of a major RMNE. When the basis of comparison is the cost structure of a factory that is at least in compliance with local laws, the perceived cost of compliance programmes is often significantly reduced.

> Our other biggest hurdle was, how much will this cost? This was from the perspective both within our own group and with our suppliers. We had senior financial directors spending hours working out the cost of this. Costs were going to be high because we had to look at paying minimum wages, overtime at 150% and ten statutory holiday days. The cost of the actual compliance programme in contrast was low. It was basically just me and my air fare (UKS 3, Compliance Manager).

4. Implementing the code in operations

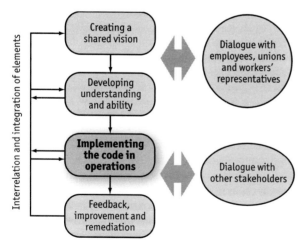

Implementation of the code of conduct within the operations of an organisation requires more than just the development of a coherent message. As the following sections illustrate, it requires the establishment of specific enabling mechanisms, including the creation of a CSR department or allocation of responsibility for CSR issues both at the MNE level and at the supplier level.

a. The structure of corporate social responsibility

As with the footwear and apparel sectors, the structure of CSR units within RMNEs interviewed varied greatly. Factors influencing the structure of a CSR department included both objective and subjective criteria, including the complexity and size of the organisation, as well as the underlying commitment made by RMNE senior management to social responsibility. The CSR units were further influenced by the degree to which the RMNE was centralised, with, for example, a majority of planning and decision-making emanating from a single office, as opposed to a decentralised structure, in which both personnel and decision-making authority is meted out to individuals in the field.

Some RMNEs have retained authority for all CSR responsibility with a single group at headquarters, as shown in Figure 19. This was usually the case with smaller companies interviewed, or those that seemed to be struggling to determine precisely what commitment to CSR their organisation was willing to make. Some of these RMNEs had a single individual responsible for all elements of compliance and CSR. Other entities, usually the larger RMNEs, had a much more developed system and were further along with the integration of compliance and CSR-related responsibilities in their overall corporate structures. These included a diversified approach, with field personnel either regionally placed, or within specific countries. As has been identified throughout this book, the commitment to CSR has much to do with past experience with compliance and labour, social and ethical issues: those firms that have received significant attention for poor past performance have advanced with respect to design and implementation of compliance and CSR systems.

Further, the most challenging task we observed was the need to integrate compliance and CSR-related decision-making authority into the operating systems of other corporate departments. Part of this challenge has to do with the fact that many busy RMNE corporate departments are accustomed to their existing operating procedures

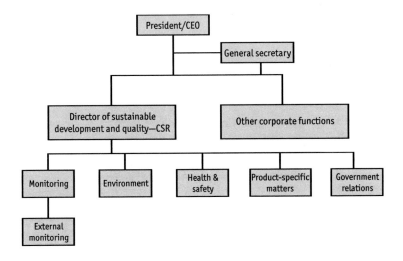

FIGURE 19 EXAMPLE OF THE ORGANISATIONAL STRUCTURE OF AN RMNE

and, therefore, we heard, are resistant to change. On a related point, the development of CSR functions and responsibilities is fairly recent and is often perceived as an added burden to the already intense and stressful corporate operations. As RMNE CSR departments continue to evolve, the real challenge for RMNEs of all sizes is to determine the most effective and least costly means with which to integrate compliance and CSR responsibilities in an appropriate manner across all relevant corporate departments.

b. Implementation at the supplier level

Implementing compliance and CSR requirements at the supplier level of RMNEs poses a major challenge. Again, the great diversity of operations, high supplier churn, inconsistent production demands, and high employee turnover in some regions lead to complexities not necessarily experienced in the headquarters of the RMNE. Thus, special attention needs to be given to understanding the operating structures of suppliers, so as to assist them in the adequate implementation of systems to ensure that code provisions are understood, implemented and continuously improved and verified.

When interviewed, suppliers raised their own concerns, primarily driven by what is specifically or contractually mandated of them. This somewhat reactive approach is seen by the following supplier's reference to the burden of regular auditing, and a focus on environmental, health and safety requirements.

> The demands made by customers, apart from production and quality on the social side, are safety standards. Companies come informally and weekly to audit us, sometimes daily. They can come anytime, according to our contract. We meet those requirements of ISO 9000, 14000. None of these codes include social standards except health and safety. In the future ISO might add social standards, for example working hours, discrimination, etc. It will consolidate all standards, that is, QS 9000 and other standards, so we will have a single standard (THS 10, Assistant Manager).

Suppliers appoint personnel to manage code compliance

Suppliers have evolved a variety of approaches to deal with the responsibilities related to CSR and code compliance. The approaches are as varied as the products they produce. Similar to the internal structure of RMNEs, some suppliers have a highly centralised approach, while others have integrated CSR responsibilities across various departments.

Generally, management structures have been created that assign responsibility in a very direct and 'top-down' fashion, often with little or no specific role definition, but with more of an ad hoc approach, as can be seen from the following comments and diagram (Figure 20).

> I have one manager responsible for [the code] and also for the accounts division. I tell him, he follows my instructions. He also has to check that it is implemented. He must check the regulations. He is in an accounts position and comes from Hong Kong [China]. His assistant is a local person. There are two people for this job, in case one is away (CHS 1, Chairman).

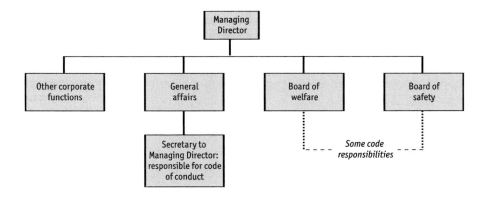

FIGURE 20 EXAMPLE OF THE ORGANISATIONAL STRUCTURE OF A RETAIL SUPPLIER

I am the person responsible but I have three colleagues working with me. They implement the code of conduct. I am the admin manager of the factory reporting into the Managing Director (CHS 3, Production Manager).

I, with the CEO, am responsible for CSR for all groups. Our business was built on the autonomous nature of all of our divisions, so what I do is to simply be the co-ordinator in an advisory capacity to each of these business units and all of the information funnels back to me. I am responsible for the individual divisions and the managing directors are responsible for CSR. No one in our company has job specs. The top-level managers undertake verbal appraisals with the CEO. Although there are no job specs within each division, informally we network and there is a strong interest in communication and training (UKS 2, Head of CSR).

The fact that some suppliers have one individual responsible for multiple tasks appears to have led to the assignment of multiple and overlapping responsibilities for CSR and non-compliance matters. In some cases this was regarded as a beneficial thing as these individuals were seen as understanding 'the business'.

I was recruited here for both quality and for social auditing. I was the first person to do audits. Why? My boss said it is clear that quality and female rights are becoming more important in our business. Someone else is responsible for trade union activities and human rights. My responsibilities are to ensure that the rights and interests of workers are protected and not discriminated against, and that there is no excessive working time (CHS 2, Quality Supervisor).

Because I am so long-standing in this company I know who to speak to. Things are shaped a bit like an egg timer. I communicate everything to the managing directors and make sure that they are well informed. Generally I also deal with the procurement people and the merchandising. Also I visit the quality people. They don't do audits but that is growing (UKS 2, Head of CSR).

We heard from one supplier who appears to have created a management structure for the systematic integration across organisational departments of matters related to code compliance and CSR. This structure included assigning specific responsibility for code-of-conduct issues to various groups within the firm and conducting regular meetings to discuss progress, achievements and improvements that needed to be made. It should be pointed out that this was rare. No other RMNE supplier reported the existence of such a structure. While it was difficult to determine the real driver behind this supplier's approach, when questioned, they cited ISO-related processes as the reason that compliance was integrated with other processes.

> The Safety Committee does the environment, and ISO is a small part, too. The Welfare Committee has a PR person who provides information on codes to the workers. The HR manager and safety officer (his title) says he is responsible for RMNE codes. Codes were here when the HR manager came one year ago. It was the first time he had heard of these. His responsibilities are payroll, compensation, training, general affairs, safety and labour regulations (THS 13, HR Manager).

Interestingly, our research indicated that CSR and compliance managers in the supplier factories were somewhat consistent in their approach to and implementation of the aims and objectives superimposed by RMNE codes. As noted by one of the experts during our field research,

> Managers of supplier factories did not differ as much as anticipated in their attitudes to codes. This may have been an artefact of the interviewing process—exhibiting a positive attitude anticipating that was what we desired—however, it may also have something to do with an emerging perspective on what constitutes a modern factory. In essence, managers gave three rationales for implementing codes. First, that codes boost the image of the factory by showing the customer that management is doing the right thing. Being clean and tidy may encourage more orders from one or other of the global firms. Second, by instituting improvements in health and safety there are fewer problems and workers see that management respects their rights. These actions increase worker satisfaction and commitment to the company, so enhancing the attractiveness of the factory to job applicants, reducing labour turnover, and increasing productivity and quality. Third, codes help management to do what is legally and ethically right. The only disadvantage managers stated was the increased cost of implementing codes. One manager explained that codes were like R&D, a longer-term investment—in people (E 2).

Implementation guidelines benefit the supplier

As discussed in Chapter II, the importance of guidelines for the implementation and ongoing management of compliance and CSR-related matters is essential. As important as guidelines are for implementation at the RMNE level, they are even more important at the supplier level. The following statements from suppliers demonstrate the reliance of suppliers on the RMNE for advice in fulfilling the requirements of CSR or code compliance, along with specific reference to the level of detail provided by the RMNE. It may be noted that these statements represent what is involved in the very detailed and interdependent relationship that often exists between the RMNE and supplier in today's world. Such intimate business relationships highlight a quantum step forward from past relationship structures of arm's-length dealing and specific contractual barriers motivated by legal liability concerns.

> Brands don't give us [an audit] checklist, but they have some manuals from which we can develop our own checklist (CHS 1, Logistics Manager).

> FMNE 2 has a whole set of codes of conduct for us but OMNE 20 and others don't. They just come to explain piece by piece and explain it in an oral way or give us presentations about it. FMNE 2 has a checklist including 126 provisions or articles to check against or implement. FMNE 2 is now pushing hard for environmental protection and health and safety in our workshops so we are trying hard to implement this (CHS 4, General Manager).

> They have created a global sourcing principles manual and developed 'supplier handbooks' which are effectively a consultant in a book. All technologists are given this handbook and it is also on the central database. Also all suppliers and subcontractors are given it (RMNE 6, Central Co-ordinator, Ethical Issues).

As has been highlighted in previous sections of this book, an important requirement of most codes is compliance with local law. The degree to which this information is available, understood, interpreted or enforced varied greatly in the retail sector. While the national government retains ultimate responsibility for enacting and enforcing applicable laws and regulations, we heard that RMNEs and suppliers have at times interacted with local regulatory authorities in a mutually beneficial manner. However, in general, suppliers have had difficulty accessing this information and reported being in need of guidance regarding interpretation and application of legal and regulatory provisions. Our research indicates that there is a need for additional government intervention in providing applicable information, along with clarification of enforcement and compliance policies at the factory level in regard to compliance with local law.

> We obtain our labour law information from the Internet, by networking, through RMNE 6, RMNE 3, AMNE 4, books and anything we can get our hands on. On my last trip to China I met with the FMNE 3 rep and he gave me new information regarding changes in dormitory regulations and minimum wages in China. I scanned this information and then sent it to RMNE 6 (UKS 3, Compliance Manager).

c. Field personnel

The degree to which CSR and code compliance manifests in the field directly relates to the quality and capacity of field personnel to handle these matters. The level of training and education, along with the level of authority for related decision-making, relates to how well CSR and code functions are fulfilled. Field personnel uniquely possess a multifaceted position for dealing with code issues. With the ability to access the factory floor, together with the ability to interact with local authorities, they can be a critical resource for the RMNE. Given the difficulty in obtaining information on local laws, an explanation or interpretation of relevant regulations such as those on health and safety, working hours or wages is another important role they can fulfil.

The degree to which RMNEs recognise or have taken advantage of field personnel varies greatly. Some RMNEs seemed to want to avoid the cost and overhead of additional employees in the field, particularly the costs associated with expatriates. Nevertheless the real benefits of having qualified field staff cannot be overlooked. Further, while some RMNEs do have high-quality compliance individuals in the field, the diversity of responsibilities or the size of the territory appeared in some cases to be too extensive for them to do the job adequately. Accordingly, ensuring an adequate number of field staff, along with adequate training and resources, can be one of the most important assets for RMNEs in implementing CSR and compliance requirements.

An expert from our field research offers a summary and insight into the role of global CSR and code team members regarding code implementation and compliance.

> Global firms employ few code compliance managers and officers relative to the workplaces they need to cover. For example, FMNE 2 [one of the firms with the largest CSR staff] employs 15 compliance team members in China. They must cover 140 supplier workplaces, some of which employ over 5,000 employees. Other global firms have much smaller ratios of compliance members to supplier workplaces. For example, AMNE 8 appears to have a team of seven compliance members in East Asia covering 350 suppliers whose average size is between 400 and 500 employees. Put simply, code implementation cannot rely on global firm monitoring because in many cases visits are too superficial and infrequent while factory managers are usually notified of impending formal audits and so have sufficient time to prepare the factory for inspection. Codes require that both factory managers and workers develop commitment. A final point to note in regard to compliance teams is that this is an arduous and skilful job that may need more senior management support. Compliance officers are constantly visiting factories, having to use their analytical and social skills to understand problems and offer advice. Audits need to be rigorous with reports completed soon afterwards. This work keeps team members away from home frequently while learning is mainly from on-the-job experience and advice from senior colleagues. There is often no clear career path or succession planning. Thus, these managers and workers risk isolation and demotivation if they are not sufficiently recognised by senior management and integrated into the wider organisation (E 3).

d. Sharing good practices

We found a noteworthy development in the sharing of good practices among RMNEs and suppliers. While this occurs to varying degrees, and not uniformly across the industry, it appears motivated by self-interest, efficiencies and recognised advantages. Primarily, this has to do with the fact that many RMNEs share multiple suppliers. As our research indicates that many code requirements are in fact similar or at least consistent, any RMNE could benefit from sharing the mechanisms that it found to be most effective in keeping a supplier functioning adequately within the parameters of its CSR and code requirements.

Further, external drivers have also encouraged the sharing of best practices. In particular, some multi-stakeholder initiatives discussed in Chapter II have formed advisory groups among industry participants as part of their approach in assisting with CSR implementation and compliance. According to MSI representatives and some MNE managers interviewed, these advisory groups have proven to be quite effective platforms for the sharing of information and practices related to CSR and code matters. At least one RMNE has adopted the approach of advisory groups as an internal function, and has further extended this to its suppliers. The following diagram (Figure 21) highlights the multiple layers of information and data sharing that can contribute to the effective design, implementation and management of CSR and code requirements.

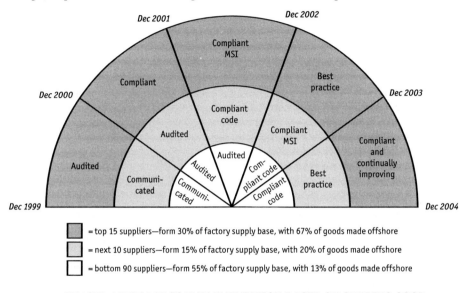

= top 15 suppliers—form 30% of factory supply base, with 67% of goods made offshore

= next 10 suppliers—form 15% of factory supply base, with 20% of goods made offshore

= bottom 90 suppliers—form 55% of factory supply base, with 13% of goods made offshore

FIGURE 21 PHASED APPROACH TO IMPLEMENTATION BASED ON SHARING GOOD PRACTICES

Source: Adapted from retail MNE materials

5. Feedback, improvement and remediation

The role of feedback, improvement and remediation systems in supporting the management systems that have been discussed in the previous sections is an important one. In fact, as the following sections reveal, in many instances these processes are regarded as the linchpins of the entire code-of-conduct implementation process. In this section we examine the types of information systems that have been developed, their role and, importantly, who has access

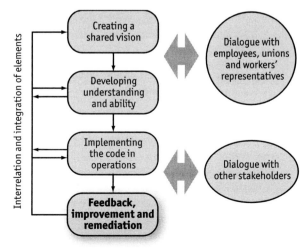

to such systems. We also consider the various types of monitoring systems that have developed, both internal and external, and the role that corrective action plans play in the continuous improvement process of supplier factories.

a. Information systems

As in the other sectors researched, IT systems have evolved in varying degrees to form a critical component of CSR programmes in the retail sector. The sheer volume of information generated by the global operations of RMNEs in managing the production of billions of dollars of merchandise, through vast, distant and competing supply chains, can be overwhelming. As in the footwear and apparel sectors, information systems have become a key tool for managing the diverse requirements of operations, including compliance. Originally developed to assist in sorting and managing huge amounts of information, our research, and the stories we heard, illustrated the fact that information systems are now evolving from mere electronic data storage systems into robust management tools that provide key guidance on how to best meet sourcing, production, delivery and overall compliance requirements. One of the repeated issues heard relates to the need to integrate all management functions into a single, complementary system. Such integration would provide efficiencies by making necessary information available throughout the business and operational decision-making processes.

Role of information systems

Information systems are used for a variety of purposes by RMNEs. Again, given the vast numbers of suppliers utilised in the global sourcing operations of RMNEs, information systems were predominantly used to gather, track and manage information related to suppliers. This includes software programs that flag audit requirements as well as generate reports regarding suppliers.

> We operate in excess of 50 countries and have about 30,000 factories on our database with about 10,000 which are 'live'. The others are inactive or terminated. The database was developed in-house (RMNE 3).

> We enter the details onto the system which triggers automatically when the audit should be conducted. Risk is based on type of product (food, toys, and apparel) and country (for example, China). (Almost all of Asia except for Japan, Korea, New Zealand and Australia are considered high risk.) When the trigger goes off, a factory audit notification is created. It gets issued by [corporate headquarters] and is sent to the licensee. We ask for confirmation within 15 days. If there is no feedback, the audit is scheduled (RMNE 3).

Some RMNE managers uniquely used their information system to track the quality of external monitors, by analysing and scanning for consistencies or inconsistencies throughout audit reports. Specifically, one RMNE determined that the audit reports from one particular auditor raised suspicion in that the reports were coming back too consistent and showing too good a performance, based on experience in other markets. Thus, having an information system that was able to screen and search for specific features allowed this RMNE to improve overall performance and save itself from potential negative consequences. This further demonstrates that the benefits of an information system are only as good as the quality of the data and information being entered, represented in the IT slogan: 'GI–GO', for 'garbage in–garbage out'.

> There is ongoing monitoring based on audits we receive. Our database has five years of audits and we have benchmarks. If the findings do not fit with our experience, we delve into it. Our report reviewers do this daily. The more formal extensive country reviews are done by year. For example, we knew something was wrong with the third-party audits that were happening in Turkey a few years ago because the findings were too clean (RMNE 3).

Types of information system

Information systems were found to consist of a variety of software packages and platforms. This includes everything from Excel spreadsheets to commercial and individually designed databases. Further, the criteria which set the parameters for required data may vary, including everything from buyer information to code provisions.

> I have an Excel spreadsheet that lists the name of the supplier, the department, audit number, audit company, country, liaison office and then the respective criteria, audit date, score and whether I have a factory profile, corrective action report and liaison follow-up report. The grading for the criteria can be A, acceptable; NA, nearly acceptable; I, insufficient; or TU, totally unacceptable. The score can be from 2 to 3. There are also weightings given to the criteria. The weightings are: child labour, 6; forced labour, 2; discrimination, 2; FOA [freedom of association], 2; working hours, 6; compensation, 7; general working conditions, 1; health, 2; safety precautions, 6. Then a total score is given (RMNE 1, Administrative Manager).

> Our current database is an Access database. I built it. I used information from our previous system and I looked at what was involved. The two key things were the information on the suppliers and the information on the factories. We needed to make sure we had general information such as contact details and location, and then information on products and buyers. Previously the buyer information was not there. We tended to talk a lot in code which was very important for other parts of the business, but not for ethical trading. So now we include things like the product name, the QA details, and if anybody else wants information on our database they have to come and ask us. The factory details will be there as well as the product details. Audit results get recorded. We have added a comment box where there can be comments placed on serious non-compliance corrective actions (RMNE 10, Ethical Trading Auditor).

Further, some RMNEs reported having no database, struggling instead with a hard-copy system of printed reports. Given the availability and customary usage of technology for information management, it is quite surprising that a paper system would be the primary tool. It may be questioned as to whether such a limited information system implies a lack of commitment or resources for a key component of compliance.

> Basically the results are fed back to the buying department. We do not have a database. All tracking is done by a hard copy and we have summary sheets that form part of the supplier file. The information is passed on to the com-

pliance manager. There are two people who are responsible for all assessment schedules and follow-ups (RMNE 9, Group Company Secretary).

The origin of the information system is another important factor that needs to be considered as, we heard, it can impact on its effectiveness; specifically, whether the system was developed internally by the RMNE compliance department or the IT department, or developed by an external contractor. Generally, we were told that organically developed information systems have benefits in that there is the opportunity to reach an understanding and a meeting of the minds when the criteria for the system are developed by individuals or groups sharing a common experience, language and philosophy from within a single organisation.

> Our database was developed one and a half years ago and IT built it. I can do a country search and input information. The supply chain report is input by myself. This information comes from our suppliers but we treat different sites differently. For example, we insist that, on all new sites, a robust external audit is carried out. In [supplier] situations where there is a direct supplier and an agent as well as somebody from our office such involved, then what happens is that the database cannot be accessed, for instance, from Hong Kong, because the portal is not big enough (but it can be accessed by e-mail). The difficulty of course is that it's an involved and prolonged process (RMNE 6, Central Co-ordinator, Ethical Issues).

> Our database was first launched in 1996 or 1997. It was built on a Lotus Notes platform because of security and flexibility but it is limited in its reporting capabilities. It is now evolving to a more relational database. To date, it has met the accumulation, management and storage of data goal. However, now we need more analysis and sharing of information (RMNE 3).

Access

Access to the data contained in the information system varied among RMNEs. Internal limitations on access were found, as well as varying degrees of sharing information externally. Access ran the full spectrum. One RMNE provided access to the information for all employees, some limited it to just managers in particular departments, and others shared some of the data with suppliers. Some of the information systems were reserved specifically for the compliance function, while others were attempting to integrate other departmental functions, such as supplier sourcing, into the process. The degree to which different departments were integrated into the information system varied greatly and was reported to be a key factor in the effectiveness and efficiencies of such a system.

> We have over 32,000 factories on the database, listing their basic information, audit history. This is the central hub to the entire department globally. It is a secure link and has three main user groups: policy-makers [complete access], internal/external monitors [limited and controlled access], and relationship builders [for example sourcing, consumer products—limited access]. The goal is to get the licensees and vendors to disclose their factories. Because of their reluctance, our aim has been to maintain confidentiality (RMNE 3).

Audit reports and corrective action plans are entered on the database. Information is available electronically. Different [compliance] team members have different levels of access to the information. For example, the Korean [compliance] person only has information for Korea (RMNE 3).

It is called our supplier-sourcing directory. All RMNE 6 employees have access to it, but in particular it is the 60 technical people that use it and it is not externally visible as yet. I want it to be, but there is a great deal of concern about security, particularly with our suppliers. Our system is a push system and not a pull system. This means that I don't have the ability to be flagged when an audit is due. I have to rely on the information from my suppliers (RMNE 6, Central Co-ordinator, Ethical Issues).

In our view, greater integration is required so that all departments and personnel with responsibilities related to compliance and code implementation can communicate effectively and efficiently. The overall objective of the information system should be the creation of a system that functions as a seamless web of communication.

Ranking of suppliers

Many information systems were created for the express purpose of ranking and managing suppliers. Some attempt to measure and assess supplier performance using differing criteria, including labour and environmental standards. One of the key challenges appears to be the need to develop measurable indicators that can be applied consistently across varying situations.

We have evaluated the basic points of our [code]. We have our merchandisers give an initial impression of whether suppliers are OK, or not OK because we don't want to have bad suppliers in our database. In 2000, we developed a ranking of A, B, C, D for our suppliers once audited. We have a first form evaluation and then a thick separate report for audit. Together with IA 10 we have defined our country risk assessment. We do social responsibility for our imported goods, for countries who are poor. You have to ask, where is the risk? Now we focus on risky countries such as China. The risky issues are salaries, unions, child labour and working conditions. Other risky countries are Bangladesh and India. Since 2000, we do not work at all with Burma (RMNE 2, Global Sourcing Manager).

Our suppliers are ranked by turnover, not by compliance performance. We have no rankings based on compliance. Instead, we have decided to aggregate the information. Using our top 13 suppliers I print out a summary document, approximately 37 pages long. What I now want to do is to put these factories into a traffic-light system. I am prepared to publish something against the fan diagram [see Figure 21 in Section 4d] to show how we as a group are performing (RMNE 6, Supply Chain Compliance Manager).

We have a five-star ranking system. We initially started with the traffic-light system but didn't think that three categories were enough because there was overlap on serious non-compliance issues. Now our ranking is one to five. One is for life-threatening child labour and serious breach-of-conduct issues. Two is for poor fire safety, no use of personal protective equipment and no immediate life-threatening issues. Three is an average factory and four and five are good factories. It is just a judgement thing, a gut feeling thing. I cannot think of any five-star factories that we have. For ones, we get back to them as soon as possible and agree time-scales. It's a question of priority. For two we go back again in priority, threes perhaps 12 to 18 months, and for fours and fives we might not go. For the Far Eastern teams the majority reports are ones (RMNE 10, Ethical Trading Auditor).

There is a lot of subjectivity in [ranking]. All buying and quality merchandising teams grade from one to ten and we wanted to be able to fit in. In our last training session we discussed rankings. Any supplier with employment issues in terms of terms and conditions is a 'one'. So it's not just that non-paid sick leave is a 'one' (RMNE 10, Ethical Trading Manager).

Suppliers are given a rating of 'Needs Improvement' or 'Acceptable'. There are only two categories of ratings. The auditors give an overall assessment in the free text field (RMNE 3).

We rank our [audit] findings from severe to low. Severe leads to termination. High leads to a follow-up audit in 30 days. Medium leads to a follow-up audit 60 days later and this is what happens in the majority of cases for things such as wages, hours and health and safety. In low cases we only require written proof of remediation (RMNE 3).

Questions remain regarding the usage of the ranking system by functional departments. In particular, the purchasing department has direct contact with suppliers on a regular basis and is responsible for the placement of new orders. The ideal situation would be to have purchasers and buyers take account of the ranking data prior to establishing new business relationships, or when evaluating existing supplier performance. From our research this appears to be some years away.

Finally, commenting on what an effective information system should entail, one of the experts that participated in this research offers the following suggestions:

I believe that there is a need for an effective IT base which captures audit results and highlights targets, review dates and categorises suppliers according to a robust set of criteria and a grading system. This also avoids the problem that was identified in some companies interviewed that the effectiveness of the audit process depended on the individuals involved, their enthusiasm and their commitment to the issues at stake. While this is important and clearly an explanatory factor in terms of the types of systems developed and the commitment to promoting decent work on the part of some companies, there is a danger that information is personalised.

An effective IT system will provide the necessary 'audit trail' and also provide an objective register of problems to be addressed and targets to be achieved as well as penalties administered. It would also provide assurance that criteria are being met and could be accessed widely within the company. Furthermore, such an IT base allows designers and buyers to operate proactively when developing their products or when looking for potential suppliers of a certain product (E 2).

b. Internal monitoring: factory self-audits

Another important aspect of overall compliance is internal monitoring. While monitoring conducted internally may at times lead to criticism if it is the only form of compliance verification undertaken, it is still an important tool for generating feedback regarding the ongoing implementation and operation of code management. RMNEs that undertake both internal and external monitoring reported being viewed in a more positive light by stakeholders, as they were told such dual monitoring provided the perception of a balance between self-auditing and the reinforced security of information due to the independence of third-party auditors.

> Let me summarise what happens for us. There is an original audit carried out by a third party. We then carry out mini internal audits and then, every second year, there is another third-party audit carried out (UKS 2, Head of CSR).

We heard that the criteria for monitoring used by RMNEs in conducting internal reviews can come from a variety of sources, and can include issues as diverse as environment, health and safety, as well as criteria from other sources such as MSIs, which have gathered broad input on issues related to labour, social and ethical behaviour.

> We do our own social audits between audits by brands, once every three or four months (not on a regular basis). We have a checklist. We got the idea from NGO 7 developed in 2000. We save the information in different departments because it affects different departments. I evaluate the checklist overall. I will set a time afterwards with the departments to make improvements. We sometimes have meetings with various departments together to sort out these problems (CHS 2, Quality Supervisor).

> We have an important feedback process. I have a person responsible for our internal audit who reports to me every day on Six-S [a quality management approach] and environmental, safety and health issues. I read these reports every day. If there is a need to improve, I write on the report and he takes it to the person in charge. They then do an action plan. We have a form, a piece of paper asking what needs to be seen and where needs to go. We developed this form ourselves. We have experienced people here who are innovative (CHS 3, Administration Manager).

> We have Seven-S [a quality management framework]. We have our own evaluation form with ten points on it, which include hygiene and health and safety. The Seven-S Committee developed this and the Health and Safety committee (THS 14, HR Manager).

As can be seen from the above comments, internal monitoring is seen as an effective tool by RMNEs for providing detailed information that, when properly considered and analysed, can assist various internal departments in assessing problem areas or areas that require improvement. A secure internal feedback loop for such information requires that serious consideration be given to the specific parameters to be monitored.

c. Verification (RMNEs and third-party auditors)

The subject of much attention due to its importance in determining the level of compliance with code provisions is the role of third-party auditors (TPAs). Beyond the internal monitoring discussed previously, external TPAs are seen as a critical element in verifying compliance and determining whether corporate behaviour is consistent with public claims and commitments. While some critics question the veracity or independence of auditors that are contracted and paid for by the RMNE, there is growing evidence that a forum of legitimate independent auditors is evolving to fill the niche of verifying the performance of RMNEs within the context of labour, social and ethical standards.

MNE budgets for auditing

An important aspect that we discovered regarding the effectiveness of compliance systems is the great differential on budget allocated for auditing. This is indicative of the variety of approaches taken by RMNEs, and takes into account the differing reliance on internal monitoring versus the reliance on third parties—with the latter generally being more expensive. The resources dedicated to auditing directly influence the effectiveness of the programme and are linked to the need for upper management to show its commitment as outlined in Section 2 of this chapter.

> We have a budget of 300,000 F for 30 audits and 150,000 F for our school project. One audit costs between $2,000 and $4,000 depending on the size of the factory. Now we do about 30 [audits] but we must do at least 100 but right now we don't have the budget . . . Also, we need to think about what to do with the results. Right now, I can take care of 30 reports but I could not do it for 100 (RMNE 1, Administrative Manager).

> We proposed our [code] and programme to our executive board and they gave us a budget for NGO 15 and for [our headquarter operations] (RMNE 2, Global Sourcing Manager).

> In terms of resources, I have very limited resources. I have only just recently been given the go-ahead to have a secretary work for me one day a week. The thing about this job is that it takes a long time to do the administrative parts of it (RMNE 6, Supply Chain Compliance Manager).

> I have a [personal] budget of £100,000. With this I conduct my one-day workshops in China, I do the 20 audits per year and cover my own travel costs, and publish manuals (RMNE 6, Central Co-ordinator, Ethical Issues).

> In our first year, our budget [for the overall programme] was £1 million, the second year £920,000, the third year £827,000. As you can see it has been decreasing (RMNE 10, Ethical Trading Manager).

Tracking subcontractors as an obstacle to verification/auditing

As in the footwear and apparel sectors, subcontracting is a common factor in the retail sector as well. It is one of the most contentious issues and RMNEs acknowledge the need for systems to track and respond to issues related to this practice. Frequently, RMNEs reported increasing challenges in identifying and managing this level of their supply chain. However, our research indicates that RMNEs and their responsible field staff are aware of the subcontracting issue and are attempting to address the situation in a variety of ways.

> [We know there are subcontractors] because our suppliers say they have them. Also because we know that we have a number of suppliers who cannot meet both our competitors and our needs given the quantity we are asking for, without subcontractors (RMNE 1, Administrative Manager).

> We try to know who the subcontractors are, but it is difficult because they change all the time (RMNE 1, Administrative Manager).

> We recognise that there is subcontracting there that we do not know about. The audit process is a tool that is a way for us to learn where this [subcontracting] exists (RMNE 3).

Dealing with homeworkers

In the retail sector, the issue of homeworkers is relevant, given the variety of products that can be contracted to them in any given season. Interestingly, most RMNES reported that they believed that there were no homeworkers involved in their supply chain. However, one of the interviewees gave the following comment that might be more reflective of the real situation. This RMNE has chosen to work with its suppliers and actively attempt to make a difference. This should be distinguished from the apparel sector where there were quality control managers in the factories every day, but where the problems of subcontracting and homeworkers persist, according to independent studies. Our research suggests that homeworkers, a by-product of subcontracting, exist in the retail sector despite the fact that many RMNEs are adamant that they do not exist.

> In India the majority of employment is cottage-worker employment, apart from the clothing sector. So what we do is that we do assessments on the types of factories and organisation that exist there. The attitude is that you shouldn't be working with them. We have to deal with reality. We form a short list of suppliers and look at issues such as child labour, health and safety, and craft workers. When it comes to things such as the brassware industry we have to pick up and fetch the best of the worst. We give them qualified approval based on the condition that workers are managed in a sensible way. For example, if children are working then we want to make sure that they get an education first before they work. We will write a paper to our compliance officer giving a list of recommendations of what we can and cannot do. We are trying to work out our best approach regarding India and we are looking at working with some NGOs to give a percentage of our profits to them to improve the situation there (RMNE 9, Group Company Secretary).

Use of independent standards

An important development in the RMNE sector is that some supplier companies are developing their own performance standards. This is a unique and positive development, as we believe it demonstrates that suppliers are starting to receive the message regarding the responsibility that RMNEs seek to impose upon them, and are therefore proactively taking steps to address a variety of performance issues—in particular, environmental standards.

> We were approving supplier factories from a quality point of view and we decided that we needed to compare like for like and also look at the environment. So, we realised that we needed to have some sort of guidance or guidelines for our suppliers. Therefore we developed specific questions on environmental conditions in our questionnaire. Media attention, however, is always on the exploitation of labour, so therefore we included this also. Our QA structure consists of managers, senior technicians and technicians, all of which have auditor training such as ISO 9000. Our documents that we use for our complete ethical compliance, quality and environmental audits come from the quality management side. Some of our auditors have had training on SA8000 and ISO 14001. We needed to determine what was the best approach for RMNE 9 (RMNE 9, Group Company Secretary).

While meritorious, questions remain regarding the source or origin of these standards, how they are developed, and how they are, or are not, reconciled with internationally recognised standards or the standards embraced by the RMNEs.

Need for uniform standards

Given the fact that corporate codes of conduct developed as voluntary initiatives across several industry sectors, a great diversity of approaches and performance criteria has evolved. Our research indicates that this has not necessarily led to confusion and frustration among RMNE suppliers.

> There are not so many differences between them. The main concern is with workers' rights: wages, overtime, how living conditions are for workers, and safety for workers (CHS 1, Logistics Manager).

> The codes are not totally the same, but on the whole they are much the same. The things that are a little different are, for example, the different emphasis of the code—some focus mainly on human rights, others on fire and safety and health (CHS 2, Personnel Manager).

> There is not really any problem having different codes since most of the items are the same (CHS 4, Deputy Manager).

> We had some difficulties with all these provisions but after several years we have a good understanding of the details so we can achieve the standards. On the whole, all the codes are the same, but they each have something special of their own (CHS 5, Production Manager).

However, there were some reported instances where inconsistent, overlapping or onerous standards have led to calls from suppliers for uniform or harmonised performance criteria.

> We have some very good factories that are suffering from audit fatigue because of other brands. We need a flag saying 'approved by the ILO' to place outside these factories (UKS 4, Ethical and Quality Manager).

Everybody is working on their own agenda. There are different standards and different areas of focus. We need some sort of universal standards, some kind of rule and we are still debating that with the NGO 5. Will it still just be a lot of sitting around a table? That's what I wonder (RMNE 10, Ethical Trading Coordinator).

In addition to the creation of a standardised industry-wide code, there may also be a need for a standard for the audit process itself, as expressed in interviews with RMNEs. Presently, the quality of TPAs varies considerably among TPA firms as well as within them, according to RMNE managers and supplier managers.

The words in the codes are very similar but the depth of probing is different with respect to how long, how hard and how deep the audit is. I don't think that e-mailing a questionnaire is very good and I do think that we need to get more involved with NGOs. The audit reflects on who did it individually and there are great variations between individuals. There are big differences in individuals in audit companies. There are some exceptionally good people and some exceptionally bad ones. It really is up to the individual. I suspect that in more developing places you go, the more important it becomes the number of audits that you have done. In Cambodia and in Viet Nam I have had problems. China has been much better than expected and India is interesting because, there, people are matter of fact about horrendous abuses. Thailand tends to be very good. A key thing is whether the audit organisation has an office in-country. For example, in Cambodia there was no office for the company that did our audit while in Viet Nam it was a completely new office without experience. They didn't even pick up things that I picked up and I wasn't even a local! (UKS 4, Ethical and Quality Manager).

[The quality of external monitors]—globally it is difficult to say. In China, TPA 4 is superior in terms of quality to TPA 7 in terms of detail. TPA 7's approach particularly for worker interviews tended to be more aggressive than I was comfortable with. They were demeaning and not on the same level. TPA 4 in contrast talked to people on their level. The comments from other suppliers are that they all rank TPA 4 first. I have never used NGO 9 or TPA 1 because generally at all our GSP meetings a TPA 4 or TPA 7 rep is there. Therefore they are up to speed and are integrally involved in producing our audit paperwork (UKS 3, Compliance Manager).

Due to questions of quality with TPAs, as well as other issues such as control of information, proprietary auditing processes, unique standards and supplier relations, some RMNEs reported a preference for using their own personnel for audits rather than TPAs. A similar comment made by some AMNEs is discussed in Chapter IV.

We have a higher level of confidence in our own team. We do hands-on training [for the third-party monitors] and focus and ensure that they get access and visibility to developments in the field. Because it is a relatively new field, the amount of business an accounting or auditing firm can generate is limited in relation to other areas. There is the challenge with the way that firms are structured (RMNE 3).

The great diversity of approaches and systems developed for auditing, even within a single RMNE, along with the significant inherent costs, has resulted in calls from field staff for a single consistent, objective and transparent auditing process, as reflected in the following statements.

We have tried to maintain a consistency of approach regardless of where in the world we are operating, from a policy point of view. That is, all the audits are managed and assessed in [corporate headquarters]. The basic process and protocol is centralised as are decisions as to which factory to monitor (RMNE 3).

Our programme is really cut and dry. We tend to be more black and white [than other brands] and not give the auditors room to make decisions. We do not let them make any decisions. The implications of their findings are determined here (RMNE 3).

Benefits of multiple overlapping audits

Notwithstanding the push for a single audit process, some interviewees indirectly identified benefits related to overlapping audits or competing performance criteria.

We only deal with Korean factories in Latin America. These factories have turned a corner. Why? Because of the proximity to the United States and more people going to the factories. They are very good at production and also produce for big brands. Thus, we can piggyback off each other's efforts (RMNE 7).

Sometimes, yes [other audits make a difference] and sometimes they don't. The factory may make a change because another brand has come along after us and advised the factory to do the same thing as we suggested. So they might then do it (AMNE 8, Quality Assurance Manager).

In factories where there are other MNEs there is increasing awareness of this issue which is reinforcing, in particular, in Europe (RMNE 10, Ethical Trading Auditor).

While overlapping audits may provide some level of added assurance, at some point, we heard that when an RMNE still finds faults in factories that have already been audited by other RMNEs, it draws into question the effectiveness of the auditing process of these other RMNEs. Unfortunately, this seemed to be a common occurrence among the RMNEs interviewed.

There are many situations in the Far East where other MNEs have audited the factories, for example, such as RMNE 3, where there are still serious employment problems. One factory that I can think of was audited three times by different MNEs and obviously either they just weren't looking at employment or they just missed it, but things in this factory were very bad (RMNE 10, Ethical Trading Co-ordinator).

Training of auditors

A number of the RMNEs we spoke with stated that they held their own training for auditors and required fairly high standards of expertise from them, such as demonstrated certification to internationally recognised auditing standards. The following examples highlight how a number of RMNEs have taken the initiative to train auditors to their own standards and implemented systems to track the effectiveness of the audits.

Auditors meet on an informal and ad hoc basis. We held training sessions with TPA 4 to review and clarify what they were to do. We also have an assurance programme to review the records and audit processes (RMNE 3).

RMNE 6 has an auditor training course in which 400 people have been trained so that people can audit from within the supply chain (RMNE 6, Central Co-ordinator, Ethical Issues).

[Suppliers] also do a three-day training course with TPA 4. This is because new factories have to do external audits. For existing factories, direct suppliers can audit their own supply chains. The key is to find that the audit methodology is robust and, because I wanted this robustness, I developed my own social compliance course. So what I say is that anybody who is going to do one of our audits must either do an auditing skills course, such as ISO 9000 or ISO 14000 or a two-day auditing course which is Inerca registered because I want this to have a professional badge; and they must do our three-day course. The purpose is to ensure that they can walk away with the knowledge and skill to run an audit (RMNE 6, Supply Chain Compliance Manager).

One RMNE we spoke with highlighted the unique challenges of operating in China, along with the innovative steps they have initiated to address them.

For our own auditors, the China process is most rigorous. Our auditors are put on a 30- to 60-day training period as well as a probationary period. They come off the probationary period after about 90 days and it is approximately 60 days before they undertake a self-audit. We recruit people from different backgrounds. We had 80 applications for a position just advertised. Ideally we want someone with a factory background. There is the issue of turnover because, after two to three years, the auditors suffer a burnout period. We are now looking for new, young auditors. For more senior positions, we want experience either in the factory (HR or production), financing background, people with a background in occupational health and safety or something like NGO 2. We have tried to develop area experts over time and we use them initially to deepen the two-person audit teams. The biggest hiring criteria is integrity and this is something that you do not necessarily find in a resume. It is important because of corruption, bribery, etc. Monitors have reported to us being tempted. It is a very real issue because a tremendous amount of pressure is exerted by the factory. Also, the salary for auditors tends to be low, particularly in China. The bribery temptation has also been reported in Thailand. It probably exists more than we hear about. The policy that we have for our internal team is the same for our external reports but we get less reports externally. This is where we need our systems checks. It has never been a concern for these people and that is the hardest step (RMNE 3).

Use of in-house auditors versus TPAs

Some RMNEs use a combination of internal and external auditors, while others exclusively use one or the other. The utilisation of a combination of auditors was justified by a variety of factors, as demonstrated in the following statements.

RMNE 3 has its own audit for factories and we also use third-party audits. The determination of in-house audit or third-party audit is based on the location.

> In-house is done in the United States, China and Taiwan [China]. In other countries we use third parties. In China we also do third-party audits (RMNE 3).

> Forty per cent is done in house and 60% by third party. The procedures are identical. We currently have two multi-country, third-party auditors, one focusing on an individual country and another one coming on stream. They are TPA 4, TPA 1, O 8, O 9 and a third-party auditor that is specific to Guangzhou. O 9 are currently getting up to speed. We established a pilot programme with O 9 (RMNE 3).

> It was decided to have a bi-programme. On direct sourcing we decided to have our own people to go into factories. On indirect sourcing we saw that it was too big and needed external people (RMNE 7).

> We use TPA 4, TPA 6, O 10 and TPA 2. TPA 4 is our preferred provider. A third-party auditor is used in locations where they have local capacity, for example Korea [the Democratic People's Republic of Korea], Cambodia but we ask them. In the United States we use TPA 2 and that is the one country where we pay 13 weeks of back wages (RMNE 7).

> In other countries we use third-party monitors such as TPA 4, TPA 1. We have pretty much worked with every firm out there. This remains a challenge for us. We have found that there is a need to implement our own QA programme with respect to third-party auditors so we do not blindly rely on them. We have produced a training programme that they must follow and we follow up on them in the field (RMNE 3).

However, other considerations have gone into the decision of whether or not to engage TPAs, and the degree to which to utilise them. We heard that a variety of factors have influenced RMNE decisions, including cost, language abilities and an established working relationship.

> For new sites, we decided we would also use a third-party audit system and that we would use TPA 4. All of our audits which we 'deem to be an audit' are third-party audits. The reason for this is because our own people cannot speak the local language and I feel that if we want to have meaningful employee interviews we need trained staff, local nationalities and often women to do the interviews. Our trained people internally are only for the pre-audit process (UKS 2, Head of CSR).

> Trial and error is involved in determining which system to adopt when it comes to deciding between self-auditing and third party. I think you need a professional company to give you the lead in and tell you things that you don't know. RMNE 6 has tapped into NGO 2's pool of law and therefore we have a system to find out the country laws (we get these directly from RMNE 6). They give us country briefs which are by no means foolproof but they cover 80% of all the issues. What don't they cover? The things that I don't know about, the little, fine laws aren't covered. It is the big, in your face, things that really concern me. So, the professional guys provided the background that I needed and then I did it myself (UKS 4, Ethical and Quality Manager).

> TPA 6 are our auditors, that is our financial auditors. We looked at the market, looked at the scale of fees and decided that TPA 6 were competent in terms of looking at other issues than financial issues for us. We benchmarked against

TPA 5 and another boutique company. We worked with TPA 7 and have a close relationship with them. They carried out some assessments for us, both quality and environmental ones, and they did inspecting and testing for us. Basically they were our eyes and ears (RMNE 9, Group Company Secretary).

While rare, we heard from some suppliers and MNEs that they exclude the use of TPAs altogether.

We don't do external audits because we can't afford them and we can't trust them. We find that TPA 4 and TPA 7, etc. do audits and then there are still issues concerning employment conditions. Is it that we are that much better or is it simply that these things are not being followed up? (RMNE 10, Ethical Trading Manager).

Further, criticism has been levelled at the use of TPAs, particularly on the quality and performance of the auditor. However, as the following academic notes, the quality of TPAs is expected to improve over time.

Monitoring is not getting anything. External monitoring is virtually useless. They have less experience than internal brand monitors and no credibility in the marketplace. FMNE 2 does a far better job than the external monitors. As for the model for external verification, I think that the NGO 16 model works. There should be a group of people involved from various backgrounds— accounting, religious, monitoring etc. At the moment they are all bad but gradually will improve in quality. There is a role for the NGO 16 model in terms of a fire alarm system but that model is not the solution (O 6).

Methodology of audits

We heard that there are a number of factors that go into establishing the methodology of both internal audits and TPAs. Considerations include the timing of the audit, the length of time allowed to conduct the audit, the level of detail of the audit, and the specific criteria that will be reviewed. Additional elements that we have seen included are interviews with workers and management, as well as exit interviews.

As in the apparel sector, we heard that the length of an audit varied, ranging from several hours to days. We have included a number of RMNE and supplier comments on this point because it is important to point out that discrepancies exist between what RMNE managers reported and what supplier managers reported.

The length of the audit: one full day with two auditors or two days for a larger factory that produces for major brands (RMNE 7).

Our audits are one day. Two auditors are sent for every initial audit. We try to have a male and female auditor so that the sexes can be matched for the interviews (RMNE 3).

An audit lasts for one to two days. If the auditor is aware of issues, he may get at the problem, but most are not aware of any issues (USS 5, Compliance Officer).

Audits take one day. Every month I have visitors (USS 6, Owner).

AMNE 8 came only once this year. They will interview the HR manager and others relating to the code. They will walk through the factory and give recommendations on improvements. It will take half a day. They have a checklist. RMNE 10 comes once a year. They came about four months ago and did very similar to AMNE 8 (THS 13, HR Manager).

Recently TPA 4 audited our joint-venture factory in China where there are 700 employees. There were two or three auditors and it took them six or seven hours. I think that this is probably sufficient because all they need to be really sure about are the documents looked at (UKS 3, Compliance Manager).

They take two to four days and involve factory interviews etc. In doing basic audits, we will usually do two factories in one day. We do the same as for a robust audit but go into less detail. We look at some EHS issues and may do some interviews of workers, say two or three and even look at documents. But as I said, it will be in less detail. I have developed a tick list for EHS issues. We endeavour to ensure that documents are in date and concentrate on key issues such as age, pay and hours worked but we go no deeper. If we could do three factories in a day, we would (UKS 4, Ethical and Quality Manager).

The audit happens two or three times a year, and lasts one day (THS 9, Personnel Manager).

They come informally and weekly to audit us, sometimes daily. They can come anytime, according to our contract. In our contract with them it stipulates that they can come. Once a year there is a formal audit (THS 10, Assistant Manager).

Audit methodology reflects the great range of operations and the breadth of suppliers that may be used, including the seasonal pressures of the retail sector. Our research revealed that the specific methodology employed by RMNEs in undertaking an audit showed a significant disparity in detail and approach.

We have a procedures document, about 60 pages long, talking about things like sample size, communication, employee interview etc. (RMNE 7).

We have two-person audit teams. We make an appointment with the supplier and we ask them to nominate a factory for us to visit. We send a letter of confirmation by e-mail and also a pre-evaluation form. There is a self-evaluation form sent by e-mail. It used to be a four-page document, but is now two. We ask it to be returned before the audit. We explain the purpose, the background to our programme and tell them what we will be looking at. Our four-page document used to flag more issues but it was too long and people weren't filling it in. We also let them know the agenda of the day and we make arrangements to come to visit them (RMNE 10, Ethical Trading Auditor).

There are slight differences [with each brand]. We haven't agreed programmes that we're not comfortable with. We always include employee interviews and our audits take a minimum of two days for a small factory. We want to do a thorough audit rather than skimp on it because it's our name. Therefore the United Kingdom team is more conservative than the other TPA 4 teams in the world. As a result of the push by RMNE 6, we have developed our own skills and systems, for example the reporting. Previously, it was very much just a tick in the box. In the United Kingdom now, you can tick and explain. There are also options to note improvements and things the factories are doing well. This has been a cultural change for us really because we were US oriented. It has filtered through regional managers' information on what we do and it gets cascaded down (TPA 4, Business Development Manager).

> The audit is scheduled. The licensee is notified and the audit party establishes the schedule. An introductory meeting laying out the scope prior to the audit is held. The audit party lists things that it wants to cover and the documentation needed. For example, accident records if this is built in within the local law requirements. This introductory meeting takes between 30 minutes and 60 minutes. The audit party then calls in the records. We often go in pairs for the initial audit depending on the size of the factory. We do the factory tour and select the people to be interviewed. We have a training manual listing criteria for selection but much of it is built up on working knowledge (RMNE 3).

Finally, we also learned how individual firms adjust to the variables involved in auditing. This includes the need to take into consideration differing audit standards, different departmental functions and roles, and the diversity of issues across multiple product lines and levels of the supply chain.

> The audit is different for each company, as each company places a different emphasis. RMNE 3 pay attention to safety; RMNE 8 to environmental protection, RMNE 7 to human rights and wages, AMNE 8 to safety, health and human rights. My job is to escort them round. Audits usually take around three hours for all of them. It is a similar process for each company. The content is similar, but each is in a different form. Some first look at documents, others are different. They all interview workers. It is hard to judge the quality of the audit because they all have a different emphasis (CHS 2, Quality Supervisor).

> The audit process starts with management interviews and analysis, followed by questions to the management, and then a factory site visit. We have a checklist of items, which we look at and if necessary take photos so we can support any observations we make. We look at fire safety, the emergency system, safety of other kinds, for example machinery, working conditions, protective equipment, first aid, employment terms and conditions, etc. After the visit we randomly select some workers from various departments—men and women of different ages—and interview them with the help of a questionnaire. We ask factory management for documentation on certain things, such as terms and conditions of employment, government certificates, factory documents, medical and fire policy, maintenance, needle policy, etc. After the worker interviews and inspection of the documents, the auditor will combine and give his views to the management within ten working days (AMNE 8, Quality Assurance Manager).

> He has a checklist on chemicals, storage area, health and safety; he will show what other firms/countries are doing which will be beneficial to the factory. Sometimes he gives feedback to improve. Documents—he will look at the document and comment (THS 9, Personnel Manager).

> The quick audit has little credibility but it is better than nothing. All factories in giftware have quick audits. Detailed audits take place in volume areas each year (UKS 4, Ethical and Quality Manager).

Worker interviews

An associated aspect of audit methodology is the degree to which feedback from workers is obtained. As in the apparel sector, we heard that the format and methodology for selecting workers to be interviewed during the audit process varied greatly, often appearing as though it was specific to the person undertaking the audit. Again, time constraints and a focus on core operational issues tended to take precedence in the worker selection process.

> We either interview 25% or 25 workers, whichever comes first, based on time-cards, operational performance and what age they look. Management are notified about the interviews and they are conducted on site. People are interviewed individually for about 15 to 20 minutes. We try to have a balanced approach—one male and one female auditor. In Guangzhou we have three female auditors (RMNE 3).

> Our sample size in terms of employee interviews depends on the size of the company. We have done groups of ten interviews, but generally we will have five or six. If it's a small factory then we'll do two groups of three interviews. We always interview workers in groups, never individually. I don't know why this is so, but this has always been the process from the beginning. I think it's too intimidating to have one-to-one interviews. The questions that we ask are similar questions to those for management. The employee interview will probably last about 40 minutes for the first group and then it would be shorter for the second group (RMNE 10, Auditor).

> Half of those interviewed are selected through the visual walk-through and the other half through documentation. There are 60 questions on the interview sheet and it takes anywhere between 10 and 20 minutes to interview the employees. Auditors reconvene throughout the day to discuss their findings—another check and balance. We are concerned about retaliation for anyone that speaks with us and we hope that 25 is a sufficiently large enough number to ensure that this does not occur (RMNE 3).

> In this particular audit they had three auditors in one room. One was looking at document trails and the other two were both doing worker interviews so there were two people being interviewed in the same room. I felt the interviews were rushed and there were questions of confidentiality. The auditors said they had to do this because they did not have enough time for the audit (UKS 3, Compliance Manager).

Announced versus unannounced audits

We learned that in the retail sector most audits are announced, which is quite different from the footwear and apparel sectors. The issue of announced audits has been explored in the earlier sectoral chapters. It is worth noting, however, that the reason cited by most RMNE managers for audits being announced was that compliance was not viewed as a pass or fail matter but rather as a goal that suppliers could work progressively towards achieving.

> We inform the factory who will be the auditor, giving them advance notice. Ninety-five per cent of audits are announced. In the early days we had problems getting access and this is why they are announced. We have found

that we don't really have a problem if they can clean up house 30 days beforehand. In any case, we ask them for 12 months of records. We recognise that announced audits may not reveal the full scope, but they are not restrictive (RMNE 3).

So far all audits are scheduled, that is announced. We expect to conduct unannounced audits in year three of our programme (RMNE 7).

They will inform you twice beforehand, and come once unannounced (CHS 5, Production Manager).

Frequency of audits

As the relationship between the RMNE and supplier develops, it is common for the RMNE to adjust the frequency of auditing. We found that internal audits carried out on a regular basis by CSR field staff may decrease in frequency as suppliers demonstrate consistent compliance and build confidence that they will remain in compliance.

Depending on the grade, then the assessment schedule will kick in. A 'C' grade requires an audit once a year, a 'B' grade an audit every two years, and an 'A' grade an audit every three years, but I have to tell you that this is a tall order. Approximately 80% of our factories are 'C' grade (RMNE 9, Group Company Secretary).

We are now moving towards audits every two years in very good factories with no problems as agreed with RMNE 6 (UKS 4, Ethical and Quality Manager).

Pre-audits

Pre-audits are utilised by RMNEs as a tool to filter out factories that will likely not be compliant with the required performance standards. Also, pre-audits are a means to minimise time delays. We heard from RMNE managers that given the JIT manufacturing approach common in the retail sector, having to get a supplier approved or back into compliance slows down the process. However, while pre-audits may be common in some RMNEs, our research leads us to suspect that the true position in the field is that audits occur after production has already commenced, as represented in the last statement below. The evidence gathered from our interviews suggests that the sheer volume of suppliers engaged, along with high supplier churn, does not allow for an effective utilisation of pre-audits. This further adds weight to the argument for integrating code requirements and compliance responsibilities more fully into the overall management systems of the firm.

Three opportunities for existing factories before termination. For new factories we require compliance before any orders would be placed (RMNE 7).

Before you receive the order you must follow their regulations, for example code. They audit the factory before placing the order (CHS 1, Chairman).

We insist that on all new sites, a robust external audit is carried out (RMNE 6, Central Co-ordinator, Ethical Issues).

> Our commitment is that we will audit new suppliers within ten days. However, it may be many months later that we actually audit them because of the pure volume. For example, in China, this week we just completed an audit of a supplier that was raised in February (RMNE 10, Ethical Trading Auditor).

> [For indirect sourcing] there is no pre-approval as it is too difficult. The audits are always after the fact and the audit is based on sampling (RMNE 7).

d. Remediation

'Comply or die' versus remediation

Some RMNEs reported taking a very rigid approach to compliance or performance requirements with suppliers, in which orders can be pulled or contracts terminated on the basis of risks associated with certain code violations. In general these risk areas appeared to be determined by the potential for negative publicity.

> Production will only be stopped in certain situations, for example, let me give you the situation in India where we did a pre-assessment and approval and discovered that there were only about half a dozen machines and that the rest of our product was being subcontracted. In this situation, we stopped production because we could have no control over our quality or over the environmental and ethical issues. Much of this is driven by media attention and we cannot afford to take risks (RMNE 9, Group Company Secretary).

> We will fail factories for key [code violations] and there is no opportunity for remediation (UKS 4, Ethical and Quality Manager).

A variety of approaches to requirements for compliance and performance are more the norm throughout the retail sector. We heard a number of comments that demonstrate an evolving level of awareness regarding the benefits of working proactively with suppliers, so as to ensure a consistent source of product, along with a higher level of quality. As such, RMNEs appear to be making a more concerted effort to work with suppliers to improve performance and compliance with code and operational standards.

> We are vested in building a long-term relationship with the suppliers. If it is a minor violation, we allow them to go into sampling, on condition that they improve. This is a minimum threshold. We want to develop a dedicated source of production. For a new factory, this relationship is not established without compliance. We choose long-term relationships because it does put our best face out there and because of the learning curve. We want less risk and there is a lower learning curve with long-term suppliers. We think of our vendors as our partners in success (RMNE 3).

> The compliance process is an ongoing process. We don't play cop with them. We ask them when they can rectify things and provided that a factory or supplier is willing to work with us we then give them a lot further time. Generally these things are dealt with via paper. Provided there is communication and the buyer is in communication then we don't have to go back to the factory (RMNE 10, Ethical Trading Auditor).

Working with non-compliant current suppliers appeared to be a more common approach for RMNEs while delisting or eliminating suppliers based on a lack of compliance with code elements appeared to be by far the exception rather than the rule. In general, RMNEs appeared to be more willing than other sectors studied to give a supplier additional opportunities to improve, working with them in what was sometimes termed a 'developmental approach'.

> In terms of going back, a supplier that is given a ranking of one is usually brought into RMNE 10 to discuss things if they haven't rectified it. We enter a rough time on the database. If they refuse to rectify things then we will delist things. This has only happened about eight to ten times in the United Kingdom, Morocco, the Far East, and usually it's been a case of a factory saying well I'm just not doing it (RMNE 10, Ethical Trading Auditor).

> We don't pass or fail factories. Suppliers are given an opportunity to sign up to our code of conduct and, if they say no, then we need to have a conversation with their director and their trading director (RMNE 10, Ethical Trading Manager).

One specific story shared with us is worth mentioning for the positive results that can accrue from the investment of time, effort and money in suppliers.

> In the last four years, from the approval process we have never had to disengage from one supplier. The nearest that we came to was on a site in China, and in that site what we ended up doing was ensuring that we actually conducted an audit every single month and helped them with their action plan. Why did that happen in that instance? Because we didn't have the option of placing the orders anywhere else. Yes it was hurtful on our wallet, but it ended up resulting in significant improvements in that particular workplace (UKS 2, Head of CSR).

Flexibility in the time frame for implementation is necessary, but there must be some measurement of progress. An open-ended time frame for improvement of specific identified issues is, in many cases, tantamount to non-enforcement of the code.

> The good thing about this is that RMNE 6 never gives a deadline. RMNE 6 recognised that you cannot make changes overnight, especially in China, and therefore she sent this message to my people. This approach was echoed by RMNE 3's compliance manager. The key measure is continuous improvement. You have to realise that continuous improvement is the path to total compliance and that you have to measure the rate of progress. It cannot be simply a case of 'we were not compliant yesterday but today we are' (UKS 3, Compliance Manager).

The compliance manager for UKS 3 adds that, 'We cannot change the world overnight but we need to demonstrate improvements.' It is in the demonstration of improvement that time frames play a crucial role. As the UKS 3 compliance manager continues to explain:

> For example, RMNE 3 did a first audit for us and they split their findings into two parts. The first part required rectification within 60 days. Issues such as 'no smoking' signs, emergency lighting on stairwells and payment below minimum wage were included in this part. The second part dealt with excess working hours, overtime and statutory holiday pay. It needed rectification within nine months (UKS 3, Compliance Manager).

High churn = low leverage

In the retail sector, the issue of supplier churn is more significant than in footwear or apparel. While the economic equation for global sourcing systems leads to 'least cost' production facilities, it also leads to inherent problems in trying to manage and influence the behaviour of suppliers. We were told that when an RMNE uses a particular supplier for a limited number of production runs, or for a single season, it is hard to enlist the efforts of the supplier in undertaking a meaningful investment in upgrading or installing management systems related to labour, social or ethical standards. Accordingly, many RMNE managers reported beliefs that until suppliers are adequately motivated by economic incentives, most likely in the form of long-term contracts, little initiative will be made in winning them over to the side of responsible corporate and social behaviour. The clearest indicator in support of this contention, that supplier churn poses a significant challenge to compliance, comes from our interviews that reference the huge number of suppliers that are continuously engaged and dropped.

> Our supply base is about 3,000 suppliers and it changes very often. For example, our suppliers in China change a lot. We have 50% of suppliers who are the same. This means that they might have been with us maybe five or six or seven years. It is easier to do something with them. We change suppliers because of price (RMNE 1, Administrative Manager).

> Our supply base is moving around constantly. For example, we are working with a unit in the Ukraine, but before we have been able to do a three-month follow-up we may have moved on to another supplier. You need a minimum of six to nine months to get buy-in and understanding when it comes to compliance issues. Approximately 50% of our suppliers need lots of input because they are the big boys who are opening up units all the time (RMNE 6, Head of Quality Management).

> Quick audits also have CAPs but we are weak at enforcing them because we may not even go back to the factory. We have a real ethical and moral problem ourselves on this issue. Should we even ask the factories to do these things if we aren't going to place another order? (UKS 4, Ethical and Quality Manager).

Use of CAPs

CAPs are an important tool for the remediation of supplier factories. CAPs continue to evolve in scope, format and application, and are a key component for remediation issues in the retail sector. Working with suppliers is a key function of RMNEs, and CAPs are seen as being able to provide a framework for ongoing management and enhancement of supplier performance. The approach for designing and implementing a CAP varies across the industry, but usually involves both the RMNE and supplier agreeing through dialogue to the parameters of the CAP. The level of specificity in the CAP varies, including prescribed performance requirements as well as general recommendations for standard policies, practices and operating procedures. Usually, the CAP then forms the measure against which the supplier is measured during subsequent auditing.

As is seen from our interviews, RMNEs demonstrated significant differences and consistencies in their approach to CAPs. The degree to which the supplier was engaged in development of the CAP varied, but generally involved a close working relationship between the RMNE and supplier. Further, by assessing and comprehending the consistencies in historical usage of CAPs, RMNEs are able to better allocate resources based on what is to be expected from suppliers in a particular country or region.

> We discuss what we expect the factory to do and then fill in a CAP and discuss the time frames for delivery. At the beginning we had a list of what we had to rectify with them, but now we no longer have this. With the European team this is constant. This is because the team has been together for a long time. In contrast, the team in the Far East is changing all the time. For example, there is no one in our current team that was there 12 months ago. It's a no-win situation in the Far East. In every case, factories have problems and it is often frustrating. The people who are doing these jobs are arguing the same issues all the time and therefore they often leave (RMNE 10, Auditor).

> After the audit, we hold the closing meeting. We leave the audit report with management and the corrective action plan is developed. Auditors devise it and the factory management signs off. The audit reports are entered electronically either by the auditor or the support staff. HQ reviews the report and then generates the corrective action plan letter—a formal letter to the licensee. This letter pretty much covers all that is in the corrective action plan. The letter issues locally (RMNE 3).

RMNEs also spoke with us concerning their approach and philosophy in sharing CAP results, findings, required changes and follow-up. In general a 'reasonable' time seemed to be agreed with supplier factories for improvements to be carried out. In most cases the supplier factory management appears to be directly involved in the setting of CAP time frames—a matter discussed later in this section.

> We create a CAP letter to the business partner. There is communication at the factory level—the auditor leaves a one-page summary of findings, and is followed up with a business letter from HQ summarising the findings in the audit. Because of our volume, we get clarifications or complaints from the factories. The CAP period is typically 60 days, through that depends on the follow-up (RMNE 3).

> We have a follow-up call and conference with the factory to suggest ways to reach any goals we give them. If something is serious we will request immediate rectification; otherwise we give them a reasonable time to comply (AMNE 8, Quality Assurance, Manager).

> The CAP is summarised to the business unit (partner and vendor) so they can understand the findings. They are grouped into different remediation deadlines. We expect the business partner to work with the factory to fix the findings. We expect them to discuss the findings and to ensure that appropriate measures are taken. We try to be as explicit as possible with respect to appropriate changes. There is negotiation on time-frames. Our office has weekly meetings, factory managers are given training on things like legal clarification and simple book-keeping (RMNE 3).

The role of auditing is integral to CAPs. An initial audit is usually undertaken and will reveal the deficiencies and corrections that will form the basis of the CAP. Additionally, follow-up, verification or re-audits are taken to verify that the requirements of the CAP have been adequately implemented.

RMNE 3 expects the licensee to respond to the corrective action plan letter. Typically we have a three-audit cycle—the initial audit and the two follow-up audits. The time between them depends on the violations but generally they are between 30 and 60 days. Ideally we have the same auditors do the follow-up. The idea is to review violations and look for progress (RMNE 3).

We do an initial audit and then a follow-up audit either one or two years later, depending on how good the factory was on the initial visit (AMNE 8, Quality Assurance Manager).

After the corrective action, the liaison office will go back and re-audit the supplier factory and give me the new report. And then, to be honest, I don't know. I will study the follow-up report and see which actions are not okay. It is a question of time. I will send our liaison office people again to follow up. This is just new. I have many audits which do not have the follow-up. I have to see how it will work (RMNE I, Administrative Manager).

We can re-audit after the factory has corrections. If there are corrections and we do a re-audit, they have to show that they have been able to hold these improvements for a one-month cycle and then we will start business (RMNE 6, Supply Chain Compliance Manager).

Negotiable aspects of CAPs

In most instances, the only negotiable aspects in a CAP are the time frames for improvements to be carried out. Only one supplier manager reported negotiating with the RMNE on physical improvements that needed to be undertaken at the facility.

[After the audit] the management manager gets a report and he and I agree via e-mail and phone what has to be done to improve (CHS I, Chairman).

The process for planning to implementation depends on different aspects, for example if the light is not working, we change the bulb. For other issues, the auditor will discuss it with us if it is a more complex problem. So it is possible to negotiate. Concerning implementation, we discuss with auditors and I will report to my superior to see whether we can do it in time and then discuss with the departments concerned and tell auditors by what date we can implement (CHS I, Logistics Manager).

After the audit has taken place, the customers give us a report and advice, and time to make improvements. Then they will check that we have implemented. This is negotiable. We have a meeting to agree on the timing (CHS 2, Quality Supervisor).

We develop an action plan and negotiate the time-frames (THS 13, HR Manager).

The auditing process as consultation

Through our interview process, we learned that many RMNEs have learned to utilise the audit function beyond that of simple compliance verification. The 'policing' role of audits has evolved to reflect a more positive approach in which the audit is utilised as a tool for supporting operational improvements, while still providing insight to, and verification of, current levels of compliance and performance. Generally, auditing has become an integral part of a wider supplier development process. This process includes direct interventions on the part of the RMNE to assist the supplier by providing advice and consultation regarding such matters as quality control, quality assurance, management systems, operational improvements and IT systems.

From the perspective of the RMNE, the logic behind their approach in utilising audits in a constructive engagement with suppliers reflects a commitment to responsibility for labour, social and ethical standards across the supply chain, as well as recognition that such standards are good for business overall.

> I do not think that anything we place on the action plan is beyond the realms of the supplier factory management team to do themselves. The standards of the factories which we go into are high. Most things that come to surface are not about corrupt management but rather about lack of awareness . . . I think that we could give help to people on how to introduce a system into their factories, for example to manage overtime. At the moment we give advice, but they often have no systems. I can tell you, however, that if there are complicated health and safety issues we do have people that we can call on because we are leaders in this field . . . I think that as factories become more aware of maintaining compliance it will change the culture where factories will actually be asking the multinational corporations for increases in time. Now I wouldn't be surprised to see this whole process being driven from the back end. The key is management, skills, knowledge, particularly about critical path planning, because you cannot just blame the brand, you have to ask when, for example, did a manager in a factory know that a label or some buttons were going to be late, and what did they do about it (UKS 1, Compliance Executive).

All suppliers expressed a desire to keep working with RMNEs in the remediation process. Many recognised their limited capacity to carry out the changes required, with a number citing the resulting improvements as positive for workers and managers—as well as for business.

> We need assistance in order to change the mentality of workers. Customers are the ones who know the procedures and the work so they can help (CHS 1, Logistics Manager).

> We receive some assistance from the companies. Last time, AMNE 8 gave us advice on alarm mounting—they showed us another factory to see where to position the safety alarm. We also looked at other things they were doing better than us, such as fire-prevention equipment—actually we found we are doing better than them. Normally, other suggestions we can solve ourselves so this was somewhat unique (CHS 2, Quality Supervisor).

> We were quite happy to improve [from the audit] because we could see the benefit of that. From EHS concerns we could see the benefit of that because our environment compared to other factories is better. Depending on issues, it did not take too long to implement the plan. Usually we could do it within a week except some things over which we do not have any control, for example overtime permits, insurance policies (CHS 3, Production Manager).

Specific operational improvements were recognised by some suppliers from an enhanced RMNE audit process which included a collaborative approach in remedying deficiencies discovered from audits.

> All codes and audits are not difficult; it is more a chance to improve our management, as some of the questions they ask makes us aware. For example, fire-fighting equipment. We aren't so aware of the latest equipment so they will advise us on this (CHS 2, Quality Supervisor).

> It made things more systematic and improved productivity. Before that, things were not so organised—for example, workers spent more overtime producing goods—and, since code reduces working hours, we needed to find ways to improve productivity. They are less tired and work harder with less working hours. Workers do eight hours and four days of overtime but no more than 60 hours. Before [MNE codes] it was 80 hours and sometimes 100 hours. We don't have hard data on this. It has been good for our company (THS 12, Manager).

e. Other reporting

It is important to note that in addition to internal reporting, additional opportunities for external reporting exist. This includes such social initiatives as sustainability reporting, represented, for example, by the Global Reporting Initiative (GRI). To undertake such reporting, some RMNEs develop the reports themselves, while others formally engage outside third parties, such as TPAs. The impact of such diverse reporting varies, but generally it has been positive for awareness raising, stakeholder dialogue and, to some degree, performance improvements. Other dimensions of reporting include a greater emphasis on stakeholder engagement and transparency, as social and sustainability reporting requires that information previously considered confidential or proprietary be made available to public scrutiny. This may be seen most significantly in the more recent phenomena of MSIs, which include a major role for NGOs. The inclusion of additional stakeholders, especially NGOs, has required further adjustments by RMNEs to compliance and operations systems for engagement of these stakeholders in some aspects of internal processes.

6. Interrelation, integration and dialogue

Given the massive scale and complexity of global retail operations, it is a monumental task to integrate adequately new roles and responsibilities across diverse and disparate organisational departments. However, as the labour, social and ethical standards reflected in publicly embraced commitments of corporate codes of conduct become more a requirement of operation, RMNEs are faced with integrating compliance and related functions into the complex maze of pre-existing management systems. The approach chosen by an RMNE to ensure that code provisions are met is key, and must consider the implicit responsibility for working with suppliers in implementing overall CSR.

a. Interrelation and integration

The importance of the governance and management structure should be a priority for RMNEs, as the responsibilities and authority for compliance with code and related operational standards must be clearly delineated. The approach in selecting responsible departments is reflected in the following statements, and reflects differences between home-country management structures versus the realities of field implementation of a global compliance strategy.

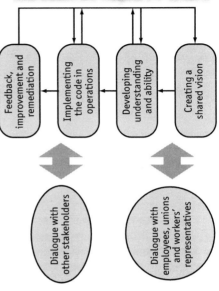

Interrelation and integration of elements

> Our CSR team is not based in legal because it is concerned with operational issues. The American point of view generally comes from a litigation perspective and therefore those companies always have to be in denial. It is their legal department that is always denying what is taking place. That is not the case with us (RMNE 6, CSR Representative).

> Compliance was part of the Department of Consumer Products but a conflict of interest arose. Therefore it was decided to move it out and now it reports into 'management audit' which reports into the CFO. There is an ILS board comprised of senior executives, the president of CP and it reports into the firm's second in command (RMNE 3).

> The compliance group is part of the corporate division. This means that we are not beholden to any business units, for example licensing, consumer products or sourcing (RMNE 3).

The considerations in establishing an actual structure for code of conduct implementation vary, though, with common operational structures shared by various RMNEs.

> The CSR working group meets every quarter to discuss issues either face-to-face or on a conference call. The structure of the group—it includes the business-unit heads (consumer products, stores, legal, corporate communications, parks and resorts) plus the CSR senior management group. It also meets on a quarterly basis. The group was set up in 1997 and has held meetings since then (RMNE 3).

> I am responsible for imports. I must control the payments and deal with customs problems and transport [logistics]. I am also responsible for social compliance. Because buyers do not always know the details, I have the power of veto. If I think that they are not doing good business, I can say no, they cannot take on this supplier. In France we have 1,200 in total for the team in our section. They are broken up into legal, IT, buyers and their assistants (RMNE 1, Administrative Manager).

> We also have a tutoring group made up of the CSR head, environmental head and the person with a marketing background to facilitate the group. It meets

with the Board of Directors to discuss things such as the CSR Committee or the role of [our code]. We are actually going to give ourselves a score as to how we are performing on compliance. It is important to have these sorts of things as the aspirations need to be driven [from the] bottom up but at the end of the day we want to make sure that we are leading in CSR (RMNE 6, CSR Representative).

Finally, two individuals shared in detail their experiences, highlighting the challenges and importance of integrating compliance functions across the entire firm and supply chain.

I am responsible half-time for social compliance and half-time for quality. In terms of how do I actually carry out my functions, I try to sign off a new factory for both issues at the same time. This is the case for clothing. So basically for social compliance we have an independent third party doing the audit and I do diligence checking. It is useful to do it through diligence particularly in terms of quality because it ties in easily in terms of looking at issues like working hours, and at the end of day if I am not happy with, say, social compliance issues, conditions in the factory, but don't have anything that I can approve, then I can reject it for lack of quality systems because I often find that these two go hand in hand (RMNE 6, Supply Chain Compliance Manager).

I receive the report and I study it. I give a copy, via e-mail, to the buyer and to the liaison office. My idea is that the liaison office will go to the supplier and ask for corrective actions. Together with the supplier, they decide the corrective action and the date for completion. The people in the liaison office are quality people. This means that they are also in charge of quality and know the people in the supplier factories. My hope for the future is to try to have an extra person in the liaison office responsible just for this because it is a lot of work and demands time. In China we really need someone else (RMNE I, Administrative Manager).

b. Dialogue

While our research indicated that MNEs and suppliers identified stakeholder engagement as a critical element in developing code-of-conduct implementation programmes in the retail sector, companies in this sector had the fewest examples of formal systems or mechanisms for this purpose. Historically, the retail sector has only recently begun to embrace the need for ongoing dialogue in the development of its CSR and code programmes, and many retail MNEs are still struggling with the management requirements of their vast supplier networks. Despite the fact that certain retailers such as RMNE I are quite advanced in their stakeholder engagement process, such examples are rare in this sector. Overall, much more could be done to formalise the structures for input from workers and their representatives, and from the public, in this sector.

Our research did uncover a general shift overall within the retail sector towards at least an acknowledgment of the need for and value of stakeholder dialogue. However, the lack of integration of mechanisms for such dialogue, along with a general lack of transparency in current dialogue, demonstrates the need for serious attention to this subject.

Many questions remain regarding whether the systems developed by MNEs and suppliers will be sufficient to achieve the aims and objectives of the CSR and the labour, social and ethical obligations they embrace. As O'Rourke (2003) asks, 'Can these systems be implemented beyond the first tier of suppliers? Can southern stakeholders be brought into discussions and have a real say in the structure and implementation of these programmes?' Such observations underscore the need for further developments in this area, in particular the effort by both MNEs and their suppliers to engage in a broader dialogue with both external and internal stakeholders on social performance issues.

The following sections outline in further detail some of the findings on this issue in the retail sector.

Dialogue with consumers

Increasingly, RMNEs reported that pressure is being placed on them to communicate directly with their customers on the broader issue of CSR and on specific issues relating to code-of-conduct implementation, such as child labour. This has led some RMNEs to develop training programmes for their store employees so that they can communicate directly with consumers.

> I am in charge of communication with stores. My idea is to explain what we do because more and more customers and NGOs are asking our store employees. It is dangerous for us if our employees do not answer. I am planning on training them this year. Last year we sent an information leaflet to management in each of our stores telling them about our programme (RMNE I, Communications Manager).

A number of RMNEs interviewed are not only disseminating information regarding their own compliance programmes but are also obtaining input and feedback from consumers on this issue. The importance of this communication was explained to us by RMNE I which had suffered financially due to a media exposé regarding alleged use of child labour in an Asian-based supplier factory. In order to restore consumer confidence and ensure that their compliance programme was reflective of consumer concerns, RMNE I decided to regularly poll its customers on code-of-conduct issues. It reported that this engagement has yielded positive results both financially and in terms of their reputation with customers.

Dialogue with NGOs

Importantly, RMNEs reported seeing the value in proactive behaviour and the engagement of NGOs. Furthermore, they reported that engaging local and global NGOs on specific matters has led to practical benefits, particularly within the context of public perception. An added benefit of this is of course the bottom line, although retailers stated it was difficult to measure the size of this benefit. Nevertheless, a number of RMNEs cited poor financial performance during certain periods as being linked to public perception of poor performance in CSR issues, particularly those alleging child labour in supplier factories.

Through ongoing international stakeholder links, RMNE 6 has avoided three press exposures. We want to ensure that they are adding value and that they can diffuse things before they hit the press. If you believe that what you are doing is right, the press will leave you alone. They have also continued networking with NGO 5 (RMNE 6, Central Co-ordinator, Ethical Issues).

Our biggest problem is that we don't talk about what we are doing. At a conference five weeks ago when I shared what we were doing, people were amazed. Many fringe NGOs are also not aware of what we are doing. We plan to do a social and environmental report. At the moment, however, we are just at the stage of doing a scene-setting document and hope that possibly we will be able to issue one next year that may coincide with our annual report (RMNE 6, CSR Representative).

Dialogue with workers

An additional factor that is critical to the effective implementation of code provisions and which facilitates improvements across global supply chains and operations is the engagement of workers in the ongoing dialogue on workplace performance. While labour standards and workplace issues may be at the forefront of both management and worker dialogue, our research indicates that it is essential to ensure that workers are apprised of a variety of corporate and factory information, so as to address mis-perceptions and build trust.

If you are aware you are compliant, why don't you start by telling your workers? This will enable you to keep your best people. If workers don't know, then you have to understand that their perception is just as risky. Let me give you an example. In Sri Lanka, there was one worker who was interviewed who thought that he was on a probation status after having worked for the factory for nine months. When in reality, six months after the probation had ended, he had been placed on to the normal employee status and given a pay rise, but because the administration was lagging and the appropriate letter hadn't been sent, that worker was not informed. This is the classic story of why the worker's perception is important. What ended happening in this case was that during an audit that worker said that he wasn't being treated fairly (RMNE 6, Central Co-ordinator, Ethical Issues).

Further, as demonstrated in the following statement, some supplier management has recognised the benefit from engaging workers directly in implementation of code standards rather than simply relying on management.

As management have too much to do, it is good to have a workers' committee to help us with code implementation. It is still something new so has not yet been implemented. We now have managerial staff inviting workers. We will invite specific workers, but it is not working yet. The idea is maybe to have voting by the workers. We will also have line supervisors (CHS 1, Logistics Manager).

The underlying issue is communication with workers, as discussed in both the apparel and footwear sections.

> The biggest issue is communication. We have a public announcement posted up in the workplace and in dormitories and have a global communication, that is, broadcasting used to announce things or if there is nothing to say, then we play music. Another important channel is through the management. We have two meetings per week. If there is something important, we call managers and supervisors to meet with us (CHS 3, Administration Manager).

Dialogue between MNEs

A significant development in the nature of RMNE behaviour is the degree to which dialogue, conversation and the sharing of information has evolved. Our research indicated that this is due, in part, to the fact that those individuals responsible for compliance and code implementation see the challenges and frustrations of multiple overlapping audit, compliance and verification systems. In the desire to realise efficiencies, some RMNEs have chosen to freely share information, with the expectation that they too will benefit from similar responses.

Of particular import is the realisation among RMNEs that they share many of the same interests across supply chains. As such, a number of RMNEs have realised that they could benefit from establishing an informal dialogue on topics of mutual interest.

> In 2001 we began our partnership with the IA 10 and other retailers to exchange ideas about what we do. We decided to have the same audit questionnaire. Because we are all using the same suppliers, by working together we may represent 10 to 15% of turnover in the supplier factory and we may have more pressure then. We decided to have our audits done by the same companies. We also decided to give IA 10 information about our audits. The IA 10 has a database and we can ask them if an audit has already been done. The company [retailer] who did the audit can then decide to give us the copy of the audit. The database is confidential. We give the IA 10 the name of the supplier factory, address, date of the audit and name of the company who did the audit. In this way, we can share audit reports, save money and do more. We decided to work together because we are not competitors for social accounting. We each decided not to advertise this or profit from it. If we have to advertise, then the IA 10 will do it (RMNE 1, Administrative Manager).

> Our top 13 [RMNE 6 supplier] group has an open, sharing relationship, unlike many other retailers. I believe that this is because of the personalities involved and the inherent way that RMNE 6 deals with their suppliers. The best example of this is that if they find child labour in one of our factories, contracts will be withdrawn and financial penalties incurred. Therefore it is best to share and be open (UKS 3, Compliance Manager).

Dialogue with external stakeholders

A few RMNEs have even evolved to the level of sharing compliance information or audit results with key stakeholders. Nevertheless there still exists a great deal of distrust even among retailers that share suppliers, with a number of RMNE compliance managers reporting that for legal and internal company reasons directing sharing of information was not possible.

RMNE 10 are active but we don't do a lot of business with them. We have a good relationship with them and often talk to them to ask what they would do in a difficult situation. They have audited two of our factories and we have cases where we share factories. We try to have multi-customer factories. Originally, all the brands wanted auditors to fit under each of their systems. RMNE 3 and RMNE 6 have pooled to share audits. It is ridiculous for this not to happen (UKS 4, Ethical and Quality Manager).

I have learned that everybody else is now getting active. Three years ago everyone was secretive. In terms of grey areas we have been talking with RMNE 3 about the possibility of partnering up because we have more people and we also do site visits, but the question is, what will we get back from them? We are also in the same factories as RMNE 6 and therefore we could look at a way of sharing our audits. You just have to come across it by accident. I think that this will just be another step forward (RMNE 10, Ethical Trading Manager).

c. Some implications of codes for functions

As we have seen in the other sectors, the implementation of a code of conduct has important implications across corporate functions. The following sections outline some of the comments that we heard on this topic from the retail MNEs and suppliers interviewed.

i. Role of CSR groups

The CSR and compliance department of a RMNE can be structured in a variety of ways. As outlined in previous sections, the diversity of requirements associated with codes, along with the myriad operational requirements related to managing the production of diverse and seasonal merchandise, provides a significant challenge to ensuring that compliance with CSR and code provisions is adequately implemented throughout an MNE and its supply chain.

A variety of factors assist in the effective implementation of required commitments. These include a systematic approach for managing code-related issues; an adequate number of trained and knowledgeable personnel dedicated specifically to this function; the integration of CSR and code responsibilities across all requisite departments; a commitment to the code from the top level of the organisation; close co-operation with suppliers on code and CSR-related matters; and adequate resources and a realistic workload for staff responsible for CSR and code implementation.

It is increasingly clear at both the RMNE level and the supplier level that managing code compliance requires dedicated personnel. This is a dominant theme in the previous comments on the operational challenges faced by CSR groups and the need for field personnel. As a supplier in China observes, 'The code of conduct is a long-term task. You must have one person concentrated to doing this task. For me as director, or my two partners, we do not have the time to do this by ourselves' (CHS 3, Administration Manager).

Some RMNEs have found that the CSR function is so important that it requires significant resources in the form of a departmental business structure, with highly defined roles and responsibilities. The following statements highlight the degree of detail that some RMNEs have gone to so as to ensure appropriate implementation of CSR requirements.

> Sixty-six people are part of the compliance organisation and they have no other responsibility. They work in three broad areas: 1) education and communication [internal business units, external business partners on the expectations of the programme], 2) monitoring including internal resources [largest group in Guangzhou, China], and 3) reporting—the group takes the output of the mentoring results and converts the results into action plans and programmes (RMNE 3).

> There is an international labour standards working group made up of all the senior executives of all business units, senior management and corporate management. It consists of our Senior Counsel, the Executive Vice President of Planning and Control, and Consumer Products individuals (RMNE 3).

> The three of us, that is the two people who are responsible for homewares and myself, we sit close next to each other, we often benchmark and go to each other's factories. You see, before any factory can be signed off [on] we need approval and the supply chain report must be signed off at headquarters (RMNE 6, Supply Chain Compliance Manager).

However, the prior statements represent those RMNEs that are at the forefront of implementing CSR into operational structures. In the interim, conflict continues to arise throughout organisations that have not recognised the need to fully integrate CSR into standard operating procedures. Until corporate governance structures clearly put a priority on code compliance, a major role of corporate CSR departments will remain that of internal champion concerning code issues that are still subject to debate in relation to commercial interests.

> There is an understood rule that no one can place orders with an unapproved factory. I debate this regularly with business units. However, the commercial director has the ultimate decision. We have not had any conflict within the last four years (RMNE 9, Group Company Secretary).

> If RMNE 6 disagrees with a compliance report I cannot really do anything about it. However, if I am not comfortable with what the report has been showing I don't even present it to RMNE 6 because I want to keep the relationship with RMNE 6. Instead, what I would do is go back to the business and say we cannot start production. If we still want to persevere then we must talk to the factory. I cannot really think of any issue where RMNE 6 and I have really disagreed (UKS 1, Compliance Executive).

ii. Implications of codes for supplier-level CSR management

Uniquely, we heard that one supplier code compliance manager uses the code as a tool to influence his or her own management within the supplier factory. As the HR manager for a Thai supplier puts it,

> Code helps to push the management. For example, regarding safety—a machine needs a guard. I will argue that the customer won't be happy if we don't have a guard. I bargain with management—after the machine guards, help the

workers as well. Concerning worker welfare, we make sure there is clean drinking water and glasses. I argued that if workers have their own clean water and glass, it is very important for their health and for the customers' view of the factory. Codes enable me to manage easier as HR manager (THS 13, HR Manager).

iii. Purchasing and selection of suppliers

In some cases, our research indicated positive developments regarding the integration of CSR and compliance responsibilities into other departmental functions of the RMNEs. The following statement represents an organisational evolution to include evaluation of existing and potential licensees within the context of CSR and code compliance.

> Within the business units themselves, there are people designated to look at compliance. For example, licensing may have many offices throughout the world. There is a designated person who does compliance as part of their job (RMNE 3).

However, in general, the impression that we gained from the RMNEs interviewed is that integrating CSR into purchasing departments remains a challenge due to the price-driven nature of the retail industry. Some RMNEs, such as RMNE 1, appear to be more advanced in this area due to the corporate strategy of working with a smaller, more easily identifiable, supply base, which reportedly facilitates the integration of CSR responsibilities into purchasing decisions.

iv. Human resource management

There is a perceived need to incorporate CSR performance criteria in the personal performance reviews of MNE managers from different departments, especially operational departments.

> There was an initiative to have corporate compliance as a general performance indicator for all of consumer products. I am not sure of where we are at (RMNE 3).

> My responsibility is about 30% [of my time] but I have no job description for this and it is NOT included in my performance evaluation. [I continue to do compliance] because of my personal values (RMNE 1, Administrative Manager).

> We have agreed that it would be good to put these code requirements, that is the responsibility for ethics, on the job profile. But this still hasn't happened. Because I can't do it openly I do it covertly. For example, over a six-week period between March and April I conducted half-day workshops which I called 'GSP: where are we up to?' but really, it was training (RMNE 6, Supply Chain Compliance Manager).

> Ethical trading is in my job specification; however, I am not particularly assessed on this. The Board of Directors takes guidance from me on what is acceptable and what isn't (RMNE 9, Group Company Secretary).

At the supplier level, code compliance issues were not reported as being part of performance evaluations. This was not surprising as few of the companies interviewed had formal performance assessment mechanisms, including job specifications and assessments; rather, performance was assessed 'on the job' in terms of whether daily tasks were achieved.

v. Manufacturing and quality

A challenge for RMNEs and their supply chain is the need to assess the integration of CSR and compliance issues into global operational systems that have extreme time constraints. As mentioned throughout this book, the JIT manufacturing approach leaves little time to integrate or assess CSR compliance. The fundamental driver for suppliers, in particular, is to meet the deadlines imposed on them by the RMNEs. Only by meeting delivery timetables will the supplier be assured that additional contracts will be forthcoming. The overall economic model requires the RMNE as buyer to allow for flexibility in delivery requirements if the supplier is to have a realistic chance to integrate CSR and related code requirements. However, the RMNE is also in fierce competition with other RMNEs from countries in which CSR and code requirements may not be as critical and therefore do not make their way into the buyer–supplier relationship, or with RMNEs that do not consider CSR or compliance of their suppliers with labour standards as a priority.

The following statements highlight the fact that time is of the essence in the RMNE–supplier relationship.

> We plan production every two and a half months. We cannot plan so much in advance as a lot of changes can occur in specifications once orders have been placed. Changes are not uncommon. Sometimes they change and sometimes we will ask for earlier or later shipment dates because of their changes (CHS 1, Chairman).

> When we have to produce within a particular period we may need to extend the time if it means we are going to violate the law or a code. That's how it might affect me. Normally, we just insist that we can't do it in the time and imply that otherwise the quality will suffer. Designers normally know how much lead time is needed so they don't normally insist on the time limit (CHS 2, Assistant Manager).

> The shipment dates are getting shorter and shorter in this competitive world. We need to respond more quickly. The current time to market is 45 days. There are changes by customers in the orders. Now the customers place the orders very late but they need the shipment fast. I think the reason why is that they do not want to keep an inventory and want to see if the product sells. Our lead times are much shorter than before. We need to work hard to control our suppliers, to work with those we can co-operate with and can have good quality of materials (CHS 3, Production Manager).

> Everything is governed by the timetable of the industry. I am not saying that critical path squeeze doesn't happen, but the customer, that is the brand multinational corporation, is partly to blame because its availability dates never change no matter what happens. This means that factories need

> assistance to meet the law and meet the standards (UKS 1, Compliance Executive).

> Lead times of orders vary. Many comments that I get from our customers require changes to orders or changes at the last minute. The challenge with this is that we are still required to deliver the garment at the end of time. At the moment we target production and procurement people to improve standards and understand this whole process, but let me tell you, it should be the designers who are understanding the impacts (UKS 2, Head of CSR).

d. Role of government

Consistent with the previous coverage given to the importance of compliance with national or local legal and regulatory requirements, is the role of government at both the national and local levels. One of the biggest challenges that we heard about facing RMNEs and their suppliers is the discrepancy between promulgated legal performance requirements and the degree to which they are actually enforced. RMNEs and suppliers face realities associated with corruption, favouritism, cronyism and similar inequities, which have been known to result in a hidden, but actual, part of business operation. In the absence of consistent enforcement across this sector, RMNE compliance managers are left to their own resources to determine how best to implement and enforce code compliance across their operations. The following statement highlights one approach of an RMNE to the absence of consistent government involvement.

> It is based on the laws in the country, but it isn't enforced. For example, in many countries the law is ignored. In Indonesia, a government inspector has 10,000 factories to inspect and it is impossible for them to do, so therefore it is up to businesses like ours to enforce it. Let me give you another example: the national law in China regarding working hours says that you can obtain a dispensation and work whatever hours you want to if you have that dispensation. This puts businesses at risk and therefore we have to invent our own intermediate standards (RMNE 6, Supply Chain Compliance Manager).

VII
Implementing specific areas addressed by codes

1. Background

In the previous three chapters we examined various management systems used by MNEs in the footwear, apparel and retail sectors to implement their codes of conduct. We heard of many different systems and approaches. In essence, the objective for each MNE was the same; namely, to adequately and appropriately address the specific issues reflected in their codes. Previously, we looked at *how* MNEs attempt to implement their labour, social and ethical commitments. In this chapter, we focus on *what* actually occurs in practice, on the ground and in the factories. By communicating directly with various stakeholders involved with the MNEs, their suppliers and related business partners, we highlight shared comments, concerns and criticisms. Given the commonality of code provisions across these three sectors, this chapter examines them as a single group, taking examples and quotes from all, as they refer to the common principles of code provisions.

The MNEs interviewed for this book face the challenge of having to consider an array of management, labour and manufacturing practices, addressing the social, labour and environmental goals embodied in their codes. The following statements are intended to demonstrate the broad scope of what is covered. In this chapter, we will consider what some of the managers and workers suggested with regard to their experience with specific issues. The intent is to provide insight for others facing similar challenges.

> We want better-quality lunches. And a stable job. And we would like a higher salary (VIS 3, Factory Worker).

> We have zero tolerance for child labour, pay rates, but it is tough with work hours. We push for VOC [volatile organic compounds]; we try to help them (FMNE 2, CSR Manager).

> The worker is an asset, not an expenditure. Our code emphasises human dignity, therefore it helps managers to think of their workers in terms of [productivity] (FMNE 2, CSR Manager).

This last statement concerns, we were told, the philosophy behind the training programme this particular MNE gives to the managers of its suppliers. Based on data gathered by this MNE, it was suggested that after these training sessions the workers are better treated and, as a result, are more productive, with up to 25% productivity growth. We were told that workers manifest more positive attitudes. Yet the nature of what is said, namely, addressing the concept of human dignity and reframing the way both the supplier and the MNE view workers, has wide-ranging implications for those carrying out this company's code. MNEs and suppliers may benefit from assessing how they view staff and what managerial culture exists in their organisations. They also need to consider who is going to move their code efforts forward. The complications of implementing diverse or unfamiliar code standards are highlighted by the following points.

Main code provisions:

- Freedom of association
- Child labour
- Forced labour
- Discrimination
- Environment, health and safety
- Harassment
- Working hours/overtime

The challenge with health and safety is much clearer than with social or labour issues—for example, 'treat your employees with respect'—it is tough to show how this impacts bottom lines, tough to measure in the first place. The same with after-hours entertainment for workers. There are always other factors that could be considered to be the reason for improvements or benefits (FMNE 2, CSR Manager).

The labour set of skills is different from health and safety. The EHS [personnel] tend to be ex-pats, they don't have or have to have the language skills. The labour people have to have a better ability to deal with local staff and HR issues (FMNE 1, Regional CSR Manager).

None of the myriad code provisions has evolved, nor has to be implemented, within a vacuum, however. Indeed, as the previous chapters indicate, most codes are developed against a background of existing legislation, policies and international principles that speak directly to MNE behaviour. Many of the provisions are interconnected, as are the strategies which MNEs use to implement them. Reiterating the intent of this chapter, we seek to provide insight for others facing similar challenges regarding the implementation of code provisions. Where appropriate, we provide an outline of key legislative references relating to the code provisions. However, for more in-depth details, refer to Chapter II.

a. Freedom of association

As already outlined, almost all MNE codes provide some recognition and respect for the right of employees to freedom of association and collective bargaining. However, few codes stipulate that the MNE or their business partners must take positive steps to support that right. One of the more progressive code provisions in supporting the right of freedom of association states:

> Business partners should ensure that workers who make such decisions or participate in such [trade] organisations are not the object of discrimination or punitive disciplinary actions and that the representatives of such organisations have access to their members under conditions established either by local laws or mutual agreement between the employer and the worker organisations.

Yet even this provision might be criticised by some due to its reliance on local laws, which may not fully uphold the right to freedom of association. Freedom of association is a fundamental international labour standard; indeed it is one of the principles on which the ILO is based.[43] The ILO has defined freedom of association as the right of workers to establish and join organisations of their own choosing without previous authorisation.[44] The ILO has also stipulated that the workers' organisations should 'not be liable to be dissolved or suspended by administrative authority',[45] and that workers should enjoy adequate protection against acts of anti-union discrimination in respect of their employment.[46]

Freedom of association, along with the right to collective bargaining, is represented in various ways in the codes of the companies we studied. Considered from both a management and a workers' perspective with regard to achieving the goals set in the codes of conduct, the firms have a considerable set of challenges in the area of freedom of association and collective bargaining. These challenges include the perceived large gap in power between managers and workers (particularly in developing countries from which the MNEs purchase), the lack of a strong, independent free trade union movement, and a lack of trade union tradition in the suppliers studied.

> The most important standard is the right of association. If we can get the workers to see the importance and the benefits of this then it will have an important benefit on the worker situation (FMNE I, Regional Manufacturing Manager).

Clearly this situation cannot be changed overnight. Freedom of association cannot be introduced simply through the adoption of a code of conduct. Rather, what is envisaged by a number of MNE managers interviewed is a process of evolution that requires vigilance and strong support from the MNE. Some would even suggest that MNEs have the direct responsibility of ensuring adequate code implementation.

In one of our interviews with worker representatives in a Viet Nam shoe factory, they stated that, at the beginning of factory operations, the union existed because it was law but that it was not clear what role the union had. Over time, they had developed the role, under the encouragement of the MNE buyer, so that the union now served as an important bridge between workers and management. While this is commendable, it is suggested that it is important that the union continues to evolve beyond a 'bridge' role, to function adequately as an independent trade union in terms acceptable to the ILO. Local managers in Viet Nam told us that each line has a trade union representative with some responsibility for ensuring that workers are supported by the code and that code requirements are met. Once again, care must be taken to ensure that the union

---

43   International Labour Organization Constitution.
44   Freedom of Association and Protection of the Right to Organise Convention, 1948 (No. 87), Article 2.
45   *Ibid.*, Art. 4.
46   Right to Organise and Collective Bargaining Convention, 1949 (No. 98), Article 1: 'Such protection shall apply more particularly in respect of acts calculated to: (a) make the employment of a worker subject to the condition that he shall not join a union or shall relinquish trade union membership; (b) cause the dismissal of or otherwise prejudice a worker by reason of union membership or because of participation in union activities outside working hours or, with the consent of the employer, within working hours.'

functions are not simply an extension of the management, but are genuinely representing the workers' interests.

Freedom of association was cited as one of the most challenging issues for MNEs in terms of code implementation. MNE managers in each of the sectors studied mentioned a number of obstacles in attempting to recognise and respect the right to freedom of association. In some countries without a long tradition of freedom of association, neither workers nor suppliers' managers appeared to have a good understanding of the role of a union. In other instances, suppliers and MNEs have viewed unions as too politicised to hold an effective dialogue with management. Conversely, unions have reported that supplier management has often been hostile to union development and that the MNEs have not engaged to actively counteract that attitude. Unions and some MNEs have described instances of factory management dismissing, discriminating against or disciplining workers seeking to participate in workers' organisations.

> There are no unions in the factory. If workers have a problem they should tell the personnel manager or factory managers. The complaints from workers are on incentives (GS 2, Director).

> Unions in Sri Lanka are politicised. I have only met 2% of union guys. There is the one factory with a union (AMNE 4).

> We talk with those in the industry and probably some unions but not in China. I personally have not come across many unionised factories nor union members. I don't think it is common for people to be union members. We have between 4,000 and 5,000 factories in China. If anything, workers don't understand what a union is about (RMNE 3).

> I have heard about union organisations, but believe freedom becomes too libertarian—the workers transform the freedom that the code gives them into disorder. For example, in a nearby factory, somebody came and spoke about organisation and getting involved in trade unions. Before trade unions, the factory was profitable but, once a trade union was formed, it went bankrupt and closed. The workers burned the products. They had heard that if they paralysed the factory, they would get results (GS 2, Personnel Manager).

> It is impossible to organise workers in the Maquila industry because there the owners are foreign and they do not respect freedom of association. They are attracted to Honduras because of low wages, poor education and good workers (HU 1).

> There are approximately 1,000 apparel factories in Thailand and approximately 30 unions in textiles and members. The number of paid union memberships in the whole country is about 1,200. Today, not even 20 factories have unions. There has been a decline in the number of members because employment has declined. Many factories closed after the 1997 crash, including three with big unions. Very few factories organise now because workers don't want to lose their jobs. Some still have CB [collective bargaining] but less so as there is difficulty with concession bargaining. At the moment in CBs, the goal is just to try to maintain the wage (NGO 1, Chairman).

Several MNEs defined freedom of association differently from the ILO or by unions for code implementation purposes. For those unions interviewed, freedom of association meant the ability to form or join a union. For some MNEs, successful freedom of association measures could extend to parallel means of association such as workers' grievance committees or the established, functional worker complaint procedures.[47] Indeed, as one of the participating academic experts noted, 'even FMNE 1, which is one of the more pioneering MNEs interviewed uses the crude criterion of "good labour management communication" as a proxy to measure freedom of association which local auditors are free to interpret in their own way' (E 1).

> Parallel means [of freedom of association] will do for now and they are positively encouraged. A factory cannot ban unions but this is difficult to prove. If it does not have a union we ask them to put a workers' committee in place or health and safety committees. These things get discussed at benchmarking groups (RMNE 6, Central Co-ordinator, Ethical Issues).

> In Indonesia, each of our sites has a union and the site rules are approved by the Department of Labour. There are collective bargaining agreements in place in some of our facilities. In our factory in Indonesia we have regular meetings with the representatives of the workforce. There are formal agendas and minutes kept. They will discuss things like holiday arrangements and site rules. I cannot remember whether anyone has ever discussed wages or whether the workers have brought up this topic. In Morocco, this is down to the individual site managers. There is a legal requirement that employees have some form of democratic organisation with worker representation. Out of our seven sites there, four have followed the letter of the law and have created a complete democratic process, including elections, etc. The other three have communication groups, but they are exactly the same as the four with the democratic process. The reason why they have called these communication groups, rather than workers' groups, is because of the fear that trade unions may be politically affiliated. We have had no strikes in any of our facilities (UKS 2, Head of CSR).

As a result, some unions have viewed MNE codes, particularly those that promote non-union worker grievance procedures in their implementation process, as weakening freedom of association.

> Code of conduct is put on the wall, but when workers want to form a trade union, to negotiate, they don't allow workers freedom of choice. A factory that had an order for AMNE 4 . . . used the police to intimidate the trade union leader. After being threatened with death, they resigned. The employer denied any involvement. The workers were forced to do overtime. When the trade union tried to negotiate, there was no effect (U 2).

In some countries that we visited, particularly those in Asia and Central America, the representatives of the MNEs, as well as factory management in various cases, recognised that the unions in these regions are particularly weak and need to be strengthened. In part, they are discussing some of the issues that allow for a strengthening of unions, a debate that, apparently, from the comment below, is also taking place at the governmental level.

> The activities of the trade union also can make things work better. The job of the union is to protect the workers, but the unions in this country are not very good. Some factories are very so-so. Here the union head has his salary paid

---

47   For a discussion of the concept of 'parallel means', see Chapter II.

for by the company. There is much discussion about how to strengthen the union within the government, but no solution has been found (FMNE 2, CSR Manager).

However, some representatives of MNEs, as well as factory management in various cases, recognised that the unions could be an integral and effective partner in solving factory problems and improving conditions for workers.

> Brands respect the freedom to organise. If the union submits a letter requesting negotiation, they will meet (U 3).

> This factory has a union. Before the union was established here, I wasn't regarding them very highly. However, after I had a union I realised that it is very easy to adjust. Let me give you an example. During our Easter week we have two or three days off and often people want to go home all week. Before it was hard to agree with the workers to change the days off. It would take me one week to go around and ask all the workers for their opinions. But now it is easy. We go to the nine people in the union and we get them to ask the workers what they want. The union was formed in 1994. Let me give you another example of what the union does. When it comes to discipline, if people don't co-operate we have very good relations with our unions and it is very functional. They will deal with things (HS 3, General Manager).

Overall, MNEs exhibited different approaches to fostering freedom of association, including requiring suppliers to create and enforce non-discrimination policies with regard to union organisers or members and training on worker representation systems. However, given the vast cultural and operational differences between host country and buyer, vast disparities in code implementation exist. In most cases a strengthening of dialogue between social partners and a critical review of implementation experiences appears necessary. In particular, the experiences encountered on the factory floor should aid in the continuing evolution of mechanisms and systems to promote and ensure the right to freedom of association and the right to collective bargaining. Furthermore, education and training is needed on the important role that workers can play in achieving the principles encompassed by codes of conduct. As one academic member of our research team pointed out:

> Workers can be a most positive force for change in terms of securing and sustaining decent conditions of work. Once awareness is built and conditions are improved then worker organisations and individual workers could perhaps be the most formidable agent of positive change and the promotion of a safer more responsible work environment (E 2).

b. Child labour

MNE codes have taken a strong stance against employing child labour in production, generally specifying that suppliers cannot employ anyone younger than 15 years or younger than the age for completing compulsory education in countries of manufacture where such an age is older than 15.

Again, many MNE codes adhere closely to established international standards, particularly to the ILO standard minimum age of employment, outlined in the Minimum Age for Employment Convention, 1973 (No. 138). Article 2 of Convention No. 138 sets the minimum age for employment for state parties at the age of completion of compulsory education or 15, whichever is higher. The ILO provides an exception for countries the economy and educational system of which are insufficiently developed, holding these developing countries to the age of 14.[48] Further, the Worst Forms of Child Labour Convention, 1999 (No. 182) specifically outlines standards in the workplace that should be met when dealing with the issue of child labour.[49] Also, the Convention on the Rights of the Child (1989) obligates state parties to provide a minimum age for admission to employment.[50] The United Nations Global Compact reiterates the ILO standard, stating that the minimum age for admission to employment or work should 'not be less than the age for completing compulsory schooling and in no event less than the age of 15 years, and the worst forms of child labour, including hazardous work, should be prohibited for those under 18'.[51]

Neither suppliers nor MNE managers interviewed regarded child labour as a recurrent code compliance issue in the industries studied. Many suppliers reported that they only hire employees with proof of age over 18, in order to avoid the perception of child labour. Further, by adopting policies that they will only hire workers of 18 years of age, suppliers are creating a cushioning system intended to ensure that, even if the worker is not 18, they will likely be over the minimum age of 15. However, this leads to a situation wherein children who finish compulsory schooling at age 15 are restricted from working in some factories or sectors for the three years until reaching 18 years of age.

> For the last five years we have had a policy of only hiring people of the age of 18 and above. Why? Because by law people who are between the age of 14 and 16 require special permits to work and [according to the] codes of conduct they are still considered to be children. So, unless they are close to being 18, we won't hire them. The labour code says that we must employ people at the age of 18 and above and our internal policy is that we don't hire people who are below this age. Codes simply say that no work for children is allowed without actually specifying the age (GS 3, HR Manager).

> In relation to hiring, we only recruit those that are 18 [and above]. However, the country minimum is 16. There are too many questions if we employ younger people that come from brand compliance groups. There are lots of false identification cards and it takes a long time to get, and therefore accept, other forms of ID. Also, there may be some restrictions in hours and the type of work that can be performed. Most codes are lax in that regard. This is interesting, though, because some states say that you can only employ workers that are 17 and 18, and others have it at 14. In certain cases, companies work in the same factories in different locations (HS 1, Manager).

> I am only against the work age limits because [they are] based on the brand codes and because we are a third-world country and we cannot stay in school longer. We were having problems with our customers and the problem has been because of age verification. It is very difficult (HS 3, Plant Manager).

48 *Ibid.*, Art. 2(4).
49 Worst Forms of Child Labour Convention, 1999 (No. 182).
50 Convention on the Rights of the Child, Article 32 (2 September 1999).
51 UN Global Compact, Principle 5.

The MNEs interviewed generally required their suppliers keep employment records, including an original, official document verifying each employee's age. Such documentation could be a national identification document, birth certificate, etc. Almost all MNEs also specified that their field representatives or agents could check these employment files at any time. We were told that auditors routinely review records for worker age documentation. Audits also provide MNE auditors with an opportunity to observe the apparent age of the workforce, and to follow up with specific inquiry (either in worker interviews or in employment records) on workers that appeared to be younger than 15.

> I can ensure in my factories that there is no forced labour, no child labour (AMNE 4).

While the MNEs studied did not perceive child labour as a significant problem in the firms studied, comments were still made that suggested that it has not been totally eliminated.

> In a [apparel] factory we found a large number of underage workers, 120, and so we and the factory are paying these workers their wages and paying their education (FMNE I, CSR Manager).

> If a factory hires children and they get caught, then they have to send the children back to school, paid by the factory—which is a type of negative incentive (FMNE I, Regional EHS Manager).

Disturbingly, our research indicated a trend that requires attention. While the focus on elimination of child labour within the context of MNEs and the export market may have all but eliminated child labour in this sector, our research indicated that, in some cases, child labour has now simply shifted to production of goods for the local market.

> Today there are on average five to six cases of child labour per year. Today also there are the O 16 (India, Bangladesh and Pakistan—in co-operation with Japanese inspectors), O 15 and NGO 3, so the problem is seldom. Suppliers are also aware of the problem. I am, however, totally convinced that there are as many children working today as yesterday, but they have transferred to the domestic industry where no one is looking—not the media nor NGOs (RMNE I, Compliance Director).

c. Forced labour

Code provisions for forced labour generally stipulate that MNEs and their business partners not use forced labour in the manufacture of products. Forced labour is commonly defined in MNE codes as including prison, indentured or bonded labour.

The MNE codes closely reflect international standards against forced, bonded and prison labour. The ILO set out a prohibition against state use of forced labour in the Forced Labour Convention, 1930 (No. 29), defining forced or compulsory labour in Article 2 as 'all work or service which is exacted from any person under the menace of any penalty and for which the said person has not offered himself voluntarily'. The Universal Declaration of Human Rights offers a broader standard, stating that every individual has the right to 'free choice of employment'.[52] The more recent UN Global Compact defines forced or compulsory labour exactly as Convention No. 29, specifically including bonded labour.[53]

Neither MNE managers nor supplier managers reported use of prison labour as a significant concern. More pressing were impingements on workers' freedom of movement, which some MNE managers considered a type of forced labour. For example, freedom of movement was sometimes violated when factory owners took the workers' passports and refused to give them back until the end of the contract. The payment of recruitment fees or deposits to factory management was also mentioned as inhibiting freedom of movement, as the financial obligation can limit the ability of workers to leave jobs until fees have been paid in full.

> For advances and payments to middlemen, we would consider that [something to consider with regard to] forced labour issues. And we can find this out. We would encourage companies to handle more of their own recruitment. But [the situation is not so simple] if you have someone living on an island in Indonesia they would not be able to get their own job in Jakarta without help (FMNE I, Regional Manufacturing Manager).

> We are looking at recruitment fees, trying to get rid of middlemen, so there isn't the skimming of money. This is not really a big issue (FMNE I, Regional CSR Manager).

MNE managers shared that they used both internal and third-party audits as the main mechanisms to determine that forced labour, or related restrictions, were not used in a business partner's factory. The worker interview was of particular value, as the auditor could uncover practices of recruitment fees and deposits not apparent in other aspects of the audit process. To uncover impingements on workers' freedom of movement, the employment records review was useful in identifying whether supplier factory management regularly held employees' passports.

d. Discrimination

Some MNE code provisions dealing with discrimination stated that no employee shall be subject to any discrimination in employment, including hiring, salary, benefits, advancement, discipline, termination or retirement, on the basis of gender, race, religion, age, disability, sexual orientation, nationality, political opinion, or social or ethnic origin. Other codes stated that while cultural differences are respected, workers should be employed on the basis of their ability to do the job, rather than on the basis of personal characteristics or beliefs.

There exists a wealth of international standards proscribing the practice of discrimination in employment. The ILO defines discrimination as, 'any distinction, exclusion or preference made on the basis of race, colour, sex, religion, political opinion, national extraction or social origin, which has the effect of nullifying or impairing equality of opportunity or treatment in employment or occupation'.[54] The Declaration of Phila-

---

52   Universal Declaration of Human Rights (1948), Article 23(1).
53   UN Global Compact, Principle 4.
54   Discrimination (Employment and Occupation) Convention, 1958 (No. III), Article 1(1).

delphia (adopted as an annex to the ILO Constitution in 1944) states that 'all human beings, irrespective of race, creed or sex have the right to pursue their material well being in conditions of . . . equal opportunity'. The UN Declaration on Human Rights also has a sweeping bar on discrimination, stating that all individuals are 'entitled to equal protection against any discrimination in violation of the Declaration' (Article 7), which includes the rights to work.

More recently, international organisations have codified norms specifically addressing the need to eradicate discrimination in the workplace against women and against migrant workers. The ILO addressed the issue of equal pay between genders in the Equal Remuneration Convention, 1951 (No. 100), outlining the goal that members 'ensure the application to all workers of the principle of equal remuneration for men and women workers for work of equal value' (Article 2), with equal remuneration meaning 'remuneration established without discrimination based on sex' (Article 1). The Convention on the Elimination of All Forms of Discrimination Against Women, adopted by the UN General Assembly in 1979, gives a general prohibition against discrimination against women by any 'organisation or enterprise' (Article 2e). For legal migrant workers, the ILO set a standard of 'equality of opportunity and treatment in respect of employment and occupation'.[55]

Anti-discrimination measures are also a part of the Global Compact. The definition of discrimination in the Global Compact (Principle 6) is the same as the ILO definition, but commentary to the Global Compact warns of specific instances of discrimination in the workplace, such as access to employment and to particular occupations, access to training and vocational guidance, and various terms and conditions of employment, such as equal remuneration, hours of work and rest, paid holidays, maternity leave, security of tenure, advancement, social security, and occupational safety and health.

Implementing and verifying compliance with code provisions related to discrimination, we were told, requires a range of practices, from training and awareness building, to enforcement through auditing and other forms of monitoring, as well as sanctions to encourage better compliance. It was even suggested that a positive obligation exists for MNEs to consider broadening the scope of requirements to include maternity leave and part-time work for men and women with family responsibilities.

> We have no problem with discrimination, 80% of the workers are female. We don't really have any issues in this area [in Viet Nam, according to a locally recruited CSR inspector] (FMNE 2, Labour Practices Inspector).

> You get some things like northern workers with provincial biases, with supervisors tending to discriminate, but we are working on that. I am targeting the senior management, building their awareness of what and why of what we are doing. Communication, communication, communication of these things. If they have a strike they might then better understand why (FMNE 1, Regional CSR Manager).

Instances of discrimination were mentioned frequently by MNEs and suppliers, and ranged from cases involving gender and national origin to sexual orientation and reproductive status. Gender roles are tied to the local culture, and can result in apparent discriminatory employment practices. For example, it seemed that there were

---

55   Migrant Workers (Supplementary Provisions) Convention, 1975 (No. 143), Article 10.

often more men than women hired as managers in supplier factories. Very few men were reported working in the sewing sections of production, as the stitching function was perceived in many cases as 'women's work'.

> In so many other cultures, the treatment of women is regarded as discriminatory. If auditors come across an advertisement for jobs, they look for this. For example, putting only women into sewing (RMNE 3).

> The workers here are not scared. The supervisors are female. My father, the owner, is a student of Tao and in each monthly meeting with all the workers he tries to incorporate our company culture and philosophy about ethical values. Our workers are more soft (THS 7, Operations Control).

> The sewing supervisors are both men and women. The other supervisors are all men (GS 2, Director).

Other issues for women concerned their reproductive status; some MNEs and unions claimed that female workers were forced by factory management to take pregnancy tests and were fired if there was evidence of pregnancy.

> Firing of pregnant workers occurs in factories where even management says it understands the labour law (U 3).

> Here we have a policy of not asking any pregnancy questions (GS 4, Compliance Officer).

On being questioned, some MNEs reported that in many of their contract factories there was a difference in ethnic or national origin between the management and workers. Generally, this disparity could be ascribed to either a large migrant worker population or imported foreign management. Entrenched cultural and linguistic differences were a challenge for MNE representatives attempting to foster an environment of equality.

> Discrimination occurred in the past. Locals were being paid differently to migrant workers who were being paid less. Often they were getting paid the local minimum wage of the province from where they came from. But this doesn't happen so much now because of the fact that vendors conduct evaluation (AMNE 4).

> Of the 1,000 workers 70 to 80% are women. Sixty per cent of investment is Korean and they have a different culture; therefore there is a need to create a mechanism of respect (IA 2).

> Instructions are given in Sinhala. This is a problem for other ethnic groups. Discrimination, however, is not really an issue as we don't recruit from the north (SLS 3, HR Manager).

The last major area of discrimination concern reported had to do with HIV/AIDS and homosexuality.

> The most recent issue has been one of HIV testing in Thailand and we find increasingly that discriminatory pregnancy testing is used (RMNE 3).

> We do not tolerate any accusation regarding sexual conduct, nationality, age or disability. I have fired supervisors because they have required favours or

because they have been changing production. But this has only happened in three cases over the course of ten years (HS 1, Manager).

Discrimination issue—particularly regarding gay people. This may be a religious or cultural issue in the United States. In China, it is predominantly offensive language that is the problem (RMNE 3).

The MNEs studied here found it a challenge to address the discrimination provision through codes of conduct, and sought to prevent discrimination in supplier factories by a combination of policy requirements, training and auditing. Several MNEs assisted factory management in the creation of a non-discrimination policy. The MNE then used its relationship with the factory and economic leverage to require that the policy be posted in languages the workers can read. The same leverage strategy has been used to implement policies eliminating pregnancy testing and the termination of employment based on a woman's reproductive status. Through worker interviews, records review and systematic training of management, MNEs sought to ensure that job performance was the sole driver for wage scale, termination and advancement, and that workers of equal skill were provided with equal remuneration.

e. Environment, health and safety (EHS)

Most MNE codes specify that employers shall provide a safe and healthy working environment to prevent accidents and injury to health arising out of, linked with, or occurring in the course of work or as a result of the operation of employer facilities. Many times the business partner has to meet extensive MNE mandated factory/vendor environment, health and safety guidelines, some of which are specific. Although most countries have government-created occupational health and safety standards, the ILO has set out recommendations for employers' responsibilities to workers in terms of workplace health and safety:

* Employers shall be required to ensure that, so far as is reasonably practicable, the workplaces, machinery, equipment and processes under their control are safe and without risk to health.[56]

* Employers shall be required to ensure that, so far as is reasonably practicable, the chemical, physical and biological substances and agents under their control are without risk to health when the appropriate measures of protection are taken.[57]

* Employers shall be required to provide, where necessary, adequate protective clothing and protective equipment to prevent, so far as is reasonably practicable, risk of accidents or of adverse effects on health.[58]

* Employers shall be required to provide, where necessary, for measures to deal with emergencies and accidents, including adequate first-aid arrangements.[59]

---

56   Occupational Health and Safety Convention, 1981 (No. 155), Article 16(1).
57   *Idem.*, Art. 16(2).
58   *Idem.*, Art. 16(3).
59   *Idem.*, Art. 18.

- Workers and their representatives in the undertaking should be given appropriate training in occupational safety and health.[60]

- A worker who reports forthwith to his immediate supervisor a situation which he has reasonable justification to believe presents an imminent and serious danger to his life or health cannot be required to return to work until the employer has taken remedial action, if there is continuing imminent and serious danger to life or health.[61]

Environment, health and safety requirements are contained in each code, and were covered quite extensively in interviews and particularly in factory walk-throughs. All of the MNEs and their suppliers interviewed argued that they have made considerable progress in the last four years, improving everything from fire safety systems to, particularly, the use of toxic substances. In this effort, they have been aided by technology such as mass spectrometers, which can spot banned substances, as well as EHS experts on staff or on contract who have provided guidance on improving factory operations.

> We know that when our suppliers go to subcontractors they don't always check to see what was used, including banned substances. For that reason we use mass spectrometer tests. We have eliminated toluene but some of our contractors' subcontractors still do use it. For social issues we don't have this ability [to put a product through a mass spectrometer test to determine labour practice compliance] but we do have two people or more in every [footwear] factory (FMNE 2, EHS Manager, Headquarters).

> Safety and health is not such a big deal—particularly in apparel. In footwear there are many machines, but we train the workers (FMNE 2, Labour Practices Inspector).

> We have seen changes in our department from the code—there are fire extinguishers, exits are clearly marked, there are emergency lights (CHS 5, Factory Workers, China).

At the factory level, MNE managers suggested that EHS compliance required working closely with suppliers to create safety and fire teams, clear up aisles, mark fire points and exits, and provide equipment needed to protect workers, as well as detailed instructions and training related to treatment, storage and disposal of regulated wastes. Safety standards can vary. In one case an MNE requires all machines to have needle guards, while another does not, arguing that with trained workers these are unnecessary.

> Just basic health and safety would be crucial in these factories—just requiring clear aisles is needed (FMNE I, CSR Manager).

> In the past the factory had a safety team, but now with the code every group has a safety worker and for the factory we still have a safety team. Workers don't like to use safety equipment, gloves, masks and goggles. But they get

---

60   *Idem.*, Art. 19(d).
61   *Idem.*, Art. 19(f).

> used to it, they accept it. They now know that these things [the materials or work] are dangerous (CHS 5, Factory Supervisor).

> Another problem we face is the availability of safety equipment. The suppliers are finally setting up because of the demand from MNEs, but there has been a lag in getting things like face-masks and gloves (FMNE 1, Compliance Manager).

> You have to provide the equipment to carry out the code. We have had a real challenge finding masks that fit. We're not sure why, but we've had real problems that might have to do with the face shapes and sizes (FMNE 2, Manufacturing Manager).

> With the code we have learned how to use PPE; there are different types of mask for different types of chemicals (VIS 5, Line Supervisor).

One of the items that appeared to be of most concern to the MNEs and suppliers was control of the use of toxic substances (substances that can cause respiratory and other health problems to those exposed to them on a regular basis), and the degree to which they could be eliminated. Volatile organic compounds, or solvents, are used for cleaning and adhesive operations throughout these factories, although over the last few years there has been a concerted effort to eliminate their use.

> We were using 340 grams of solvent per pair of shoes before; now we use 40 grams and still we are aiming for less. We have a very close tracking system keeping records of all materials used. We want to buy things that are done right. The companies have to provide records of how many chemicals are used. We then do check (FMNE 2, Headquarters).

> If you wear a cotton mask when applying solvents, then the solvent tends to collect in the mask and you breathe it in all day. You need to go and measure the area and determine if a carbon mask would be needed or enough, and, if not, you need to look at things like ventilation (FMNE 2, Manager).

> All lines are using 100% water-based solvents for adhesive and 40% of primer is now water-based. The water-based is slightly more expensive. At first it was difficult to use the water-based. Time, speed of the conveyor both have to be right. You can't apply it too thickly or thinly [versus solvent-based adhesives, which do not require such careful application]. Production was lower at first, with our numbers falling off from 1,400 pairs a day to 900 for the first week (FMNE 1, Manufacturing Manager).

In the initial stages of code implementation, manufacturing managers, who are accustomed to working to specifications and need to guide factories in their work, were often left with very general guidelines of what was acceptable. This led to confusion within factories and the need to develop these at the field level. This work on establishing, communicating and implementing standards will be ongoing to some degree, as national laws and corporate standards change.

> We had to decide which EHS standards to use. We try to get the highest. As a new one comes up we will try to implement the most 'practicable' level. When we first brought these up it was a real fight in our factories and they had to work many hours, more than they should have. But with time it started to work and they started to believe it too (FMNE 1, Country Manager).

> For some of these we have a hard time to quantify, not VOCs [volatile organic substances or solvents]. But with fire safety, it is hard to quantify. Do you want sprinklers in the whole factory or just parts? (FMNE I, Country Manager).

In general, MNEs reported a high frequency of EHS concerns upon the first audit of suppliers, but found the EHS provisions easier than other aspects of their code. EHS compliance is tangible, logical and measurable compared to other code provisions. Additionally, many countries have passed legislation requiring the suppliers to have worker/management EHS committees, which several MNEs have used as a springboard for EHS compliance. As a result, MNEs have tended to focus on implementation of EHS measures and have reported some impressive success stories.

> The workers have a clinic and a nurse is present daily. A doctor is present from one to four-thirty and deals with such complaints as headaches, dizziness, and cuts. [Continuing] challenges in health and safety are fire extinguishers—at first they did not have a sufficient number, now they do, and open fire exits (GS 2, Compliance Officer).

> In many factories or plants there were previously no measures. Many workers do not use face-masks and are exposed to environmental pollutions from textiles, noise and noise pollution. Recently the labour department has acquired measures, but they are stored and not used. Oxygen levels need to be measured in the factories. There is an over concentration of workers in the factories and this leads to fainting (HU 2).

> The codes have also been beneficial in relation to the working environment. I have been in some factories where the bathroom is just terrible. With compliance, in Honduras we don't really have a problem (HS 3, Plant Manager).

> We don't have needle guards. Some workers get injured and there is a system for workers to inform if they have a needle accident but they normally don't inform us as it is considered to be like an ant bite. Currently we are ordering hair nets and the next step will be a uniform. We are still working on our EHS records. In the last two to three months there have been no major accidents. I am making up our records ourselves based on the lectures I attended and have also asked my friend (THS 6, Health & Safety Officer).

> The health and safety committee has ten members: accountancy manager, personnel manager, line supervisors, two cutting-section supervisors, ironing supervisors, and packing supervisor. They are all chosen by the personnel manager. This is required under legislation. The Committee meets once a month, but this has to improve. Sometimes members do not have time to meet because of production schedules. I get very angry when a person does not show up and I tell the personnel manager. The production manager and personnel manager deal with overtime, as does the Director (GS 2, Compliance Officer).

> The number of members in the security and hygiene committee depends on the size of the plant. HR chooses the members. It meets once a month. There are minutes kept, and records and training are conducted, for example for fire safety. The meetings are managed by HR (GS 2, HR Manager).

> We also had a health and safety committee, but it didn't work because of lack of communication or support from personnel management. It consisted of

> representatives from the departments. Half were workers and half were
> managers. The personnel head chose the people who were on it. It existed for
> about two months. We have other committees to deal with things like foot-
> ball, outings and sports (GS 4, Compliance Officer).

The MNEs get most of their information on EHS from the walk-through and worker
interviews. As stated above, due to the tangible nature of health and safety, and its
apparent effect on productivity, there is less resistance from suppliers than on other
provisions. The exception was PPE, which suppliers cited as being a superfluous,
Western imposition. The main strategy used by both MNEs and suppliers to implement
EHS code provisions was training.

> We have training about once per month for about 150 workers in things like
> product quality, first aid. We try to do it ourselves. All workers attend the
> training. For new workers we have a 20- to 30-minute induction programme.
> We explain the company rules, background and our buyer list. We use the
> buyers' codes and Thai law. For working hours and product safety, I talked to
> the personnel manager and handed over a handbook on Thai legal require-
> ments. I looked at all the codes and tried to understand them, to see the
> critical points and where there was conflict with the codes (THS 3, Assistant
> Manager).

We heard that there was a need for further training related to EHS and, specifically,
the integration of EHS policies, standards and procedures with other code provisions.

f. Harassment

Some of the MNE code provisions examined stipulated, in one form or another, that no
employee should be subject to physical, sexual, psychological or verbal harassment or
abuse. This definition of harassment illustrates that the notion of harassment is quite
wide for many MNEs and this can present a challenge in itself, particularly in terms of
the identification of instances of harassment.

Thus far, international labour standards addressing freedom from harassment have
not been specifically codified. A harassment-free workplace may be seen as an extension of an employee's right to a favourable and dignified working environment, which
has been mentioned in several international instruments. For example, the ILO
Declaration of Philadelphia states that pursuing material well-being in 'conditions of
freedom and dignity' is a right of all persons.[62] The United Nations Declaration on
Human Rights speaks of the right of all to 'just and favourable conditions of work'.[63]

MNEs stated that establishing a harassment-free workplace was very challenging.
Given the time pressure involved in production, supplier factories are stressful environments. MNEs and suppliers found that instilling a culture of communication without
physical or verbal abuse was especially difficult in supplier factories with expatriate
managers.

> The management here are Hondurans, as are the supervisors, but there are a
> couple of Filipinos. I don't think that you can control [verbal abuse]. You can

---

62   Declaration of Philadelphia, IIa.
63   Universal Declaration of Human Rights, Art. 23.

only do that which is acceptable. The species mutates and what doesn't survive dies out. You're trying to legislate justice and it's not possible. The good guys are going to live up to the code and the bad ones just require a signature (HS 2, Director).

In considering the issue of harassment, several factors need to be considered. In particular there is the issue of the demographics of the workforce. As discussed earlier, workers in the footwear, apparel and retail sectors are predominantly female. Furthermore, the majority of these female workers in countries such as China are young (under the age of 25), single migrants with very little or almost no support provided to them once they leave their homes to work in the factories. In contrast, their managers are often older, expatriate male managers who often do not speak the same language as the female workers. In such an environment we heard that workers may be subject to verbal abuse and various types of harassment, including sexual harassment ranging from verbal to physical assault.

> There is a problem with management abusing employees verbally. The culture of shouting has to go. This is more ignorance (SLS 3, Director).

> How to treat people is also part of the code. No yelling at workers is allowed. They find it hard at times, when they are under pressure. Me, I am here almost five years. We have to learn that here the workers want to be treated with respect, not yelled at (FMNE 1, Manufacturing Manager).

Other examples of harassment raised by a number of MNEs interviewed related to attempts by workers to organise. In such instances, it is apparently not unheard of for the leader of the organising movement to be harassed verbally and/or physically, if not fired.

> Problems of associating workers tend to be with harassment, leaders being fired, and physical violence (NGO 6, Cambodia).

Furthermore, even in regions where we heard that performance on other issues encompassed by the code may have improved, this improvement has yet to be made when it comes to harassment.

> Things have changed for the better in such areas as Central America and South Asia—they're smarter about local law and about protecting their business—but they still have a long way to go on harassment and discrimination, but this is a longer-term effort. Another real problem is the whole question of migrant workers, who are more vulnerable, who accept whatever they can get, who pay fees to get their jobs, and who want to work excessive hours to send money back home (RMNE 7, Compliance Director).

Identification of harassment issues within a factory may present quite a challenge to auditors as it requires the workers to voluntarily raise the issue during the interview process or feel comfortable discussing such an issue when questioned. In many instances, the fear of social stigmatisation and cultural norms may prevent the worker from freely speaking of such abuse.

In other areas of this book we have discussed some of the challenges associated with worker interviews, including the amount of time spent in conducting these interviews, whether they are conducted on an individual basis or in a group setting, and the skills and ability of the interviewer to elicit honest responses from workers. All of these factors coupled with the simple economic importance of job retention may prevent many workers from openly discussing harassment issues, reinforcing the view by many MNE managers that well-qualified, experienced and trained personnel, knowledgeable in local norms and culture, are vital when it comes to worker interviews.

> Particularly strong worker interviews are required to get at the issues of harassment, discrimination, and freedom of association (RMNE 7, Compliance Director).

> The difficulty of defining psychological or verbal harassment shows why monitors should be drawn from local culture. They need to make sensitive, subjective judgements (RMNE 3, Senior Counsel).

For the reasons outlined above, we heard that in implementing code provisions related to harassment, MNEs generally relied heavily on a multi-faceted approach. Worker interviews were the primary method for assessing whether harassment was present in the workplace. However, MNEs repeatedly stated that establishing the requisite trust between the auditor and the worker, enabling the worker to reveal instances of harassment, was extremely difficult. Nevertheless some of the MNEs interviewed were attempting to deal with the limits of worker interviews by implementing specific strategies to address instances of harassment. Strategies used to prevent physical and verbal abuse of workers included the institution of non-harassment policies, formulation of grievance procedures, education for workers and management in alternative methods of communication, worker interviews, and sanctions against non-compliant suppliers.

Challenges remain, though, particularly those relating to the costs of implementing such strategies. As one of the leading apparel MNEs interviewed pointed out,

> All factories have worker committees to educate workers on issues such as sexual harassment. The problem is that it is expensive (AMNE 3, Compliance Director).

g. Working hours and overtime

The ILO provided guidelines for working hours and overtime in its first Convention in 1919. The maximum working hours were given as an eight-hour day over a period of six days culminating in a 48-hour week due to the additional requirement that there be not less than 24 consecutive hours of rest in the course of a seven-day work period (not applicable to supervisors or managers).[64] The Convention made several exceptions to the working limitation. If one or more of the working days was less than eight hours (due to custom, law or agreement with a union), then the working day could be extended on the remaining days of the week to a maximum of nine hours (Art. 2[b]). Another exception for the eight-hour day was shift work, but the ILO stipulated that the working hours per week should still average 48 (Art. 2[c]). There was also an exception

---

64   Hours of Work (Industry) Convention, 1919 (No. 1), Article 2(a), and Weekly Rest (Industry) Convention, 1921 (No. 14).

Change at the factory level

At one factory visited, experience with the MNE code of conduct was still limited—only about two years. Initially there was quite a large amount of resistance and doubt about the benefits of the code. Now, according to the factory managers, there have been tangible results that management tends to associate with the code. Workforce turnover fell from 4% in 1998 to 2% per month in 2000. In the same time, orders from the buyer MNE rose from 1998 to 2000 by 10%. The MNE CEO actually visited the factory, and expressed his satisfaction with the factory's efforts at complying with code. Now over 3,000 job applicants are on the waiting list for possible positions. (This could reflect local labour market conditions as much as factory conditions.)

In a similar case where a code was introduced, productivity rose quite considerably over the first two years of implementation, while working hours fell. In 1998 workers put in about 300 hours a month. Under the code the factory had to bring the working week down to a maximum of 250 hours per month. Output, though, while in the beginning falling off, was within two years back at previous levels (about 400,000 pairs per month), resulting in a considerable net productivity gain during the period. Workforce turnover had again fallen, in this case from 6–7% to about 4%.

Other changes can be seen, other than limitations on the use of overtime. In another factory, preference is given to referrals and married couples in the recruitment of new staff. In both locations, the worker cafeteria or canteen has been improved. A typical worker complaint in factories across the region is the quality of food—a particular challenge in China, where many line workers come from other regions and cooks may come from the local area. In one case, the factory introduced a food court to provide greater variety; in another, management decided to outsource canteen operations to improve quality. In the outsourced canteen, canteen workers were not laid off. Rather, they had a choice—to work for the catering company or to work on the assembly line. In both cases they needed training, provided by the factory. In the case of those workers who still elected to leave the company, they were given severance pay equal to one to two months' salary.

---

for 'urgent work', but 'only so far as may be necessary' (Art. 3). The Convention also set a minimum rate of pay for overtime at one and one-quarter times the regular rate (Art. 6[2]).

Overtime was one of the most frequently mentioned issues during our field research, particularly in Asia. Changing from a system where a factory would work the hours necessary to get the job done to one where it was limited to 60 hours per week, a limit set by many codes of conduct, has required the firms to change in various ways.[65] New accounting and information systems were needed to keep track of hours worked, bonus systems set in place to encourage higher productivity to make up for lost output, and both workers and managers needed to understand why this was necessary. Good documentation of pay and hours is important, something that appears to be achieved in the footwear sector, yet would require a much more in-depth audit to ensure this is the case.

> Overtime is the biggest challenge to meeting the code, due to the nature of the business. In low season, we can't lay off the workers, and then we don't have enough for the high season. We can't use temporary workers, because

---

65   Normal hours of work in the countries of the factories studied are China 40, Viet Nam 48 and Thailand 48. Overtime hours are China 36 a month, Viet Nam 200 a year and Thailand unspecified. Source: *Conditions of Work Digest: Working Times Around the World* (Geneva: International Labour Office, 1995).

they don't have the skills—these take several months to learn (FMNE 2, Labour Practices Inspector).

We insist that a factory meets the requirement [regarding hours of work] for all workers—not just those making our products but for all workers. This just avoids problem, otherwise they will just play games (FMNE 2, Regional Manager).

We pushed for every other Sunday off, then every Sunday. Now some factories are working half days on Saturdays. But in combination with reducing hours you need to have some form of bonus, for quality and quantity. Otherwise they will quit and go somewhere else where they can make money on overtime (FMNE 1, Country Manager).

I am really convinced, and I think you are going to hear this, that we have things on overtime under control. And the factories agree that it is better than before. The managers didn't really have a grip on how many hours they were working and the costs they were paying. Factories now have less overtime and it is easier to control—things are more documented. It is a matter of systematisation (FMNE 1, Country Manager).

There are still workers who would like to see more working hours. They have to support family and would like to make more money. Now, they have one or two days of work off a week. One day is OK, two days is too much (CHS 2, Workers' Representative). [In other words, working time was reduced with loss of pay, contrary to Convention No. 1.]

The codes of companies that participated in this report generally require that the supplier observe either local labour laws or the code requirements, whichever is more stringent. In some cases, this can be a challenge. In Viet Nam, for example, the law at the time of this research restricted the working week to 48 hours, with a total of 200 overtime hours per year. In order to ensure that they follow national labour laws, we heard that some MNEs seek a waiver from the government for overtime hours. In this way, MNEs seek to adhere to their codes of conduct as well as meet national legislative requirements. This appears to be more usual in the apparel than in the footwear sector.

Local government limits overtime to 200 hours a year from a base of 48 hours a week. And we follow the law. We are closed on Sundays, except for maintenance. We have had informal discussions to increase the overtime limits, and workers are supportive about this (FMNE 2, Manufacturing Manager).

Due to high unemployment the government does not want to allow overtime, thereby increasing the number of employed workers (FMNE 2, Manufacturing Manager).

With 200 hours of overtime allowed a year, we had 2,000 transgressions in 1997, and have had zero in 1998, 1999 and 2000 (VIS 7, Manager).

The introduction of stringent parameters for overtime appeared to be a difficult undertaking in the factories over the last several years. We heard that, initially, the factories and their employees did not understand these boundaries, and for this reason there was resistance. Gradually, as the factories learned to boost productivity and keep track of the costs of overtime, they found that the limitations of overtime—the costs of paying overtime wages—were not what they expected.

One of our biggest worries was implementing working hours. HQ told us 'you can't work more than X hours', but nothing else. We had to go figure out how to do it, without scaring away the workers. They would leave. We started on EHS at first, and monitoring the hours. We didn't even know where we were with that. We were given a time period by headquarters, some months, to reduce OT [overtime]. People here were very worried; they thought it was punishment. It was a difficult time; we had to communicate that this work-hour reduction was not punishment. Since then the turnover rate has dropped from 6% to 2% and this has a big impact on quality and productivity. We plan to cross-train across departments and within departments. We'll have workers learn other areas and that should help reduce OT needs as well (FMNE 1, Manufacturing Manager).

Overtime tends to be a crucial area, and the question is whether it is forced or voluntary. Cross-training helps, since workers may be a bottleneck. We are doing a programme on this [cross-training], since if for a specific job you have a larger pool, then you can avoid bottlenecks (FMNE 1, Regional CSR Manager).

When the code first came out they [the workers] hoped to work more over-time. We told them we want to work less overtime but pay bonuses. Workers tended to link hours with money. So we had a hard time but they started to see that things were as we said (CHS 5, CSR Manager).

When the code came out in the beginning we had lots of problems. We had to cut hours and there was lots of resistance. But my boss said we would have to boost productivity to pay productivity bonuses. We met with supervisors and said 'you will have to go back to your employees and boost productivity'. And they know their jobs, so they know where things can be improved (CHS 5, Assistant Factory Manager).

Given the highly seasonal nature of the industries studied, and the correspondingly tight shipping requirements, the MNEs and suppliers found the limitation on working hours and overtime the most difficult code provisions to consistently and successfully implement. In general, we heard that MNEs allow voluntary overtime beyond their code limits, if (a) it does not have a negative effect on the quality, (b) it is adequately compensated, (c) it is reasonable, and (d) it complies with national norms and legislation. Of course, the definition of 'reasonable' is a matter left for the MNE and supplier factory to determine.

We live or die by the 60-hour rule. It is the most heinous thing ever written on a piece of paper (HS 2, Director).

In our production plans we insert room for these special plans. It is a very complicated process because I don't want to be doing overtime. It is a bitter experience but you still cannot control everything. Living in this country, facing every day a new problem is a hard life. Every day is tense (GS 4, General Manager).

We exceed overtime and take the slap on the hand often from the brands. It hasn't stopped them though from placing more orders with us, has it? (HS 2, Director).

Working hours are an issue for us in the factories. Our problem is that we have low capacity in the factories and no leverage (AMNE 9, CSR Manager).

We went over 60 hours very often, at least 30 to 40% of the time. They would work over 60 hours and below 84 hours. The buyers were aware of this. There were a couple of responses. They would either grade the factory lower in their evaluation or they would give initiatives to educate the factory such as FMNE 2 and Agent 1. They looked at things like the checking of the lighting levels and the payroll system (THS 4, Production Manager).

Consumer products (CP) make the requirements for review of working hours for Thailand, Malaysia and Singapore. Singapore just slightly exceeded the requirements. Thus, CP asked for a review because, they said, they would lose business there without an increase in working hours. They presented their information to the board. The board didn't even have to vote. It just reached a general consensus not to increase the hours (RMNE 3).

The issue of adherence to national norms and legislation is a complicated one and has been discussed throughout this book. It is an important issue when it comes to working hours because local labour law on working hours often does not accord with international standards. It places MNEs in a difficult position. For example, one of the academic research team members pointed out during a research visit to Thailand,

Thai labour law conflicts with codes in two main areas making it difficult for global companies to secure legitimacy for their codes and hence enforce them effectively . . . The Labour Protection Act (1998) stipulates that standard hours should be no more than 48 per week. However, workers may be employed on overtime hours (paid at higher rates) up to 36 hours a week. So, effectively, the maximum hours allowed is 84 per week and this is what two of our factories were working. For the others who follow, or who are trying to reduce hours to the code requirements (maximum of 60 hours per week including overtime), they are constrained compared to local competitors (however, they are protected by the agreement with the global firms) (E 3).

Our research indicates that, at the very least, many MNEs require that overtime be voluntary. However, given the many punitive mechanisms at the disposal of supplier managers, it can often be difficult for workers to turn down the offer to work extra hours. An area of concern is the very fact that many of these extra hours worked are required to be 'voluntary'.

Overtime is a problem. We demanded that workers get paid or work fewer hours. There is no way that these factories are working 84 hours and are paying premiums for overtime (AMNE 4, VP CSR).

Working hours are seven-thirty to twelve, one to four-thirty, with one-and-a-half hours of voluntary overtime. Workers want to work overtime (GS 2, Compliance Officer).

Overtime is a challenge. The biggest problem is that people look forward to it. They want the dollars. Here it is voluntary and some volunteer every day. We always try to limit their hours. The HR department has 45 people. The company process is that red flags are raised as to who is reaching overtime limits. The maximum hours are 60 hours per week (GS 2, President).

We work a six-day week, and need to explain to workers why they can't work more overtime. We display the overtime policy (HS 2, Director).

Overtime here is all voluntary. But when it comes to shipment times, some-times you just need to work. Workers complain to me that they need the money to work also (HS 3, Plant Manager).

One of the primary means of reducing working hours in factories is increasing productivity. Faced with the need to meet the same production goals but within the work-hour limitations set by codes and national laws, some suppliers reported that there was little option but to increase output per work hour. The surprising finding for many of the supplier managers was that this was possible; by setting limits and paying bonuses, they were able to meet the goals set. Cross-training has also helped, eliminating bottlenecks in areas where longer hours were previously needed to keep up with the output of other sections.

[Not all factories pay productivity bonuses] We don't have a productivity bonus. We plan and implement according to plan, and we have experienced people (VIS 5, Factory Manager).

Workers tended to go slow during the day so they could get overtime to make money. Factories didn't really measure how things were working; there was no measurement system on hours versus productivity. So now we introduced a bonus time system to support productivity. If they finish early, it feeds into the bonus. The less they work, the higher the bonus. We don't pay piece work for the most part, we pay a group bonus. So since line balancing on a stitching line is so tough, if you train workers there is a group incentive to work better (FMNE 1, Manufacturing Manager).

At the beginning managers thought that reducing work hours would have a great cost, but we didn't really keep track of the costs of overtime. We now have workers work less than 60 hours. We had to spend a lot of time explaining to workers, and setting up a bonus system so that workers could make as much as before in the reduced work hours (CHS 2, Factory Manager).

Our [the MNE's] biggest role is to work with the factory to allow them to improve efficiency while reducing working hours. Otherwise it won't be possible (FMNE 1, Manufacturing Manager).

Some pioneering MNEs had a role other than just setting the limits and advising the factories on how to meet these limits. They have also set examples, as the first comment below illustrates. However, some have made requirements that make meeting work-hour limitations difficult, such as very short time frames for delivery of samples, as a reaction to the 'just-in-time' manufacturing model prevalent in the sector. We heard that the latter practices have in some cases been addressed, but in others change is difficult due to the nature of the sector.

You have to live what you say, so we close the office at six-thirty. Otherwise people here would work all night sometimes. So we now kick them out—if not the factory manager would say 'your pricing people were here working until eleven-thirty' (FMNE 1, Country Manager).

With the changes in work rules we don't get samples back in 24 hours like before, but the quality is getting better (FMNE 1, Product Designer).

We have multiple buyers, and neither one of them can guarantee us 12 months of orders. In 2000 we had at least one full month without orders. So,

> when we have orders, workers work a lot [overtime beyond limits set by national law and the MNE] (HS 3, Manager).

We also heard that, in the apparel sector particularly, the situation created by rising and falling demand makes overtime limitations even more challenging to carry forward.

> I was talking to another MNE about overtime and they asked 'you actually follow the law?!' Two hundred hours is really not much. The 200 is not a real problem with all workers, but it depends on the job. In footwear in some cases 200 is not an issue. But with apparel it is a problem (FMNE 2, Regional Manager).

One result of the reduction in work hours has been the creation of free time, creating a new twist for the supplier factories—how to occupy people's time. In this, they have sought the help of the MNEs.

> We change the culture in the factories. People now have free time. This is something new. More and more people are moving their families down, less we see the migration and return of workers. They [the MNE] could give us more information on what we can do to occupy people's time (CHS 5, CSR Manager).

Notwithstanding the attempts to control work hours, the most commonly reported issues of supplier non-compliance were double book-keeping, incorrect overtime payment and faulty overtime records. This was particularly the case in China. In some instances, MNEs have stopped auditing against their working hours standards as they fear that focusing on this topic will merely drive the practice 'underground'.

> Double book-keeping is one of the biggest challenges for us. As time goes by, the factories are getting much smarter at concealing the facts from us. We are trying to eliminate double books and have been revoking orders [in China] (AMNE 4, Vice President, CSR).

> Double record-keeping is common in Sri Lanka. The abuse is because of the overtime legislation. The law isn't clear. They are now asking for an increase to 70 hours per month (TPA 3).

> For workers in China, people are now paid for overtime. There has been a general reduction in hours and there has been increased understanding of knowledge regarding hours of work and we have eliminated fines (SUK 1, Compliance Executive).

> In India we had a case where there was high absenteeism in a factory that was linked to overtime. Because the factory paid double rates for overtime, workers would work a double shift and not come in the next day. This meant that the production manager couldn't plan production. The factory ended up eliminating overtime but shutting the factory early on a Saturday. Productivity improved and workers got their time off and their wages increased. This shows clarity of thought on the part of management. The example fits into a pattern of productivity, quality and ethical standards (SUK 4, Ethical and Quality Manager).

> When I first looked at payroll records in China, I was horrified. There were no computer printouts that you could check against. China was using old clock cards to clock time attendance. I had to look at the payroll records and then compare them with the time attended and see if people were paid the correct amount. Now we have swipe cards but we still have no common system (SUK 3, Compliance Manager).

Simply ignoring the problem won't make it go away. Some would argue that to do so could be interpreted as implicit acceptance of the practice, and thereby set a new norm. MNEs that are in the public eye and have faced the most vociferous criticisms of their practices have attempted to deal directly with this issue. We heard that the primary tools used to assess compliance with working hours and overtime were the records review and worker interviews during the audit. To prevent and redress difficulties with these issues, the MNEs used a variety of strategies including:

- Requiring a policy of voluntary overtime from suppliers, posted in the factory in the language of the workers

- Training suppliers in methods to improve productivity (so as not to resort to overtime)

- Installation of a swipe card computerised timekeeping system to record working hours

As working hours and overtime limitations have thus far proven to be a challenge to implementation, continuing multi-stakeholder dialogue is imperative for identifying policies, procedures and mechanisms to address the unique situations in the field. As has been seen, the simple adoption of new or prohibitive code language is insufficient to effectuate real changes within the workplace. Engagement of workers and management in a collaborative effort to find realistic solutions is required. Training on principles of working hours, EHS and other related subjects was emphasised as a requirement for effective and efficient implementation of code provisions.

h. Living conditions

The ILO does not have detailed standards that address living conditions within the context of employment. The primary issue related to this subject involves factory-based accommodation. In some cases, the conditions in the factories visited would be regarded as quite poor by Western standards. However, some argue that the question of whether these conditions are acceptable or not needs to be considered within the local context. As such, this raises an important question as to what the standards should be, and is likely a matter that requires further research.

Notwithstanding a lack of applicable regulations, living conditions in the workers' dorms were found to be a major concern for MNEs, particularly for operations in China, where dormitories are common, and are one of the most important issues addressed during both initial screening and monitoring.

> I am also responsible for living conditions, and we are always fighting on this. Managers say 'this is better than they [the workers] have in their hometowns'. Which may be true, but we adopted OSHA conditions and standards (FMNE 1, Regional EHS Manager).

> First we put in a supermarket. Now we are going to have a food court, so workers will have a choice of things to eat. And they are opening a bank branch on the grounds, so the workers don't have to go outside with their earnings. Also public phones, because otherwise outside they would have to pay a telephone surcharge. Now we are trying to fill workers' spare time. We have dance classes, hobbies—something not normal for grown-ups to have— and other activities. We are asking the local university for help (FMNE I, Manufacturing Manager).

The MNE managers for two of the companies researched emphasised their interest in getting the factories to support workers in moving into their own accommodation, outside the factories.

> We now have 1,800 people living outside, but for each person moving out we need to get approval of the local government. But we want them moving out, then it is not our concern. Hot water, hygiene, social issues, etc. etc.—these are always problems (FMNE I, Manufacturing Manager).

> Dormitories are always going to be a problem—you have problems with the conditions. So we are encouraging the factories to support people in finding their own housing. We are even using local recruits or having manufacturing of components in areas where the workers are located (FMNE I, Country Manager).

Interviews included discussions on moving more production to areas where labour was more freely available and workers could remain in their home communities, rather than the coastal export processing zones (EPZs) of China. According to the MNEs, this is being considered but is complicated by several factors. First, the infrastructure needed to support operations is not available at an acceptable level in these areas—the electricity is not reliable, the transportation for bringing components and supplies to the factory and the finished goods from the factory is difficult. Perhaps more importantly, locating work further from shipping points to consumer markets would result in greater lead times. In a market where rapidly shifting market demand requires closer linkages and shorter lead times, this could make using locations where lead times are lengthened prohibitive. At the same time, while the MNEs may want the workers to live outside the factory in their own accommodation, in part so that they will not be held responsible for living conditions over which they have limited control, factory managers may not be so interested in seeing workers move outside.

> Workers are like our children . . . We do not encourage them to live outside the dorm. It's dangerous outside! [Supplier CSR Manager China]

In another factory in China, the CSR manager expressed similar sentiments:

> We want our workers to live in the dorm! They can't live outside! It's dangerous for these girls—we are like their parents. We look after them. We write a letter to their parents saying: 'Your daughter is safe' (FMNE 2, China).

Finally, food was consistently raised as an issue. It was brought up again and again, by workers, by supplier managers and by the MNE representatives: the challenge of providing quality food that meets workers' needs. Being from a variety of regions, many of the workers find the food either too bland or too spicy or spicy in the wrong way. At the same time, the MNEs have had a hard time in some cases getting local staff to maintain hygiene levels that are acceptable according to local levels but not acceptable according to the code. More than one MNE manager pointed out the challenge of getting locals to use hot water for washing plates and utensils.

> The most important thing for dorms and the canteen is to improve the food. Before they made Cantonese food then just spiced it up to make it like Szechwan. There are three main provinces represented, so we need to cook authentic food for each of them (CHS 2, Canteen/Dorms Manager).

> The manager of [a supplier factory] heard that the food was not good, so he now eats in the canteen (FMNE 1, Regional EHS Manager).

The general sense is that, over time and as incomes rise, investments will be made in housing infrastructure, and living conditions will improve accordingly. Further, government provision of social services is expected to increase as well. However, until basic needs and living conditions are adequately met, many we spoke to felt that the responsibility rests with those that have the most resources to directly contribute to providing for basic needs, namely the MNEs.

i. Wage rates

There is implicit or explicit reference in a number of MNE codes that wages are 'essential' to meeting workers' needs. However, the codes generally state only that MNEs will seek business partners that pay their employees the local legal minimum wage or local industry standard—whichever is higher.

The ILO's Conventions concerning wage rates recommend several elements be taken into consideration when determining the minimum wage rate.[66] These suggested elements are relevant to an examination of the MNE code provision on wage rates, as the ILO elements indicate the possibility of needing to balance workers' needs with the state's overarching economic needs. The ILO proposes that:

1. The needs of workers and their families be taken into account, including the general level of wages in the country, the cost of living, social security benefits, and the relative living standards of other social groups

2. Economic factors be considered, including the requirements of economic development, levels of productivity and the desirability of attaining and maintaining a high level of employment[67]

Although the MNEs studied have faced pressure from civil society to pay workers a wage that meets the supplier's workers' basic needs, sometimes referred to as a 'living wage', thus far the MNEs have not publicly entered the debate. MNEs with codes that were interviewed stated that they require their suppliers to adhere to their stated provisions of paying the local minimum or prevailing industry wage. However, in many of the

---

66   See Minimum Wage-Fixing Machinery Convention, 1928 (No. 26), Art. 1, and Minimum Wage Fixing Convention, 1970 (No. 131), Art. 3.

67   ILO Convention No. 26, Art. 3(a).

suppliers visited, the local minimum wage did not seem sufficient to meet the workers' needs, according to comments made by some union representatives.

> When it comes to minimum wages it is not the minimum that covers your basic food needs. For example, for a five-member family this wage would only be adequate if they just ate 50 grams a day, so that would be that only food was covered. If you take public transport, then you need more. And if you have to pay your room for a month, it will probably cost you about 3,500 per month and, yet, even bank workers do not earn 3,500 per month. A cashier makes 1,800 lempiras per month and yet to get this type of job you need to have a university degree and a suit and tie (HU 1, Manager).

> Sometimes even buses come to our factory doors offering our workers marvels. They get in the bus and then one week later they are coming back. The main reason that they return to GS 3 is because of the benefits and pay. GS 3 pays in excess of the minimum wage. The minimum wage is 1,150 quetzals per month divided by eight, so the base is 900 quetzals and the legal bonus is 250 quetzals. The legal minimum is US$145. We pay US$215. The wages here are better than in Asia (GS 3, HR Manager).

Our conversations indicated that wages were a point of common concern for both workers and managers. Consistently, in talking with workers, while salary was mentioned and the desire for higher pay was prominent, job security also figured highly. Wage rates are, of course, a contentious issue. Some discussion took place regarding 'living wage' issues, with some of the challenges this presents outlined in the following comments by some managers interviewed.

> Workers make an average of $53 a month in a district where the requirement is $35. We had problems at first with health-insurance deductions and other things, but we have ironed those out (FMNE 2, Manufacturing Manager).

> TPA 3's code is very much like [our code] but has living wage, and that is almost impossible to figure out. Should this include local issues of things like number of children, local costs, dormitories and other benefits, local traditions like supporting your family? But just because something is difficult doesn't mean you shouldn't attempt to do anything about it. We need to look at it, but it is not simple. We can't just look at the situation, though, and say that 'as long as people are taking these jobs, then they are making enough'. I would want to make sure that these people can get adequate meals, get long- and short-term healthcare, some form of retirement benefits (FMNE 1, Regional Manufacturing Manager).

> The corporation [MNE] should really push more to control wages [to increase wage levels beyond what is currently paid by suppliers] (FMNE 1, Manufacturing Manager, China).

One important change that has occurred in a number of supplier factories as a result of MNE code implementation is the transparency of the payments, which has meant a reduction in the possibility of 'game playing' by the factories with pay rates or hours worked. In almost all of the factories we visited, computer printouts were made available, presenting hours worked including overtime, pay rates, bonuses, deductions and the like.

Now [after the introduction of the code] our pay check is easy to understand—we can see the number of hours worked, including overtime hours, and what we are paid for (CHS 2, Factory Worker).

Putting the issue of 'living wage' to one side, our research indicated that the primary issue of concern with regard to wage rate involves accurate payment. We heard that even MNE compliance managers find that calculating the pay rate at supplier factories can be difficult, as suppliers use different combinations of piece-rate and hourly rate pay.

We give the workers a pay slip and if there is something wrong; they talk to me and I correct it. Things might go wrong because we use a bar code system and sometimes the workers swipe it too fast. In such a case the worker must talk to the supervisor and prove that he or she was at work on the day but there hasn't been any problems doing this (HR Manager, Supplier).

Most violations occur with new factories that haven't worked for us before. This is revealed in the pre-evaluation. They pay below minimum wage. Often they don't even know about minimum wage. And they always hold up part of the workers' wages as 'savings'. For revision in local minimum wage we require them to back-pay. In China there is a separate law for each province and an annual revision (AMNE 4).

We pay an hourly wage. In the knitting factory, a piece-rate system is used (GS 2, Director).

The average wage for sewers is approximately $50 or 800 lempiras. The minimum wage is approximately $30 a week. A good worker gets about 50% above the minimum wage. They are paid an individual piece rate. There are no team rates except where we are experimenting this in the cutting room. We use a progressive bundle system here, not a modular one. On our lines we still use the individual piece rate. These rates are based on the skill level of the workers, the effort level and attitude level. So, for example, an employee standardly will do 100 bundles and work every day at work for, say, approximately 249 days of the year. We will look at the stopwatch and see whether they are capable of 125 bundles per day, though, because workers are classic underachievers (HS 2, Director).

The MNEs use the audit, especially the records review and worker interview, to ascertain code compliance on wage payment. The strategies used by the MNE to redress non-compliance are similar to that of correct payment of overtime. Today, many MNEs require use of electronic swipe cards to document working hours. Other MNEs are training workers in how to calculate their pay and check it against their pay stub. Generally, the collaborative efforts have resulted in positive changes and improved levels of trust between workers and management.

j. Atmosphere

Our research indicated that many of the MNE codes of conduct include reference to treating workers with respect and dignity, and not allowing physical or other types of abuse. The instances where these elements are lacking have led to some of the most damaging publicity for the MNEs involved. Some of the interviews revealed continuing problems in this area:

> [With primary contractors, brands] really implement their codes. Subcontractors on the other hand often abuse their workers, with shouting, harassment (O 9).

> Rules say she cannot go to the toilet after three-thirty (Sri Lanka, Worker Interview).

Accordingly, it is logical that MNEs include these issues among the most important to address in order to implement code provisions. Our interviews with various parties—workers, MNEs and suppliers—indicated that the situation has generally improved in this regard, though is far from perfect.

We also heard, though, that changing the style of the managers, particularly expatriate managers from other countries in the region, can be very challenging. In this matter, the MNEs have had to rely on a multi-faceted approach of education, monitoring and sanctions.

> The new management practices are very respectful of the workers. We have seen continuous improvement in the factory since 1996. On the management perspective, supervisors would, to reach production targets, be punished by a higher manager. They might have to carry a bucket of water around the line as punishment. The code of conduct helps people know better what is wrong and what is right (CHS 2, Workers' Representative).

In terms of the actions by the MNEs, they appear to be able to set an important example for both the workers and the factory managers. Given that the MNE manufacturing manager and his staff in the factory are considered high-level officials by the workers, their actions can send a powerful message regarding the correct treatment of employees by managers.

> As workers see that our CSR staff can be trusted, then if things don't work out for workers in going through regular channels then they can work with us. We don't want to interfere in the work of the factories—we want the factories to handle these things—but we do want to establish a good atmosphere (FMNE 2, CSR Manager).

> Four or five years ago when I walked the line there was a feeling of 'oh no, we are going to be in trouble'. But now, they see and have interacted with us, and the more they do this the more they develop feelings of equals. For a new factory there has to be an attempt to figure out how to be more approachable, be considered part of the team (FMNE 2, Manufacturing Manager).

k. Turnover

Workforce turnover is not explicitly covered in the principles of the ILO, and rarely showed up as an element of the codes of conduct we reviewed for this book. However, our conversations revealed that worker turnover was a reality and concern that has led to attempts to reduce the problem. Turnover is a challenge, particularly in China, where workers see their positions as temporary, as they often have plans to move back to their hometowns.

Regardless of country, turnover is consistently experienced by management as a challenge in working with the workforce.

> Five to six per cent, approximately ten people per month, leave the factory (SLS 2, Personnel Manager).

> We lost somewhere between two to ten workers per month. They leave because of family reasons, personal reasons or to visit family (THS 6, Manager).

> About 10% turnover in a year because the husband gets a job in another area and they have to move or because they have to go back to look after their families (THS 3, Assistant Production Manager).

> Ten people leave each month to go back to the field (THS 2, Owner).

> We need training more on productivity and overtime. We still pay a daily rate minimum wage. Higher salaries are based on seniority. Our turnover is 10 or 11%. There are always about 100 people coming and going. The factories compete for workers and there are a lot of factories. The workers are young and often come in groups of five from the countryside. They all tend to leave together (THS 7, Operations Control, Supplier).

Some of the code provisions may have directly or indirectly led to improvements in workforce turnover. In one case we heard about, after the introduction of a code of conduct, turnover went down from 10% per month four years ago, to 4 to 5% two years ago, to 2% at the time of the interview. The average stay at this particular factory is now six years, with the peak turnover period just after Chinese New Year, when workers decide to stay at their homes in the provinces rather than return to the factory in the coastal EPZ.

Another factor influencing turnover is related to the percentage of the workforce sourced locally. At one state-owned apparel factory that we visited, all the workers were from the local urban area, and the turnover was two to three people per month, or about 0.3%.

In the factories that scored high on audit reviews, turnover rates were lower. However, one can attribute lower turnover in some instances to the fact that it is getting more difficult to find other jobs, including lower-paid jobs and ones with lower working conditions in the state sector.

> Turnover here [in the Viet Nam factories] is very low, since other jobs are hard to find. And people have much better benefits here, good pay, free lunch or a subsidised lunch, literacy training, adult learning. We pay for each week of training, including an allowance of 3,500 dong per night of training (FMNE I, Manager).

> Turnover here is 2% a month and anything below 10% is very good. Part of the reason is the social situation and demographics. We try to keep the people here (CHS 2, Assistant Factory Manager).

> We want our workers to stay longer. And some of them stay for five to seven to ten years—some for 13 years. The number of veterans is growing. One of the reasons is the increased labour standards (CHS 5, Factory Manager).

Seasonal cycles in production are another factor that leads to intermittent hiring and increased workforce turnover.

> [The] law says you can work 60 hours [overtime] per month max., 100 hours per year. Thus to cope during peak seasons we have to bring in more workers. However, there is a high turnover of rural employees due to marriage and family commitments (SLS 6, HR Manager).

Other MNEs approached the problem more systematically, developing responses and solutions that have assisted in improving their unique concerns.

> In Sri Lanka we came to an understanding of this scenario. We were training and putting people into factories and they were disappearing. We conducted exit interviews using an independent body and found that most of the problems were at the beginning with new operators. You see, usually a line runs at about 60% but a new person creates defects and bottleneck to the whole line and this percentage automatically disappears. These new people often wouldn't say anything but would just disappear. This was a burden for training costs. We developed a programme to train the production lines. We got a full-time instructor to talk to the lines every day and to classify the workers and put the new ones into easier operations until they got up to speed. In Thailand in this area we hire skilled workers. We have overturn problems but these aren't directly related to production problems. In most cases that I have seen, the husband either changes the house because of a new job and the wife follows or the wife goes back to the hometown to look after her family. Most of the workers here are from the northeast. There is a difference. Here it is a problem at every level. If you give people a task, everything needs to be clear. If there is an unclear area, they don't bother to study up about it which is not the case in Sri Lanka (THS 4, Production Manager).

As market forces, worker migration and global market trends continue to shift and transform the workplace, flexibility and innovation—with contributions by all concerned stakeholders—is required to address the challenges of workforce turnover.

VIII
Summary and conclusions

1. Summary

Two primary questions formed the basis for this research. First, we sought to provide an understanding of the various management systems implemented by enterprises at both the MNE and the supplier level to establish, communicate, implement and evaluate progress towards attaining the social objectives represented in their voluntary code-of-conduct commitments. Second, we sought to evaluate the dynamic of how these management systems are linked between MNEs and supplier levels, and how they interact.

Acknowledging the historical developments from which code-of-conduct implementation processes have evolved, management systems varied across the three sectors studied. Taking into consideration the unique operational requirements of each business sector and at each of the enterprises within sectors, we saw that management systems generally originated with the MNE. However, there were examples of some suppliers that manufacture products for multiple sectors having developed their own systems due to their ability to build on the initial forays into social performance made in the footwear sector. The retail sector, which of the three sectors included in this study was the most recent to embrace code-of-conduct issues relatively speaking, has been able to benefit to some degree from the learning curve already travelled by suppliers. This phenomenon, coupled with the evolution of MSIs, has pushed the social performance agenda overall.

The framework outlined in Chapter III set the context for documenting the relationship between MNEs and their suppliers in

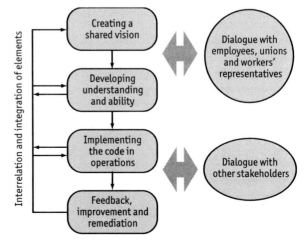

designing and implementing management systems for codes of conduct. The framework was intended to be used as a tool to depict what MNEs and suppliers are implementing, and not as a proposed standard for all management systems. However, our research indicated that, overall, the principles contained in the framework are consistently present in successful compliance operations, and thus may provide a good foundation from which to build.

The specific elements that appeared with greatest consistency at both the MNE and the supplier levels include:

- Creating a shared vision

- Developing understanding and ability

- Integrating code into operations

- Feedback, improvement and remediation, with a permeating theme of dialogue both internally and externally throughout these elements

Concerning the topic of dialogue with workers, unions and worker representatives, our research highlighted that successful engagement for dialogue provides a significant challenge. Repeatedly we were told that successful code implementation programmes required the clear and consistent involvement of workers, with defined roles relating to labour, social and ethical performance standards. This was particularly the case with regard to verification systems to ensure the right to freedom of association and the right to collective bargaining were upheld.

On the issue of dialogue with stakeholders, the interviews and research we conducted portrayed a relatively low level of involvement in engaging the various external individuals, groups and organisations with an interest in issues of CSR. This was demonstrated by a low number of sustainability reports. Some managers also reported that a contributing factor to this low level of stakeholder dialogue was the fear of negative public relations or media exposure, such as has occurred in the past regarding exposés of hazardous working conditions. Further, our findings highlight the need for trust to be built between MNEs, suppliers and stakeholders in all sectors. This may potentially occur through the establishment of a multi-stakeholder forum for discussing the private and voluntary approaches to social performance.

Generally, many similarities exist in the approach that MNEs in the footwear, apparel and retail sectors utilise for the design, implementation and management of CSR and codes of conduct across their supply chains. Across all three sectors, more consistencies were found than differences. However, those areas that were unique or specific to a sector are important to highlight.

Overall, MNEs in all sectors shared a common vision regarding the aims and objectives of CSR and their individual code. Consistently, firms demonstrated tangible top-level commitment for their legal and voluntary labour, social and ethical obligations. This often took the form of public statements by the CEO and was reflected in mission statements on the company website or in the annual report. One opportunity to communicate that such commitment exists is the provision of a sustainability report. As mentioned, our research indicated that only a few firms actually have produced such reports, thereby identifying an element of CSR that leaves potential for improvement among all sectors. As we heard from some MNE managers, sustainability reporting can be a useful tool not only for communication of the company vision but also for transparency and dialogue with stakeholders.

Most MNEs across all sectors have developed and demonstrated a persuasive and rational message regarding their code of conduct. We found that in a number of cases this message was being communicated both internally and externally. However, discrepancies existed regarding the depth of understanding of the recipients of such communication. Several firms demonstrated a deeper integration of code issues into their operational structure, specifically by communicating the economic and cost–benefit proposition that they experienced in the implementation of code provisions.

There appeared to be a mix of abilities among firms and sectors, with all firms having made some inroads in understanding, designing and implementing the principles encompassed in their codes of conduct. Our research suggested that this was due in part to the fact that relationships that exist today between suppliers and MNEs, in which CSR and codes of conduct increasingly are playing an important role, are more sophisticated and complex than those that have previously existed. Historically, MNEs had much greater legal and operational distance from suppliers, exemplified by contractual relationships that maintained an 'arm's length' for commercial interactions. In the sectors studied, factors such as increased public scrutiny, capital movement and streamlining of relationships with suppliers have led many MNEs to strengthen ties to suppliers and, in a complementary fashion, implement compliance programmes.

Recognising the need to integrate code provisions both horizontally and vertically throughout their organisational structures, MNEs in all sectors generally have embraced capacity-building in the form of education and training. However, it was in this area that clear differences appeared. Differences were not specific to a sector, but were dispersed among all sectors and various MNEs to varying degrees. Our research indicated that, while this could be due to several reasons, the primary reason stemmed from historical factors. This includes, for instance, when a firm embraced code obligations, the individual experience of the firm in designing and implementing the code and, importantly, the original motivation for voluntarily committing to labour, social and ethical obligations.

As has been noted, the major name brands in the footwear sector were among the first MNEs to be hit by public outrage at allegations of substandard and hazardous workplace standards, and accordingly have evolved the furthest in their systems for code implementation. Other factors that influenced the degree to which an MNE acted on its commitment to code provisions included the overall cost associated with the voluntary obligations, as well as the level of skill, training and availability of local managers in the field and the degree of 'lock-in' in the form of capital or relational investment that existed between the MNE and its suppliers.

It was in the area of implementing CSR and code obligations into operations that the most significant differences appeared among the three sectors studied. Again, due to historical factors such as the timing and severity of public pressure, the footwear sector, which also has fewer dominant players than the other sectors, appears to be the most advanced in this regard. It should be noted, however, that this finding is limited to the context of sports shoes, as the research conducted did not encompass all the apparel lines associated with these major footwear brands nor other general shoe manufacturers. The evolutionary approach in footwear is best represented by the fact that most manufacturers have their own CSR, code and overall compliance managers that work directly and regularly, in many cases full-time, with the supplier manufacturer. Further, an important factor to note with respect to footwear is that FMNEs have chosen to significantly reduce the number of supplier factories with which they work. This approach has been coupled with FMNEs increasing the size of their orders or production runs. In this way, the FMNEs aim to imbed themselves deeply within the operations of their suppliers, and work with them intimately to achieve the benefits and efficiencies of better quality, consistent performance, standard management and operating systems, and increased profits, among other things. Programmes to benefit from these closer relationships include those addressing CSR and code-of-conduct implementation.

In the apparel sector, our research indicated that, generally, apparel MNEs were less advanced than the footwear sector regarding CSR and code implementation, though more advanced than the retail sector. In the AMNEs interviewed, it was common to have a single manager responsible for CSR and code compliance at multiple supplier factories. It was not uncommon to find a single individual attempting to manage the labour, social and ethical obligations of between five and fifty supplier facilities and in some cases even more. Accordingly, given the extraneous factors influencing apparel manufacturing, such as frequently changing production runs, intermittent peak seasons and high workforce turnover, the apparel sector seems to be less advanced in its approach to CSR and code implementation. Further, the fact that AMNEs tend to work with hundreds of suppliers poses serious challenges to efficient and effective management of supplier activities related to CSR and code provisions.

Regarding initiatives within the retail sector related to the implementation of CSR and code requirements into internal and external operations, our findings indicate that significant challenges exist. A foundational reason for this has to do with the fact that retailers trade in a huge variety of products. Further, while there is a historical development of retailers branding their own products, the cornerstone of their business remains the marketing and sale of other brands, which provides a lower incentive to verify CSR and code compliance of their own products.

Our research revealed that RMNEs to a great extent, and certainly more than most other MNEs in the footwear and apparel sectors, rely on external monitors to verify compliance with CSR and code requirements. Further, while AMNEs may work with hundreds of suppliers, it is not uncommon for RMNEs to deal with literally thousands of often-changing supplier facilities. The vastness of such a supply base poses a serious impediment to the effective implementation and integration of a code of conduct and to the assurance that code compliance is present across the supply base.

Generally, the noticeable differences include the varying approaches across sectors in designing and implementing internal structures for the management of CSR and code obligations, as well as the degree to which they interact with suppliers. While all MNEs had individuals or departments within home-country headquarters responsible for CSR and code compliance, and many major brands in all the sectors had CSR personnel in the field, there were major differences in the degree to which CSR personnel functioned at the field level, and the degree to which interaction occurred with suppliers. Generally, the bigger the brand name, the more risk to reputation was perceived and the more resources seemed to be dedicated to CSR and code compliance. It must be acknowledged, however, that difficulty exists in determining the causality of the relationship between these factors.

The previous distinctions aside, consistencies across footwear, apparel and retail include initiatives to include employee participation in various and appropriate CSR and code activities, the development of detailed guidelines and operating procedures to direct CSR and compliance staff at both internal MNE and external supplier levels, and the establishment of clear CSR objectives along with systems of rewards and incentives that provide for continuous improvements related to CSR and code commitments. Furthermore, there appears to be a push in all sectors to move from a 'policing model' to a more consultative approach, although discrepancies exist regarding the practical implications of such a move with some MNEs further ahead than others in this regard.

MNEs interviewed across all sectors seem to have recognised the benefits of creating platforms for dialogue that allow for the sharing of 'best practices' and 'lessons learned'. Such dialogue is occurring internally with MNEs, among the suppliers of individual MNEs, as well as externally among the CSR personnel of competing MNEs and suppliers. The sharing of CSR experiences among competitors is motivated in part by the recognition of common CSR and code compliance requirements. At the same time the utilisation of multiple common suppliers provides an opportunity to reduce repetitive compliance requirements and eliminate overlapping and expensive CSR requirements.

Further, the trend for MNEs to work across multiple sectors is noteworthy. Some FMNEs interviewed focused initially on code-of-conduct implementation within the specific context of their sports shoe products lines. Apart from sports shoes, they also carry a broad variety of sports apparel and related accessories. Time will demonstrate the degree to which the apparent advances of the sports footwear brands make their way into their other product lines. Our research indicates that it is more a question of time, as the evolution of CSR and the mechanisms for the implementation and management of code commitments reach across multiple sectors, among both MNEs and the suppliers who manufacture for these MNEs. Our findings from the apparel sector suggest that some suppliers, who have met the initial CSR requirements of MNEs that also operate in the sports footwear sector, are further advanced in compliance with labour, social and ethical performance criteria. This may be due to the fact that code compliance within these MNEs as a whole is more developed and compliance managers and their field staff have more developed tools and systems at their disposal.

The management systems for monitoring, verification, reporting and continuous improvement are present in varying degrees across all sectors. Existing systems for dealing with technical requirements of matters such as EHS are being manipulated and extended to apply to other compliance issues related to labour, social and ethical standards. Again, referencing the differences previously summarised, the sports footwear sector appeared to be the most advanced in the development of integrated systems for obtaining feedback, improving existing operations and remedying problems and instances of CSR non-compliance when they are determined. The major brand footwear MNEs interact directly with daily operations of their suppliers, while both apparel and retail MNEs are generally pushing their greatly diverse suppliers, and generally approach CSR and code compliance requirements as an 'add-on' to existing operating and management systems.

Our research consistently revealed an inadequate, if not poor, level of integration of CSR and code compliance responsibilities in the internal structure of MNEs and suppliers. Interestingly, many MNEs readily admitted and acknowledged this challenge. We learned that the sourcing department, the functional department responsible for determining which suppliers to buy or 'source' from, plays the most significant role in identifying and interacting with suppliers. However, this department was often the least involved with CSR and code compliance issues. The fundamental challenge that exists across all sectors is the need to integrate CSR into sourcing, something which is occurring at a slow pace, if at all.

With regard to challenges posed by the requirement that suppliers comply with multiple codes from different RMNEs, as one of the experts who participated in this research notes below, we did not find this to be a significant challenge faced by RMNE suppliers in terms of code implementation.

> Our conjectures that multiple codes would present a problem for management was not supported. Three main reasons were given for this: first, the codes of different companies like those of AMNE 4 and RMNE 3 were quite similar in content (covering the ILO's core labour standards) though not in enforcement. The only qualification to this is that several managers suggested that global firms often had different emphases: one firm might focus particularly on health and safety, whereas another might pay more attention to working hours. Overall, however, this contributed to maintaining standards across all areas of the codes. Second, since some firms were more rigorous in enforcement—in particular, FMNE 2, FMNE 1, AMNE 4 and AMNE 8—other less enforcement-conscious firms tended to accept this as a guarantee of code compliance and so engaged in less-frequent factory visits. Third, some of the factories had instituted their own regular audit process so that a continuous focus on code-related issues meant that there were few surprises when auditors from a global company's compliance team visited the factory (E 4).

However, one of the primary challenges facing all sectors is the means to consistently and objectively measure performance related to labour, social and ethical standards. Our research revealed an obvious need for the development of indicators that will allow facilities to benchmark performance in these areas. A set of metrics that is applicable across sectors for use at the factory level would support MNEs in working with their suppliers in order to meet the principles encompassed in codes of conduct. Such metrics could also help MNEs better address principles in their codes of conduct that parallel those standards such as freedom of association, collective bargaining and discrimination, which are also encompassed by the ILO Tripartite Declaration and the OECD Guidelines. As mentioned previously, while it is fairly straightforward to measure and verify compliance related to technical environment and health and safety standards, the challenge is to objectively measure and verify compliance with the more subjective labour, social and ethical standards. The greatest challenges reported by company managers rest with the development of objective standards against which to measure supplier performance for freedom of association, collective bargaining and worker discrimination.

One of the difficulties that we heard about repeatedly centred on the issue of international labour standards that have been developed by the ILO. At the factory level, these standards are of limited assistance due to their non-specificity and by the fact that they are aimed at governments, not companies. The issues that need to be dealt with at the enterprise level differ from those at the national level. The development of factory-level metrics and guidance documents to enable comparison of performance at the factory level are matters that would directly assist in the code implementation process. Apart from translating code principles into tangible, measurable outputs, they would enable MNEs to conduct comparisons of their supplier factories while the factories themselves would be in a position to monitor their own levels of compliance.

Finally, based on our research, we would maintain that the ILO is uniquely positioned to play a lead role in facilitating the development of internationally accepted standards for labour, social and ethical behaviour. Through its constituents, dialogue on the subject matter covered by this book could be commenced, with particular emphasis on the important role that governments play in enacting and enforcing national legislation as well as adhering to relevant international Conventions and Recommendations.

2. Conclusions

In our review of the elements present in each of the management systems we studied, there were unique aspects as well as many common factors. In reviewing the factors of successful operation, we have attempted to discover what makes achieving a company's social policies possible. We found an emerging framework of systems, policies and procedures that are supported by this research project as well as other material reviewed. Nine points stand out regarding what firms do to effectively implement their codes.

a. Responsibility, vision and leadership

Each firm developed its code to reflect its unique vision of itself, comply with national laws and address civil-society pressures for social responsibility, as well as generally recognised international standards including those articulated by the ILO in its international labour standards. The companies have had to re-examine what they stand for in light of quantum changes in their markets. A result of increased consumer and stakeholder pressure, this re-examination has resulted in the development of an internal framework for acceptable practices. From this framework firms have created codes of conduct that guide them in manifesting this vision. In implementing these codes, top-management support, both in headquarters and with suppliers, is a prerequisite.

b. Stakeholder engagement

The best cases observed involved an ongoing and effective dialogue with key internal and external stakeholders whereby these stakeholders played a role in designing, developing and implementing the operating policies and procedures adopted by the companies. When this dialogue was not present, the companies often had problems. Companies that adequately understand their relationship with, and impact on, various stakeholders appropriately incorporate the views of stakeholders into corporate vision and leadership. Thereby, these firms are better positioned to carry out a logical and long-term strategy. While firms generally reach out to include primary stakeholders such as employees, owners, supplier/allies and customers, some firms have struggled to broaden their stakeholder view to include essential secondary stakeholders such as local communities, civil-society agents and governments. An additional factor is that those MNE and supplier firms that freely shared 'best practices' and 'lessons learned' with competitors generally made advances in CSR and code compliance over others in the sector. Accordingly, the need to establish forums for dialogue on the experiences of what works in the field is of utmost importance.

c. Strategy

As firms come to grip with the emerging pressures to act responsibly, they appear to have moved from an ad hoc approach, to one that is more strategic and systematic in addressing the labour, social and ethical considerations of the codes of conduct. This systematic approach would initiate with stakeholder engagement and proceed to the development of an overall strategy for achieving its vision, leadership and corporate goals. An integrated approach to implementing codes has been achieved to varying degrees from little to considerable. This best-case scenario did not appear to occur in most cases. Each firm has experienced a learning process that includes both a reactive stage and proactive strategy. Firms attempting to be strategic seek to reconcile their overarching vision with the reality they experience throughout their global operations. We saw many managers grappling with conflicting goals, increased workloads and conflicting directives. Interestingly, we heard that achieving goals and objectives was best done through rational planning, rather than 'adhocracy'.

d. Human resource responsibility

Human issues fundamentally drive each of the codes. We found that implementation depends on the support, understanding, belief and action of managers and workers. The focus on people and human resource issues was a core element in creation of the codes and implementation of the codes, and particularly for stretching beyond the MNEs' formal boundaries to include other companies in their value chain. This reflects the unique development of applying specific performance standards to entities not contractually or legally part of the company. The success of code implementation appears to depend on recognition by the MNEs that an expanded set of labour, social and ethical standards and responsibilities is fundamental. Accordingly, human resource training, performance appraisals, recruitment, retention, dismissal and wage policies need to be integrated throughout the organisation, taking into account the MNE's code. Achieving code compliance requires managers at all levels, including suppliers and buyers, to consider issues such as working conditions, training and development, and employee engagement.

e. Systems for code integration

Meeting code requirements appeared to be integral to corporate practices and relationships. This occurred in some cases as a new concept for firms. Initially, many firms perceived CSR and code compliance as the sole responsibility of the CSR group. Over time, these firms are moving in varying degrees toward management systems that explicitly integrate code implementation and compliance tasks with other parts of their organisation. Key elements from our research that are critical to integration of management systems include: reward systems; communication systems; operating, production and delivery systems; purchasing, accounting and financial systems; human resource systems; and supplier relationships. As one manufacturing manager explained, the task of truly carrying out all the elements that are required by codes is 'huge', with broad implications.

f. Measurement and information systems

The companies are undertaking, again to varying degrees, a process of building up information systems that support their CSR and code compliance efforts. Keeping track of performance against objectives, following up on CAPs established after audits, ensuring reductions in the use of toxic substances or monitoring accident rates all require some sort of measurement and information systems. The nature of such systems is pervasive and multi-dimensional. By multi-dimensional we mean that information systems provide inputs at the corporate level on the success of organisation-wide efforts, or on crises that require top-level action; they also provide inputs at the country level and within the factories: flagging local issues that require consideration, problems that exist and need action by factory personnel. By pervasive, we mean that it appeared that the integration of CSR and code requirements into decision-making processes requires wide access to information on code elements; for code compliance to impact on purchase decisions or management performance reviews, for example, then it has to be available. Data gathering for the information systems was also pervasive, ranging from audits, both external and internal, accident reporting systems, suggestion boxes, best-practice exchange networks, supplier databases, and so on. As one of the managers quoted at the end of this chapter suggested, you need to 'quantify everything' in order to manage it.

g. Transparency and accountability

We heard again and again that the firms had made progress in large part due to pressure from consumers and organisations concerned with employee rights and working conditions, and that without this pressure it was doubtful that nearly as much would have occurred to improve conditions in the factories studied. Being held accountable by stakeholders is an effective means of maintaining pressure to move forward. In the companies reviewed, a number of times managers suggested that while some of the organisations and consumer movements have been unfairly critical at times, they hoped they would continue pushing for improvement. The companies also recognised a need for increased transparency with stakeholders, that a vacuum of information was worse than providing information demonstrating that more improvement is necessary. What appears to be necessary is a system of reporting and transparency that provides external stakeholders with data they feel they can trust, data that is both reliable, in that it does not change from one day to the next, and valid, in that it is generated based on objective criteria. Linking to the previous element of measurement and information systems, the firms in question appear to recognise that they have to provide stakeholders with information they can trust to decide how the firms are doing against their goals. The path to this reliable, valid information was not always clear, in particular with regard to third-party or independent monitoring.

h. Remediation, improvement and innovation

While the previous item suggests the need for transparency and accountability externally, the same applies internally. Information and measurement should be linked into internal systems, encouraging both a problem-solving and a learning approach. Managers need to know how they are doing against their goals. They need to know how subordinates are performing, or which areas need improvement. From what we learned, the companies generally felt that some problems need to be addressed immediately—for example, that no level of forced labour was acceptable—while other issues require additional time to address. CAPs play a vital role in this process. Feedback from information contained in CAPs can demonstrate the need for increased education or training, for the introduction of new ventilation systems, or for changes in personnel. We heard that tools such as CAPs are most effective when combined with dialogue and consultation. Based on this, it appears that a learning and action approach is the most effective long-term strategy.

i. Broad-based view

Finally, we heard how the firms studied have broadened their vision of what they are trying to achieve. This includes senior managers who have changed their description of organisational goals and responsibilities to include issues covered by codes of conduct. We also heard how damaging it was when these same managers failed to provide the guidance or support for codes. Managers throughout the organisations, but particularly those dealing with suppliers, talked about the challenges of these new responsibilities. Achieving the goals of codes of conduct appears to have complicated the lives of people at all levels; no longer responsible only for profits, costs, quality and delivery dates, these managers now also have to be concerned with far-off living conditions and health and safety issues, environmental impacts and labour practices of suppliers and their workers. In our view, this is a challenge that—with globalisation, disaggregation of supply chains, and increasing consumer awareness facilitated by the ease of communication—will increasingly face managers in many industries.

In conducting this research, apart from gaining an understanding of what companies do effectively to implement their codes, we also were provided with insights into some of the challenges faced by companies associated with code implementation. The following paragraphs provide insight into four key areas of concern.

i. Ambiguous legislation

One of the things that we repeatedly heard about was that a level of ambiguity exists in many national regulatory instruments applicable to the operations of MNEs and their suppliers in the footwear, apparel and retail sectors. While this phenomenon is something that MNEs and suppliers have had to address in the past for other areas, they generally involved more technical areas such as EHS standards. Clearly defined parameters of social performance generally do not exist in most regulatory programmes. Further, within the context of international legal regimes, such as UN declarations and ILO Conventions, there is a lack of detail regarding applicable indicators at the enterprise level. This exacerbates the challenges of implementation of management systems addressing voluntary labour, social and ethical standards adopted by companies. Based on the interviews conducted, there is a need within national regulatory systems to clarify and define standards applicable to enterprises. Some interviewees suggested that this clarity may be achieved through the initiation of dialogue between industry and government or may be advanced through discussions conducted by international organisations such as the ILO. Furthermore, MSIs may provide an important pathway to such discussions.

ii. Low education levels of workers

As we discovered, workers play a key role in any successful code implementation programme. The demographic information we found in our research pointed to a majority of workers in the sectors studied being young females from distant, mostly agricultural, villages, who possess a minimal level of education. We were told that these dynamics tended to lead to a generally high rate of worker turnover among most MNE suppliers visited. To address the challenges reflected in these demographics, almost all interviewees suggested that formalised training and education programmes are needed. While we heard of some training activities targeted at the worker level, these were relatively few and further developments in this area are required.

iii. Cost

An additional conclusion shared by most participants in this research is the fact that code-of-conduct implementation is expensive unless it is offset by gains in productivity and quality. The fundamental question underlying the question of expense is that of who bears the cost for the design, implementation and ongoing management of the systems and mechanisms for labour, social and ethical performance standards. Part of the answer relates to who is in the best position to bear these costs. Generally, as with other behavioural or operational requirements that were either embraced or imposed, MNEs and supplier managers reported a preference to defer to market mechanisms that ultimately pass the cost on to the consumer. However, given the lack of data regarding the code implementation process, it is difficult to quantify the costs. This is particularly an issue the deeper one delves into a supply chain, where tangential issues arise such as the utilisation of homeworkers. Some managers suggested that an attempt be made to quantify the added costs of code design, implementation and management. This could be undertaken through a case-study comparison of costs involved with two particular MNEs and their suppliers. It could be beneficial to try to capture any of the tangible and intangible benefits from embracing codes of conduct such as goodwill and an enhanced public image, although such matters are difficult to quantify.

iv. The business case

From our conversations with various stakeholders, including those within management, we learned that those involved with codes of conduct, such as MNEs, the ILO, employers' organisations and trade unions, must do a better job at making the business case for code-of-conduct and CSR issues. This would likely take the form of establishing a more coherent, consistent and rational argument for the economic advantages and benefits, as well as the social benefits, of implementing labour, social and ethical performance criteria reflected in a company's code of conduct. To assist in developing a more rational argument for the business reasoning to implement a code of conduct, a number of MNE managers suggested that additional case studies, research and data be generated to aid in this process. Fundamentally, based on what we heard from those in the sectors that have the most experience with code implementation, such as the footwear sector, there are quantitative benefits from investing and integrating code issues deeply into the relationship between the MNE and its supplier base. A thorough analysis of these benefits needs to be conducted.

Alongside the points outlined above, these conclusions would be incomplete without consideration of the role of governments and MSIs as highlighted by the research findings.

- **The role of government.** At the very start of this book we noted that code-of-conduct implementation does not take place in a vacuum but rather occurs against a backdrop of international and national law and regulations. This was supported by our research findings which indicated that, by implementing labour, social and ethical standards espoused in their code-of-conduct implementation programmes, MNEs and suppliers are in essence fulfilling a task normally reserved by the responsible governmental authority from the jurisdiction within which they are operating. It is the national government's responsibility to establish policy, promulgate law, issue regulations and set enforcement procedures. Within the context of labour, social and ethical performance standards, MNEs and suppliers have been fulfilling this governmental role in the absence of regulation, policy and enforcement procedures. The paradox is that MNEs and suppliers are in a sense regulating themselves by creating an additional layer of social performance requirements akin to regulations. As was shown in the retail sector particularly, where MNEs have, in some instances, thousands of suppliers, the ability to self-regulate through codes of conduct can be limited without a facilitative environment.

  Accordingly, there is a need for consistent, reliable information and guidance from governments, particularly for clear and defined standards of performance. A number of interviewees suggested that government–MNE dialogue needs to be more formalised to address subjective and sometimes poorly defined social performance standards reflected in CSR programmes. Specific engagement of MNEs and supplier factories needs to occur with national ministries of labour. Further, such ministries should play an active role in defining and developing the capacity of national auditing firms to fulfil the objective of third-party verification. In addition to driving better social performance, this will potentially create a national market of service providers.

- **Role of MSIs.** A further conclusion to be drawn from the research findings is the critical role of MSIs. They represent a progression in the evolution of code implementation programmes. They play an important role in providing a forum within which all stakeholders are able to exchange data and information, along with carrying on a dialogue regarding expectations for labour, social and ethical behaviour, both nationally and abroad. Furthermore, they have provided, in some cases, an entry level for discussions between MNEs, supplier management and trade unions on issues such as allegations of breaches of workers' rights at supplier factories. The positive outcome of these discussions in a number of instances has directly resulted from facilitation and intervention of some MSIs.

   Within the context of MSIs and code-of-conduct implementation, our research indicates the need to streamline the processes that have and are continuing to develop within MSIs. MSIs can continue to provide the forum from which accepted standards and best practices will emanate, as well as to allow for innovation in managing code of conduct implementation programmes, as experiences are reported and shared among stakeholders. MSIs need to maintain an approach that is not overly prescriptive, thereby allowing for different approaches to implement code commitments, based on the unique requirements of particular industry sectors and local traditions. Further, partnerships should be encouraged with additional emphasis on the role for governments to establish clear guidance on required standards and enforcement policies.

3. Recommendations

a. An industry challenge

Interviews in all of the sectors highlighted the need for a discussion on an industry-led solution to the proliferation of auditing approaches rather than simply focusing on the standards encompassed by codes themselves. Such a discussion could be facilitated by organisations actively involved in this arena including ILO constituents. This discussion could provide a forum for various stakeholders to explore the possibility of establishing an industry-wide auditing approach applicable at the factory level.

From our research it is clear that, while the ILO Declaration on Fundamental Principles and Rights at Work and the Tripartite Declaration of Principles concerning Multinational Enterprises and Social Policy provide useful guidance to governments and MNEs, more operational guidance at the factory level is required. Other issues that could also be explored include the development of an industry-wide auditor training programme leading to consistency in practices and procedures. Given the increasing tendency of MNEs to conduct audits, a credible auditor training programme would be extremely useful. Furthermore, the forum could explore the possibility of developing a common approach for dealing with code-of-conduct issues along the lines of how the American 'Big Three' auto manufacturers developed an approach to deal with quality issues. By creating auditable standards, the Big Three were able to avoid overlap and were also able to outsource most of the cost and work of auditing to third parties. Some MNE managers interviewed suggested that, through such an approach, MNEs, particularly their purchasing and CSR departments, could continue to have a role in advising suppliers on how to qualify for certification, but they would be separated from the certification process itself. The benefits of such a system could include:

1. Lower compliance management costs for MNEs

2. Less confusion about standards and greater transparency

3. Increased consistency of audits

4. Fewer audits and their associated disruptions for each individual factory

5. Increased number of factories being audited as overlapping audits are eliminated and the additional resources are applied to factories that are currently not being audited

6. The development of metrics to monitor ongoing performance and improvements

b. Research and training

An area for further research is establishing measurements for the effectiveness of codes in practice. A recommendation suggested by a number of managers and supported by one of the experts that participated in this research is that an important area of study is the measuring of changes in working conditions over time.

> We can get to know the functions and limitations of code of conduct by studying the change in the working conditions of the workers, and different people and cultures in the supply chain (E 4).

Where conditions improve and causal links are established, successes can be claimed for code programmes. Perhaps more importantly, where weaknesses are observed, opportunities for improving compliance management may have been found. In this way, the expert observed, 'A useful way to develop the code of conduct will be formed' (E 4).

Some MNEs and organisations have already begun attempting to establish and document the causal links, particularly in the areas of quality, productivity and worker–management relations. More applied research needs to be conducted in this area, taking account of the learning to date. It is clear that, as there is no 'one-size-fits-all' approach to the content of a code, there is also no 'one-size-fits-all' to its implementation. There needs to be encouragement of various practical initiatives that attempt to address some of the problems associated with traditional 'policing' models of implementation.

Efforts need to be made to involve workers and managers in joint education and training programmes so that each understands the important role that the other plays. To date, many programmes have been delivered either to workers or to managers with most effort being concentrated on providing training in the area of health and safety.

While this is a critically important aspect of meeting some code-of-conduct principles, further steps could be taken. Indeed, many health and safety aspects can be regarded as 'soft targets' by some industry participants, with more difficult-to-detect or difficult-to-resolve issues attracting less attention from audits and corrective action programmes. Furthermore, while separate training of workers and managers is important, an attempt needs to be made to bridge the gap between these two groups.

> With regard to the general aspects of other audits I am not sure of the competence of the auditors. The only problems that they have ever come up to me about are on safety issues, and half the time they are wrong. Sometimes they have made some recommendations which have actually been beneficial, for example, FMNE 2 recommended that fire extinguishers on columns have red markings all the way round them, and AMNE 4 recommended that we have some 'no-parking' zones, but these are the soft, easy targets. When it comes to the usual suspects of wages and benefits, hours and work, there is nothing that's said, and this is why I say that I am not sure of the competence of the auditors (UKS 2, Head of CSR).

Apart from establishing the causal linkage between issues such as productivity, quality, working conditions and workers' rights, it is important to demonstrate the sustainability of changes that are made directly within the factories themselves. Documentation of these changes, how they affect workers and managers, their impact on firm competitiveness and how they can lead to longer-term benefits for the industry, could be provided through case studies and other such resource materials which could then be utilised by practitioners, policy-makers and academics in formulating constructive suggestions for future changes.

Finally, consideration of the important role that governments play—or could play given increased capacity—not only in the enactment and enforcement of legislative standards but also in the education and training of the workforce must be made. Targeted initiatives by governments to improve the capacity of the workforce from workers to managers alike, to respond to the challenges being placed on them as a result of the pressures of globalisation and the need to be competitive, are required. Furthermore, the establishment of effective labour administration departments and alternative dispute resolution fora plays a key role in the functioning of management systems established to implement codes of conduct by MNEs and their suppliers. The absence of such a facilitating environment, as we heard from the interviews conducted, creates a major hurdle to companies.

c. Expert recommendations

A number of academic experts participated in this research and provided useful guidance on the range of topics and issues to be covered. Given their expertise in the field of code implementation, it is useful to consider some of their recommendations on specific issues raised through the conduct of this research. Following the broad categories considered throughout this book, the specific recommendations made by the experts are provided in the paragraphs below.

Industry response

There seems to be a great deal of merit in exploring the role of standardised codes and joint approaches to auditing and verification, especially with the apparent increasing trend for supplier factories to be shared among MNEs. At the very least, it would be beneficial to provide guidance to firms, in all sectors, undertaking the somewhat challenging task of translating and implementing ILO core labour standards at the enterprise level.

Research and training

The framework and research rightly emphasise training and education as levers for code development. As part of the working vision, MNE buyers and suppliers need to conceive of themselves as learning organisations. Individual learning is not enough. Knowledge about high-performance work systems and organisational change—how to successfully achieve this in the fastest possible time—needs to be developed through the use of modern learning and knowledge management techniques. Integral to these processes are the development of communities of practice (especially of factory managers) and the smart use of technology. Portals can be tailored for use by managers and workers. Some athletic footwear firms have developed knowledge-sharing systems but little is known about their effectiveness. This is another area that requires more research.

Auditors

There is no substitute for a competent and tenaciously motivated corps of front-line auditors; that is, the corps of compliance officers who actually enter the factories, interview workers and managers, and oversee corrective action. Competence is not assured by compliance managers' recruitment of staff who have *generally* high qualifications. Competence instead requires specific and genuinely professional training—or years of practical experience—in the application of complex labour rights and standards to the infinite particularities of individual factories. Ideally, such professional training takes the form of legal education (particularly in the case of freedom of association and anti-discrimination rights) or certification in occupational health and industrial hygiene (in the case of workplace health and safety). After all, auditors purport to play the role traditionally played by sovereign law-enforcement personnel, such as labour-board investigators, labour courts and occupational safety administrators, on the premise that such administrative or judicial capacity is lacking or weak in low-wage countries (as well as in many high-wage countries where public enforcement is erratic). Tenacious motivation is the second necessary qualification of front-line auditors because the remediation of labour and employment violations requires sustained, detailed and aggressive attention, especially when factories are faced with potentially costly or 'redistributive' changes in the work environment such as unionisation. In this light, auditor training by MNEs alone is insufficient. MNEs should instead partner with labour unions and universities, with the facilitation of an organisation such as the ILO, to create programmes in auditor education and certification.

Linkage between compliance, productivity and worker rights

One of the most critical phases of the compliance process is that of 'corrective action' or 'remediation'. It is, relatively speaking, easy for compliance personnel to find code violations, announce them to factory managers, and require that they be corrected by the time of the next audit. It is much harder to develop systems of ongoing accountability to ensure that factory-level stakeholders have the motivation and capacity to remedy violations of labour rights and standards apart from the periodic intervention of MNE compliance personnel—especially if the ultimate goal is not the achievement of a static benchmark of labour conditions (which may simply impound a poor industry-wide performance) but instead continuous improvement (which embodies the aspiration to continue indefinitely to better conditions, including wages, throughout the industry). The twin goals of continuous accountability and continuous improvement require that compliance personnel, factory managers and workers understand the relationship between productivity and the trust and empowerment of workers. Enhanced productivity provides the economic margin that may ease managerial fears that empowered workers will excessively redistribute in their own favour. Accountability through worker participation or representation eases workers' fears that greater productivity will not be rewarded. A virtuous cycle requires that both managers and workers are trained in productivity enhancement and methods of stakeholder accountability and dialogue at the point of production. MNEs, labour unions and tripartite organisations such as the ILO have roles to play in this training process.

Integration

A distinction needs to be made between inscribing values and broad statements about the desirability of codes and social responsibility more generally at corporate level (in relation to MNEs, buyers and suppliers) and what we would call a 'working vision' that should be developed at workplace level. This would reflect what the framework and report rightly emphasise: the need for integration of elements. The working vision should be a manufacturing plan that would include an HR component. This plan should speak to the issue of high-performance work systems. In other words, the plan should be motivated by a vision of what the factory is going to look like in a year or two. There is a large literature on this topic; the most comprehensive study to date being Appelbaum *et al.* (2000) *Manufacturing Advantage*. As an aside, very little research on this issue has been reported outside of the US and Europe. This gap needs to be filled.

Role of HR

Codes can be conceived in two main ways: as a floor of rights and as a foundation for furthering HR practices within the workplace. The notion of compliance and the rationale for developing codes—mainly as a response to consumer or external stakeholder pressure—should be de-emphasised in favour of the code as an HR foundation. Thus, the code is the start of a journey to the high-performance workplace, which itself is changing in conception as technological developments are made and skills and expectations change. According to this view, responsibility for codes should be the responsibility of HR specialists who would liaise with CSR or public relations specialists to keep them informed and especially when labour practices become a public issue. In the normal course of work, this is likely to be a rare event. At present there is a disconnect between HR departments in MNEs and code development, and this is an emerging issue in supplier companies that, by and large, are tending to follow MNEs in setting up separate labour practices sections, albeit sometimes within personnel departments. However, the latter tend to be administrative rather than strategic structures. This suggests a final point in regard to code responsibility: HR departments that have oversight for codes and their development should be strategic and work closely with senior management. In short, returning to a previous point, HR should be an integral aspect of the working vision and in order to do that it must include managers at a senior level who have input into this blueprint for lifting performance.

Indicators
There is a need for a management systems approach to ethical sourcing, with key performance indicators and formalised reporting cycles and procedures. The extent to which ethical supply chain management practices and measurement—indicators—are integrated horizontally and vertically within the company, itself should be considered. There needs to be management 'buy in' and awareness building to counter ignorance with respect to the complexity, scope and potential damage of poor practice in respect of ethical sourcing of products.

Stakeholder engagement
Examination of the robustness of the audit process and the appropriate combination of constructive engagement through training needs to occur so there is first-party audit capacity; constructive engagement through the second-party audit process; and assurance through the third-party audit process. Furthermore, companies should examine the extent to which constructive engagement includes management training so that managers are empowered to deal with problems and manage them as opposed to eliminating them without systems being in place to identify any adverse consequences of changing working situations (e.g. the implications of eliminating child labour or reducing working hours but not increasing pay). They should also consider the extent to which workers and workers' organisations are involved in the social audit process, the development of solutions and future monitoring and first audit processes.

Role of governments, employers' organisations and workers' organisations
Greater government involvement could perhaps be achieved through intermediaries such as employers' organisations and chambers of commerce as well as workers' organisations. In any case, strategies should be developed to engage these organisations in understanding and promoting codes as part of their role as facilitators and disseminators of good HR practices in their respective industries and countries. The ILO could consider a project that facilitates this process.

d. Company recommendations

While this research focused somewhat narrowly on specific subject matter in the three sectors, our intent was to facilitate and forward the issues discussed. In the spirit of the following comment, we seek to highlight some of the core lessons learned.

> It has been a tough few years. But our factories are coming along. And the public is starting to understand how complicated it is. And that has helped us. Our feeling is that, if people have an unbiased factual view of things, that helps us. So any reporting of that helps us. So if your efforts [this research project] and some of the NGOs help get this out, then that works for us (FMNE 2, Senior Manager).

Some of the more significant conclusions and recommendations from the companies we dealt with include:

* The requirement to act proactively to address code-related issues before crises force action

* To adapt to the specific situation and the locations in which a company operates

* To take a systematic view, with measurement and information systems, plans and standards

* To freely share 'best practices' and 'lessons learned' within the context of CSR

These suggestions are supported by the following comments received directly from company managers:

> We will never be able to avoid all the fires, so act proactively to go where you do want to go, rather than just running ahead of the latest rules (FMNE 2, CSR Manager Headquarters).

> You cannot use a cookie-cutter approach in each sector, although the code is high enough that it can apply to all factories and suppliers, internal and external (FMNE 2, Headquarters).

> Keep in mind local culture. We tried suggestion boxes and the local people just wouldn't use them. With time [one of the factories] has gotten them to do it, and the last time I asked they had received 3,000 (FMNE 1, Country Manager).

> Systems are important. There are hundreds of factories and hundreds of thousands of employees, and we are the minority buyer in each of these. If we don't have a calendar, standards and practices for when these standards are not met, then we would have a disaster on our hands. To make the management of this whole thing effective over time you need a system. We are going to merge EHS and labour issues into one system (FMNE 2, CSR Manager, Headquarters).

Among the three sectors considered, the greatest advances in reducing supplier churn have occurred within the sports footwear sector. While the benefits of low churn among suppliers were acknowledged across all three sectors, it was reported to be a growing challenge in both apparel and retail sectors. We heard that significant advantages from low supplier turnover exist. For example, long-term engagements can exist between MNEs and individual suppliers or supplier networks, and thereby aid an MNE in quality control, quality assurance and code implementation as well as in predicting future performance requirements for the supplier. Further, working exclusively with a smaller set of suppliers allows for the joint development and implementation of CAPs, a key aspect of many compliance programmes. Similarly, a smaller set of suppliers provides for consistency in key management staff, familiarity with management and operational systems, and dedicated resources, all of which are beneficial to code-of-conduct implementation.

The need and importance of integrating CSR and code compliance functions across all functional departments is a point that cannot be overemphasised. Beyond the individual frustration expressed by compliance managers from a lack of co-ordinated planning with other departments, MNE and supplier managers acknowledged the money, time and effort lost to the lack of integration. Our research indicated that the standard experience of most firms was to initially approach CSR as an 'add-on' function. We heard that, over time, firms that took CSR and other social commitments seriously expressed the realisation that there were significant efficiencies and benefits to be achieved from early integration of CSR responsibilities into the overall management structure of global operations and the supply chain.

A fundamental element of the recommendations from corporations includes the role of employees. As CSR and the labour, social and ethical commitments embraced within corporate codes of conduct directly relate to the daily lives of workers, it is only natural to include these key stakeholders in the process to design, implement and manage CSR systems. Further, as much of the subject matter associated with CSR deals directly with the rights and responsibilities of the worker, some MNEs told us that there is much to gain from the feedback and advice provided by the intended beneficiaries of CSR and code requirements. Over time, as MNEs and supplier factories become more comfortable with the dynamics of CSR, the specific role of workers in the overall CSR process, taking into account their legislative rights, can be defined based on the unique concerns and issues of each organisation.

e. Concluding remarks

Implementing a broad-based code addressing labour, social and ethical issues in disaggregated supply chains is a complicated, multi-faceted undertaking, as outlined in this book. From what we heard it seems likely that competitive business pressures will probably lead to a reduction in the diffuseness of the manufacturing level of the supply chain. Or put simply, the challenge of providing the right product at the right price and within a short time frame will likely support a reduction in the absolute numbers of suppliers. This may present a useful opportunity for code implementation programmes to capitalise on as already appears to be occurring in some of the sectors studied, particularly the footwear sector. A high number of suppliers usually leads to a higher level of transaction costs. Traditionally these costs are thought to be offset by the price-suppressing effects of competition within so large a supply base. However, when compliance management, and particularly factory auditing, are introduced into the overall transaction costs, these can tilt the balance back towards the benefits of having fewer suppliers complementing the effect of working closely with a smaller range of suppliers on productivity and quality issues as well as on competitive issues such as speed of delivery. Moreover, we heard that it is not necessarily true that having fewer suppliers reduces competition and price competitiveness; just the opposite can be true as larger but fewer suppliers are able to exploit economies of scale and compete more intensively for orders. The comments of the agents in Chapter V make this clear.

Compliance departments may well be able to capitalise on the business imperative to streamline operations if there is increased communication across departmental functions. In particular, communication and increased integration with sourcing or purchasing departments needs to occur to ensure that compliance managers are informed of supplier factories and strategic sourcing decisions for the future. In this way, there could be a refinement of the auditing processes to ensure that the resources of the compliance department are being used effectively. Phased approaches to auditing could be introduced so that ongoing consultation and assistance could be provided to companies to address issues posing the greatest challenges such as workers' rights and discrimination.

> There have been improvements for workers. There have been significant improvements in terms of changes in management policies. For example, there have been increases in wages and the toughening of regulations. Last year we had about 8,000 assessments of many different sorts by NGO 5 members. Please remember that these assessments are of many forms and can include self-assessments done by the company. In summary I would say that we have received reports of 1,250 significant corrective actions, over 50% of which relate to health and safety, and 30% to wages and working hours. This tells me that we are not getting to the tough issues of empowerment and discrimination, that there are gaps in core labour standards (NGO 5, Director).

As was noted by one of our experts, 'the extent to which discrimination, harassment, bullying situations and equal opportunities as well as workers' organisations and rights are addressed, in addition to the more "sensational" and reputationally damaging issues such as child labour, bonded labour or excessive working hours' needs to be examined in greater depth. This may be simpler to carry out with a more limited number of suppliers.

Notwithstanding the changes in supplier numbers that may occur in some industries, industries such as the retail sector operate on a business model based on a large supply base. In such an instance, our findings suggest that the role of dialogue, particularly with workers, workers' organisations and employers' organisations as well as with external stakeholders, is critical. In particular, the limited reach of compliance managers can be supplemented by these organisations.

Furthermore, such dialogue may address one of the most disputed issues regarding code of conduct implementation, namely, its potential to oust traditional forms of worker organisation. As was pointed out by one of our experts:

> Critics argue that private auditing may displace enforcement of labour rights by both legitimate public authorities and collective organisations of workers. This concern is real and should be addressed systematically in compliance programmes. Compliance programmes should, concurrently with their auditing functions, seek to build the capacity of existing local public authorities and worker organisations, and avoid substituting managerial monitoring for the functions that might be played by emergent public authorities and worker

organisations. There is an inherent tension in these tasks. Managers who seek to build the capacity of workers' collective organisation may interfere with the legitimate autonomy of those organisations. The appropriate resolution of this tension cannot be left to managerial compliance officers alone but should instead be governed by policies that are fashioned through dialogue between employer and union federations (E 1).

Given that most of the information in this book is based on the experience of managers in both buyer and supplier firms, we thought we would leave them with the last words on how to implement codes in global supply chains.

According to one MNE country manager, the success of implementing a code could be improved in three ways:

- Convince somebody very high up at the supplier that this code of conduct is necessary.

- Copy someone else's standards; don't waste time doing your own. Look around and copy them.

- Set up a control system and hire the people that can support this system. If you want it to happen, you have to control.

From another MNE country manager we received a slightly more extensive list.

- Try to get easy successes at the start: do small things first.

- Priorities need to be established: you can't do everything at the same time.

- Show your determination!

- Communicate clear objectives and don't change them.

- Have one voice.

- Training is key.

- Use the incentives, for example factory rankings on code is a good tool, since 'face-saving' is a part of the local culture; 'best code compliance factory' awards can also be important for local managers.

- There are two levels of code: general, for all factories, and regulations specific to individual factories.

- The code helps managers to interpret national law, especially when there are inconsistencies.

- Take into account the national laws versus provincial and city laws.

- Quantify everything!

Finally, a CSR manager provided this even more extensive list of recommendations.

- Be transparent.

- Establish partnerships.

- Get support from employees through education.

- Get support from top management. It usually does not come from the very beginning—you must convince them, through inclusion of labour issues into the management meetings' agendas.

- Get support from factory managers. Internalisation is a key to success.

- Get the workers in the factory on your side, also through education.

- Implement a rigid compliance system, including continuous follow-up.

- Work closely with other business units.

- Be flexible; see the code of conduct as a living document.

- Share experience from other companies and learn from them, build and develop business coalitions.

- If you declare something, carry it out.

- You can't have many codes—you can have only one global code, and it should be internally consistent. Standards should to the degree possible be the same in each country. However, while implementing the code, pay attention to cross-cultural differences.

- It is not enough to write a code with high standards; you have to live up to them continuously.

- A good code can have an impact on the domestic [headquarters] operations of the company.

- Reinforcement of labour standards can be viewed as a short-term cost, but in the long term it will be one of the major profit-drivers.

Glossary

Bar code label. A printed label containing black-and-white coded images meeting industry standards for routing packages or retrieving information about the box or merchandise to which the label is attached (www.plunkettresearch.com).

Category killer. Discount retailer that offers a complete assortment in a *category* and thus dominates a category from the customer's perspective. Also known as a category specialist (www.plunkettresearch.com).

Channel. The set of all firms and relationships that get a product to market, including the original acquisition of raw material; production of the item at a manufacturing facility; distribution to a retailer; sale of the finished item to the customer; and any installation, repair or service activities that follow the sale (Abernathy *et al.* 2002).

Continuous replenishment. The practice of partnering between distribution channel members that changes the traditional replenishment process from distributor-generated purchase orders, based on economic order quantities, to the replenishment of products based on actual and forecasted product demand (www.infoaccess.net).

Contractor. Firm that provides sewing, assembly or speciality services. May also be referred to as a vendor, or supplier.

Convenience stores. Stores between 3,000 and 8,000 square feet in size providing a limited assortment of merchandise at a convenient location and time (e.g. 7-Eleven) (www.plunkettresearch.com).

Corporate social responsibility (CSR). Business for Social Responsibility (BSR), a global non-profit organisation helping companies achieve CSR, defines CSR as 'achieving commercial success in ways that honour ethical values and respect people, communities, and the natural environment'. Further, BSR states that CSR means addressing the legal, ethical, commercial and other expectations society has for business, and making decisions that fairly balance the claims of all key stakeholders. From a business perspective, the US Council for International Business (USCIB) approaches the issue of social responsibility from the point of view of the corporation as responsible individual: 'Corporate responsibility is a commitment to manage diverse roles in society—as producer, employer, customer and citizen—in a responsible and sustainable manner' (USCIB, 'Advancing Corporate Responsibility', a statement by the USCIB Corporate Responsibility Committee, November 2002).

Discount store. A general merchandise retailer offering a wide variety of merchandise, limited service and low prices (e.g. Kmart) (www.plunkettresearch.com).

Distribution centre. The customer's facility from which vendor orders are received and then distributed to the appropriate stores (www.infoaccess.net).

Efficient consumer response (ECR). A strategy in which the retailer, distributor and supplier trading partners work closely together to eliminate excess costs from the supply chain (www.infoaccess.net).

Electronic data interchange (EDI). The computer-to-computer exchange of business documents from retailer to vendor and back, such as purchase orders; a technological arrangement allowing rapid transmission of information across the supply chain. The main prerequisite for implementing EDI is the possession of common standards as well as of technological infrastructure by the value chain participants (www.plunkettresearch.com).

Full packaging. Full package is still a generic term for the sub-assembly or assembly supplier incorporating more of the supply chain in order to offer its clients increased service.

Homeworker. Workers who provide sewing or assembly services to contractors or other vendors. Homeworkers are also called the informal sector, as they are difficult to count and document.

Item 807/Chapter 98. A special provision of the tariff schedules that allows products to be partially made in the US then exported for further manufacturing processes. To qualify for Item 807/Chapter 98 the product has to be made from fabrics cut in the US but the manufacturer that imports the apparel does not have to be domestically owned or located in the US. Most Item 807/Chapter 98 operations are in the Caribbean Basin, Mexico and Latin America because of their proximity to the US.

Just-in-time (JIT). A manufacturing philosophy based on arrival of each component of a product just in time as it is assembled. It cuts non-value added tasks, cuts inventory, eliminates delay and requires near-zero defects and fast set-up times, particularly for repetitive, discrete manufacturing (www.infoaccess.net).

Lean production (also Toyotaism, post-Fordism, flexible specialisation, self-managing teams, high-performance work systems). Lean production is an assembly-line manufacturing methodology developed originally for Toyota and the manufacture of automobiles. The goal of lean production is described as 'to get the right things to the right place at the right time, the first time, while minimising waste and being open to change'. The principles of lean production enabled the company to deliver on demand, minimise inventory, maximise the use of multi-skilled employees, flatten the management structure, and focus resources where they were needed.

Lean retailing. Concept of providing frequent shipments on the basis of ongoing replenishment orders placed by the retailer. Orders are made based on real-time sales information at the stock keeping unit (SKU) level, that is, collected at the retailer's registers via bar code. This system reduces the need for retailers to stockpile large inventories.

Living wage. The generally accepted definition of a living wage is a wage sufficient for workers to meet their basic material needs.

Logistics. The function of sourcing and distributing material and product in the proper place and in proper quantities (www.infoaccess.net).

Maquiladoras or maquila. Offshore assembly plants that assemble cut cloth and provide only the labour for sewing. Typically associated with Caribbean and Latin American production as a result of the 807 provisions in the US tariff regulations.

Multifiber Arrangement/Agreement (MFA). Agreement reached in 1974, which provided for bilateral agreements between trading nations that would regulate trade in apparel and textiles. It is set to expire in 2005.

Non-governmental organisation. The World Bank defines NGOs as 'private organisations that pursue activities to relieve suffering, promote the interests of the poor, protect the environment, provide basic social services, or undertake community development' (Operational Directive 14.70). In wider usage, the term NGO can be applied to any non-profit organisation independent from government.

North American Free Trade Agreement (NAFTA). Regional trade agreement between the US, Canada and Mexico that includes in its provisions the phase-out of most tariffs and non-tariff barriers on industrial products over ten years, including on all textiles and apparel items that have regional content.

Original equipment manufacturing (OEM). Also called full-package production.

Point-of-sale (POS) terminals. A cash register that has the capability to electronically scan a bar code with a laser and electronically record a sale; also known as computerised checkout (www.plunkettresearch.com).

Profit margin. Net profit after taxes divided by net sales (www.plunkettresearch.com).

Quotas. Regulated quantities that can be traded.

SA 8000. A workplace standard that covers all key labour rights and certifies compliance through independent, accredited auditors. To fulfil its mission, SAI convenes key multi-sectoral stakeholders to develop consensus-based voluntary standards; accredits qualified organisations to verify compliance; promotes understanding and implementation of such standards worldwide (www.sa8000.org).

SPO. Social performance objectives, a set of goals covering various social and labour issues; the research project will focus on freedom of association, collective bargaining, child and forced labour, non-discrimination and equal opportunity. SPOs may also relate to working conditions, remuneration, occupational safety and health, and other aspects of HRM.

Stock keeping unit (SKU): An identification number assigned to a unique item by the retailer (www.plunkettresearch.com).

Subcontractor. Firm hired by contractor to provide sewing, assembly or speciality services.

Supply chain management. The optimisation of the entire fulfilment process, from consumer purchase back through retail store, retail distribution centre, wholesaler, manufacturer distribution centre, factory, raw material/component supplier, etc. for greater responsiveness, speed and efficiency (www.infoaccess.net).

Tariffs. Taxes imposed on imported goods.

Total quality management (TQM). A structured system for satisfying internal and external customers and suppliers by integrating the business environment, continuous improvement, and breakthroughs with development, improvement and maintenance cycles while changing organisational culture (www.iqd.com).

Vendor. Any firm such as a manufacturer or distributor from which a retailer obtains merchandise (www.plunkettresearch.com).

Appendix 1
International instruments

International Labour Office

Conventions

Hours of Work (Industry) Convention, 1919 (No. 1)

Weekly Rest (Industry) Convention, 1921 (No. 14)

Minimum Wage-Fixing Machinery Convention, 1928 (No. 26)

Forced Labour Convention, 1930 (No. 29)

Freedom of Association and Protection of the Right to Organise Convention, 1948 (No. 87)

Right to Organise and Collective Bargaining Convention, 1949 (No. 98)

Equal Remuneration Convention, 1951 (No. 100)

Discrimination (Employment and Occupation) Convention, 1958 (No. 111)

Minimum Wage Fixing Convention, 1970 (No. 131)

Minimum Wage Convention, 1973 (No. 138)

Migrant Workers (Supplementary Provisions) Convention, 1975 (No. 143)

Occupational Health and Safety Convention, 1981 (No. 155)

Other references

Constitution of the International Labour Organization, 1919

Declaration of Philadelphia, 1944 (Annex to the ILO Constitution)

Tripartite Declaration of Principles concerning Multinational Enterprises and Social Policy, adopted by the Governing Body of the International Labour Office at its 240th Session, Geneva, November 1977, as amended at its 279th Session, Geneva, November 2000

Official Bulletin (Geneva: ILO, 1981), Vol. LXIV, Series A, No. 1, pp. 89-90

Official Bulletin (Geneva: ILO, 1986). Vol. LXIX, Series A, No. 3, pp. 196-97

Conditions of Work Digest: Working Times Around the World (Geneva: ILO, 1995)

Instruments of the United Nations

Universal Declaration of Human Rights, adopted by UN General Assembly resolution 217 A (III) of 10 December 1948

United Nation Convention on the Elimination of All Forms of Discrimination Against Women (CEDAW), 1981, adopted by the UN General Assembly resolution 34/180 of 18 December 1979.

Convention on the Rights of the Child, adopted by UN General Assembly resolution 44/25 of 20 November 1989, entered into force 2 September 1990

United Nations Global Compact, 2000

Appendix 2
Interview schedule

1. Introduction

The object of the research project is to identify and examine the management systems used by enterprises to set, communicate, implement and evaluate social objectives in the context of globalised business operations. The enquiry will consider and will seek inputs from various levels in global supply chains, from MNE headquarters, to suppliers' regional and national offices, to factories and subcontractors. This draft interview schedule is designed to outline the questions that need to be asked of enterprises and the components of their supply chains.

The research will take the perspective of examining the implementation of firm social policies through the various cross-organisational processes on which such implementation depends. In examining these processes, the research will seek to:

- Document at which points in the various and primary organisational processes elements pertaining to the attainment of firm social performance objectives (SPOs) occur

- Establish who is involved at each of these points and what their responsibilities are with regard to SPOs

- Describe the context of the SPO system by defining broadly the processes within which it operates

- Establish the history of the SPO system, how it has evolved within the organisation and organisational processes, and what has driven these changes

1.1. Definitions

CSR. Corporate social responsibility.

Management function. A grouping of tasks within an enterprise which typically oversees the operation of a system, but may not be exclusively involved in that system.

Process. A process is a set of tasks that work to achieve an objective.

SPOs. Social performance objectives, a set of goals covering various social and labour issues; the research project will focus on freedom of association, collective bargaining, child and forced labour, non-discrimination and equal opportunity. SPOs may also relate to working conditions, remuneration, occupational safety and health, and other aspects of HRM.

SPO system. The object of the enquiry of the Management Systems and Decent Work research project. It includes the ways enterprises adopt, implement and evaluate social objectives.

System. A system is a set of processes that work to achieve a set of objectives.

1.2. Objectives of first day

- Introduce the research project

- Develop a general understanding of the firm to be studied, focusing on the manner in which it organises core areas such as human resources, production, design, supply chain management

- Examine the core intra- and inter-organisational processes with regard to how these processes impact on the attainment of SPOs

- Begin a basic mapping of processes that impact on CSR, as well as the mapping of relationships between the various functional groups within the organisations studied and their various external collaborators, i.e. suppliers

1.3. Organisational processes and SPO system

In examining the implementation of SPOs, the research team will be looking at cross-organisational processes, a listing of which is given below. Specifically, these are processes that are assumed, in a supply chain-based organisation, to stretch beyond the MNE corporate boundaries and in some way impact on the activities of the suppliers and the achievement of SPOs.

- First of all, can we have a copy of your SPOs (code of conduct)? How are these set out to staff and suppliers or others concerned? (For ILO, which of these cover core standards?)

- As an overview, *briefly* answer the following questions considering each process (these points will be covered in more detail in later sections addressing individual processes):
  - How are these processes (listed below) organised at your firm?
  - How does each of these processes contribute to the achievement of the SPOs?
    - Strategy and policy development
    - Communication
    - Information
    - HRM
    - Purchasing and logistics

- Marketing and design
- Manufacturing
- Monitoring and performance feedback
- Integration
- Stakeholder consultation

1.4. Functional involvement in CSR

Outline the tasks that each of the following functions performs for the achievement of SPOs.

- HRM
- CSR
- Purchasing
- Supply chain
- Manufacturing
- Marketing

Have you established cross-functional teams which oversee the SPO process? Please describe them.

1.5. Process and relationship mapping

For each of the primary organisational processes and CSR, to be considered in the following sections, attempt to draw out the various relationships of those involved in the process as it relates to SPO, both within the organisation and between the corporate representatives and those external (for example, suppliers) to the organisation.

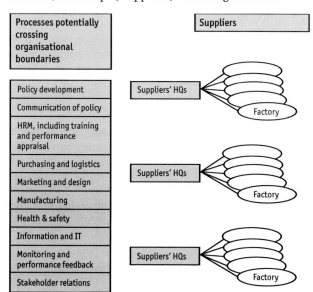

1.6. Framework of SPO system

The SPO system can be seen to incorporate four elements, closely mirroring the elements of the total quality management's Plan–Do–Act cycle. For each of the processes considered in the following sections, consider where in the following overview of the CSR system these processes impact on SPOs.

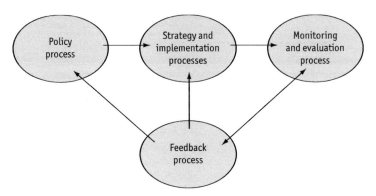

2. CSR function

2.1. Opening questions

This type of question will be asked at the start of each interview.

- What are your professional background, experience and qualifications?

- To whom do you report? (Refer to organisational chart.)

- Do you or members of your function ever visit overseas supplier factories to discuss operational issues or compliance issues?

- If so, is this on a regular programmed basis or on a required basis?

- What would be the three to four most important performance indicators by which your performance would be evaluated and rewarded?

- What has been your experience with the SPO system at your company and what is your role in this system?

- As a general introduction, what does the CSR function do?

2.2. CSR specific questions

- Does the CSR function undertake or oversee any of the following? (Points covered in greater detail in later sections)

- Cross process co-ordination
- Monitoring
- Policy development
- Training
- Information
- Other

- How does the CSR function work with other functional areas; which are its primary counterparts in other parts of the organisation?

- Where does top-level responsibility lie for SPOs?

- How many staff are part of the CSR group or organisation, and where are they located? Are these direct reports or is there a matrix management structure?

- What are the competences required of this staff? Are these mostly in place?

- Does the CSR function have specialists from other functional/process areas working within it? Which functional areas? What is the CSR staff background? Are they mainly specialists or do they typically come from other functional areas of your firm?

- What is the history of the CSR group, when was it established, and how have its roles and relationships changed over time? What were the forces behind these changes?

- Is it changing still and how do you foresee CSR in your company in ten years?

- What is the direct cost of the CSR function in your company? Is this cost based just on the cost of the CSR group or in terms of cost at all levels within the supply chain where costs are incurred?

- How is this cost viewed within the organisation: as an investment or as a cost?

- What has made it effective and what would make it more effective?

3. Integration of systems process

3.1. Overview of integration

We would like to explore how your company achieves integration between the various functional activities that constitute your supply chain across both production and support functions. The functions of manufacturing, logistics and procurement usually represent the core activities of a company's production process.

- How is integration achieved between the functions that contribute to the production process; in other words, which integrating mechanisms are used to harmonise the activities of these functions, e.g. a cross-functional co-ordination group, a supply chain manager?

- Is authority for this activity formalised and vested in a particular function, e.g. manufacturing, logistics?

- How do these integrating activities extend to your external supply chain of suppliers, contractors and subcontractors, e.g. purchasing, logistics, manufacturing?

- Which of these core activities of production maintain direct contact with suppliers, contractors and subcontractors, e.g. all of them or just purchasing or other?

- The supporting functions of CSR, HRM, marketing and finance all make some contribution to the core production process. In the case of CSR how does this happen?

- How do these integrating mechanisms relate to the SPO system, i.e. the provision of advice on SPO policy impacting the production process; in other words, the selection of suppliers?

- How does the CSR process relate to the production process? How does the CSR process relate to product design?

- Alternatively, does CSR simply relate to the external production process, e.g. monitoring, evaluation and reporting on SPOs?

A fairly recent development has been the establishment of a senior executive position of supply chain management, in some companies, to achieve the integration referred to in the above questions.

3.2. Supply chain management function

- Does your company have or contemplate having a separate function for supply chain management (SCM); in other words, a VP or department for SCM or cross-firm co-ordination?

- If so, in broad terms, what is its responsibility?

- Does it exercise authority over other supply chain components, e.g. manufacturing, logistics and purchasing?

- Does it extend to suppliers outside the internal supply chain?

- Does the supply chain management function have any responsibility for monitoring and evaluation of external suppliers?

- Does the supply chain management function have a role in developing SPO policy for the internal as well as external supply chain?

- How do the supporting functions of information and communications technologies (ICT) support the management of supply chains?

4. Policy development process

4.1. Overall policy development in the organisation

- In brief, how does the organisation develop corporate-wide policies: both in general and with regard to SPOs?
- Who does the policy development process include?
- What steps are involved in the decision-making process leading up to policy formation?
- How does the organisation maintain policy coherence?

4.2. Specific questions on SPO development

- What labour and social SPOs apply to your suppliers, contractors and subcontractors?
- Are SPOs part of the strategic planning process or a separate process?
- When deciding to develop a policy on social performance, what motivated you? (Relate to reply from the questionnaire if they replied.)
  - Analysis of risk (can we obtain a copy?)
  - Philanthropy
  - Pressure
  - Image
  - Other
- How long have policies for SPOs existed?
- What is the history or series of steps in the evolution of this policy and its formation?
- Which processes are involved in SPO development?
- How often are SPO policies reviewed and who approves them?
- What definitions and guidance documents exist to help clarify the policy?
- Have indicators been established for measuring progress in achieving the policy?
- Do you set targets for the policy? What are they?
- What stakeholders do you involve in SPO development?
- What reference points do you use in the development of SPOs?
- How do you maintain policy coherence on the SPOs through your supply chain?

5. Communication process

5.1. Process overview

- How are corporate-wide policies or decisions communicated at your company? Who is responsible for communication of corporate-wide policies?

- What media are typically involved (e.g. intranet, e-mail, corporate newsletter, other)?

- Is there a corporate mission statement or statement of values? Can we get a copy? How is it incorporated into the practices of the company?

- What are the primary themes that run through communication at the company (e.g. speed, performance, quality . . .)?

5.2. Responsibility for communication

- Which function has responsibility for internal communication of SPO policy?
  - CSR
  - HRM
  - Other _____

- In each case, what role does this group have?

5.3. SPO internal communication

- Which individuals are informed of the SPOs?
  - Managers at HQ (in which functions?)
  - Managers at production facilities
  - Supplier's managers
  - Employees at production facilities
  - Employees at HQ
  - Employees of suppliers

- How are they informed of the SPOs?

- How are SPO policies communicated within the company?
  - Policy manuals
  - SPO training sessions
  - Publications
  - Videos
  - Other

- May we have copies of these materials?

5.4. SPO external communication

- How are SPO policies communicated to suppliers?
  - Contractual provisions only
  - Contractual provisions and training for supplier management
  - Other _____
  - Can we see examples of contractual provisions?

- How are SPO policies communicated to suppliers' workers, if at all?
  - Information sessions
  - Through unions
  - Publications
  - Other

- Who has responsibility for communicating SPO policy to suppliers, their workers and unions?
  - CSR only
  - Purchasing only
  - CSR and purchasing
  - Others

- Do you have a method for checking communication effectiveness with the various parties for whom the communication is intended?

- What means are used for communicating with the general public regarding SPOs and their application? What is the role of the company's annual report? Is there an annual social report or such document?

- Again, may we have copies or examples for each: reports, documents for communicating to suppliers, employees of suppliers, corporate employees and the like?

6. Information management process

6.1. Opening questions

- Could you please describe the company's information systems?
  - Degree of centralisation
  - Types of information
  - Computerisation
  - Degree of integration
- How are they integrated?

- Where does responsibility lie for different subject areas of the information system?
  - Thematic areas of information
  - Collection
  - Input
  - Analysis
- How does the overall information system of the company contribute to the SPO system?
- How is SPO information—from internal and external sources—collected? Are they integrated into the performance monitoring system of the company; if so, where?
- Can you help us map the information relationships within the company with respect to the SPO system?
- What function/unit/person has responsibility for the management of information systems relevant to the achievement of the SPOs in the supply chain?
- Whose work relies on these SPO-related systems (e.g. purchasing, marketing, planning . . .)?
- How have the systems at your company evolved, both in general and with regard to SPOs?

6.2. Maintenance

- Who is involved in the maintenance (inputting, analysing, collecting) of a database on the labour/social practices of your suppliers, if such a database exists?
- Is the SPO information computerised?
- How often is the information in the database updated?
  - Daily
  - Weekly
  - Bi-weekly
  - Monthly
  - Annually
  - When required/occasionally
- What type of information is contained in the database or dataset?
  - Monitoring reports
  - Statistics
  - Analysis of monitoring reports
  - Corrective action request sheets
  - Corrective action timetables

6.3. Access

- Can those working with different systems or functions access the labour and social information on the suppliers with which you deal?
- Which systems require access to SPO information for the fulfilment of their SPO-related tasks?
- Which systems or functions can access and use the relevant SPO information?

6.4. Structure

- What information does the information system track?
- What are the data fields?
- What indicators does it use?
- Does it generate reports?

7. Monitoring and evaluation process

7.1. General questions

- What general monitoring and evaluation systems exist in the enterprise?
- What monitoring and evaluation systems exist which work with the company's supply chain?
- What is the relationship between SPO monitoring and evaluation and these more general systems?

7.2. Mechanisms and their structure

- What are the major mechanisms for monitoring SPO policy?
  - Site inspections
  - Records audit
  - Third-party audits
  - Complaint mechanisms
  - National Labour Inspection systems
  - Other
- Could we get a copy of any monitoring guides you may have, as well as a sample monitoring report or any other reports generated?

- What are your functional responsibility, skills and involvement in the SPO process?

- Who is involved in the major mechanisms?

- Who or which group is responsible for carrying out monitoring of SPO policy?

- Who or which group(s) is responsible for carrying out evaluation of the policy?

- Who or which group(s) is responsible for developing and implementing feedback?

- What technical skills and other competences are required for the monitoring process to be effective? Which systems require these skills?

7.3. Site inspections

- How does monitoring take place?
  - Scheduled site visits
  - Unscheduled site visits
  - Audits of supplier-submitted reports
  - Ongoing inspection by production managers
  - Ongoing inspection by workers
  - Ongoing inspection by worker organisations

- Do documents exist to guide monitors?

- What guidance is given on monitoring the core standards? (Could be determined from documentation.)

7.4. Evaluation

- How are evaluations of supplier, contractor and subcontractor performed?

- Who is involved in supplier, contractor and subcontractor evaluations?

7.5. Feedback

- What are the feedback sub-processes of the SPO process?

- How often are recommendations or information fed back to the CSR process and its sub-processes?

- Is there a standardised format for the feedback reports? Could we see examples?

- What would be the circulation of such reports?

- If violations of the SPOs are detected, what mechanisms are in place to ensure they are corrected (e.g. correction order issued, target date for correction, inspection to ensure compliance with SPO policy, training provided, etc.)?

8. Stakeholder management process

8.1. Stakeholder selection

- What stakeholders have been involved with the SPOs?
  - International NGOs
  - Local NGOs
  - National trade unions
  - Employees
  - Employers' or industry associations
  - National or local government
  - Other

- How do you select the stakeholders you would like to work with?

- What criteria do you use to select the stakeholders you work with?

8.2. Types of possible involvement

- Are stakeholders (each group) integrated into all the different processes operating in a company that address the SPOs?

- Which processes are they involved in?

- How are they involved in policy systems?

- How are stakeholders involved in information systems?

- How are stakeholders involved in the HRM process contribution to the SPOs?

- How are stakeholders involved in the marketing process contribution to the SPOs?

- How are stakeholders involved in the purchasing and logistics process?

- How are stakeholders involved in the manufacturing process?

- How are stakeholders involved in the monitoring and performance feedback process contribution to SPOs?

8.3. Stakeholder roles

- Specifically with regard to the above questions concerning stakeholder involvement in different processes:
    - Are they receivers of information?
    - Do they play an active part in the management of the process?
    - Are they informed of the activities of the process?
    - Do they provide inputs into the process?
    - Are they involved in the evaluation of any processes?
    - Are they involved in the development of any processes?

- Which specific groups have you involved in your management system? May we have permission to contact them?

9. Manufacturing process

9.1. Manufacturing specific

- To what extent does manufacturing manage the supply chain function in your company?

- Who controls the integration of supply chain activities between manufacturing, purchasing and logistics?

- Does this supply chain management function extend to your external suppliers?

- If it extends to external suppliers, in what types of activities do you interact with suppliers?
    - Manufacturing methods/systems
    - Quality
    - Workflows
    - Plant layout
    - OHS issues
    - Other

- How, if at all, do you assist your suppliers with meeting your quality standards in the mass manufacture of your products?

9.2. SPO and manufacturing

Your company outsources the mass-manufacturing of your product to suppliers in developing countries that invariably have lower mandated labour standards than the country in which your corporate offices are based.

- Is manufacturing involved in the setting of SPO policies regarding work standards and policies?

- Do you maintain a physical presence in these plants?

- Is manufacturing involved in the implementation of SPO policy in suppliers' plants?

- Is manufacturing involved in monitoring and evaluation of SPO policy in suppliers' plants?

- In the event of non-compliance with your SPO, does manufacturing get involved in corrective measures?

10. Purchasing and logistics process

10.1. Selection of suppliers

- To what extent, if any, do the company's SPO policies have an impact on the work of purchasing and logistics?

- Do SPO policy considerations form a part of the criteria for selecting suppliers from developing countries?

- Do you have standardised selection criteria that include specific SPO policy objectives? If so, can we see it?

- Who in purchasing and logistics are directly involved with the visitation and selection of suppliers from developing countries?

- What are the primary skills required of these people? Does there need to be any awareness or understanding of developing country/supplier issues?

- How is the performance of purchasers and buyers evaluated? What are the criteria for good performance? Does it include SPO matters?

- Does the CSR group have a role in the selection of suppliers? If so, what is its role?

- Who has the final authority to select suppliers?

10.2. Purchasing strategy

Traditionally, purchasing has followed a strategy of spreading risk over a number of suppliers who compete with one another on the basis of lowest cost at an acceptable level of quality.

- Is this the major consideration in the selection of new suppliers?

- Could you outline the purchasing procedures and steps in a typical purchasing situation? How do these vary and why?

- What are the primary factors driving your purchasing decisions?

- In the selection of new suppliers, do you ever require SPO improvements to be made before placing an order? Could you give us an example?

- What consistency and stability in order placement do you provide to encourage a new supplier to upgrade their facilities and work practices to meet your standards?

- Is your policy designed as an ongoing guide for suppliers to meet your social policy objectives?

- How would you balance cost and quality goals of purchasing with the SPO? For example, to meet the competitive requirements of cost and quality, suppliers may be encouraged to do the minimum in SPO areas such as remuneration, working conditions, hours of work, etc.

- When a supplier contract is terminated, what are the usual reasons (e.g. cost, quality, code violations)?

- Who makes the termination decision (e.g. purchasing alone, CSR alone, purchasing and CSR)?

- Who has the final authority to terminate a supplier?

- What procedures do you use to prevent the termination of a supplier (e.g. requirements to initiate corrective adjustments, various problem-solving techniques)?

- When you decide to expand the supply chain into a new country, which considerations are most important? Rank in order of importance.
  - Political stability/risk
  - Availability of low-cost labour
  - Human rights record of country
  - Infrastructure, e.g. roads, transport, energy supply
  - Labour standards
  - Speed to markets

10.3. Information systems and purchasing

- What role(s) does the purchasing and logistics system/function have in the management of information systems?

- Are you involved in the maintenance (inputting, analysing, discussing, collecting) of a database on the labour/social practices of your suppliers?

- Can those working in the purchasing and logistics system access the labour and social information on the suppliers with which you deal?

- Do you receive information from those maintaining the database?
- Does the person who has final authority to select suppliers have access to and time to use the information on the labour/social practices of suppliers?

10.4. Training of suppliers

- Is the purchasing and logistics system function responsible for training supplier, contractor and subcontractor managers on how to apply and achieve the SPOs?
- How often is management training done at head office, supplier, contractor and subcontractor levels?
- Do management induction courses include training on the SPOs?
- What materials are used (e.g. managers' and trainers' kits)? May we have a copy?

10.5. Stakeholder relations and purchasing

- Does purchasing and logistics work with any of the corporate stakeholders?
  - Employees
  - Trade unions
  - International NGOs
  - Local NGOs
- What other functions, apart from purchasing and logistics, may be involved in country/supplier selection?
- Who has final authority to make the decision as to which countries to source supply from?
- How do you incorporate the labour and human rights record of the country into country selection considerations?
  - Country ratification of UN/regional standards
  - Assessment of UN and regional intergovernmental organisations' reports and findings
  - Assessment of non-governmental organisations' reports and recommendations
  - Other

11. Marketing process

11.1. Marketing overview

- Marketing, with its activities of product development, marketing research and demand forecasting, is clearly important to the core production process. Is the following representative of the process?

  Marketing research suggests style → product development produces design → manufacturing produces a prototype → suppliers produce bulk production → logistics handle distribution → marketing and sales handle pricing and promotion.

- Do marketing activities have SPO implications (e.g. pricing, promotion)?

- Do marketing activities extend to the external supply chain?

11.2. Marketing organisation

- Is product design a specific marketing responsibility? Where is it located?

- Does your company use a product manager system? If so:
  - How and by whom is product management co-ordinated and controlled?
  - What kind of system?
  - What is the range of responsibilities of a product manager?
  - Who do product managers report to?
  - Do product managers exercise authority across functional lines in the supply chain?
  - Does product management extend to external suppliers?
  - Is product management a formal part of the supply chain management function?

11.3. Marketing and SPO

- Do SPO considerations figure into your marketing and design strategies? If so, how?

- Do the marketing and design functions have any direct interface with your overseas suppliers?

- If so, could you describe what that consists of?

- Does the CSR function have marketing and design expertise within their group?

- Does marketing and design have a direct input into SPO policy formulation?

11.4. Image management

- What commercial impact does your company's image for social responsibility have on your company?

- What means of monitoring the image held by customers and others is in place?

- What does the company do to improve its social responsibility image, other than attempting to reach SPOs?

- Do you have any material used to communicate to consumers and others of the company's socially responsible approach?

- How has this approach to image management changed with time?

12. Human resource management process

12.1. Internal role of HRM

- Please discuss the development and implementation of internal policies in relation to staffing, training and development, performance management, remuneration, termination, promotion, EHS and equal employment opportunities.

- Is HRM primarily responsible for internal SPO policy initiatives in relation to the above management systems?

- What role does CSR play in relation to internal SPO policy development and implementation?

- Is there a cross-functional approach to internal SPO policy development?

- Who has the final authority for internal SPO policy?

- Is HRM involved in setting HR performance targets, particularly those related to social policy objectives?

- Do you have any material documenting HR-related internal social policies, their results, the feedback managers receive on their SPO-related performance, or other similar material?

12.2. HRM in the supply chain

- To what extent does HRM and its internal subsystems, mentioned above, influence and participate in the development and implementation of SPO policy as it relates to external suppliers in developing countries?

- Is this the primary responsibility of CSR or some other group?

- If so, what is the role of HRM in this process?

- Do internal HRM systems and practices form the basis for SPO policy for external suppliers?

- Are internal SPO practices appropriate for external suppliers (e.g. policies concerning work hours, freedom of association, etc.)?

- Are the criteria in your policy patterned after internal HRM practices in relation to SPOs?

12.3. Training

- Is the HRM function involved in training of managers in developing countries on how to work towards the SPOs? May we have copies of any materials they may use?

- Which function is responsible for training supplier, contractor and subcontractor managers in how to apply and achieve the SPO?

- Which individuals are trained with respect to the SPO?
    - Managers at HQ (in which functions?)
    - Managers at production facilities
    - Suppliers' managers
    - Employees at production facilities
    - Employees at HQ

- How are policies communicated?

- How often is management training done at head office, supplier, contractor and subcontractor levels?

- Do management induction courses for a) corporate staff and b) supplier managers include training on the SPOs?

- What materials are used (e.g. managers' and trainers' kits)? May we have a copy?

- Does the communication system incorporate the use of stakeholders in training managers or employees?
    - Employees
    - Trade unions
    - International NGOs
    - Local NGOs
    - Employer and industry organisations
    - Local government
    - Suppliers and contractors

- Similarly, how are HRM functions integrated into the production process?

- Internally, one would assume that HRM makes a major contribution to: staffing, training and development, performance appraisal, remuneration and benefits, OSH and EEO considerations. Is this the case in your company?

- Do the HRM contributions extend to the external supply chain in terms of SPO policies related to their expertise? How does this happen?

12.4. Monitoring

- To what extent is HRM involved in monitoring the SPOs?
- Is HRM involved in the development of monitoring methodologies?
- Is HRM involved in the actual monitoring?
- Is HRM involved in the SPO evaluation of suppliers, contractors and subcontractors?
- Does HRM make the decision alone?
- Does HRM make the decision in consultation with other functions?

12.5. Extending SPO to the suppliers

Your company employs advanced HRM systems and practices, internally, to protect your investment in and to add value to high-quality employees.

- Are modern HRM practices appropriate for your developing-country suppliers?

- Does your company attempt to help suppliers develop their HRM practices, considering the value of a stable workforce with an enhanced skill base? Does the company see this, at least in part, as part of its responsibility? If so, how do you go about doing it?

- Does the HRM function deal with any issues of industrial relations down the supply chain, and if so, how?

12.6. HRM general questions

Questions relating to information systems and information technology:

- What role(s) does the HRM system/function have in the management of information systems?

- Are you involved in the maintenance (inputting, analysing, discussing, collecting) of a database on the labour/social practices of your suppliers?

- Can those working in the purchasing and logistics system access the labour and social information on the suppliers with which you deal?

- Do you receive information from those maintaining the database?

- Does the person who has final authority to select suppliers have access to and time to use the information on the labour/social practices of suppliers?

12.7. Integration of SPO

- How does the company ensure a balance of interests from purchasing and logistics, CSR and HRM in relation to what is required of suppliers to manage their business (cost, quality, speed) as well as SPO targets?

- Are there potentially conflicting interests?

- Do you use some sort of integrating mechanism? If so, could you explain it to us?

- Who has final authority to say what HRM SPO policy initiatives will apply to your suppliers?

- What is the HRM expertise on the CSR function's staff and what is their role in working on HRM issues?

- Is HRM involved in decisions to terminate suppliers for code violations?

- Is HRM involved in the evaluation of new suppliers? If so, in what way?

- Is HRM involved in assessment of potential new countries in which the supply chain could be extended? If so, in what way?

- Is HRM involved in preparing corrective action plans to help suppliers better meet SPOs?

12.8. Additional material

As mentioned at various points, it would be useful to have other material, if possible before our visit:

- Annual report

- Organigrams

- Mission and SPO statements

- SPO performance reports at field level or corporate overviews

Appendix 3
Experts' comments on the interview schedule: suggested additional questions

Expert 1

1. Static versus dynamic processes

The current list of questions seems to reflect a view of the corporation and its supply chains that is relatively static, at least with respect to SPOs. This view may be accurate for some or even most of the corporations and supply chains that we're exploring. But if the corporation's SPO implementation is a dynamic process—or if corporations want the process to become more dynamic—then additional or re-inflected questions may be appropriate. There's good reason to believe that a dynamic system—and a self-consciously dynamic system—achieves best practice.

What do I mean by 'static'? The current list of questions embodies the following view of SPO implementation: Some actor(s) near the 'top' or 'centre' of the corporation—whether SPO or HRM or other policy-makers at the HQ level—devises the SPO code and implementation protocols (see Sections 4.1, 4.2 of interview schedule). The code and protocols are then 'communicated to' lower level or peripheral managers, functional departments, supply chain managers and factory stakeholders (Sections 5.1, 5.2, 5.3). The latter actors may also undergo 'training' in the code and protocols by SPO, HRM or other top and centre actors, and may receive 'feedback'. Top and centre managers receive 'information' about code implementation, through monitoring (Section 6.1, 7).

In this view, the code and implementation protocols seem relatively static, once devised. Hence, the flow of information need only be a two-step or three-step process: first, information about the code and its implementation (including any training that may occur) is transmitted from top and centre to the bottom or the periphery. Then, information about the degree of code implementation, to the extent it can be extracted, is transmitted back to the top and centre. A third, subsidiary information flow, is 'feedback' to the SPO sub-processes.

If these two or three steps blur into a single process, however, then upward and downward 'transmissions' of information may transform into dialogue and deliberation among upper and lower actors. The consequence may well be that the code—and methods for implementing the code—changes over time. In implementing action plans to correct code violations, the folks 'on the ground' learn about what works and what does not work. Given resource constraints, they may need to prioritise their corrective efforts and therefore reach new understandings of what code provisions are most important to different workforces and most susceptible to managerial reform at the supplier level. They learn how to create indicators for qualitative labour conditions, and how to improve those indicators over time. In vertical discussions with folks at the top—and horizontal discussions with ground-level folks working in other countries and with other suppliers, discussions that may be co-ordinated by the folks at the top— there is even more potential for learning based on comparative experience, and therefore further potential and incentive to continually change and improve codes and implementation methods. In these ways, the SPO system becomes dynamic rather than static (Sabel 1994).

Implications for questions

When we ask questions that now refer to 'communicating' policies downwards, 'training' downwards about current policies, and 'information' transmitted upwards or 'feedback' transmitted downwards, we should perhaps be attentive to communication networks that embody dialogue and deliberation rather than mere information transmission. We should be attentive to whether these networks encourage learning and revision based on discussion about which methods of code implementation work best and which code provisions are given the highest priority by local stakeholders. We should also be attentive to efforts by corporations to co-ordinate discussion of comparative performance among different supply chains and factories.

2. Policing versus collaboration versus collusion

The current list of questions reflects a view of standard operating procedure (SOP) implementation that might be termed a 'compliance' or 'policing' mode of implementation. In this view, supply chain managers seek information about whether factories are 'violating' the (relatively static) code and seek to impose 'corrective action', perhaps under the threat of terminating the supplier's contract (Section 7.5, 9.2, 10.2). The 'policing' mode stands in contrast to a 'collaborative' mode of encouraging suppliers to meet or exceed code standards. If, in fact, code implementation is a dynamic process, then supply chain managers may collaborate with factory stakeholders to ensure that they aim at a moving target (that is, the ever-improving code) or that they *create* the moving target by exceeding existing code standards.

In the 'policing' mode, supply chain managers place their emphasis on determining whether existing code rules have been violated by suppliers and on threatening penalties that will produce corrective action. In the 'collaborative' mode, supply chain managers are more concerned about putting 'remediation' systems in place; that is, broader organisational changes that will yield long-term improvement of suppliers' labour conditions and, perhaps, long-term improvements in quality and efficiency (Sturm 2001). In these remediation systems, supply chain managers are oriented towards collaborative, organisational problem-solving to improve labour conditions rather than policing and penalties (Frenkel and Scott unpublished).

A third mode of SOP implementation—'collusion'—is outwardly similar to the collaborative mode. In the collusive mode, as in the collaborative mode, supply chain managers and local stakeholders develop close, dialogic relationships. But such relationships carry the danger that the parties will 'collude' in weak compliance efforts and exaggerated reports of improvements rather than in continual improvement.

Implications for questions

We should be attentive to the qualitative tone of relationships between supply chain managers and factory stakeholders. Are suppliers motivated by fear of penalties if they violate the code? Do suppliers instead view supply chain managers as positive collaborators in long-term remediation of organisational pathologies? If the latter, has the collaborative relationship become *too* cosy, suggesting that neither supply chain managers nor suppliers are sufficiently alert to labour problems?

3. Local context

The current list of questions mentions that suppliers operate in countries that have 'lower mandated standards' than in the headquarters' countries (Section 9.2). It also mentions the problem of measuring a country's conformance with ILO Conventions (Section 10.5). These important points might generate at least four lines of more detailed enquiry. The host country's economic and institutional context arises in several phases of the SPO process. First, many corporate codes in fact require suppliers to meet local labour regulations. Even if our research is focused primarily on SPO implementation of ILO standards, in many cases ILO standards are so abstract that corporate SPO programmes take local labour laws as proxies for adequate specification of those abstract ILO standards. This presents the corporate SPO programme with complex conceptual and practical issues. Should SPO country managers and the corporation's other in-country managers be trained in the host-country's labour and employment law, and the way in which local laws do or don't adequately fulfil ILO standards? Does this require creation and distribution of a simplified manual on local law, in addition to a manual on ILO standards? How does the *formal* baseline of host-country labour laws—or ILO standards—relate to the corporation's 'dynamic' and 'collaborative' effort to raise labour standards from the *practical* starting point of actual conditions and practices in the factory or the local area? Second, how do supply chain managers address the fact that different countries and different localities have widely varying labour relations and labour-market institutions, which may entail quite different action plans even when suppliers fail to comply with the same provisions of the codes? Third, how do supply chain managers address the thorny problem of host countries the labour laws of which violate ILO standards? Are supply chain managers authorised, or required, to source from factories that develop 'parallel' means of promoting standards which are otherwise not enforced (or affirmatively suppressed) in host-country law? Fourth, how do supply chain managers address another difficult question—the problem of factory managers who are trained and socialised in HRM and IR methods that differ substantially from the corporation's and from the host-country workers' and managers' expectations?

Implications for questions

Perhaps the questions raised in the previous paragraph should be added to the list, time permitting.

4. Meshing of supply chain management and suppliers

The question list is quite comprehensive on this issue (see especially Sections 3.1, 9.1, 9.2, 10.2). However, perhaps some more detailed questioning would be useful regarding the mechanisms of support, collaboration and implementation at the interface between supply chain managers and factory managers.

Implications for questions

Such questions as: Does the corporation require that there be a formal 'SPO management team' among factory managers? If so, which factory managers are expected to serve as members of the team? What forms of support of and interchange with the factory's SPO team are formally expected of supply chain managers, including internal monitors and their superiors, who deal directly with the team? Whether or not there is a formal SPO team at the supplier level, are there formal policies about which factory managers or which supply chain managers are responsible for implementation of action plans, and follow-up on corrective action required by those plans? At the interface level, what are the required modes of co-operation among production, quality control and SPO managers, within the factory and supply chains and between the two?

5. Questions of efficiency and distribution of costs and efficiency gains

The seventh question in Section 10.2 gives a good start to these issues. Again, some more detailed lines of enquiry might be useful. If supply chain managers and factory managers believe that SPO mechanisms increase efficiency, then they may be more likely to follow the 'collaboration' rather than 'policing' mode of SPO implementation. The question of allocating costs through supply contracts may also be less pressing. If managers believe that SPO mechanisms entail increased operating costs or investments, then supply chain managers may be more inclined to adopt a policing approach and factory managers may adopt a less co-operative and more resistant attitude to SPO. In any event, questions of how costs and efficiencies of SPO are distributed between the corporation and its suppliers may raise crucial matters of principle and practice that distinguish different SPO programmes.

Implications for questions

Does your SPO programme rest on any assumptions about whether it will provide efficiencies or, to the contrary, impose net costs on suppliers? Is the programme implemented as part of any broader reorganisation of the work process designed to achieve efficiencies or improve labour conditions, such as 'lean management', 'team production' or 'cellular production'? Have you implemented any mechanism to determine or verify the question of efficiencies or costs? Is the allocation of such efficiencies or costs a matter that you incorporate in your supply contracts? Have suppliers sought to incorporate the operating or investment costs of SPO into their contracts? If so, what has been your response?

6. Industrial relations and labour–management relations

Here are the central questions that might be included in the interview schedule in this area:

IR policies and collective agreements pertaining to suppliers

- Are IR policies and implementation included in the systems and functions of HRM?

- If not, which processes, functions and systems make and implement IR policy?

- Does your corporation have collective bargaining agreements (CBAs) with any employees? If so, describe the different bargaining units and CBAs.

- Has the corporation entered into a 'global compact' with a union or union federation or secretariat?

- Has the corporation entered into a 'framework agreement' with any union or federation?

- Does the corporation have works councils in any of its operations? Does the corporation have European Works Councils or other multinational works councils in any of its operations?

- In any of the CBAs, global compacts, framework agreements, works councils or other collective agreements, has the corporation agreed to enforce a code of conduct or implement any other SPO measures relating to labour rights or standards in its suppliers around the world?

SPO code and implementation pertaining to supplier IR

- How many of your suppliers have CBAs with unions?

- As to suppliers with CBAs, do unions participate in SPO processes and functions? If so, how? To what extent is the role of existing unions in SPOs dictated by host-country laws on mandatory collective bargaining and to what extent by your own SPO code and systems?

- If your production systems implement 'lean production', 'cellular production' or 'team production' as a way of achieving production efficiencies concurrently with SPOs, do you require that suppliers seek collective consultation or discussion with employees before or during implementation?

- Does your SPO system include policies on entering into purchase orders with suppliers operating in countries that prohibit collective organising or bargaining by employees, or that require unions to affiliate with the government or with a federation controlled by the government? If so, describe those policies and your experience in implementing them.

- To the extent your codes include protections of freedom of association, do you enquire into the validity of the formation of the supplier union or the validity of the CBA under host-country law or under ILO standards, as a precondition to entering into initial relationships with the supplier?

- Does your SPO system enquire into those same matters as a precondition to inclusion of the union in SPO processes and functions?

- Does your SPO system instead treat those same matters as potential issues to be addressed in code implementation, action plans and corrective plans?

- Does your SPO system require that suppliers establish some form of collective consultation or representation with their employees, where the supplier has no pre-existing union, CBA or works council?

- Does your SPO system require that suppliers establish some other form of communication channel between supplier managers and employees, where the supplier has no pre-existing union, CBA or works council that serves that function?

- Does your SPO system require that suppliers establish some form of grievance mechanism, where the supplier has no pre-existing union, CBA or works council that serves that function?

- Does your SPO system require that suppliers take a stance of neutrality towards employees attempting to organise unions?

Expert 2

1. Social accounting framework including audit and verification processes

a. Social accounting framework: general

- To what extent have you developed a social accounting framework? Are there certain social criteria you require a supplier to meet? If so, which criteria do you use when searching for and selecting new suppliers? How do you measure whether the potential supplier meets these criteria?

- Have the social criteria your company uses changed over time and do you anticipate them changing in the future? How frequently are criteria revised and updated? Has your company opted for an incremental approach towards raising labour standards?

- What form does the company's social accounting framework have? Did the company develop its own code of conduct? If so, did it incorporate each of the core ILO Conventions (freedom of association and collective bargaining; forced labour; child labour; non-discrimination)? Does your company subscribe to an existing social initiative (Ethical Trading Initiative, Global Compact, AA1000 . . .)?

b. Social auditing and verification

- **Measurement**. How is a supplier's social behaviour/adherence to labour standards measured? Is each of the labour standards considered separately? Do you use scales? Indicators? Which ones? Do you collate long-term data on a potential new supplier's social performance?

- **Tools**. Which tools are used to assess compliance with labour standards? Do your own staff members visit the suppliers' production units or do you rely solely on reports provided by the (potential/existing) supplier? Or is a semi- or completely independent body hired to check a supplier's social record? [Independent body: a (social)-auditing company such as KPMG; semi-independent e.g. SOCAM (C&A).] If the compliance report is prepared by the company itself, is this report then externally verified?

- **On-site auditing**. If a team visits a potential/existing supplier, are these on-site visits announced or unannounced? How much freedom (from the site manager's control) do auditors have when they inspect the production units? Is co-operation from production units required? How does the auditor work? Do they have a checklist of indicators and proxy indicators? Do they interview workers?

- **CSR targets**. Does your company have CSR targets and, if so, what do these include? For example, are you aiming to increase your audit work? Do you aim to increase the proportion of 'clean' suppliers by a certain amount per year? Do you aim for an overall improvement in working conditions of x per cent? Do you manage to reach these targets? What are the factors that prevent you from doing so? For example, simply the non-existence of reliable (time/quality) suppliers? The higher price of products made by 'clean' suppliers? Difficulties associated with auditing?

2. Management capacity of social accountants

- Are your auditors trained as social accountants? Do they have a prepared 'toolkit' to analyse the supplier? How much is it down to individual judgement?

- If the verification relies heavily on individual judgement, is your company interested in a more measurable method, or do you think that 1) every situation is different and it is better to rely on the judgement of the auditor; 2) it is simply impossible to create a whole kit of indicators that can be easily measured; or 3) . . .

- Are your accountants/auditors experienced in the sourcing and production of merchandise?

3. Performance and impact of management systems including audit processes

a. Questions on the company's strategy to choose its suppliers

- Who is responsible in your company for auditing the social performance of existing and potential suppliers? Does a separate team of verifiers exist or do the buyers control the social criteria put forward by your company? Who has the final decision about accepting (keeping/rejecting) a supplier?

- If you have a separate auditing team, how independently do they operate from the buyers? Who has the last say? Do the buyers suggest potential suppliers to the auditing team or do the auditing team suggest potential 'clean' suppliers to the buyers?

- The actual selection process: Is a supplier first selected on the basis of price/quality/reliability analysis, after which a 'social responsibility check' takes place? Or, are a range of similar suppliers selected and does the social audit take place before the price/quality/reliability analysis? Or, are all four factors given equal weight and analysed together?

- How is the trade-off between price and social responsibility managed? Do you work with a point system? Are there levels of social behaviour that are absolutely unacceptable, even at a very low price? Are there unacceptable levels of price even if no other 'clean' supplier is available?

- Is it possible to list in order of importance the factors that determine whether you accept (or keep) a certain supplier? Price; quality; reliability of the supplier (deliveries in time); social behaviour; environmental behaviour; political stability/government system of the country in which the company operates . . .

- Do you consider the company's current strategy on supplier choice is effective? In terms of ensuring that the suppliers are 'clean'? In terms of profitability? In terms of cost-effectiveness of the procedures?

b. Questions on the performance and the impact of the audit processes

- Is support given to suppliers to tackle problems of poor working conditions? For example, when an audit team observes infringements against the set of labour standards/criteria, does it provide help/suggestions to improve the conditions (short term/long term)? What about in the case of a major infringement? Is the contract with the supplier immediately suspended? Has there been any follow-up on what happened to a supplier company and its workers when the contract was suspended after a negative audit?

- To what extent have you engaged in capacity-building to empower supplier firms to manage labour issues, rather than just identify and react to problems shown up in the audit? For example, how do you deal with complex issues such as child labour, where an immediate, all-out ban on child labour could create worse problems by forcing children into more exploitative work? What kind of management training, tools and guidelines do you have for tackling the problems of poor labour standards at their roots?

- Have you evaluated the wider (external) implications of social standards and auditing? Has the elimination of child labour forced children into other industries?

c. Questions on the performance and impact of management systems

- To what extent have you implemented management systems for social and labour standards, or audit systems?

- To what extent does your management system align with the following criteria for social performance management systems:
  - Leadership and commitment?
  - Principles, policies, objectives and standards?
  - Evaluation and risk management procedures, including impact assessment?
  - Organisation, resources and documentation management structure with defined roles and responsibilities and a framework for social accounting?
  - Planning and implementation targets and management tools?
  - Performance review, in the form of a commitment to a regular process of reporting and stakeholder consultation, and a social audit, verification and evaluation process?

- Which departments in your company are involved? Do you have the support of top management? Are CSR and ethical sourcing key to decision-making in your company?

- Which factors determine the success of the supply chain management systems?

- How is the headquarters' social policy communicated to all parts of the firm's production network? Is the message being communicated effectively?

4. Costs and benefits, productivity and competitiveness

a. Costs and benefits

- **Costs.** Has an analysis of the direct and indirect costs of shifting to CSR management systems been made? What are the main costs related to CSR policies?
    - How are direct and indirect costs measured?

- **Benefits.** Has an analysis of the direct and indirect benefits of shifting to CSR management systems been made? What are the main benefits related to CSR policies?
    - How are direct and indirect benefits measured?

b. Productivity

- Has your company noticed any productivity increase among its suppliers following the introduction of new labour standards requirements? How did this manifest itself (shorter delivery times, better quality . . .)?

- Has the adoption of a CSR management system increased the productivity of the company? In what sense? How do you measure an increase of productivity and how do you determine the extent to which this is the result of improved working conditions? Has your company done such a study?

- Can you point to particular labour issues which have led to an increase in productivity? If so, which ones? (For example, more efficient use of the labour force [adults versus children], an increase in motivation . . .)

c. Competitiveness

- To what extent do the costs of a social accounting system and a possible increase in prices asked by the supplier influence the competitive position of the company?

- To what extent do higher labour standards increase the labour costs of a product? How do improved working conditions influence the competitive position of a (supplier) company?

- CSR literature points to eight areas that determine the competitive position of a company, and which could be influenced by CSR:[68] financial performance,

---

68   Business for Social Responsibility, 'Introduction to Corporate Social Responsibility', White Paper, www.bsr.org.

operation costs, brand image and reputation, customer sales and loyalty, productivity and quality, attracting and retaining employees, regulatory oversight and access to capital. To what extent are these areas positively/negatively influenced by your company's CSR policy and practice?

Expert 3

In what follows I suggest question areas rather than providing the exact questions. This can come later. These question areas have been developed after reading the Business and Decent Work Interview Schedule. I have assumed the existence of a code. If there is no code we should explore policies and practices that bear on what is in the ILO core labour standards. Note that the question areas may apply to managers and workers' representatives or workers themselves. Again, this can be discussed later.

Contextual

1. Relationships with the global firm(s), percentage of production by revenue supplied to these firms compared with other markets. Length of time and trend in sales to the firm(s). Requirements of these firms especially around code of conduct.

2. External context: local interpretations of labour law, local labour institutions and role *vis-à-vis* the factory; local social norms affecting code principles e.g. discrimination, child labour, hours of work etc. Local labour market data—unemployment, underemployment, etc.

3. Internal context: business strategy; people strategy and policies; workforce composition by age, ethnicity and occupation; special features e.g. dorms, demographic characteristics of management (mgt); technology—age and skill requirements; characterisation of manufacturing strategy (e.g. mass, lean, etc.); and HR strategy, policies and practices. Quality of mgt–employee relations (from highly co-operative to highly conflicting).

Code development and implementation

4. Code evolution and reasons for it.

5. Responsibility for code implementation: history, qualifications and experience of the person/team involved.

6. Process of code implementation, including training; check extent of formalisation and systematic evaluation and learning processes.

7. Monitoring (including third-party) mechanisms and frequency, consequences of.

8. Learning and increasing absorptive capacity: knowledge creation, importing and sharing with regard to the code.

9. Pressures on increasing effectiveness of code implementation: role of stakeholders, for example unions, line managers, global firm managers and HR or related staff.

10. Integration of code and other processes into the socio-technical system.

11. Benefits and costs of code implementation.

12. Trend in code development—lifting the bar? Reasons for, or for not, upgrading the code requirements.

Relationships associated with the code

13. Between the global firm and the supplier. Evolution of, characterisation of, especially *vis-à-vis* the code.

14. Between senior management and those responsible for code implementation.

15. Between the code implementers and junior line managers, e.g. supervisors.

16. Between the HR department (if there is one) and code implementers (if they are different personnel).

17. Within the code implementation team or section.

18. Between workers, their unions (if present) and the code implementers. For example, use of information and consultative mechanisms such as suggestion boxes.

Key issues pertaining to code implementation and improvement

19. As defined by the various parties, including their respective priorities for change.

Data worth asking for

20. Organisation chart; market-share data; cost breakdown; workforce composition by occupation, age, gender and ethnicity or home location; copy of recent code audit; list of suppliers; copy of code; labour data, e.g. pay, turnover, absenteeism, grievances, fines, labour productivity, workforce surveys etc.; local labour market data as referred to above.

Appendix 4
Multi-stakeholder initiative codes of conduct

	SAI	FLA	WRAP	WRC	CCC	ETI
Child Labour	**Definition of child:** Any person less than 15 years of age, unless local minimum age law stipulates a higher age for work or mandatory schooling, in which case the higher age would apply. If, however, local minimum age law is set at 14 years of age in accordance with developing-country exceptions under ILO Convention No. 138, the lower age will apply. **Definition of child labour:** Any work by a child younger than the age(s) specified in the above definition of a child, except as provided for by ILO Convention No. 146. **CHILD LABOUR** 1.1 The company shall not engage in or support the use of child labour as defined above. 1.2 The company shall establish, document, maintain, and effectively communicate to personnel and other interested parties policies and procedures for remediation of children found to be working in situations which fit the definition of child labour above, and shall provide adequate support to enable such children to attend and remain in school until no longer a child as defined above. 1.3 The company shall establish, document, maintain, and effectively communicate to personnel and other interested parties policies and procedures for promotion of education for children covered under ILO Recommendation No. 146 and young workers who are subject to local compulsory education laws or are attending school, including means to ensure that no such child or young worker is employed during school hours and that combined hours of daily transportation (to and from work and school), school, and work time does not exceed 10 hours a day. 1.4 The company shall not expose children or young workers to situations in or outside of the workplace that are hazardous, unsafe, or unhealthy.	**Child Labor.** No person shall be employed at an age younger than 15 (or 14 where the law of the country of manufacture allows) or younger than the age for completing compulsory education in the country of manufacture where such age is higher than 15.	**Prohibition of Child Labor –** Manufacturers of Sewn Products will not hire any employee under the age of 14, or under the age interfering with compulsory schooling, or under the minimum age established by law, whichever is greater.	**Child Labor:** Licensees shall not employ any person at an age younger than 15 (or 14, where, consistent with ILO practices for developing countries, the law of the country of manufacture allows such exception). Where the age for completing compulsory education is higher than the standard for the minimum age of employment stated above, the higher age for completing compulsory education shall apply to this section. Licensees agree to consult with governmental, human rights, and nongovernmental organizations, and to take reasonable steps to minimize the negative impact on children released from employment as a result of implementation or enforcement of the code.	**Child labour is not used.** There shall be no use of child labour. Only workers above the age of 15 years or above the compulsory school-leaving age shall be engaged (ILO Convention No. 138). Adequate transitional economic assistance and appropriate educational opportunities shall be provided to any replaced child workers.	**4. CHILD LABOUR SHALL NOT BE USED.** 4.1 There shall be no new recruitment of child labour. 4.2 Companies shall develop or participate in and contribute to policies and programmes which provide for the transition of any child found to be performing child labour to enable her or him to attend and remain in quality education until no longer a child; 'child' and 'child labour' being defined in the appendices. 4.3 Children and young persons under 18 shall not be employed at night or in hazardous conditions. 4.4 These policies and procedures shall conform to the provisions of the relevant ILO standards.

	SAI	FLA	WRAP	WRC	CCC	ETI
Discrimination	**DISCRIMINATION** **5.1** The company shall not engage in or support discrimination in hiring, remuneration, access to training, promotion, termination or retirement based on race, caste, national origin, religion, disability, gender, sexual orientation, union membership, political affiliation, or age. **5.2** The company shall not interfere with the exercise of the rights of personnel to observe tenets or practices, or to meet needs relating to race, caste, national origin, religion, disability, gender, sexual orientation, union membership, or political affiliation. **5.3** The company shall not allow behaviour, including gestures, language and physical contact, that is sexually coercive, threatening, abusive or exploitative.	**Nondiscrimination.** No person shall be subject to any discrimination in employment, including hiring, salary, benefits, advancement, discipline, termination or retirement, on the basis of gender, race, religion, age, disability, sexual orientation, nationality, political opinion, or social or ethnic origin.	**Prohibition of Discrimination** – Manufacturers of Sewn Products will employ, pay, promote, and terminate workers on the basis of their ability to do the job, rather than on the basis of personal characteristics or beliefs.	**Nondiscrimination:** No person shall be subject to any discrimination in employment, including hiring, salary, benefits, advancement, discipline, termination or retirement, on the basis of gender, race, religion, age, disability, sexual orientation, nationality, political opinion, or social or ethnic origin.	**There is no discrimination in employment.** Equality of opportunity and treatment regardless of race, colour, sex, religion, political opinion, nationality, social origin or other distinguishing characteristic shall be provided (ILO Conventions 100 and 111).	**7. NO DISCRIMINATION IS PRACTISED.** **7.1** There is no discrimination in hiring, compensation, access to training, promotion, termination or retirement based on race, caste, national origin, religion, age, disability, gender, marital status, sexual orientation, union membership or political affiliation.

	SAI	FLA	WRAP	WRC	CCC	ETI
Health & Safety	**HEALTH & SAFETY** **3.1** The company, bearing in mind the prevailing knowledge of the industry and of any specific hazards, shall provide a safe and healthy working environment and shall take adequate steps to prevent accidents and injury to health arising out of, associated with or occurring in the course of work, by minimizing, so far as is reasonably practicable, the causes of hazards inherent in the working environment. **3.2** The company shall appoint a senior management representative responsible for the health and safety of all personnel, and accountable for the implementation of the Health and Safety elements of this standard. **3.3** The company shall ensure that all personnel receive regular and recorded health and safety training and that such training is repeated for new and reassigned personnel. **3.4** The company shall establish systems to detect, avoid or respond to potential threats to the health and safety of all personnel. **3.5** The company shall provide, for use by all personnel, clean bathrooms, access to potable water, and, if appropriate, sanitary facilities for food storage. **3.6** The company shall ensure that, if provided for personnel, dormitory facilities are clean, safe, and meet the basic needs of the personnel.	Employers shall provide a safe and healthy working environment to prevent accidents and injury to health arising out of, linked with, or occurring in the course of work or as a result of the operation of employer facilities.	**Health and Safety –** Manufacturers of Sewn Products will provide a safe and healthy work environment. Where residential housing is provided for workers, apparel manufacturers will provide safe and healthy housing.	**Health and Safety:** Licensees shall provide a safe and healthy working environment to prevent accidents and injury to health arising out of, linked with, or occurring in the course of work or as a result of the operation of Licensee facilities. In addition, Licensees must comply with the following provisions: The Licensee shall ensure that its direct operations and those of any subcontractors comply with all workplace safety and health regulations established by the national government where the production facility is located, or with Title 29 CFR of the Federal Code of Regulations, enforced by Federal OSHA (Occupational Safety and Health Administration), whichever regulation is more health protective for a given hazard. The Licensee shall ensure that its direct operations and subcontractors comply with all health and safety conventions of the International Labor Organization (ILO) ratified and adopted by the country in which the production facility is located.	**Working conditions are decent.** A safe and hygienic working environment shall be provided, and best occupational health and safety practice shall be promoted, bearing in mind the prevailing knowledge of the industry and of any specific hazards. Physical abuse, threats of physical abuse, unusual punishments or discipline, sexual and other harassment, and intimidation by the employer is strictly prohibited.	**3. WORKING CONDITIONS ARE SAFE AND HYGIENIC.** **3.1** A safe and hygienic working environment shall be provided, bearing in mind the prevailing knowledge of the industry and of any specific hazards. Adequate steps shall be taken to prevent accidents and injury to health arising out of, associated with, or occurring in the course of work, by minimising, so far as is reasonably practicable, the causes of hazards inherent in the working environment. **3.2** Workers shall receive regular and recorded health and safety training, and such training shall be repeated for new or reassigned workers. **3.3** Access to clean toilet facilities and to potable water, and, if appropriate, sanitary facilities for food storage shall be provided. **3.4** Accommodation, where provided, shall be clean, safe, and meet the basic needs of the workers. **3.5** The company observing the code shall assign responsibility for health and safety to a senior management representative.

	SAI	FLA	WRAP	WRC	CCC	ETI
Freedom of Association and Collective Bargaining	**FREEDOM OF ASSOCIATION & RIGHT TO COLLECTIVE BARGAINING** **4.1** The company shall respect the right of all personnel to form and join trade unions of their choice and to bargain collectively. **4.2** The company shall, in those situations in which the right to freedom of association and collective bargaining are restricted under law, facilitate parallel means of independent and free association and bargaining for all such personnel. **4.3** The company shall ensure that representatives of such personnel are not the subject of discrimination.	**Freedom of Association and Collective Bargaining.** Employers shall recognize and respect the right of employees to freedom of association and collective bargaining. *Note:* the FLA Charter concedes that 'Implementation of some of the standards contained in the Workplace Code may be problematic in certain countries where the rights embodied in the standards are not fully recognized or enforced either through law or practice. Despite these difficulties, one of the principal goals of the Association is to promote and encourage positive change in these countries so these standards become fully recognized, respected and enforced … With regard to the standard on freedom of association and collective bargaining contained in the Workplace Code, the Association expects all Participating Companies to address this issue by taking steps to ensure that employees have the ability to exercise these rights without fear of discrimination or punishment. Such steps include contracting with factory owners that understand and recognize these rights and who shall not affirmatively seek the assistance of state authorities to prevent workers from exercising these rights.'	**Freedom of Association and Collective Bargaining –** Manufacturers of Sewn Products will recognize and respect the right of employees to exercise their lawful rights of free association and collective bargaining.	**9. Freedom of Association and Collective Bargaining:** Licensees shall recognize and respect the right of employees to freedom of association and collective bargaining. No employee shall be subject to harassment, intimidation or retaliation in their efforts to freely associate or bargain collectively. Licensees shall not cooperate with governmental agencies and other organizations that use the power of the State to prevent workers from organizing a union of their choice. Licensees shall allow union organizers free access to employees. Licensees shall recognize the union of the employees' choice.	**Freedom of association and the right to collective bargaining are respected.** The right of all workers to form and join trade unions and to bargain collectively shall be recognised (ILO Conventions Nos. 87 and 98). Workers' representatives shall not be the subject of discrimination and shall have access to all workplaces necessary to enable them to carry out their representation functions (ILO Convention No. 135 and Recommendation No. 143). Employers shall adopt a positive approach towards the activities of trade unions and an open attitude towards organisational activities.	**2. FREEDOM OF ASSOCIATION AND THE RIGHT TO COLLECTIVE BARGAINING ARE RESPECTED.** **2.1** Workers, without distinction, have the right to join or form trade unions of their own choosing and to bargain collectively. **2.2** The employer adopts an open attitude towards the activities of trade unions and their organisational activities. **2.3** Workers representatives are not discriminated against and have access to carry out their representative functions in the workplace. **2.4** Where the right to freedom of association and collective bargaining is restricted under law, the employer facilitates, and does not hinder, the development of parallel means for independent and free association and bargaining.

	SAI	FLA	WRAP	WRC	CCC	ETI
Harass-ment or Abuse	**DISCIPLINARY PRACTICES** **6.1** The company shall not engage in or support the use of corporal punishment, mental or physical coercion, and verbal abuse.	**Harassment or Abuse.** Every employee shall be treated with respect and dignity. No employee shall be subject to any physical, sexual, psychological or verbal harassment or abuse.	**Prohibition of Harassment or Abuse –** Manufacturers of Sewn Products will provide a work environment free of harassment, abuse or corporal punishment in any form.	**8. Harassment or Abuse:** Every employee shall be treated with dignity and respect. No employee shall be subject to any physical, sexual, psychological, or verbal harassment or abuse. Licensees will not use or tolerate any form of corporal punishment.	None.	**9. NO HARSH OR INHUMANE TREATMENT IS ALLOWED.** **9.1** Physical abuse or discipline, the threat of physical abuse, sexual or other harassment and verbal abuse or other forms of intimidation shall be prohibited.

	SAI	FLA	WRAP	WRC	CCC	ETI
Working Hours	**WORKING HOURS** **7.1** The company shall comply with applicable laws and industry standards on working hours. The normal workweek shall be as defined by law but shall not on a regular basis exceed 48 hours. Personnel shall be provided with at least one day off in every seven-day period. All overtime work shall be reimbursed at a premium rate and under no circumstances shall exceed 12 hours per employee per week. **7.2** Other than as permitted in Section 7.3, overtime work shall be voluntary. **7.3** Where the company is party to a collective bargaining agreement freely negotiated with worker organizations (as defined by the ILO) representing a significant portion of its workforce, it may require overtime work in accordance with such agreement to meet short-term business demand. Any such agreement must comply with the requirements of Section 7.1.	**Hours of Work.** Except in extraordinary business circumstances, employees shall (i) not be required to work more than the lesser of (a) 48 hours per week and 12 hours overtime or (b) the limits on regular and overtime hours allowed by the law of the country of manufacture or, where the laws of such country do not limit the hours of work, the regular work week in such country plus 12 hours overtime and (ii) be entitled to at least one day off in every seven day period.	**Hours of Work** – Manufacturers of Sewn Products will comply with hours worked each day, and days worked each week, and shall not exceed the legal limitations of the countries in which sewn product is produced. Manufacturers of Sewn Products will provide at least one day off in every seven-day period, except as required to meet urgent business needs.	**2. Working Hours:** Hourly and/or quota-based wage employees shall (i) not be required to work more than the lesser of (a) 48 hours per week or (b) the limits on regular hours allowed by the law of the country of manufacture, and (ii) be entitled to at least one day off in every seven day period, as well as holidays and vacations.	**Hours of work are not excessive.** Hours of work shall comply with applicable laws and industry standards. In any event, workers shall not on a regular basis be required to work in excess of 48 hours per week and shall be provided with at least one day off for every 7 day period. Overtime shall be voluntary, shall not exceed 12 hours per week, shall not be demanded on a regular basis and shall always be compensated at a premium rate.	**6. WORKING HOURS ARE NOT EXCESSIVE.** **6.1** Working hours comply with national laws and benchmark industry standards, whichever affords greater protection. **6.2** In any event, workers shall not on a regular basis be required to work in excess of 48 hours per week and shall be provided with at least one day off for every 7 day period on average. Overtime shall be voluntary, shall not exceed 12 hours per week, shall not be demanded on a regular basis and shall always be compensated at a premium rate.

	SAI	FLA	WRAP	WRC	CCC	ETI
Wages and Benefits	**REMUNERATION** **8.1** The company shall ensure that wages paid for a standard working week shall always meet at least legal or industry minimum standards and shall be sufficient to meet basic needs of personnel and to provide some discretionary income. **8.2** The company shall ensure that deductions from wages are not made for disciplinary purposes, and shall ensure that wage and benefits composition are detailed clearly and regularly for workers; the company shall also ensure that wages and benefits are rendered in full compliance with all applicable laws and that remuneration is rendered either in cash or cheque form, in a manner convenient to workers. **8.3** The company shall ensure that labour-only contracting arrangements and false apprenticeship schemes are not undertaken in an effort to avoid fulfilling its obligations to personnel under applicable laws pertaining to labour and social security legislation and regulations.	**Wages and Benefits.** Employers recognize that wages are essential to meeting employees' basic needs. Employers shall pay employees, as a floor, at least the minimum wage required by local law or the prevailing industry wage, whichever is higher, and shall provide legally mandated benefits. **Overtime Compensation:** In addition to their compensation for regular hours of work, employees shall be compensated for overtime hours at such premium rate as is legally required in the country of manufacture or, in those countries where such laws do not exist, at a rate at least equal to their regular hourly compensation rate.	**Compensation and Benefits –** Manufacturers of Sewn Products will pay at least the minimum total compensation required by local law, including all mandated wages, allowances and benefits.	**1. Wages and Benefits: Licensees** recognize that wages are essential to meeting employees' basic needs. Licensees shall pay employees, as a floor, wages and benefits which comply with all applicable laws and regulations, and which provide for essential needs and establish a dignified living wage for workers and their families. [A living wage is a 'take home' or 'net' wage, earned during a country's legal maximum work week, but not more than 48 hours. A living wage provides for the basic needs (housing, energy, nutrition, clothing, health care, education, potable water, childcare, transportation and savings) of an average family unit of employees in the garment manufacturing employment sector of the country divided by the average number of adult wage earners in the family unit of employees in the garment manufacturing employment sector of the country.] **3. Overtime Compensation:** All overtime hours must be worked voluntarily by employees. In addition to their compensation for regular hours of work, hourly and/or quota-based wage employees shall be compensated for overtime hours at such a premium rate as is legally required in the country of manufacture or, in those countries where such laws do not exist, at a rate at least one and one-half their regular hourly compensation rate.	**Living wages are paid.** Wages and benefits paid for a standard working week shall meet at least legal or industry minimum standards and always be sufficient to meet basic needs of workers and their families and to provide some discretionary income. Deductions from wages for disciplinary measures shall not be permitted nor shall any deductions from wages not provided for by national law be permitted without the expressed permission of the worker concerned. All workers shall be provided with written and understandable information about the conditions in respect of wages before they enter employment and of the particulars of their wages for the pay period concerned each time that they are paid.	**LIVING WAGES ARE PAID.** **5.1** Wages and benefits paid for a standard working week meet, at a minimum, national legal standards or industry benchmark standards, whichever is higher. In any event wages should always be enough to meet basic needs and to provide some discretionary income. **5.2** All workers shall be provided with written and understandable information about their employment conditions in respect to wages before they enter employment and about the particulars of their wages for the pay period concerned each time that they are paid. **5.3** Deductions from wages as a disciplinary measure shall not be permitted nor shall any deductions from wages not provided for by national law be permitted without the expressed permission of the worker concerned. All disciplinary measures should be recorded.

	SAI	FLA	WRAP	WRC	CCC	ETI
Forced Labour	**FORCED LABOUR** **2.1** The company shall not engage in or support the use of forced labour nor shall personnel be required to lodge 'deposits' or identity papers upon commencing employment with the company.	**Forced Labor.** There shall not be any use of forced labor, whether in the form of prison labor, indentured labor, bonded labor or otherwise.	**Prohibition of Forced Labor –** Manufacturers of Sewn Products will not use involuntary or forced labor – indentured, bonded or otherwise.	**5. Forced Labor:** There shall not be any use of forced prison labor, indentured labor, bonded labor or other forced labor.	**Employment is freely chosen.** There shall be no use of forced, including bonded or prison, labour (ILO Conventions Nos. 29 and 105). Nor shall workers be required to lodge 'deposits' or their identity papers with their employer.	**1. EMPLOYMENT IS FREELY CHOSEN.** **1.1** There is no forced, bonded or involuntary prison labour. **1.2** Workers are not required to lodge 'deposits' or their identity papers with their employer and are free to leave their employer after reasonable notice.

	SAI	FLA	WRAP	WRC	CCC	ETI
Other	**MANAGEMENT SYSTEMS** **Policy** 9.1 Top management shall define the company's policy for social accountability and labour conditions to ensure that it: a) includes a commitment to conform to all requirements of this standard; b) includes a commitment to comply with the national and other applicable law, other requirements to which the company subscribes and to respect the international instruments and their interpretation; c) includes a commitment to continual improvement; d) is effectively documented, implemented, maintained, communicated and is accessible in a comprehensible form to all personnel, including directors, executives, management, supervisors, and staff, whether directly employed, contracted, or otherwise representing the company; e) is publicly available. **Management Review** 9.2 Top management shall periodically review the adequacy, suitability, and continuing effectiveness of the company's policy, procedures, and performance results vis-à-vis the requirements of this standard and other requirements to which the company subscribes. System amendments and improvements shall be implemented where appropriate. **Company Representatives** 9.3 The company shall appoint a senior management representative who, irrespective of other responsibilities, shall ensure that the requirements of this standard are met. 9.4 The company shall provide for non-management personnel to choose a representative from their own group to facilitate communication with senior management on matters related to this standard. **Planning and Implementation** 9.5 The company shall ensure that the requirements of this standard are understood and implemented at all levels of the organization; methods shall include, but are not limited to: a) clear definition of roles, responsibilities, and authority; b) training of new and/or temporary employees upon hiring;	None	**Compliance with Laws and Workplace Regulations –** Manufacturers of Sewn Products will comply with laws and regulations in all locations where they conduct business. **Environment –** Manufacturers of Sewn Products will comply with environmental rules, regulations and standards applicable to their operations, and will observe environmentally conscious practices in all locations where they operate. **Customs Compliance –** Manufacturers of Sewn Products will comply with applicable customs law and, in particular, will establish and maintain programs to comply with customs laws regarding illegal transshipment of apparel products. **Drug Interdiction –** Manufacturers of Sewn Products will cooperate with local, national and foreign customs and drug enforcement agencies to guard against illegal shipments of drugs	**10. Women's Rights:** a. Women workers will receive equal remuneration, including benefits; equal treatment; equal evaluation of the quality of their work; and equal opportunity to fill all positions open to male workers. b. Pregnancy tests will not be a condition of employment, nor will they be demanded of employees. c. Workers who take maternity leave will not face dismissal nor threat of dismissal, loss of seniority or deduction of wages, and will be able to return to their former employment at the same rate of pay and benefits. d. Workers will not be forced or pressured to use contraception. e. Workers will not be exposed to hazards, including glues and solvents, that may endanger their safety, including their reproductive health. f. Licensees shall provide appropriate services and accommodation to	**The employment relationship is established.** Obligations to employees under labour or social security laws and regulations arising from the regular employment relationship shall not be avoided through the use of labour-only contracting arrangements, or through apprenticeship schemes where there is no real intent to impart skills or provide regular employment. Younger workers shall be given the opportunity to participate in education and training programmes.	**8. REGULAR EMPLOYMENT IS PROVIDED.** 8.1 To every extent possible work performed must be on the basis of recognised employment relationship established through national law and practice. 8.2 Obligations to employees under labour or social security laws and regulations arising from the regular employment relationship shall not be avoided through the use of labour-only contracting, sub-contracting, or home-working arrangements, or through apprenticeship schemes where there is no real

SAI	FLA	WRAP	WRC	CCC	ETI
c) periodic training and awareness programs for existing employees; d) continuous monitoring of activities and results to demonstrate the effectiveness of systems implemented to meet the company's policy and the requirements of this standard. **Control of Suppliers, Subcontractors and Sub-Suppliers** **9.6** The company shall establish and maintain appropriate procedures to evaluate and select suppliers/subcontractors (and, where appropriate, sub-suppliers) based on their ability to meet the requirements of this standard. **9.7** The company shall maintain appropriate records of suppliers'/subcontractors' (and, where appropriate, sub-suppliers') commitments to social accountability, including, but not limited to, the written commitment of those organizations to: a) conform to all requirements of this standard (including this clause); b) participate in the company's monitoring activities as requested; c) promptly implement remedial and corrective action to address any nonconformance identified against the requirements of this standard; d) promptly and completely inform the company of any and all relevant business relationship(s) with other suppliers/subcontractors and sub-suppliers. **9.8** The company shall maintain reasonable evidence that the requirements of this standard are being met by suppliers and subcontractors. **9.9** In addition to the requirements of Sections 9.6 and 9.7 above, where the company receives, handles or promotes goods and/or services from suppliers/subcontractors or sub-suppliers who are classified as homeworkers, the company shall take special steps to ensure that such homeworkers are afforded a similar level of protection as would be afforded to directly employed personnel under the requirements of this standard. Such special steps shall include but not be limited to: a) establishing legally binding, written purchasing contracts requiring conformance to minimum criteria (in accordance with the requirements of this standard); b) ensuring that the requirements of the written purchasing contract are understood and implemented by homeworkers and all other parties involved in the purchasing contract; c) maintaining, on the company premises, comprehensive records detailing the identities of homeworkers; the quantities of goods			women workers in connection with pregnancy.		intent to impart skills or provide regular employment, nor shall any such obligations be avoided through the excessive use of fixed-term contracts of employment.

SAI	FLA	WRAP	WRC	CCC	ETI
produced/services provided and/or hours worked by each homeworker; d) frequent announced and unannounced monitoring activities to verify compliance with the terms of the written purchasing contract. **Addressing Concerns and Taking Action** **9.10** The company shall investigate, address, and respond to the concerns of employees and other interested parties with regard to conformance/nonconformance with the company's policy and/or the requirements of this standard; the company shall refrain from disciplining, dismissing or otherwise discriminating against any employee for providing information concerning observance of the standard. **9.11** The company shall implement remedial and corrective action and allocate adequate resources appropriate to the nature and severity of any nonconformance identified against the company's policy and/or the requirements of the standard. **Outside Communication** **9.12** The company shall establish and maintain procedures to communicate regularly to all interested parties data and other information regarding performance against the requirements of this document, including, but not limited to, the results of management reviews and monitoring activities. **Access for Verification** **9.13** Where required by contract, the company shall provide reasonable information and access to interested parties seeking to verify conformance to the requirements of this standard; where further required by contract, similar information and access shall also be afforded by the company's suppliers and subcontractors through the incorporation of such a requirement in the company's purchasing contracts. **Records** **9.14** The company maintain appropriate records to demonstrate conformance to the requirements of this standard.					

Bibliography

Abegglen, J. (1994) *Sea Change: Pacific Asia as the New World Industrial Centre* (New York: Free Press).

Abernathy, F., J.T. Dunlop, J. Hammond and D. Weil (2002) *Globalisation in the Apparel and Textile Industries: What is New and What is Not?* (Cambridge, MA: Harvard Center for Textile and Apparel Research, Harvard University).

Alber, K.L., and W.T. Walker (1997) *Supply Chain Management Practitioner Notes* (Falls Church, VA: APICS Educational and Research Foundation).

Appelbaum, E., T. Bailey, P. Berg and A.L. Kalleberg (2000) *Manufacturing Advantage: Why High Performance Systems Pay Off* (Ithaca, NY: Cornell University Press).

Asia Research Centre, Murdoch University (1992) *Southern China in Transition* (Canberra: East Asia Analytical Unit).

Barrientos, S. (2002) 'Mapping Codes through the Value Chain: From Researcher to Detective', in R. Jenkins, R. Pearson and G. Seyfang (eds.), *Corporate Responsibility and Labour Rights: Codes of Conduct in the Global Economy* (London: Earthscan Publications): 61-76.

Boje, D., and L. Prieto (2000) 'What is Postmodern?', found at www.horsenseatwork.com/psl/pages/postmoderndefined.html, 10 April 2003.

Bonacich, E., and R.P. Applebaum (2000) *Behind the Label: Inequality in the Los Angeles Apparel Industry* (Los Angeles: University of California Press).

Brill, L. (2002) 'Can Codes of Conduct Help Home-Based Workers?' in R. Jenkins, R. Pearson and G. Seyfang (eds.), *Corporate Responsibility & Labour Rights: Codes of Conduct in the Global Economy* (London: Earthscan Publications): 113-24.

Business Korea (1992) 'Footwear: Wearing Out Fast', *Business Korea* 10.5: 33.

Cestre, G. (2002) 'Social Accountability and Performance: The Switcher/Prem Group Experience in India', paper presented at the *6th International Conference on Corporate Reputation, Identity and Competitiveness*, organised by the Reputation Institute, Boston, MA, 23–25 May 2002, www.cepaa.org/Document%20Center/ImpactAnalysisDocuments.htm.

Chandra, C., and S. Kumar (2001) 'Enterprise Architectural Framework for Supply-Chain Integration', *Industrial Management & Data Systems* 101.6: 290-303.

Chen, X. (1999) 'Business over Politics', *China Business Review* 26.2: 8-14.

Connor, T. (2004). 'Time to Scale Up Co-operation? Unions, Non-Government Organisations and the International Anti-Sweatshop Movement', *Development in Practice* 14.1–2: 61-70.

Daft, R.L. (1995) *Organisation Theory and Design* (St Paul, MN: West Publishing, 5th edn).

Doehringer, P.B., A. Watson, L. Oxborrow, P. Totterdill, B. Courault and E. Parat (1998) *Strengthening Apparel Production Channels: Public Policy for the Clothing Industry in the US, UK and France* (Geneva: International Institute for Labour Studies).

Eisenhardt, K.M. (1989) 'Building Theories from Case Study Research', *Academy of Management Review* 14.4: 532-50.

Elkington, J. (2001) 'Jobs and Money: Management: From the Top', *The Guardian*, 17 February 2001: 45.

ETI (Ethical Trading Initiative) (1999/2000) Annual Report 1999/2000, www.ethicaltrade.org, 20 September 2004.

Frenkel, S. (2001) 'Globalisation, the Athletic Footwear Commodity Chain and Employment Relations in Southern China', *Organisation Studies* 22.4 (Thousand Oaks, CA: Sage).

—— and D. Scott (2002) *Compliance, Collaboration and Codes of Labour Practices: The Adidas Connection* (unpublished).

Friedman, M. (1970) 'The Social Responsibility of Business is to Increase Profits', *New York Times*, 13 September 1970: 32 & 125.

Gereffi, G. (1999) *A Commodity Chains Framework for Analysing Global Industries* (Brighton, UK: Institute of Development Studies).

—— and L. Hempel (1996) 'Latin America in the Global Economy: Running Faster to Stay in Place', *NACLA's Report on the Americas* 29.4: 18-27.

Glaser, B.G., and A.L. Strauss (1967) *The Discovery of Grounded Theory* (New York: Aldine De Gruyter).

Glock, R.E., and G. Kunz (2002) *Apparel Manufacturing* (Upper Saddle River, NJ: Prentice Hall, 3rd edn).

Gu, Q. (1999) *The Development of the China Apparel Industry*, report presented jointly by China Textile University and Harvard Center of Textile Research, November (Cambridge, MA: Harvard Center of Textile Research).

Hopkins, M. (1999) *The Planetary Bargain* (New York: St Martin's Press).

ICFTU (International Confederation of Free Trade Unions) (2001) 'The International Trade Union Movement and the New Codes of Conduct', www.ICFTU.org, 10 April 2003.

IFBWW (International Federation of Builders and Wood Workers)–IKEA (2001) 'Agreement on Rights of Workers, Geneva and Leiden', www.ifbww.org, 20 September 2004.

ILO (International Labour Office) (2002a) *Codes of Conduct for Multinational Enterprises* (CD-ROM; Geneva: ILO).

—— (2002b) *The World of Work: The Magazine of the ILO* 45 (December 2002): 4-7.

—— (2003) *Information Note on Corporate Social Responsibility and International Labour Standards* (GB.286/WP/SDG/4 [Rev.] 286th Session, Geneva, March 2003).

IOE (International Organisation of Employers) (1999) 'Codes of Conduct: Position Paper', Geneva, IOE, www.IOE-emp.org, 20 September 2004.

Jenkins, R. (2001) *Technology, Business and Society* (Geneva: United Nations Research Institute for Social Development [UNRISD]).

—— (2002a) 'The Political Economy of Codes of Conduct', in R. Jenkins, R. Pearson and G. Seyfang (eds.), *Corporate Responsibility and Labour Rights: Codes of Conduct in the Global Economy* (London: Earthscan Publications): 13-30.

—— (2002b) *Corporate Codes of Conduct: Self-Regulation in a Global Economy* (Geneva: United Nations Research Institute for Social Development [UNRISD]).

——, R. Pearson and G. Seyfang (eds.) (2002) *Corporate Responsibility and Labour Rights: Codes of Conduct in the Global Economy* (London: Earthscan Publications): 13-30.

Johnson, E. (2002) 'Product Design Collaboration: Capturing Lost Supply Chain Value in the Apparel Industry', Tuck School of Business Working Paper No. 02-08 (Hanover, NH: Tuck School of Business at Dartmouth).

Joshi, G. (2002) *Garment Industry in South Asia: Rags or Riches?* (New Delhi: ILO).

Justice, D.W. (2000) 'New Codes of Conduct and the Social Partners', 26 January, ICFTU website, www.icftu.org, 20 September 2004.

Kahn, G. (2003) 'China Firm Takes Aim at Nike', *Wall Street Journal*, Brussels, 28 January 2003.

Klein, N. (2002) *No Logo* (New York: Picador).

Kyloh, R., and J. Murray (1998) *Mastering the Challenge of Globalisation: Towards a Trade Union Agenda* (Geneva: ILO).

Lau, Ho-Fuk, and Chi-Fai Chan (1994) 'The Development Process of the Hong Kong Garment Industry: A Mature Industry in a Newly Industrialised Economy', in E. Bonacich, L. Cheng, N. Chinchilla, N. Hamilton and P. Ong (eds.), *Global Production: The Apparel Industry in the Pacific Rim* (Philadelphia, PA: Temple University Press).

Levy, D.L. (1997) 'Lean Production in an International Supply Chain', *Sloan Management Review* 38.2: 94-102.

Levy, M., and B. Weitz (1998) *Retailing Management* (New York: Irwin McGraw-Hill).

Lincoln, Y.S., and E.G. Guba (1985) *Naturalistic Inquiry* (Beverly Hills, CA: Sage Publications).

Marshall, C., and G.B. Rossman (1995) *Designing Qualitative Research* (Newbury Park, CA: Sage Publications).

Mason-Jones, R., and D.R. Towil (2000) 'Coping with Uncertainty: Reducing "Bullwhip" Behaviour in Global Supply Chains', *Supply Chain Forum* 1: 40-45; www.supplychain-forum.com.

McGrath, J.E. (1982) 'Dilemmatics: The Study of Research Choices and Dilemmas', in J.E. McGrath, J. Martin and R.A. Kulka (eds.), *Judgement Calls in Research* (Beverly Hills, CA: Sage Publications): 69-102.

McIntosh, M., R. Thomas, D. Leipziger and G. Coleman (2002) *Living Corporate Citizenship: Strategic Routes to Socially Responsible Business* (London: Pearson Publications).

Miles, M.B., and M. Huberman (1994) *Qualitative Data Analysis* (Thousand Oaks, CA: Sage Publications).

Mooney, P. (1991) 'Taking Steps to be the Best', *Asian Business* 27.5: 46.

Murray, J. (1998) *Corporate Codes of Conduct and Labour Standards* (Geneva: ILO, Bureau for Workers' Activities).

OECD (Organisation for Economic Co-operation and Development) (1999) *Codes of Corporate Conduct: An Inventory* (Paris: OECD).

—— (2000) *Codes of Corporate Conduct: An Expanded Review of their Contents* (Paris: OECD).

—— (2001) *Making Codes of Corporate Conduct Work: Management Control Systems and Corporate Responsibility* (Paris: OECD).

O'Rourke, D. (2002) 'Monitoring the Monitors: A Critique of Third-Party Labour Monitors', in R. Jenkins, R. Pearson and G. Seyfang (eds.), *Corporate Responsibility and Labour Rights: Codes of Conduct in the Global Economy* (London: Earthscan Publications): 196-209.

—— (2003) 'Outsourcing Regulation: Analyzing Non-Governmental Systems of Labour Standards and Monitoring', *Policy Studies Journal* 31.1: 1.

Parnell, C. (2000) 'Retailers, Manufacturers Collaborate Toward Success', *Executive Technology*, www.executivetechnology.com/ViewSOFull.cfm?SOID=22, 11 April 2003.

Patton, M.Q. (1990) *Qualitative Evaluation Methods* (Beverly Hills, CA: Sage Publications).

Ries, A., and J. Trout (1997) *Marketing Warfare* (New York: McGraw-Hill).

Rohitratana, K. (2002) 'SA8000: Tool to Improve Quality of Life', *Managerial Auditing Journal*, 17 January 2002: 60-64.

Sabel, C. (1994) 'Learning by Monitoring: The Institutions of Economic Development', in N. Smelser and R. Swedberg (eds.), *The Handbook of Economic Sociology* (Princeton, NJ: Princeton University Press): 137-65.

——, D. O'Rourke and A. Fung (2000) *Ratcheting Labour Standards: Regulation for Continuous Improvement in the Global Workplace* (Social Protection Discussion Paper No. 11; Washington, DC: The World Bank).

Sajhau, J.-P. (2000) *Labour Practices in the Footwear, Leather, Textiles and Clothing Industries* (Geneva: ILO, Sectoral Activities Programme).

Shaw, L., and A. Hale (2002) 'The Emperor's New Clothes: What Codes Mean for Workers in the Garment Industry', in R. Jenkins, R. Pearson and G. Seyfang (eds.), *Corporate Responsibility and Labour Rights: Codes of Conduct in the Global Economy* (London: Earthscan Publications): 101-13.

Silverman, D. (1993) *Interpreting Qualitative Data* (Thousand Oaks, CA: Sage Publications).

Sito, P. (2002) 'HK's Role as Sourcing Hub under Threat', *South China Morning Post* (Hong Kong), 3 December 2002.

Spinanger, D. (1992) 'The Impact on Employment and Income of Structural and Technological Changes in the Clothing Industry', in G. van Liemt (ed.), *Industry on the Move* (Geneva: ILO): 83-116.

Sporting Goods Intelligence (2003) 'US Branded Athletic Footwear Market', www.sginews.com, 21 March 2003.

Stiglitz, J. (2000) *Frontiers of Development Economics* (Oxford, UK: Oxford University Press).

Sturm, S. (2001) 'Second Generation Employment Discrimination: A Structural Approach', *Columbia Law Review* 101: 458-568.

Tuck, L. (2002) 'Get Ready for the Retail Revolution', *Frontline Solutions*, 1 December 2002.

UNCTAD (United Nations Conference on Trade and Development), Officer-in-Charge, Masataka Fujita, Investment Trends Section, Division on Investment, Technology and Enterprise Development, personal communication.

United States Department of Labor (1996) *The Apparel Industry and Codes of Conduct: A Solution to the International Child Labour Problem?* (Washington, DC: United States Department of Labor).

—— (2002) *Development of a Methodology for the Regular Reporting of Working Conditions in the Production of Apparel Imported into the United States* (Washington, DC: Bureau of International Affairs).

Urminsky, M. (2001) *Self Regulation in the Workplace: Codes of Conduct, Social Labeling, and Socially Responsible Investment* (Geneva: ILO).

USCIB (United States Council for International Business) (1998) 'USCIB Position Paper on Codes of Conduct', December, www.uscib.org/index.asp?DocumentID=1358, 10 April 2003.

Utting, P. (2002) 'Regulating Business via Multistakeholder Initiatives: A Preliminary Assessment', in *Voluntary Approaches to Corporate Responsibility: Readings and a Resource Guide* (UN Non-Governmental Liaison Service Development Dossier; Geneva: UNRISD): 61-130.

Vijaybaskar, M. (2002) 'Garment Industry in India', in G. Joshi (ed.), *Garment industry in South Asia: Rags or Riches?* (New Delhi: ILO).

Villamor, R.J. (2001) 'Philippines has Potential to Become Call Center Hub', *Business World* (Manila), 26 January.

Waddock, S. (2001) *Leading Corporate Citizens: Vision, Values, Value-Added* (New York: McGraw-Hill).

WEF (World Economic Forum) (2001) Summary of the annual meeting entitled, *The Corporation and the Public: Open For Inspection*, 25–30 January 2001, Davos, Switzerland. www.weforum.org.

White, H., and F. Munger (1998) 'Dynamics of the Global Assembly Line', in P. Varley (ed.), *Quandary: Corporate Responsibility on the Global Frontier* (Washington, DC: Investor Responsibility Research Center).

Wick, I. (2001) *Workers' Tool or PR Ploy?* (Bonn: Friedrich-Ebert-Stiftung; Siegburg, Germany: SÜDWIND Institut für Ökonomie und Ökumene).

Yin, R.K. (1994) *Case Study Research: Design and Methods* (Thousand Oaks, CA: Sage Publications).

Websites

BASI: www.ilo.org/basi
Business for Social Responsibility: www.bsr.org
Clean Clothes Campaign: www.cleanclothes.org
International Confederation of Free Trade Unions: www.icftu.org
International Federation of Builders and Wood Workers: www.ifbww.org
International Labour Organization: www.ilo.org
International Labour Rights Fund: www.laborrights.org
Organisation for Economic Co-operation and Development: www.oecd.org
Stanford University: www.stanford.edu
Transparency International: www.transparency.org
United Nations Conference on Trade and Development: www.unctad.org
United Nations High Commission for Refugees: www.unhcr.ch
United States Department of Commerce, Office of Textiles and Apparel: http://otexa.ita.doc.gov
World Trade Organisation: www.wto.org

Abbreviations

Note: For an explanation of the abbreviated codes use to identify organisations, see Table 3 on page 18.

AA1000	AccountAbility Standard 1000
AIDS	acquired immuno-deficiency syndrome
BASI	Business and Social Incentives database of the ILO
BIAC	Business and Advisory Committee to the OECD
BSR	Business for Social Responsibility
CAD	computer-aided design
CAP	corrective action plan
CB	collective bargaining
CBA	collective bargaining agreement
CBI	Caribbean Basin Initiative
CCC	Clean Clothes Campaign
CD-ROM	compact disc–read-only memory
CEO	chief executive officer
CFO	chief financial officer
CIP	continuous improvement programme
COO	chief operating officer
CP	Consumer products
CPFR	collaborative planning, forecasting and replenishment
CSR	corporate social responsibility
EDI	electronic data interchange
EEO	equal employment opportunity
EHS	environment, health and safety
EPZ	export processing zone
ERP	environmental resource planning
ETI	Ethical Trading Initiative
FDI	foreign direct investment
FIFA	Fédération Internationale de Football
FLA	Fair Labor Association
FOA	freedom of association
FOB	free on board
GM	general manager
GNX	Global Net Exchange
GRI	Global Reporting Initiative
GSP	generalised system of preferences
GUF	Global Union Federation
H&S	health and safety

HCTAR	Harvard Center for Textile and Apparel Research
HIV	human immunodeficiency virus
HR	human resources
HRM	human resource management
ICC	International Chamber of Commerce
ICFTU	International Confederation of Free Trade Unions
ICT	information and communications technologies
IFBWW	International Federation of Building and Wood Workers
IFC	International Finance Committee
ILO	International Labour Office
ILS	International Labour Standards
IOE	International Organisation of Employers
IR	industrial relations
ISO	International Organisation for Standardisation
IT	information technology
JIT	just-in-time
LDC	less-developed country
LMDP	local manager development programme
MD	managing director
MFA	Multifiber Arrangement/Agreement
MNE	multinational enterprise
MSI	multi-stakeholder initiative
NAFTA	North American Free Trade Agreement
NCP	National Contact Point (OECD)
NGO	non-governmental organisation
NIE	newly industrialised economies
ODM	original design manufacturing
OECD	Organisation for Economic Co-operation and Development
OEM	original equipment manufacturer
OHS	occupational health and safety
OSH	occupational safety and health
OSHA	Occupational Safety and Health Administration (USA)
PBS	progressive bundle system
PPE	personal protection equipment
PR	public relations
PVC	polyvinyl chloride
QA	quality assurance
QC	quality control
QS9000	Quality Standards 9000
R&D	research and development
RFC	ready for commercialisation
RMB	Chinese renminbi
SA8000	social accountability standard 8000
SAI	Social Accountability International
SCM	supply chain management
SKU	stock keeping unit
SME	small or medium-sized enterprise

SOP	standard operating procedure
SPO	social performance objective
TLV	threshold limit value
TPA	third-party auditor
TQC	total quality control
TQM	total quality management
TUAC	Trade Union Advisory Committee to the OECD
UNCTAD	United Nations Conference on Trade and Development
UNEP	United Nations Environment Program
UNHCR	United Nations High Commissioner for Human Rights
UNI	Union Network International
UPS	unit production system
USCIB	United States Council for International Business
VND	Vietnamese dong
VOC	volatile organic compound
VP	vice president
WRAP	Worldwide Responsible Apparel Production Program
WRC	Workers' Rights Consortium
WTO	World Trade Organisation
WWRE	Worldwide Retail Exchange

Index